CASES IN INTERNATIONAL FINANCE

MICHAEL H.
MOFFETT

Thunderbird, The American Graduate School of International Management

With contributions by:

M. Edgar Barrett, Thunderbird

Robert F. Bruner, Darden

Dale Davison, Thunderbird

Kenneth R. Ferris, Thunderbird

Mark D. Griffiths, Thunderbird

Gabriel Hawawini, INSEAD

F. John Mathis, Thunderbird

James L. Mills, Thunderbird

Graeme Rankine, Thunderbird

H. Lee Remmers, INSEAD

Arthur I. Stonehill, University of Hawaii, Manoa

Anant K. Sundaram, Thunderbird

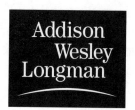

Addison
Wesley
Longman

Boston San Francisco New York
London Toronto Sydney Tokyo Singapore Madrid
Mexico City Munich Paris Cape Town Hong Kong Montreal

Michael H. Moffett, *Cases in International Finance*

Copyright © 2001 Addison Wesley Longman, Inc.

ISBN: 0-201-70086-7

2 3 4 5 6 7 8 9 10-VG-0403020100

"Well, in *our* country," said Alice, still panting a little, "you'd generally get to somewhere else—if you ran very fast for a long time as we've been doing."

"A slow sort of country!" said the Queen. "Now, *here*, you see, it takes all the running you can do, to keep in the same place. If you want to get to somewhere else, you must run at least twice as fast as that."

Through the Looking Glass, And What Alice Found There
Lewis Carroll, 1871

CASES IN INTERNATIONAL FINANCE

Preface

The growth of international business continues to know no bounds. With the coming of the year 2000, the world's access to information technology—and to capital—has reaffirmed the need to explore and expand our understanding of international finance. Finance is integral to the conduct of global business, and the increasing access to capital by enterprises and institutions from Bangalore to Beijing, is giving rise to competitors which many multinational firms in traditional industrial markets have not yet seen on their radar screens. As a recent slogan on the Internet noted, "The future is here, it is simply not evenly distributed."

This collection of cases in international finance is intended to provide current material for the exploration of these global financial challenges and trends. These cases are the product of academics from some of the leading educational institutions in the world in the fields of international business, generally, and international finance, specifically. Many of the cases have benefitted from extensive co-authorship with the practitioners in the field, the professional financial managers who are on the front lines of global business. Many of these same professionals are our former students, who (thankfully for us) continue to reeducate us, the educators.

The key words in the selection of cases for this collection were *currency* (timing of case events, not money) and diversity (geographic, not ethnic). Twenty-seven of the 30 cases involve events occurring in the 1990s, with ten cases in the period of time between 1997 and 2000 alone. To our knowledge, this is also the first major financial case collection in which the majority of the case events occur outside of the United States. This geographic diversity includes Pakistan, Italy, Honduras, China, Denmark, Brazil, Germany, Malaysia, and Ecuador to name but a few. As the leaders in international business and finance have reiterated time and time again over the past 30 years, global business and financial practices reflect much of the culture and history of the geographic environments. It is hoped that this case collection provides an opportunity for students of international finance to understand the differences and complexity of international financial management on a truly global landscape.

Topical coverage is wide. In addition to the traditional international financial issues of currency exposure and global funding, topics of contemporary managerial concern such as international performance evaluation, valuation and recapitalization, mergers and acquisitions, global tax management, remittance and repatriation, pricing, project financing, ratio analysis, and multinational capital budgeting are also covered. Few if any of the cases are confined to a single topic; most cases present the complexity of financial decision-making within a competitive business environment. The challenges presented by these cases are intended to go far beyond simple exercises in financial mathematics, to real world financial issues faced by real world managers in real world companies.

The organization of the collection follows that of *Multinational Business Finance* (MBF), ninth edition, 2001, Addison-Wesley Longman Publishing, coauthored by

David Eiteman, Arthur Stonehill, and myself. It is intended that the casebook be used as a supplement to MBF, but also as a supplement to a traditional financial management text, or independently on a stand-alone basis. Although the title of the collection is *International Finance,* each case could be viewed as focusing on a variety of financial dimensions of global business in general. The selection of cases for the volume was intended to expand the scope of international finance, not narrow it.

These cases have been extensively field-tested in both undergraduate and graduate level degree programs at a variety of educational institutions around the globe, as well as within a variety of executive education programs, including here at Thunderbird. I wish to thank all the authors for allowing me to use their cases, several of whom have revised in their cases specifically for this volume. Thank you. And of course, any remaining errors of content or omission are mine alone.

M.H.M., *Flagstaff, Arizona*

CONTENTS

PART I
THE INTERNATIONAL
FINANCIAL ENVIRONMENT

BENECOL: RAISIO'S GLOBAL NUTRICEUTICAL

The discovery and launch of a revolutionary new margarine—Benecol—scientifically proven to cut cholesterol without known side-effects, has transformed Raisio into the hottest stock on the Finnish stock exchange. When Benecol was launched in Finland early in 1996, it sold out quickly, even though it cost seven times more than ordinary margarine. As talk of "miracle margarine" began to filter out of Finland, Raisio's slumbering share price jumped. It has risen 16-fold since Benecol's launch, helped by a surge in foreign ownership. Overseas investors held 10 percent of the shares at the start of 1996. Today the proportion is 63 percent.

"Benecol's Spread of Riches," *The Financial Times,* July 9, 1998.

The share price of Raisio Oy, a Finnish grain and chemicals company, had recently exhibited all the characteristics of a roller-coaster ride. The ride up had been on the back of Benecol, a *nutriceutical,* a human nutrient-based product with pharmaceutical qualities. The firm had rolled-out its new margarine product in Finland under the patented Benecol name in November 1995 with enormous success and fanfare. Sales had grown rapidly, but global interest in both Raisio and Benecol had grown even faster. The share price had skyrocketed, rising from 6.2 Finnish marks (FIM) in December 1995 to 64.7 in December 1997. Kenza Medici, food and pharmaceutical analyst for Sinagua Capital, had picked and promoted Raisio.

But 1998 had proved difficult for both Raisio and Kenza. The share price continued upward in the spring with the signing of an international licensing agreement with the U.S. consumer and pharmaceutical conglomerate, Johnson & Johnson (J&J). But forces out of Raisio's control inflicted severe damage to the firm's earnings potential in late summer and early fall. First, two of Raisio's four major business units had been seriously hit by the Russian economic and financial collapse in August. Both the margarine and grain divisions were expected to end the year at a loss. The second hit was worse: the U.S. Food and Drug Administration (FDA) blocked J&J's McNeil Consumer Products Group from test-marketing Benecol in the United States. All bets on earnings for Benecol-based products were off. As 1998 drew to a close, Kenza revisited her valuation of Raisio.

Raisio Oy

The Raisio Group was a Finnish foodstuffs, animal feeds, paper, and chemicals conglomerate. Founded in 1939, Raisio had grown from a single flour mill to a

EXHIBIT 1 Selected Financial Results, the Raisio Group (million Finnish marks)

	1992	1993	1994	1995	1996	1997
Turnover (sales)	3,070	3,549	3,518	3,224	3,928	4,947
Percent change	33%	16%	-1%	-8%	22%	26%
Profit before extraordinary item	158	199	165	141	166	209
Percent of sales	5.1%	5.6%	4.7%	4.4%	4.2%	4.2%
Return on Equity (ROE)	14.6%	19.7%	10.8%	7.5%	4.5%	7.8%
Return on Investment	15.5%	13.5%	11.1%	9.2%	9.2%	10.1%
Share price (eoy), FIM	40.3	83.9	70.2	61.9	280.0	647.0
Earning per share (EPS)	8.0	11.0	9.4	6.2	6.0	10.0
Price/EPS ratio	5.0	7.6	7.5	10.0	46.7	64.7

Source: The Raisio Group and Handelsbanken. Share price and EPS on a pre-split basis. The Raisio Group approved a 10 to 1 split in June 1998.
eoy = end-of-year.

FIM 4.9 billion firm in 1997 ($912 million at FIM5.37/$) with more than 2,800 employees working in 17 countries. Raisio characterized its various business lines as being linked by their common input—renewable natural resources, and took pride in its continued investment in research, innovation, and development. Raisio's strategy was to improve the quality, reduce the cost, increase the availability, and expand the uses of all products in its value chain.

Sales growth and profitability at Raisio had been quite volatile in the 1990s. As illustrated by Exhibit 1, the turnover of the traditional business lines of Raisio, heavily chemical and foodstuff in composition, had grown rapidly in 1992 and 1993, falling dramatically in 1994 and 1995, only to resume a rapid growth path in 1996 and 1997. Sales growth for 1998 was expected to be flat. That was, however, before Benecol. Although Benecol's actual sales were not yet significant, contributing only 2% of total Group sales in 1997, the earnings potential for the product globally was thought to be enormous. The growth in corporate earnings and prospects in 1996 and 1997 had led the share price to increase ten-fold.

Raisio first listed on the Helsinki Stock Exchange in 1989. Raisio's free shares of the parent company (Series V) are quoted on the Helsinki Exchanges (RAIVV) and the firm's restricted shares (Series K) on the brokers' list (RAIKV). Restricted shares of the company, limited to qualified buyers according to the firm's Articles of Association, possess 20 votes per share, while the free shares, sold to all buyers (both domestic and foreign), possess one vote per share. Acquisition of restricted shares must be approved by the firm's Board of Directors with the exception of that by Finnish citizens. Both kinds of shares were entitled to equal amounts of profits.

Benecol

Raisio's scientists had started searching for a cholesterol-decomposing food product in the late 1980s. The firm's knowledge and background in wood- and plant-based sterols led it to believe it could be found (the potential for plant sterols to inhibit cholesterol absorption was known as early as 1950). Raisio became the first to successfully isolate and manufacture *stanol ester,* a by-product of wood and vegetable pulping. *Stanol ester* had been shown in clinical trials in Finland to reduce total blood serum cholesterol in the human blood stream by up to 15%. Benecol could be ingested from within a product like margarine and actually inhibit cholesterol absorption.

Fats (lipids) are generally insoluble in water. Lipids are therefore transported through the human blood stream via proteins—lipoproteins—which are water soluble. Water-soluble lipoproteins are classified according to density, and fall into three primary categories: very low-density lipoproteins (VLDL), a relatively rare complex; low-density lipoproteins (LDL), often termed "bad cholesterol," making up roughly 60% of the average cholesterol in the human blood stream; and high-density lipoproteins (HDL), "good cholesterol," which transport excess cholesterol from the body's cells to the liver for excretion. It was Benecol's impact on LDL which was of value.

The human digestive tract receives cholesterol from two sources, ingested food and from the body itself. Once cholesterol enters the digestive tract, roughly half is eliminated and half absorbed by the body. *Stanol ester,* the active

EXHIBIT 2 Margarine Prices in Finland (August 1998, per 250 gm container)

Margarine Brand	FIM	US$
Benecol	24.90	4.61
Becel (reduced cholesterol)	4.94	0.91
Keiju (table margarine)	3.33	0.62
Flora (table margarine	4.06	0.75
Soila (table margarine)	2.88	0.53

Note: U.S. dollar prices at FIM5.40/US$.

ingredient in Benecol, inhibits the body's ability to absorb this cholesterol. Specifically, it reduces the body's absorption of LDL, which the body compensates for by increasing its own production of cholesterol. The net result is a reduction in LDL, a reduction in VLDL (a precursor to some LDL), leaving the levels of good cholesterol (HDL) unchanged. Clinical studies in Finland indicated that total blood serum cholesterol was reduced by 10% and LDL reduced by 15%.[1]

Benecol—the margarine product—was launched in November 1995 in Finland. Though the product was initially priced at about seven times the average margarine product, store shelves were emptied in days. Although hoping for such success, Raisio had not anticipated the level of demand. Nearly a year passed before sufficient quantities of stanol ester could be produced to meet the Benecol product demands simply within Finland itself.

---

[1] A study published in the *New England Journal of Medicine* (T.A. Miettinen, H. Gylling, H. Vanhanen, and E. Vartiainen, "Reduction of serum cholesterol with sitostanol-ester margarine in a mildly hyper-cholesterolemic population," *New England Journal of Medicine*, 1995, 333, 1308-1312), documented a 10% reduction in total blood-serum cholesterol levels and a 14% reduction in low-density lipoprotein (LDL) levels among Finnish consumers who used Benecol margarine regularly.

Developing a Global Strategy

Time was the critical element. Raisio had a unique product with enormous market potential, but, if it could not be brought to the global market quickly, competitors would succeed in reaping many of the gains from Raisio's long and expensive research and development process.[2] Unilever already was thought to be nearing a very similar product. Time to penetrate the global market was running short. Tor Bergman, Director of the Benecol Division, estimated Raisio had an 18- to 24-month lead on the competition. The problem, however, was that Raisio had little experience with a business line like that of Benecol.

In late 1996, Raisio had formed a 12-person panel to aid in formulating a five-year development plan for Benecol. The panel, comprising current and former executives from Nestlé, Kraft, and Heinz, among others, provided valuable insights into food products that Raisio did not possess. Together, they worked to develop an understanding of the potential Benecol value-chain, and where Raisio should position itself in the chain. The resulting strategy focused on international licensing, requiring Raisio to find a global partner for market penetration. Raisio itself, however, would maintain the control of stanol ester production, which was consistent with the company's traditional core businesses.

Raisio, as a result of its determination to maintain productive control over stanol ester, launched a global effort both to increase production of stanol ester (esterification) and to secure increasing supplies of stanol ester's primary component, plant sterol. In addition to the existing production facility in Finland, four new sterol production facilities were now under construction: in France with a joint-venture partner, DRT; in Chile via a joint venture (named Detsa S.A.) with one of Chile's largest private companies, Harting S.A.; in the United States via a joint venture with Westvaco Corporation in Charleston, South Carolina; and a second facility in Finland itself. Even with this build-up in production capacity, if the global distribution of Benecol was anywhere near as successful as thought possible, there would be insufficient production capacity of stanol ester.

The J&J Agreements

Johnson & Johnson's McNeil Consumer Products group had proposed a comprehensive production, promotion, and distribution strategy. Kenza, like all segment analysts, had pieced together what she could find out (neither Raisio nor McNeil was talking). First, J&J would purchase all stanol ester from Raisio. Second, it would make a number of lump-sum payments to Raisio, *milestone* payments, based on unspecified product or sales goals. Third, J&J would pay Raisio a royalty on sales of all products containing Benecol. Kenza was unsure of the exact royalty rate; it was also unclear

---

[2] Raisio's U.S. patent for stanol ester, Benecol7, was initiated in 1992 and awarded in March 1996. The patent will expire in the year 2008, 17 years after the initiation of patent request protection.

whether the milestone payments were payable only upon specific stanol ester capacity or production goals. Kenza did know that royalties were to be based on the final product retail price, not on the cost or internal transfer price associated with the stanol ester input. Although the milestone payments were thought to be substantial in 1998 and 1999, they were expected to quickly become minor in magnitude relative to the royalty payments arising from J&J's prospective global sales (see Appendix 2 for additional detail).

McNeil's proposed product strategy included the introduction of two different varieties of Benecol margarine and a line of four Benecol-based salad dressings, all to be introduced by March of 1999.[3] In January of 1999, McNeil would introduce boxes of 21 individually wrapped servings of light and regular margarine containing Benecol. The four Benecol-based salad dressings, 8-ounce bottles of French, Creamy Italian, Russian, and Thousand Islands, would retail for $5.99 per bottle.[4] This was a significant price increase over normal salad dressings, and reflected the underlying product strategy shared by Raisio and McNeil: low population penetration rates with high margin product sales. Raisio estimated that approximately 40% of the Finnish population had tried Benecol, and 3.5% of the population continued to use the product on a regular basis. The product-packaging and marketing strategy was to use the green coloration of *better-for-you products* to help rationalize the higher prices.

In addition to the product commitment was the promotional commitment: McNeil had slated over US$80 million in national television, print, radio, and free-standing inserts (FSIs) to promote the new product lines, in addition to substantial educational promotions for doctors and pharmacists. Saatchi & Saatchi had been retained to handle the advertising campaign. The promotional campaign would combine the general health benefits of Benecol usage with an explicit recommendation to use Benecol three times per day to lower cholesterol (hence the individually wrapped servings). McNeil, a firm with extensive experience in healthcare-based product promotion and distribution, planned to use retail brokers to get the products into supermarket and grocery chains.

Raisio signed an exclusive North American marketing rights agreement with J&J in July of 1997 (the United States, Canada, and Mexico), and a similar global marketing agreement in March 1998.[5] In June 1998, the share price reached its peak at just over FIM1,000 (pre-split basis). The strategic plan was to introduce Benecol in the United States and Continental Europe in 1999, followed by Japan in 2000. Raisio moved quickly to assure adequate production capacity of stanol ester was available in the United States and Europe for 1999.

---

[3] McNeil planned to introduce a slightly altered form of Benecol which contained even more cholesterol-lowering mono-unsaturated fats and less cholesterol-raising saturated fats than the original Finnish version. Additional product deliveries of Benecol currently under study by J&J included mayonnaise and ice cream.

[4] "McNeil Loads Up $80M Warchest for Benecol," *Brandweek*, New York, October 5, 1998.

[5] Although the J&J agreement provided specific detail over individual responsibilities, the partners agreed to share joint responsibilities on continuing clinical studies and product development.

Exhibit 3 depicts the Benecol value-chain and Raisio's now assembled corporate partners. Raisio wished to focus the majority of its actual equity interest and control in the middle phase, the production of stanol esters, and partner with those possessing existing capabilities and resources for the initial sterol supply and final Benecol production and distribution.

EXHIBIT 3   The Benecol Value-Chain and Raisio's Corporate Partners

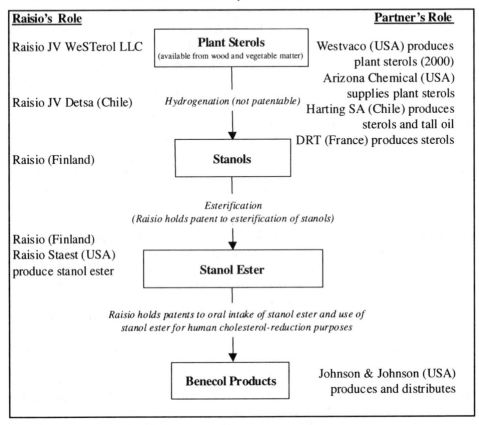

Potential Competitors

One potential competitive product was under development by Unilever, trade-named *New Flora*, but slated for U.S. distribution by Unilever's Lipton subsidiary as *Take Control*. Although Unilever planned to introduce *Take Control* as a cholesterol-reducing margarine, it was actually a *sterol ester*, not a *stanol ester*. Sterol esters are also colorless, odorless, and fat-soluble, but clinical studies indicated LDL cholesterol reduction of only 7-8%. This was only half of that thought achievable by Benecol. A second, but potentially more serious concern for Unilever, was the possibility that some human bodies absorb sterol esters. Absorption could possibly lead to the development of arteriosclerosis. Benecol, a stanol ester, was not subject to absorption. Analysts expected Unilever to introduce *New Flora* to the European Union's (EU) regulatory process sometime in early 1999, but given its potential side-effects of absorption, the timing of regulatory approval was uncertain. The primary advantage to Unilever was its well-established brand name in Europe.

A number of other competitive products were also on the horizon. Forbes Medi-Tech, a Vancouver-listed firm, was studying the possibility of marketing *CardioRex*, a blend of plant sterols derived from wood pulp. Novartis, a Swiss-based pharmaceutical firm, had taken an equity stake of C$7 million in Forbes in early 1998 to aid in the product's development and to position itself for potential global marketing. While *CardioRex* was thought to have some LDL cholesterol-reducing benefits and was relatively cheap to produce, its efficacy was still much less than Benecol. Like *New Flora*, it was based on sterol esters which could be absorbed. Very limited clinical tests had been completed.

Monsanto Life Sciences (U.S.) was studying the possibility of extracting sterols from maize products, but the development process was still in its infancy. An added complexity for Monsanto in 1998 had been its preoccupation with its attempted merger with American Home Products (which failed). Fytokem (Canada) was rumored to be investigating extracting sterols from rapeseed oil, but no information was currently available on their success. Nabisco (U.S.) was similarly experimenting with sterol derivation from wheat.

Kenza and other analysts had concluded that Unilever posed the greatest competitive threat. Tor Bergman, Director of the Benecol Division, was quoted in the *Financial Times* as saying "Benecol patents will run 15-20 years. We are sleeping well at night."[6]

Regulatory Hurdles

There were, however, substantial regulatory hurdles facing Benecol in both Europe and the United States.

Europe. In Europe, functional foods like Raisio's Benecol and Unilever's *New Flora* were regulated by the Novel Foods Regulation. In effect since May of 1997, it specified that *functional foods* must follow one of two potential regulatory development paths prior to commercial sale, a *fast-track process* or a *full-assessment track*. *Fast-track approval* was available to new functional foods which were "substantially equivalent to a counter-party," meaning that if the food was similar to other food products already in the marketplace, it could enter the EU market immediately. The local food authority of the member state in which the functional food's firm is established was still required to forward its opinion and relevant data to the central Novel Foods Commission in Brussels for approval. This would not likely apply to Benecol simply because it was the first nutriceutical of its kind. Benecol had been registered

---

[6] "Benecol's Spread of Riches," *The Financial Times*, July 9, 1998.

in Finland as a *dietary product*, according to both Finnish and European Union (EU) legislation.

Full-assessment track approval was a much more complex and time-consuming process. The representative member-state food authority must file an application with the Novel Foods Commission and submit a detailed report within 90 days of the application filing. This report was then distributed to all other 15 member states for evaluation, the results of which must be returned to the Commission within 60 days. If there were no substantial queries or objections, the Standing Committee of the Novel Commission could issue a permit for the food to be sold within the EU immediately. If, however, there were objections arising from the member states, the questions were referred back to the member state authority and the individual firm for evaluation and potential testing or explanation. The firm then re-submitted to the same permit process until all concerns were resolved.

Benecol might, however, might fit through a regulatory loop-hole. Benecol had been sold in Finland since November 1995, meeting the food authority regulatory needs in Finland, an EU member state, <u>prior</u> to the inception of the Novel Foods Commission. It was possible that the Commission's authority did not apply, and Benecol would only need apply to each individual member state's food authority for commercial approval.

United States. The regulatory process was different in the United States, and arguably more difficult. Benecol or McNeil Consumer Products had three basic paths: 1) *food-additive path*; 2) *pharmaceutical path*; and 3) *dietary-supplement path*.

1. **Food-additive path.** Acquiring approval directly from the Food and Drug Administration (FDA) for commercial sale of a food additive was a lengthy and costly process.[7] This process could, however, be superceded if the food was *generally regarded as safe* (GRAS). This standing could be acquired through the firm's own self-affirmation, in which it assembles a panel of independent experts that declares the product safe, and then informs the FDA of its findings. Baring any exceptional objections to submitted data and clinical studies, the product may be introduced commercially in 60 days.

2. **Pharmaceutical path.** Once approved as a pharmaceutical, Benecol could potentially be marketed in a variety of ways (as a drug, a food additive or a dietary-supplement), giving substantial flexibility to exploiting its profit potential. It required, however, an arduous, costly, and time-consuming process of clinical testing. This would take several years.

3. **Dietary-supplement path.** This was by far the easiest and fastest of the three approval paths, although it represented a significant level of risk if questions arose over product properties or claims. To register Benecol as a dietary-supplement,

---

[7] For example, Johnson & Johnson received FDA approval in early 1998 for a product first submitted for direct FDA approval in 1987, 11 years earlier.

the sponsoring firm must simply file a notification letter with the FDA 60 days prior to commercial rollout.[8] Firms would typically file complete data and clinical studies following the notification letter. The dietary supplement was not considered either a drug or a food under this path.

McNeil had chosen the third alternative, to introduce Benecol as a dietary supplement. This would allow the fastest route to market in order to maximize profit and market-growth opportunities. (Introduction of Benecol as a dietary supplement would not preclude a subsequent application as a pharmaceutical.) Although clearly the cheapest and most expeditious, this approach posed significant additional risks to Benecol's profit potential. Marketers would have to walk a fine line in outlining and promoting Benecol. Dietary supplements had traditionally been sold as pills, powders, and tonics. As a dietary supplement, it was unclear whether McNeil could promote Benecol's cholesterol-reducing effects or its added benefits in reducing heart disease.

What troubled Kenza was the possibility that the dietary-supplement/food approach was leaving too much money on the table. If Raisio or Raisio's agent was able to guide Benecol through the troubled waters of FDA approval as a pharmaceutical, it was possible that the value-margins could be substantially larger. On-going clinical tests were not only showing stronger and stronger cholesterol-reducing benefits, but also the clear competitiveness of Benecol with the cholesterol-reducing pharmaceuticals on the market.

The second question was whether Benecol could be promoted for the reduction of coronary heart disease (CHD). CHD, considered one of the top two or three causes of death in most industrialized countries, is principally caused by arteriosclerosis.[9] Arteriosclerosis is the condition in which *fibrous plaques,* fatty streaks, adhere to the walls of blood vessels. This reduces blood flow to the brain and heart. These fibrous plaques are created when free radicals (chemical compounds) cause LDL cholesterols to peroxidize (a process called *lipid peroxidization*). If the LDL levels in the blood serum are reduced, so are the probable levels of fibrous plaques.

The medical profession has tended to focus on three ways to reduce the risk of CHD: 1) reduction of serum cholesterol, via diet or medication; 2) stopping smoking; and 3) increased exercise, which not only encourages HDL cholesterol production but also reduces weight and stress. Reduction of serum cholesterol is considered fundamental to true risk-reduction. Benecol could potentially fall into a very discrete but valuable niche between a low cholesterol diet (the cheapest alternative) and prescribed pharmaceuticals (the most expensive).

---

[8] Although the U.S. Congress largely exempted dietary supplements from FDA regulation in 1994, the FDA still retained the right to pursue additional investigation and study at future dates if health questions arose.

[9] The risk factors for coronary heart disease, in rank-order, are: 1. smoking; 2. serum cholesterol (LDL-based); 3. high blood pressure; 4. obesity; 5. lack of exercise; 6. stress; 7. sex at advancing age; 8. genetics.

Fall 1998 Events

The August crisis in Russia greatly reduced the profitability of grain and margarine sales, dominated by Russian buyers. Raisio reported in October that Benecol sales in Finland were essentially flat, even with the introduction of a lighter version. This implied the new light product had simply replaced existing Benecol sales. Raisio's share price appeared to be headed toward a year-end close of FIM60.

One bit of good news had come from Dr. Tu T. Nguyen of the Mayo Clinic in Rochester, Minnesota, who reported in October that McNeil's slightly altered recipe of Benecol performs comparably to that studied and marketed in Finland. LDL concentrations were reduced by 14% on average. According to Nguyen, "we got the same response in eight weeks that [the Finnish study] got at one year."[10]

In late October, however, the FDA notified McNeil of its objections:

> The purpose of this letter is to advise you that marketing this product with the prototype label that the agency was shown at the meeting would be illegal under the Federal Food, Drug and Cosmetic Act (FD&C Act) .... The label for the Benecol spread, through statements that the product replaces butter or margarine, vignettes picturing the product in common butter and margarine uses, statements promoting the texture and flavour of the product, and statements such as "...help(s) you manage your cholesterol naturally through the food you eat," represents this product for use as a conventional food. Therefore, the product is not a dietary supplement.

Kenza and other analysts had interpreted this to mean that if McNeil wished to distribute Benecol as a dietary supplement, it must be that—a *supplement*—and not a food like margarine (a yellow-colored *spread* applied to food much like butter or margarine).

Although it was known that the FDA and McNeil had a number of additional meetings in November, the impasse was still without official resolution. The FDA argued that Benecol in margarine form was a *food*, not a *dietary supplement*. And FDA had the rights and responsibilities of regulating foods with additives which had not yet been approved as safe. Several analysts had speculated that if McNeil had introduced Benecol in tablet form, it would not have been a problem. McNeil countered FDA arguments with the contention that consumers were not likely to pay $16 a pound for a food (the planned price of the margarine product to be test-marketed). McNeil spokeswoman Amy Weiselman noted that this distinction makes Benecol "less a food substitute than a supplement delivered in the guise of a food."

Kellogg's, in a surprise announcement on November 2nd, unveiled a line of products under the *Ensemble* name containing psyllium, a cholesterol-reducing substance. *Ensemble* would include a variety of food products (cookies, bread, breakfast cereals, among others), and was already approved by the FDA to be marketed as a dietary supplement. Similar to Unilever's *Take Control*, cholesterol reduction was estimated at 8-9%, relative to Benecol's 10%. *Ensemble* was slated for a March 1999 launch.

---

[10] *Science News*, November 14, 1998, Volume 154, Issue 20, p.311.

Raisio's Valuation Revisited

The key to Raisio's value rested on both the global volume and value of Benecol sales. Given the timing delays of FDA approval and the entry of new competitors, forecasts for Benecol sales and Raisio's share price were all over the map. Kenza reviewed various analysts' opinions on Raisio's shares over the past year (Appendices 2 and 3), and returned to her own valuation (Appendices 4-11).

Credit Suisse First Boston (CFSB) has upped its 12-month target price for Finnish food, animal feeds and chemicals group Raisio to 1,200 markka from 900 markka in a report dated January 28. It said it is maintaining its buy recommendation on the stock because it expected the company's cholesterol reducing agent Benecol to get wider application in the second half of 1998.

"We are looking to announcements of Benecol sub-contracts with food manufacturers during the second half of 1998," it said. CSFB said it believes there is a possibility of Benecol being launched in 1998 without full approval, with very limited medical claims.

"Assuming that the 2.5 percent market penetration could be reached after four years in every country, and that the total penetration of the western world could reach 3.5 percent in ten years, our model points to a stock-price target of FIM 1,200," it said. It forecast earnings per share of 10.9 markka in 1997, 20.7 markka in 1998 and 32.9 markka in 1999.

"If the product is a clear success once commercialization in large countries has started, we believe penetration rates could rise further and, as consequence, our target price could also rise," it said.

CSFB said Raisio would face competition from others trying to develop agents similar to Benecol, such as Swiss drug maker Novartis. Novartis agreement with Forbes Medi-Tech to have an exclusive option on a worldwide license to use Forbes' plant-based sterol composition, FCP, in nutritional products is a cheap way of entry into Benecol's potential market, it said.

"If Novartis succeeds in developing FCP with 'scientifically proven benefits,' we believe it will take a share of the market a few years from now," it said. This would, however, stimulate the cholesterol-lowering food market as a whole and therefore not be detrimental to Raisio, it added.

Appendix 2 A Survey of Investment Bankers' Opinions on Raisio

Analyst	Date of Analysis	Recommendation	Title	Current Price	12 Month Price
Credit Suisse First Boston	June 1998	Strong Buy		100	
	September 1998	Strong Buy	"Buoyant Market Before Birth"	67	107.5 - 55
	October 21,1998	Buy		84	107.5 - 55
	November 9,1998	Upgrade to Strong Buy	"Market Overreaction"	50	107.5 - 50
	December 1998	Strong Buy		60	107.5 - 49.2
Merrill Lynch	October 6, 1998	Neutral: Long Term Neutral		76	96
	October 20,1998	Reduce: Long Term Neutral	"Cholesterol Klondike?"	91	76
	November 9, 1998	Neutral: Long Term Neutral		53	45
Dresdner Kleinwort Benson	June 1998	Buy	"Benecol Goes from Strength to Strength"	96	135
	October 6,1998	Buy (unchanged)	"Benecol Goes Pan-US on 7 January"	83	
Warburg Dillon Read	October 8,1998	Buy	"It's Not Over Until the Fat Lady Sings"	82	57 - 108
	April 15, 1998	Buy	"Fear Not the Free Market"	90	175
Nordic Equities	October 14,1998	Outperform/Medium Risk	"Unilever Meets the Misery of EU"	77	
	September 3, 1998	Outperform/High Risk	"Benecol Fears Overrated"	62	
Handelsbanken	December 1998	Reiterate Strong Buy	"Greasing for US Launch"	58	120

Appendix 3 Raisio's Historical Performance

Millions of FIM	1992	1993	1994	1995	1996	1997
Turnover (Net Sales)	3,070	3,549	3,518	3,224	3,928	4,947
Percent change	33%	16%	-1%	-8%	22%	26%
Earnings Before Interest & Taxes	252	294	230	183	196	246
Percent change	5%	17%	-22%	-20%	7%	26%
Shares, Earnings & Dividends						
Average Shares Outstanding (000s):						
Free shares	4,447	4,626	7,060	9,174	10,690	11,709
Restricted shares	8,092	7,914	6,676	5,848	5,200	4,624
Total shares	12,539	12,540	13,736	15,022	15,890	16,333
Share Price (free shares):						
Share price, average (FIM)	29.40	69.54	101.65	59.25	228.01	497.65
Share price, December 31 (FIM)	40.33	82.32	69.98	61.48	290.81	646.82
EPS (FIM)	10.32	18.74	9.68	6.16	4.08	8.27
Dividend per share (FIM)	1.13	1.40	4.58	1.76	2.00	3.00
Price to Earnings Ratio, free shares (PE)	3.9	4.4	7.2	10.0	71.2	78.2

Appendix 4 Raisio's Benecol Sales in Finland

	Size (grams)	Stanol Ester (grams)	Price (FIM)	Daily Need (grams)	Days per Package	Price/day (FIM)	1998e	1999e	2000e	2001e	2002e	2003e	2004e	2005e
Individual Use of Benecol														
One package of Benecol margarine	250.0	20.0	25.00	2.0	10.0	2.50								
Per kilogram	1,000.0	80.0	100.0	2.0	40.0	2.50								
Raisio's Finnish Market														
Population: Finland							5,100,000	5,100,000	5,100,000	5,100,000	5,100,000	5,100,000	5,100,000	5,100,000
Penetration Rate							3.50%	3.60%	3.70%	3.80%	3.90%	4.00%	4.00%	4.00%
Consumption population							178,500	183,600	188,700	193,800	198,900	204,000	204,000	204,000
Gross revenue per person per year (FIM)							912.50	912.50	912.50	912.50	912.50	912.50	912.50	912.50
Accruing to Raisio after distribution costs							593.13	593.13	593.13	593.13	593.13	593.13	593.13	593.13
Raisio's revenues in FIM							105,872,813	108,897,750	111,922,688	114,947,625	117,972,563	120,997,500	120,997,500	120,997,500
Sales price, Benecol margarine (FIM/kg)							100	100	100	100	100	100	100	100
Less distribution costs							35	35	35	35	35	35	35	35
Net revenue accruing to Raisio (FIM/kg)							65	65	65	65	65	65	65	65
Cost of margarine input per kg							10	10	10	10	10	10	10	10
Cost of stanol ester input							27	22	20	15	15	15	15	15
Total cost of inputs in Benecol per kg							37	32	30	25	25	25	25	25
Raisio's gross profit per kg of Benecol							28	33	35	40	40	40	40	40
Gross margin							43%	51%	54%	62%	62%	62%	62%	62%
Raisio's costs of Benecol (FIM)							60,266,063	53,611,200	51,656,625	44,210,625	45,374,063	46,537,500	46,537,500	46,537,500

Appendix 5 Raisio's Global Market Penetration

Individual Use of Benecol	Size (grams)	Stanol Ester (grams)	Price (FIM)	Daily Need (grams)	Days Per Package	Price/day (FIM)	1998e	1999e	2000e	2001e	2002e	2003e	2004e	2005e
One package of Benecol margarine	250.0	20.0	25.00	2.0	10.0	2.50								
Per kilogram	1,000.0	80.0	100.00	2.0	40.0	2.50								
North America														
North American population							284,000,000	284,000,000	284,000,000	284,000,000	284,000,000	284,000,000	284,000,000	284,000,000
NA penetration rate, all product							0.0%	1.0%	2.0%	2.5%	3.0%	3.5%	3.5%	3.5%
Benecol market share								70.0%	65.0%	60.0%	50.0%	40.0%	40.0%	40.0%
Benecol consumers								1,988,000	3,692,000	4,260,000	4,260,000	3,976,000	3,976,000	3,976,000
Retail price of Benecol, kilo (USD)							$20.00	$20.00	$20.00	$20.00	$20.00	$20.00	$20.00	$20.00
Gross revenue per person per year (USD)							$182.50	$182.50	$182.50	$182.50	$182.50	$182.50	$182.50	$182.50
Gross revenue, NA market (USD)								362,810,000	673,790,000	777,450,000	777,450,000	725,620,000	725,620,000	725,620,000
Distribution costs (% of retail)							30.0%	30.0%	30.0%	30.0%	30.0%	30.0%	30.0%	30.0%
Revenues accruing to J&J (USD)								253,967,000	471,653,000	544,215,000	544,215,000	507,934,000	507,934,000	507,934,000
European Union														
European population (EU11)							372,000,000	372,000,000	372,000,000	372,000,000	372,000,000	372,000,000	372,000,000	372,000,000
European penetration rate, all product								0.2%	0.5%	1.0%	1.5%	2.0%	2.5%	3.0%
Benecol market share								50.0%	45.0%	40.0%	40.0%	40.0%	40.0%	40.0%
Benecol consumers								372,000	837,000	1,488,000	2,232,000	2,976,000	3,720,000	4,464,000
Retail price of Benecol, kilo (USD)								$20.00	$20.00	$20.00	$20.00	$20.00	$20.00	$20.00
Gross revenue per person per year (USD)								$182.50	$182.50	$182.50	$182.50	$182.50	$182.50	$182.50
Gross revenue, EU market (USD)								67,890,000	152,752,500	271,560,000	407,340,000	543,120,000	678,900,000	814,680,000
Distribution costs (% of retail)								30.0%	30.0%	30.0%	30.0%	30.0%	30.0%	30.0%
Revenues accruing to J&J (USD)								47,523,000	106,926,750	190,092,000	285,138,000	380,184,000	475,230,000	570,276,000
Japan														
Japanese population							126,000,000	126,000,000	126,000,000	126,000,000	126,000,000	126,000,000	126,000,000	126,000,000
Japanese penetration rate, all product									0.2%	0.4%	0.5%	0.8%	1.0%	1.5%
Benecol market share									100%	75%	50%	50%	50%	50%
Benecol consumers									252,000	378,000	315,000	504,000	630,000	945,000
Retail price of Benecol, kilo (USD)							$20.00		$20.00	$20.00	$20.00	$20.00	$20.00	$20.00
Gross revenue per person per year (USD)							$182.50		$182.50	$182.50	$182.50	$182.50	$182.50	$182.50
Gross revenue, Japanese market (USD)									45,990,000	68,985,000	57,487,500	91,980,000	114,975,000	172,462,500
Distribution costs (% of retail)							35.0%		35.0%	35.0%	35.0%	35.0%	35.0%	35.0%
Revenues accruing to J&J (USD)									29,893,500	44,840,250	37,366,875	59,787,000	74,733,750	112,100,625

A06-99-0004

Appendix 6 Raisio's Proceeds from Global Agreement with Johnson & Johnson

	Size (grams)	Stanol Ester (grams)	Price (FIM)	Daily Need (grams)	Days Per Package	Price/day (FIM)	1998e	1999e	2000e	2001e	2002e	2003e	2004e	2005e
Individual Use of Benecol														
One package of Benecol margarine	250.0	20.0	25.00	2.0	10.0	2.50								
Per kilogram	1,000.0	80.0	100.0	2.0	40.0	2.50								
J&J Agreement: Royalties														
Gross revenues, US market (USD)							-	362,810,000	673,790,000	777,450,000	777,450,000	725,620,000	725,620,000	725,620,000
Gross revenues, EU market (USD)							-	67,890,000	152,752,500	271,560,000	407,340,000	543,120,000	678,900,000	814,680,000
Gross revenues, Japanese market (USD)							-		45,990,000	68,985,000	57,487,500	91,980,000	114,975,000	172,462,500
Total revenues (USD)							-	430,700,000	872,532,500	1,117,995,000	1,242,277,500	1,360,720,000	1,519,495,000	1,712,762,500
Exchange rate (FIM/USD)							5.0000	5.0000	5.0000	5.0000	5.0000	5.0000	5.0000	5.0000
Revenue base for royalties (FIM)								2,153,500,000	4,362,662,500	5,589,975,000	6,211,387,500	6,803,600,000	7,597,475,000	8,563,812,500
Royalty rate to Raisio for Benecol products							5%	5%	5%	5%	5%	5%	5%	5%
Royalty payments to Raisio (FIM)								107,675,000	218,133,125	279,498,750	310,569,375	340,180,000	379,873,750	428,190,625
J&J Agreement: Stanol Ester														
Sales price of stanol ester to J&J (FIM/tonne)							600	600	600	600	600	600	600	600
Cost price of stanol ester							300	244	222	167	167	167	167	167
Gross profit on stanol ester (FIM/tonne)							300	356	378	433	433	433	433	433
Gross margin							50%	59%	63%	72%	72%	72%	72%	72%
Stanol ester per person per year (kg)							0.730	0.730	0.730	0.730	0.730	0.730	0.730	0.730
Total consumers (US, EU, Japan)								2,360,000	4,781,000	6,126,000	6,807,000	7,456,000	8,326,000	9,385,000
Total stanol ester, kilograms								1,722,800	3,490,130	4,471,980	4,969,110	5,442,880	6,077,980	6,851,050
Total stanol ester, tonnes								1,723	3,490	4,472	4,969	5,443	6,078	6,851
Sales of stanol ester to J&J (FIM)								1,033,680	2,094,078	2,683,188	2,981,466	3,265,728	3,646,788	4,110,630
J&J Agreement: Milestone Payments														
Payments to Raisio from J&J (FIM)							110,000,000	150,000,000	100,000,000	50,000,000	-	-	-	-

Appendix 7 Raisio's Division Results (in millions of FIM)

	1996	1997	1998e	1999e	2000e	2001e	2002e	2003e	2004e	2005e
Chemical Division										
Revenue	1,360	1,634	1,733	1,819	1,910	2,006	2,106	2,211	2,322	2,438
Revenue growth	24%	20%	6%	5%	5%	5%	5%	5%	5%	5%
EBIT	101	93	90	102	107	112	118	124	130	137
EBIT margin	7.4%	5.7%	5.2%	5.6%	5.6%	5.6%	5.6%	5.6%	5.6%	5.6%
Implied cost of sales	1,259	1,541	1,642	1,717	1,803	1,893	1,988	2,087	2,192	2,301
Margarine Division										
Revenue	864	1,678	1,309	1,322	1,361	1,402	1,444	1,488	1,532	1,578
Revenue growth	45%	94%	-22%	1%	3%	3%	3%	3%	3%	3%
EBIT	12	106	7	20	27	35	43	45	46	47
EBIT margin	1.4%	6.3%	0.5%	1.5%	2.0%	2.5%	3.0%	3.0%	3.0%	3.0%
Implied cost of sales	852	1,572	1,302	1,302	1,334	1,367	1,401	1,443	1,486	1,531
Grain Division										
Revenue	1,627	1,725	1,725	1,759	1,812	1,866	1,922	1,980	2,039	2,100
Revenue growth	45%	6%	0%	2%	3%	3%	3%	3%	3%	3%
EBIT	79	58	60	69	78	80	83	85	88	90
EBIT margin	4.9%	3.4%	3.5%	3.9%	4.3%	4.3%	4.3%	4.3%	4.3%	4.3%
Implied cost of sales	1,548	1,667	1,664	1,691	1,734	1,786	1,840	1,895	1,952	2,010
Benecol										
Revenue	-	99	216	368	432	447	432	464	505	553
Revenue growth	na	na	118%	70%	18%	3%	-3%	8%	9%	10%
Revenue Summary										
Benecol	-	99	216	368	432	447	432	464	505	553
Chemicals	1,360	1,634	1,733	1,819	1,910	2,006	2,106	2,211	2,322	2,438
Margarine	864	1,678	1,309	1,322	1,361	1,402	1,444	1,488	1,532	1,578
Grain	1,627	1,725	1,725	1,752	1,812	1,866	1,922	1,980	2,032	2,100
Total Sales	3,851	5,136	4,982	5,268	5,516	5,721	5,904	6,143	6,398	6,670
Benecol	0%	2%	4%	7%	8%	8%	7%	8%	8%	8%
Chemicals	35%	32%	35%	35%	35%	35%	36%	36%	36%	37%
Margarine	22%	33%	26%	25%	25%	25%	24%	24%	24%	24%
Grain	42%	34%	35%	33%	33%	33%	33%	32%	32%	31%
Total Sales	100%	100%	100%	100%	100%	100%	100%	100%	100%	100%

Appendix 8 Raisio's Pro Forma Income Statement (millions of FIM)

Year-end (December)	1996	1997	1998e	1999e	2000e	2001e	2002e	2003e	2004e	2005e
Benecol, Raisio's sales	-	69	106	109	112	115	118	121	121	121
Benecol, milestones	-	30	110	150	100	50	-	-	-	-
Benecol, stanol ester	-	-	-	1	2	3	-	3	4	-
Benecol, royalties	-	-	-	108	218	279	311	340	380	428
Benecol Revenues	-	99	216	368	432	447	432	464	505	553
As percent of total	0%	2%	4%	7%	8%	8%	7%	8%	8%	8%
Chemicals	1,360	1,634	1,733	1,819	1,910	2,006	2,106	2,211	2,322	2,438
Margarine	864	1,609	1,309	1,322	1,361	1,402	1,444	1,488	1,532	1,578
Grain	1,627	1,725	1,725	1,759	1,812	1,866	1,922	1,980	2,039	2,100
Other income	-	68	-	-	-	-	-	-	-	-
Non-Benecol Revenues	3,928	5,036	4,766	4,900	5,083	5,274	5,473	5,679	5,893	6,117
As percent of total	100%	98%	96%	93%	92%	92%	93%	92%	92%	92%
Total Revenues	3,928	5,135	4,982	5,268	5,516	5,721	5,904	6,143	6,398	6,670
Percent growth	22%	31%	-3%	6%	5%	4%	3%	4%	4%	4%
Cost of sales	(3,535)	(4,604)	(4,277)	(4,356)	(4,472)	(4,596)	(4,770)	(4,950)	(5,139)	(5,335)
As % of Cost-Revenue	90.0%	92.1%	91.0%	90.0%	89.0%	88.0%	88.0%	88.0%	88.0%	88.0%
EBITDA	393	531	705	912	1,044	1,125	1,134	1,193	1,259	1,335
Gross Margin	10.0%	10.3%	14.2%	17.3%	18.9%	19.7%	19.2%	19.4%	19.7%	20.0%
Depreciation	(212)	(229)	(249)	(263)	(276)	(286)	(295)	(307)	(320)	(333)
Goodwill amortization	(12)	(22)								
EBIT	169	281	456	648	768	839	839	886	940	1,002
Operating Margin	4%	6%	10%	13%	15%	16%	15%	16%	16%	16%
Associates	3	10	12	12	12	12	12	12	12	12
Investment income & other	19	3	3	3	3	3	3	3	3	3
Net interest	(51)	(50)	(72)	(46)	(30)	(30)	(30)	(30)	(30)	(30)
EBT	140	244	399	618	753	824	825	872	925	987
Extraordinary income	(4)	(90)	-	-	-	-	-	-	-	-
Tax	(63)	(64)	(132)	(204)	(249)	(272)	(272)	(288)	(305)	(326)
Minorities	(8)	(21)	(9)	(10)	(10)	(10)	(10)	(10)	(10)	(10)
Net Profit	66	110	258	404	495	542	542	574	610	651
EPS	0.40	0.67	1.57	2.44	3.00	3.28	3.28	3.48	3.69	3.94
Tax rate	33%	33%	33%	33%	33%	33%	33%	33%	33%	33%
Distribution rate	50%									
Dividends	32.76	55.22	129.24	201.89	247.36	271.13	271.23	286.96	304.79	325.59
Retained earnings	32.76	55.22	129.24	201.89	247.36	271.13	271.23	286.96	304.79	325.59

Notes:
1 "Cost-Revenue" refers to all revenues which possess actual production costs; it excludes milestone and royalty payments.
2 Cost of sales line item includes differing cost assumptions by the following categories: traditional product lines; stanol ester sales to J&J; Benecol sales by Raisio.
3 The line item "change in deferred tax liability" included in Raisio's Finnish income statement (just prior to net profit) is excluded here.
4 As a result of the differences between Finnish accounting standards and US GAAP, these 1996 and 1997 results may not match those reported by Raisio exactly.
5 Depreciation assumed to be 5% of sales throughout.

Appendix 9 Raisio's Prof Forma Balance Sheet (millions of FIM)

Year-end (December)	1996	1997	1998e	1999e	2000e	2001e	2002e	2003e	2004e	2005e
Cash & Marketable Securities	306	247	582	604	769	1,016	1,266	1,525	1,800	2,094
Receivables	677	668	682	722	756	784	809	842	876	914
Inventory	669	775	797	843	883	915	945	983	1,024	1,067
Current assets	1,652	1,690	2,062	2,168	2,407	2,715	3,020	3,350	3,700	4,075
Intangible	556	529	529	529	529	529	529	529	529	529
Net fixed assets	1,385	1,491	1,491	1,491	1,491	1,491	1,491	1,491	1,491	1,491
Investments	86	116	116	116	116	116	116	116	116	116
Total Assets	3,679	3,826	4,198	4,304	4,543	4,851	5,156	5,486	5,836	6,211
Payables	431	450	498	527	552	572	590	614	640	667
Other creditors	347	617	498	474	441	458	472	491	512	534
Current liabilities	778	1,067	996	1,001	993	1,030	1,063	1,106	1,152	1,201
Total debt (long term)	928	988	800	700	700	700	700	700	700	700
Equity	1,098	1,611	1,740	1,942	2,189	2,461	2,732	3,019	3,324	3,649
Minorities & Provisions	875	161	161	161	161	161	161	161	161	161
Total equity	1,973	1,772	1,901	2,103	2,350	2,622	2,893	3,180	3,485	3,810
Total Liabilities & Equity	3,679	3,827	3,698	3,804	4,043	4,351	4,656	4,986	5,336	5,711
Sales	3,928	5,135	4,982	5,268	5,516	5,721	5,904	6,143	6,398	6,670
Days sales outstanding	63	47	50	50	50	50	50	50	50	50
Inventory as % of sales	17%	15%	16%	16%	16%	16%	16%	16%	16%	16%
Payables days outstanding	40	32	40	40	40	40	40	40	40	40
As % of sales	11%	9%	10%	10%	10%	10%	10%	10%	10%	10%
Other credits % of sales	9%	12%	10%	9%	8%	8%	8%	8%	8%	8%

Year-end (December)	1997	1998e	1999e	2000e	2001e	2002e	2003e	2004e	2005e
Net income	110	258	404	495	542	542	574	610	651
Add back depreciation:	229	249	263	276	286	295	307	320	333
Add back goodwill amortiz	22	-	-	-	-	-	-	-	-
Increases in A/R	9	(14)	(39)	(34)	(28)	(25)	(33)	(35)	(37)
Increases in stocks	(106)	(22)	(46)	(40)	(33)	(29)	(38)	(41)	(44)
Increases in A/P	19	48	29	25	21	18	24	25	27
Increases in credit	270	(119)	(24)	(33)	16	15	19	20	22
Other	(10)								
Operating Cash Flows	543	400	587	689	804	816	853	900	953
Capital expenditure	(106)	(249)	(263)	(276)	(286)	(295)	(307)	(320)	(333)
Investing Cash Flows	(106)	(249)	(263)	(276)	(286)	(295)	(307)	(320)	(333)
Dividends paid	(55)	(129)	(202)	(247)	(271)	(271)	(287)	(305)	(326)
Change in net debt	60	(188)	(100)						
Financing Cash Flows	5	(317)	(302)	(247)	(271)	(271)	(287)	(305)	(326)
Cash (boy)	306	748	582	604	769	1,016	1,266	1,525	1,800
Change in cash flow	442	(166)	21	166	247	250	259	275	294
Cash (eoy)	748	582	604	769	1,016	1,266	1,525	1,800	2,094

Appendix 11 Valuation of the Raisio Group (millions of FIM)

| Year of DCF | | 1 | 2 | 3 | 4 | 5 | 6 | 7 | Terminal |
Calendar Year	1998	1999	2000	2001	2002	2003	2004	2005	Value
EBIT	456	648	768	839	839	886	940	1,002	1,032
Less calculated taxes	(151)	(214)	(253)	(277)	(277)	(293)	(310)	(331)	(340)
EBIT after-tax	306	434	515	562	562	594	630	671	691
Plus depreciation	249	263	276	286	295	307	320	333	383
Less capital expenditure	(249)	(263)	(276)	(286)	(295)	(307)	(320)	(333)	(383)
Less added working capital	(107)	(80)	(82)	(28)	(29)	(30)	(32)	(34)	(34)
Free Cash Flows	198	354	433	534	533	564	598	637	657
Terminal Value	—							13,386	
CFs for Discounting		354	433	534	533	564	598	14,023	
Discount factor (WACC)		0.9267	0.8588	0.7958	0.7375	0.6834	0.6333	0.5869	
Discounted CF @ WACC		328	372	425	393	385	378	8,230	
Cumulative PV of Cashflows	10,513								

Valuation

Firm Value	10,513
Less Debt	(800)
Equity Value	9,713
Shares Outstanding	165.15
Equity Value Per Share	59

Note: Terminal Value makes up the following percentage of total valuation: 75%

FCF compound growth rate, 1999 to 2005: 10.3%

WACC Calculation

Cost of equity	8.30%	Atx Cost of debt	4.36%	Debt
Risk premium	4.00%	Borrowing rate	6.50%	Equity
Beta for Raisio	1.00	Tax rate	33.0%	Firm Value
Long bond (risk-free rate)	4.30%	L.T. growth	3.00%	
Current share price	62	Shares out (m)	165.15	WACC

Debt	800	7%
Equity	10,239	93%
Firm Value	11,039	100%
WACC	7.91%	

Notes:
1 Recalculation of taxes on EBIT eliminates the tax shields associated with interest, which are in turn eventually included in the discounting by the WACC.
2 Depreciation and CAPEX are assumed equal into the future.

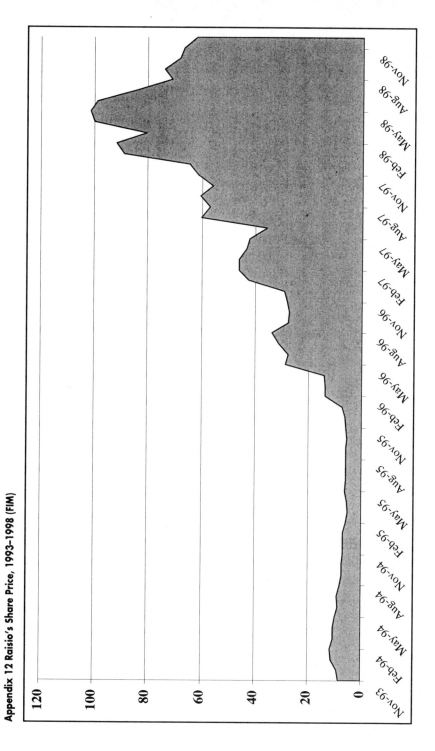

Appendix 12 Raisio's Share Price, 1993–1998 (FIM)

GLAXO ITALIA S.P.A.: THE ZINNAT MARKETING DECISION

The laws of the marketplace now apply as much to pharmaceuticals as to consumer electronics: once armed with a new product, a company must establish its market share as quickly as possible, before rival firms produce competitive brands. . . . In the past, drugs brought in good profits for a decade or more.

—Ernest Mario, chief executive officer of Glaxo Holdings PLC [1]

In September 1990, the laws of the pharmaceutical marketplace prompted Emilio Rottoli, financial controller of Glaxo Italia S.p.A.,[2] to evaluate competing strategies for the launch of a promising new product in Italy. Zinnat was a new formula of oral antibiotic. After a research-and-development cost of more than 200 billion Italian lire,[3] the product represented a significant innovation in its market segment. However, the huge quantity of competing antibiotics and antihistaminics made success of the product launch unpredictable.

Glaxo's general approach to launching a new product called for rapid and massive distribution into the target market in order to capture a large market share quickly, but Rottoli had decided to evaluate two competing strategies for selling Zinnat:

◆ *Co-marketing distribution,* under which Glaxo would permit another pharmaceutical company to make and market the same product but under a different brand name. Glaxo would receive a fee from the co-marketer, plus profits on the sales of certain ingredients to that firm. This arrangement would sacrifice some market share for Glaxo's own brand, Zinnat. Glaxo had used co-marketing arrangements to promote other products. The major market for Glaxo's best selling product, Zantac, an anti-ulcer drug, was developed under a co-marketing agreement with Hoffmann-La Roche, whose sales teams organized

---

[1]Quoted in *The Economist,* September 6, 1990.
[2]Societa per Azioni; literally, a business under share ownership, like a public corporation in the United States. Also, PLC means a public limited company.
[3]On September 14, 1990, one U.S. dollar could purchase 1,165 lire.

This case was prepared from field interviews and public information by Matteo Davoli, Giuseppe Geneletti, Marco Ghiotto, Diogo Rezende, and Professor Robert F. Bruner. Some financial information has been disguised. The cooperation of Emilio Rottoli and Glaxo Italia S.p.A. is gratefully acknowledged, as is the financial support of the Citicorp Global Scholars Program. Copyright (c) 1992 by the University of Virginia Darden School Foundation, Charlottesville, VA, and INSEAD, Fontainebleau, France. All rights reserved. To order copies, send an e-mail to dardencases@virginia.edu. No part of this publication may be reproduced, stored in a retrieval system, used in a spreadsheet, or transmitted in any form or by any meansCelectronic, mechanical, photocopying, recording, or otherwiseCwithout the permission of the Darden School Foundation.

Exhibit 1 Annual Value of £1 Invested in Glaxo Holdings Stock in 1979 (indexed so that the value for 1979 equals £1; uses yearly median stock prices; adjusted for 100% stock dividends in 1983 and 1985)

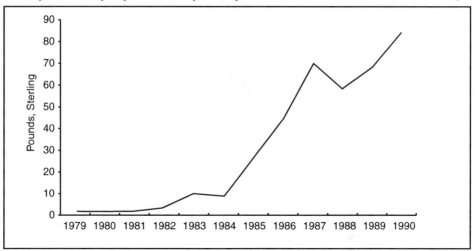

the introduction of the product among doctors in the United States. The tremendous success of this initiative had built up an appetite (and an expertise) within the company for such arrangements.

♦   Direct sales, under which Glaxo's own sales force would be the sole channel of distribution. This approach would permit the company to exploit the potential gains from its new product most fully. Under this approach, demands on Glaxo's sales organization would be greater than in co-marketing, however, and market penetration for the product would take longer.

The choice between the two approaches would hinge not only on financial criteria (such as payback and internal rate of return) but also on qualitative factors such as the potential strength of the brand, uncertainties about the future regulation of a possible over-the-counter (OTC) product, the need to generate cash in the short term to sustain a large R&D budget, uncertainties about the rate of technological change in the pharmaceutical industry and the development of products competitive to Zinnat, potential price wars, and the peculiar aspects of the Italian market.

Glaxo Holdings PLC

Glaxo Italia S.p.A. was a wholly owned operating company of Glaxo Holdings PLC, headquartered in London. Glaxo Holdings was the world's second largest pharmaceutical company in terms of sales, which totaled £2,894 million in the fiscal year ending June 30, 1990, and were expected to grow to £3.4 billion in 1991.[4] The company's growth had been phenomenal: £1 invested in the company in 1979 was

---

[4]On September 14, 1990, £1 = 2,212 Italian lire and US$1.898.

Exhibit 2 Shares of Pharmaceutical Market (Italy, 1990)

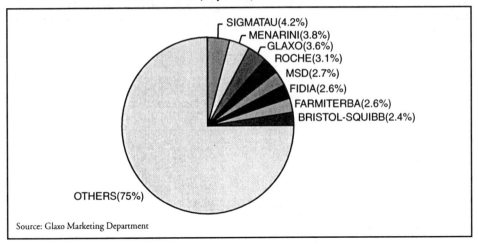

SIGMATAU(4.2%)
MENARINI(3.8%)
GLAXO(3.6%)
ROCHE(3.1%)
MSD(2.7%)
FIDIA(2.6%)
FARMITERBA(2.6%)
BRISTOL-SQUIBB(2.4%)

OTHERS(75%)

Source: Glaxo Marketing Department

worth £85 in 1990, approximately a 50 percent annual compound rate of growth in value (see Exhibit 1). Glaxo's shares were listed for trading in London, New York (as American Depositary Receipts), Tokyo, and Paris. With an equity market value of $23 billion, the company had the distinction of being the largest capitalization stock traded on the London stock market and the 26th largest traded in the United States.

Glaxo was a leader in products for the relief of peptic ulcers and of asthma and was a major supplier of antibiotics and of treatments for skin disorders. For several reasons, many of Glaxo's new drugs eventually achieved dominant market positions. First, Glaxo focused its research on unmet medical needs. Second, the company always coupled its R&D strategy with a fast track record in new-drug approval time. Third, Glaxo had built up one of the world's biggest sales forces for drugs, 9,500 representatives. Fourth, its marketing machine went into action early in a product's life. While the new drug was being developed, Glaxo held costly symposiums to which it invited opinion leaders who knew about the disease the drug was designed to treat. The idea was to build and gauge market potential. Once a drug was presented to regulators for approval, the marketers used public-relations firms to work out ways to create demand. Doctors were flooded with medical literature and given guidelines on how to diagnose the disease. Medical authorities were persuaded of the economic savings from the product introduction. Almost immediately after a drug had been launched, Glaxo established small studies to monitor the performance of the drug in a normal population in order to spot any new adverse effect. Doctors were paid for their contributions to these studies.

Glaxo Italia S.p.A.

Glaxo Italia S.p.A. was the oldest Glaxo subsidiary. Exhibit 2 reveals that the subsidiary had the third largest market share in the highly fragmented Italian pharmaceutical

Exhibit 3 Glaxo Italia Financial Performance, Historical and Projected, 1989-1995

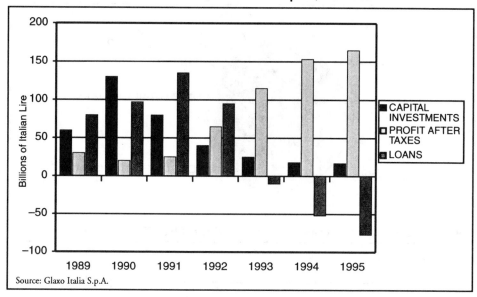

Source: Glaxo Italia S.p.A.

market. Based in Verona (in the northeastern part of the country and the setting of Shakespeare's Romeo and Juliet), Glaxo Italia had manufacturing facilities producing most of Glaxo Holdings' products. The company work force was about 2,000 people, 400 of whom were involved in research.

Glaxo Holdings granted unusual autonomy to its operating subsidiaries, including discretion over product positioning, the choice of promotional mix, the timing of line extensions, and resource allocation to various products. Glaxo Italia's objectives were to achieve a turnover [5] of 2 trillion lire, which would represent 9 percent of the market, with a 50 percent profit margin, by the turn of the century. In order to achieve these challenging goals, the company was rapidly expanding its sales force and had invested heavily in new research facilities (156 billion lire), which was one of the five most important R&D centers for Glaxo Holdings. Last but not least, Glaxo Holdings had selected Italy as the site for the Glaxo Management School.

As shown in Exhibit 3, this expansion strategy was expected to dampen profitability in the short term, but within five years, the heavy investment and debt-based financing were forecasted to pay off in a sevenfold growth of profits. Glaxo Italia sales in 1991 were expected to be 719 billion lire, which included 183 billion lire of sales by licensees and co-marketers. The total would represent 6.2 percent of the pharmaceutical market (3.8 percent through direct sales only). Exhibit 4 reveals that a quarter of these sales would derive from licensees in co-marketing agreements; Exhibit 5 indicates that continued sales growth depended significantly on new products and sales by licensees.

---

[5]"Turnover" is equivalent to sales revenue.

Exhibit 4 Glaxo Italia Product Portfolio, 1991 (projected revenues, 720 billion ITL)

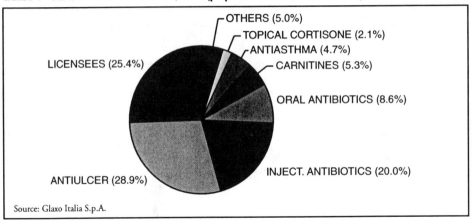

OTHERS (5.0%)
TOPICAL CORTISONE (2.1%)
ANTIASTHMA (4.7%)
CARNITINES (5.3%)
LICENSEES (25.4%)
ORAL ANTIBIOTICS (8.6%)
INJECT. ANTIBIOTICS (20.0%)
ANTIULCER (28.9%)

Source: Glaxo Italia S.p.A.

Exhibit 5 Glaxo Italia Sales Composition, Historical and Projected, 1980–1995

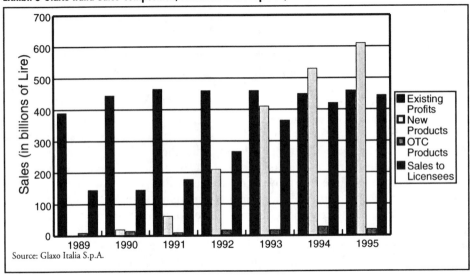

Source: Glaxo Italia S.p.A.

Zinnat

The Zinnat oral antibiotic offered a new competitive remedy to current drugs for influenza-like feverish diseases. Zinnat's launch would be a major opportunity and challenge for the company to support and expand its presence in the antibiotic segment. The product would be introduced in two formulations: (1) a package of 12 pills of 250 milligrams each with a retail price of 34,400 Italian lire (ITL) and (2) a 2.5-g. syrup with a retail price of 29,880 ITL. The manufacturer's price was 61 percent of the retail price. Gross margin was 53 percent of the manufacturer's price. The cost of goods sold consisted mainly of costs of raw materials, local production, bottling, and fees. The raw material was sold to Glaxo Italia S.p.A. and any co-marketers from Glaxo Holdings at a transfer price of 1,566 ITL/gram. Glaxo

Italia would pay an additional 4 percent of this price for customs fees, transportation, etc. The transfer price consisted of variable costs (20 percent) and the product's share of R&D expenses incurred (80 percent). Glaxo Italia and any co-marketers had to anticipate a 20 percent cost for local production and bottling.

The Ethical and OTC Pharmaceutical Markets

Glaxo planned to introduce Zinnat solely into the ethical-drug market, although at some point in the future, Zinnat might convert into an OTC drug. (When a drug was prescribed over a long period of time, it could develop a strong brand image.) These two main segments of the market were significantly different.

In the ethical-drug market, a doctor's prescription was necessary to obtain the product; therefore, the doctor was the "gate keeper" to the end user and the target of marketing efforts by the manufacturers.

Italian doctors were renowned in Europe for their interest in new drugs. As a result, the average life cycle of ethical drugs tended to be shorter in Italy than elsewhere. Glaxo managers believed that aggressive use of sales-force marketing (both direct and co-marketed) would have a strong effect on Zinnat's market share.

OTCs, by definition, could be purchased directly from retailers (usually, but not necessarily, pharmacies). No patents applied in the case of OTCs, and all OTCs were branded. In most countries, OTCs could be directly advertised to the public, while ethical drugs were subjected to government regulations that allowed them to be advertised only in media targeted to the medical profession.

In general, manufacturers decided whether a drug they were developing fit the ethical or the OTC market, but a final decision was made by national drug-control authorities. OTC drugs were usually established remedies for minor illnesses such as coughs, colds, and flu or preventive preparations such as vitamins and tonics. For a new drug to be launched straight into the OTC market was extremely rare.

Ethical drugs might, however, be sold over the counter when their patents expired. This conversion could occur when an ethical drug, after a number of years on the market, was found not to have significant side effects and its potency for conditions other than those for which it was prescribed was limited. When government regulators were satisfied that a drug's side effects and potency were limited, they would permit the drug to be sold without a prescription.

Marketers at Glaxo believed that OTC marketing would increase for several reasons: (1) tighter control of national health-service budgets was leading to increasing incentives for self-medication; (2) patients were becoming more and more able to take on active roles as consumers; (3) liberalization in national drug-approval agencies had increased the number of products in this market (for instance, in Denmark, H2 antagonists[6] such as Zantac had been permitted to go OTC since 1989).

Antibiotics, because of their consumption patterns and intrinsic characteristics, were one product category that might experience movement into the OTC market

---

[6]H2 antagonists (also called H2 blockers) block the histamine receptor (H2) in the body and thus reduces the production of gastric acids believed to cause stomach ulcers.

early in their life cycles. Glaxo Holdings wanted to enter this segment first, however, because of its large share of revenues. But Glaxo Holdings considered itself an ethical-drug company and was structured accordingly (substantial R&D facilities and investments, marketing and distribution organizations centered on sales representatives rather than on advertising or brand management). One Glaxo Holdings executive was quoted as saying that "strong brand images were not our area. OTC was a different sort of business."[7] But the company was prepared to adapt.

The Policy of Rapid Product Launch: The Role of Co-Marketing

Glaxo's strategy of rapid market penetration for new products sought to create several advantages: (1) the "snow-ball" effect of word-of-mouth advertising within the medical community; (2) economies of scale and scope (the introduction costs, such as presentations to doctors and hospitals, conferences, advertising, were relatively fixed) could be gained if the costs were spread across the largest possible volume; and (3) raised barriers to entry (preemption of market space). Rapid penetration also served the fundamental need to generate positive cash flows in the shortest possible time in order to finance investments in R&D for future products. Glaxo Holdings' new products that reached the launch phase were, in fact, extremely profitable, with internal rates of return generally greater than 200 percent. In the pharmaceutical industry, one R&D project in ten became a commercialized new product; thus new-product development in a growing company such as Glaxo required significant investment.

Glaxo Italia possessed two direct sales-force teams (called "lines") currently employing 320 sales representatives each. In co-marketing agreements, Glaxo would pursue rapid market penetration by adding the sales efforts of the co-marketer as each marketed its own brands of the same product.[8] With co-marketing, Glaxo anticipated various benefits: volumes would be higher and reached in shorter times than when marketing alone. In addition, establishing close ties with other firms could provide additional lobbying leverage in regulatory environments where the registration process for new products was particularly slow and bureaucratic. The co-marketer could benefit in two ways. First, that firm's sales force could carry more products and thereby make each sales call more productive. Second, a broader product line might help keep the sales force productive during any trough in the firm's business cycle.

On the other hand, the presence of a distribution partner had several disadvantages. First, Glaxo had to increase its sales force and marketing efforts to compete against the co-marketer's products. Second, the co-marketer, which was also a pharmaceutical company in 90 percent of the cases, might be tempted to reformulate the product (and thus side-step licensing fees) if it proved to be successful. Co-marketing strategies were also vulnerable to price wars and litigation over allocation of resources and territories, and risked saturation of the doctors' attention.

---

[7] In the *Financial Times,* November 8, 1989.

[8] Another classic joint marketing arrangement called co-detailing (same product, same brand name).

Product Life and Patent Life

Product life and patent life were important influences on the Zinnat marketing decision. Product life consisted of the remaining years of effective patent life, plus any years thereafter when the product might continue to be sold without the benefit of patent protection. In theory, the product life of Zinnat could be infinite. Even after the patent expired, Zinnat might continue to be prescribed. The earliest antibiotic—penicillin—was still being prescribed by doctors, well after the expiration of patent protection. But the rate of innovation in the development of new antibiotics was increasing, raising the likelihood that Zinnat would be displaced by some new drug. Practically, Mr. Rottoli doubted there would be any appreciable sales of Zinnat after the fifteenth year.

Patent life was the number of years of protection for inventors from uncompensated direct imitation of their invention. The total patent life in the United States was 17 years, whereas in Europe it was 20 years. Patent life was taken up by (1) the time required to develop the specific application after the new compound had been developed, (2) the time necessary for registration, (3) the time required to introduce the product, and (4) the remaining "effective" patent life. Exhibit 6 shows that effective patent life fell from 13 to 5 years between 1965 and 1985. As Sir Peter Girolami, chairman of Glaxo, had recently said,

> Medicines, which are now emerging from the development pipeline, are more complex and more powerful than their predecessors; this inevitably complicates the necessary process of satisfying regulatory authorities.

A shortening of effective patent life could reduce the period of time during which protected profits on a drug could be made. Rottoli forecasted the Zinnat cash

Exhibit 6   Effective Patent Life of Drugs in EC, 1965 and 1985

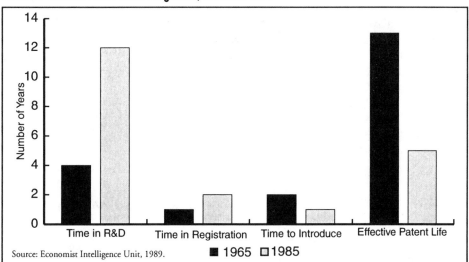

Source: Economist Intelligence Unit, 1989.   ■ 1965 □ 1985

flows out to the sixth year in the belief that the product should prove that it could earn its return during that window of effective patent protection.

While patent life had shortened, R&D expenditures were constantly increasing. One widely accepted estimate of the average cost to discover and bring a major new drug to the market was US$100 million. The implication of these high costs was that large revenues had to be generated to pay for them. According to one study of The Wellcome Foundation, to achieve an adequate return on an R&D expenditure of US$100 million, a drug had to reach peak annual sales of over US$200 million and total sales revenues of 11 times the R&D spent.[9] Rottoli estimated that a delay of just one week in development time represented a loss in terms of revenues of US$1–US$2 million. At the same time, the reduction in effective patent life led to a quicker significant drop in sales revenues when the price had to be reduced to face competition from the generic product. Co-marketing could increase the risk of competition when a patent expired, because the co-marketer might be prepared to manufacture the product in house. To manufacture Zinnat, for instance, the co-marketer would have to pay a licensing fee and would be required to purchase some ingredients from Glaxo Holdings. Without the protection of a patent, the fee and the supply arrangement would disappear.

Financial Criteria

Glaxo Italia used two main criteria as the basis for evaluating decisions about sales strategies: payback and internal rate of return (IRR).

♦ Payback. Any new product launched had to have a payback period of less than three years. This period reflected the company's strategic emphasis on rapid market penetration. The use of the payback criterion was justified on two grounds. First, given the extended industry practice of "cross-subsidization" among products, senior managers needed to know when a new product would start to generate cash surpluses that could be used to finance new R&D projects. Payback helped focus managers' attention on the cash-flow breakeven. Second, uncertainty about the time at which competitors could launch a similar product made it relevant to know how much time was necessary to recover the additional investment to market the product.

♦ IRR. The more desirable strategy would have the higher IRR. Glaxo's minimum required IRR on projects in Italy was the firm's cost of debt there (12.5 percent in September 1990).[10] Exhibit 7 contains information on current capital-market conditions.

---

[9]Trevor M. Jones, "Improving the Development Process," paper presented at the World Pharmaceutical Conference, London, March 1990.

[10]The yield-to-maturity of Glaxo holdings' long-term debt in the United Kingdom was 12.5 percent. Its book value of debt amounted to £420 million. Its market value of equity was £12,193 million. Also, Glaxo could borrow long-term funds in Italian lire at 12.5 percent.

Exhibit 7   Capital-Market Conditions, September 1990

Yield on long-term government bonds			
	United Kingdom	Italy	
June	11.01%	11.32%	
September	11.32%	11.60%	
Expected inflation rate	5%	4%	
	Price/Earnings Ratio	Share Price (US$)	Beta
Glaxo Holdings PLC	**15.6**	**30**	**.90**
Bristol Myers-Squibb	18.5	66	1.00
Eli Lilly	17.6	77	1.10
Pfizer	16.1	81	1.05
Rhône-Poulenc Rorer	7.5	9 3/8	1.05
Schering Plough Corp.	17.5	16	1.15
Equity market risk premium			
(64-year geometric mean)	5.6%		

Sources: *Financial Times, Risk Measurement Services, Value Line Investment Survey.*

When asked if an appropriate discount rate should take into account the cost of equity capital as well as the cost of debt, Rottoli answered:

> Investors expect to get higher returns? Well, if I produce good returns, they'll get them. If I don't, they won't! To begin with, let's start from zero cash and a new project on the way. At this point in time, the firm, hypothetically, can borrow money from a bank at, say, 12.5 percent; that represents the cost of debt. After this initial cost is entirely paid back from the project cash flows, what is left to the shareholders is the project net IRR (i.e., net of financial charges). Thus we do not fix any a priori target for shareholders' returns, be they based on market averages or historical trends or even future forecasts. It is sufficient for the net IRR to be greater than zero to justify the investment. It then falls to the investors to accept the expected rate of return on the project or to reject it. However, the net IRR is still clearly higher than what the shareholders will ultimately get from the business. I mean, we need yet to include and subtract all the fixed and structural costs necessary to run the business before getting to the investors' payoff. These are basically the reasons why I tend to consider discounted cash flow based on the project WACC (weighted-average cost of capital) premature at this stage.

Referring to the choice of costs and cash flows included in the forecast, Rottoli said,

> Only manufacturing and promotional cost are considered relevant. The remaining items—such as G&A (general and administrative), historical and future R&D (at local and group level), medical testing cost, real financial charges, taxes—are not taken into account. [11] Not at all! We are really interested in evaluating the marginal profitability between direct sales

---

[11]Glaxo Italia's marginal tax rate was 47 percent. Glaxo holdings' marginal tax rate in the United Kingdom was 29 percent.

and co-marketing. Therefore, all of those items being shared by the two alternatives end up complicating the measures while not dramatically improving the final decision.

Financial Projections

To evaluate the strategic choice between direct sales and co-marketing, Rottoli had prepared a financial model as presented in Exhibits 8, 9, and 10. Assumptions underlying the model are summarized in Exhibit 8. Aspects of the forecast that required some judgment were the following:

♦ *Product mix.* In the first year, the model assumed this mix: 85 percent pills and 15 percent syrup. From the second year on, the mix was assumed to be 80 percent pills and 20 percent syrup. The licensee was assumed to weight the product mix differently: 40 percent pills and 60 percent syrup. These assumptions were based on prior experience.

♦ *Marketing costs.* These costs included (1) the cost of drug samples given to doctors and clinics, (2) the cost of medical promotions (trials to hospitals, clinics, and local health-care units), (3) the cost of seminars, congresses, and social promotions (one-hour short conferences plus dinners held by technical/scientific sales reps), (4) the cost of training the sales force, and (5) sales force compensation. Assumptions about these costs were based on prior experience. Sales-force compensation costs could be saved if Glaxo chose to market Zinnat directly, rather than with a co-marketer. Rottoli believed that the sales force would spend about 25 percent less time on Zinnat if the product were marketed directly, instead of with a co-marketer—this reflected the highly motivational effects of competition.

♦ *Market share.* The effect of competition from the co-marketer would be reflected in higher market share for Zinnat in the antibiotic market, and earlier attainment of a notable position. Figure 1 (on page 13) compares the two market share forecasts projected by the Glaxo Italia staff. The lower market shares for Zinnat under the direct sales strategy were consistent with experience on other products, though Rottoli believed that the share forecast for direct sales was perhaps conservative. The market shares for the direct sales strategy could be as much as one, two or three percent higher.

♦ *Sales force.* Zinnat was assigned principally to the sales force named "Line 1." In the first year only, sales force "Line 2" would support the launch. The cost of the direct sales force was calculated according to the estimated percentage time to be spent on the specific product. Historically, the cost per salesperson had increased by 12 percent each year on average; the forecast assumed this growth rate in salesperson costs over the forecast period. [12] The sales force in Line 1 was supposed to grow from 320 to 440 reps within three years, but Rottoli

---

[12]Beyond year six, one could assume that the cost per salesperson would grow at the rate of inflation in the lira, 4 percent.

Exhibit 8   Forecast Assumptions

	First Year Product Mix	Years 2+ Product Mix	1990 Price to Retail Cust. lira	Content of Key Raw Materials (gr)	1990 Manufacturer Price to Retailer	1990 Transfer Price Of Ingredients (lira/gr)
Pills sold by Glaxo	85%	80%	34,400.0	3.0	20,984.0	1,566.0
Syrup sold by Glaxo	15%	20%	29,880.0	2.5	18,226.8	1,566.0
Pills sold by Licensee	40%	40%				
Syrup sold by Licensee	60%	60%				
Marginal tax rate - Italy	47.0%					
Marginal tax rate - UK	29.0%					
Expected inflation rate - Italian lira	0.0%					
Expected inflation rate - UK, pounds, sterling	5.0%					
Yearly percentage increase in cost per sales rep.	12.0%					
Yearly decline in market share after year 6	4.0%					
Savings in promotional effort direct sales vs. co-marketing	25.0%					
Licensee fee (% of Zinnat revenues to licensee)	4.0%					
Working capital required/Sales	16.7%					
Glaxo Holdings, interest rate and internal charge for capital	12.5%					

	1990	1991	1992	1993	1994	1995	1996
Market forecast of antibiotic demand (millions of units)		52.3	46.6	46.6	44.6	46.3	47.2
Market share for Zinnat, direct sales strategy	0.0%	5.1%	9.0%	9.0%	9.1%	9.1%	9.1%
Market share for Zinnat, co-marketing strategy	0.0%	9.0%	13.0%	12.5%	11.5%	11.0%	10.0%
% Zinnat volume sold by Glaxo, co-marketing strategy		45.35%	61.79%	63.78%	67.40%	71.38%	71.63%
Years from Sept. 1990	0.25	1.25	2.25	3.25	4.25	5.25	6.25
Transfer price of ingredients per gram (lira)	1,566.0	1,566.0	1,566.0	1,566.0	1,566.0	1,566.0	1,566.0
Glaxo Price to customer - pills (lira)	20,984.0	20,984.0	20,984.0	20,984.0	20,984.0	20,984.0	20,984.0
Glaxo price to customer - syrup (lira)	18,226.8	18,226.8	18,226.8	18,226.8	18,226.8	18,226.8	18,226.8
Gross margin/direct sales, Glaxo Italia	53%	53%	53%	53%	53%	53%	53%
Gross margin/Ingredient sales, Glaxo Holdings	80%	80%	80%	80%	80%	80%	80%
Sales force #1—salespeople	320	320	350	400	400	400	440
% time on Zinnat (if direct marketing)	20%	20%	20%	18%	16%	17%	17%
% time on Zinnat (if co-marketing)	26%	26%	25%	24%	21%	23%	23%
Sales force #2—salespeople	320	320	350	400	400	400	440
% time on Zinnat (if direct marketing)	18%	18%	18%	18%	18%	17%	17%
% time on Zinnat (if co-marketing)	13%	13%	13%	13%	13%	13%	13%
Cost per sales rep (millions of lira)		105.0	117.6	131.7	147.5	165.2	185.0

Figure 1 Zinnat Market Share by Strategy

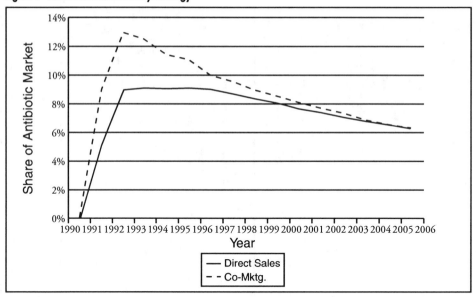

wrestled with the question of whether this increased sales-force promotional time was a marginal item or just a reallocation of corporate resources that would be needed anyway. He said,

> It was an eternal source of discussion between me and Mr. (Giuseppe) Ferrari, the Sales V.P. I told him that as long as new employees were hired for new-product promotional support, the sales structure was an incremental expense of this product launch. Mr. Ferrari argued that the sales force supported the company as a whole and that, therefore, the cost of new sales recruits should not be included in the forecast.

The financial forecast prepared by Rottoli charged Zinnat for the percent of actual sales force time that the product was assumed to require.

♦ *Group profit on parent-subsidiary transfer of ingredients.* This figure was the profit that Glaxo Holdings PLC (the parent) made on the sales of the key chemical compounds to Glaxo Italia (the subsidiary). Glaxo explained that this profit was a means of reimbursing the parent for R&D expenses. The ingredients could be directly packaged by Glaxo Italia or possibly resold to the co-marketer. The price per gram of the ingredients was 1,566 lire, which included a gross profit of 80 percent to Glaxo Holdings.

♦ *Capital generated and interest.* Glaxo Holdings viewed the product launch as having a cash flow (or flow of "capital generated") equal to the product margin less the working-capital requirement (equivalent to two months of sales.) The Zinnat product line in Italy would be charged interest for capital used, or credited interest for net capital supplied to Glaxo Holdings. The interest charge

Exhibit 9 Financial Forecast: Direct Sales (all figures in ITL billions)

	1990	1991	1992	1993	1994	1995	1996
Quantities of units (000)							
volume sold direct		1958	3491	3644	3656	3816	3948
samples		710	700	600	400	400	350
Glaxo Italia: Profit							
Revenues	0.0	40.28	71.34	74.46	74.70	77.97	80.67
Gross margin		21.4	37.8	39.5	39.6	41.3	42.8
Marketing expense, direct sales:							
Samples expense		3.3	3.2	2.7	1.8	1.8	1.6
Medical promotions (trials)	0.2	0.4	0.7	0.7	0.7	0.8	
Seminars, congresses, etc.	0.2	5.6	5.1	4.5	2.2	2.4	2.5
Sales force training	0.3	1.4	0.4	0.4	1.2	1.2	1.3
Compensation: sales force #1		6.6	10.2	9.5	9.3	11.4	14.0
Compensation: sales force #2		5.9					
Total marketing expense	0.7	23.1	19.6	17.9	15.3	17.7	19.4
Profit: Direct sales	-0.7	-1.8	18.2	21.6	24.3	23.7	23.3
Glaxo Holdings							
Profit on sales of ingredients to Glaxo Italia		9.8	15.2	15.4	14.7	15.3	15.6
Capital charge (-), income(+)	0.0	-0.1	0.1	3.6	8.6	14.6	21.2
Profit: Zinnat product line	-0.7	7.9	33.5	40.6	47.7	53.5	60.1
Investment in NWC	0.0	6.7	5.2	0.5	0.0	0.5	0.4
Capital Generated	**-0.7**	**1.2**	**28.3**	**40.1**	**47.6**	**53.0**	**59.7**
Cumulative Capital							
Used (-) or Generated (+)	-0.7	0.5	28.8	68.9	116.6	169.6	229.2
IRR on Capital Employed	**690%**						
Payback Period	1.1 years						

or credit was equal to the current yield on Glaxo Holdings' debt, multiplied by the cumulative capital used or generated at the end of the previous year. The initial phase of a project was somewhat similar to an entrepreneur venturing upon a new business. Initial exposure for a new-product launch was burdened by interest expenses at the stated rate until the early outlays were recovered. From then on, the business's profits would be "loaned" to new emerging projects at the same stated rate, according to the following logic: "One line generates cash, while another—internally—absorbs part of it," as Mr. Rottoli said. The capital employed then turned from a use (–) to a generation of cash (+). Investors expected higher returns from a project, however, than from purchasing securities on the market.

♦ *Time horizon.* Although the product life cycle of pharmaceutical products was typically between 10 and 20 years, the forecast was carried out to only 6 years. Product managers and marketing directors found extending a forecast beyond

Exhibit 10 Financial Forecast: Co-Marketing (all figures in ITL billions)

	1990	1991	1992	1993	1994	1995	1996
Quantities of units (000)							
volume sold direct by Glaxo	1,813	3,308	3,336	3,185	3,352	3,132	
samples distributed free	50	710	700	600	400	400	350
sold by licensees	200	2,895	2,746	2,494	1,941	1,744	1,591
Total	250	5,419	6,754	6,430	5,526	5,496	5,073
Glaxo, Italia: Profit							
Direct sales by Glaxo Italia	0.0	37.3	67.6	68.2	65.1	68.5	64.0
Gross margin, direct sales	0.0	19.8	35.8	36.1	34.5	36.3	33.9
Marketing expense, direct sales:							
Samples expense	0.2	3.3	3.2	2.7	1.8	1.8	1.6
Medical promotions (trials)	0.2	0.4	0.7	0.7	0.7	0.7	
Seminars, congresses, etc.	0.2	5.2	4.7	4.1	2.0	2.1	1.9
Sales force training	1.0	1.3	0.3	0.3	1.0	1.1	1.0
Compensation: sales force #1		8.7	13.6	12.6	12.4	15.2	18.7
Compensation: sales force #2		5.9					
Total marketing expense	1.6	24.8	22.5	20.5	17.9	20.9	23.2
Profit: Direct sales, Glaxo Italia	-1.6	-5.0	13.3	15.6	16.6	15.4	10.7
Glaxo Holdings: Profit and Fees							
Ingredient sales to Glaxo							
Italia and licensee	1.1	22.9	28.6	27.2	23.4	23.2	21.4
Profit: ingredient sales, Glaxo HIdgs.	0.8	18.3	22.8	21.7	18.7	18.6	17.2
Fee from licensee	0.2	2.2	2.1	1.9	1.5	1.3	1.2
Capital charge (-), income(+)	0.0	-0.1	0.6	4.7	10.2	16.3	22.6
Profit: Zinnat product line	-0.6	15.5	38.9	44.0	47.1	51.7	51.8
Change in working capital	0.2	9.9	6.0	-0.1	-1.2	0.5	-1.0
Capital Generated	**-0.8**	**5.6**	**32.9**	**44.2**	**48.2**	**51.1**	**52.8**
Cumulative Capital							
Used (-) or Generated (+)	-0.8	4.8	37.7	81.9	130.1	181.2	234.0
IRR on Capital Employed	**1013%**						
Payback Period	**0.2 year**						

Sources: Company analysis and casewriters' analysis.

6 years difficult. They believed that Zinnat in Italy would enjoy its strongest competitive standing in its first 6 years of life. From the seventh year on, the product's share of the antibiotic market would decline. Mr. Rottoli estimated that a reasonable rate of decline would be 4 percent per year. [13] He wondered, however, whether the rate of decline and/or the cash flows beyond the forecast horizon mattered.

◆   *Fees from the licensee.* Under the contemplated arrangement, the Italian co-marketer would pay Glaxo Holdings an annual fee equal to 4 percent of its revenues from Zinnat sales. However, the size of this fee would be the

---

[13]That is, share of market in year 2 would be 95 percent of the share of market in year 1.

focus of tough negotiation. The ultimate arrangement could entail a fee lower or higher than 4 percent.

Conclusion

The data in the forecasts Rottoli was holding (Exhibits 8, 9, and 10) suggested he should undoubtedly recommend that the company go forward with co-marketing instead of direct sales:

	Direct Sales	Co-marketing
IRR	690%	1013%
Payback	1.1 years	0.2 year

He wondered, however, whether these base-case results adequately captured the richness of the problem. For instance, how robust was the preference for co-marketing to considerations such as these:

♦ What combinations of license fees, sales force savings and market share would leave Glaxo indifferent between the two marketing strategies?

♦ Taking Mr. Ferrari's argument, should the cost of the field sales force be considered to be incremental to the Zinnat launch?

♦ The combined action of two firms would allow reaching a high maximum market share in 24 months, whereas the effort of only one firm required 36 months in the forecast to achieve a lower market share. How significant was the benefit of the incremental speed and market penetration?

♦ After the product proved itself in the marketplace, a co-marketer might defect to its own brand; thus direct selling could have a distinctly different set of cash flows beyond year 6. In addition, the appearance or nonappearance of newer products could affect the more distant cash flows. What should be done about cash flows beyond the five-year forecast horizon?

On top of these concerns, Rottoli wondered if the forecasting system with which he was endowed captured the best insights. Glaxo had delivered abundant value to shareholders. Would the current financial evaluation of the Zinnat marketing decision promote that value? Were IRR and payback the best decision criteria? Was he missing any relevant cash flows?

AVICULAR CONTROLS &
PAKISTAN INTERNATIONAL AIRLINES

Gabriel Benguela had just walked into his office from attending an operations review when the telephone rang. Gabriel guessed that this late in the day, the call must be from one of his Marketing Managers based in the Far East. It was indeed; Peter Mai was calling from Avicular's Singapore office. Peter was the lead negotiator on a deal under negotiation with Pakistan International Airlines (PIA). It was July 6, 1997.

Peter: "Gabriel, we have a problem with the PIA proposal. Although our local agent keeps assuring me that we have won this competition and we will get the deal, I'm not so sure. Pakistan's negotiations with the International Monetary Fund (IMF) to secure yet another loan to finance their current account deficit is causing more problems for this deal. Recent economic data for the country is also not very good, with low economic growth and continuing employment problems. There have been more demonstrations in Lahore because of the European Union's recent anti-dumping ruling imposing high tariffs against several cotton exporting countries including Pakistan. The export of cotton is not only a major source of employment, but also a source of badly needed hard currency. All this on the heels of the IMF's austerity program."

Gabriel: "What does PIA want now? How long have we been trying to finalize this deal?"

Peter: "Seven months. PIA has asked that we accept local currency."

Gabriel: "That's just great! Peter, you know our division never accepts payment in local currency. Although nearly 50% of our business is international, we are just not set up to accept the risk that denominating sales in other currencies would bring. In fact, the whole aerospace business is conducted in U.S. dollars."

Peter: "Hey, blame the IMF. They should be charged for inciting riots and billed for our expenses."

Gabriel: "We need this program badly. These large cockpit retrofit opportunities are hard to find and it seems that our division's management has already committed this $23.7 million sale to Corporate on our latest stretch goal."

Peter: "There is an alternative. Our agent, Makran, advised me that they can buy the receivable from us at a 5% discount and take all of the currency risk. Their Los Angeles subsidiary would pay us 30 days after our invoice."

Gabriel: "But we can't take another hit to the return on sales on this deal. As the deal stands, we had to go to Group Level for approval on this one. This isn't good. I'll speak with the finance people and call you back within 24 hours."

Avicular Controls

Avicular Controls, Inc. (ACI), based in Chicago, had dominated the field of automatic controls since its founding in 1903. Beginning with furnace controls for the steel and power industries in 1903, it continued to grow for over 90 years. By 1996, Avicular employed 13,000 people and conducted business in 52 countries. ACI was composed of two major business units: Industrial Process Controls (AvIPC, 1996 sales of $1.75 billion), and Aviation Control (AvAC, 1996 sales of $1.21 billion). In the summer of 1997 ACI was positioned to achieve its sales growth goal of $4 billion by the year 2000.

AvAC was once again on a growth path after several tough years. Avicular was recognized as the dominant force in the avionics market; market share had grown to a hefty 53% by 1996. But the industry had suffered a severe downturn beginning in 1992, and was only now reaching the sales levels achieved last in 1991. In fact, AvAC sales had been $1.6 billion in 1991, and would hopefully once again break the $1.5 billion line in 1997. The commercial aircraft industry returned to a healthy growth path in 1996 and early 1997, and growth was expected to stay robust through the year 2000.

ACI, specifically the Air Transport Systems division of the Space and Aviation Control business unit had recorded a number of major wins in 1996. These wins included the contract for the cockpit retrofits for a major overnight package delivery firm's fleet of DC-10s, and numerous orders for the firm's new enhanced airborne collision avoidance system. Although U.S. government spending for electronic components was leveling off, international opportunities for military avionics retrofits and space systems were on the rise. Commercial space programs were also projected to grow rapidly, and ACI had landed key initial contracts with NASA and Lockheed Martin.

ACI was not new to international business, establishing its first foreign subsidiaries in 1936. Global treasury was headquartered (along with corporate) near O'Hare International Airport outside Chicago. Corporate treasury was a profit center, and charged 1% commission on all sales. Treasury, however, passed on the currency risk to the business unit. If a local affiliate, joint venture, or subsidiary required local currency, then Treasury would try and match those requirements by accepting the A/R in the local currency. For many developing countries where ACI had little or no activities (such as Pakistan), this was only done on an exception basis. Treasury did agree that Aviation Controls could use their local affiliates to manage the sale of aviation products, but would have to pay between 3% and 8% for currency cover (the final fee would have to be negotiated between Treasury and Aviation Controls). This was something that the division had an unwritten policy of *not* doing; the standard transfer charge imposed by Treasury cut into sales margins.

Pakistan International Airlines (PIA)

Pakistan International Airlines Corporation (PIA) was the national flag carrier of the Islamic Republic of Pakistan. Founded in 1954, PIA operated both scheduled passenger and cargo services. The firm was 57% state-owned, with the remaining 43% held by private investors internal to Pakistan. PIA had been Pakistan's only airline for over 40 years, but in 1993 Aero Asia International Ltd. was born. By 1996, however, it had captured little of the domestic or Pakistan international market (only 5% of Aero Asia's sales were international). Two other recent entrants into the domestic market, Bhoja Airlines Pvt. LTD and Shaheen Air, had captured little of the market.

The International Air Transport Association's (IATA) latest projections indicated that passenger and cargo traffic would double in Asia by the year 2010. Asia was expected to surpass Europe and North America in both size of fleets and passenger/cargo hauled. PIA was experiencing some of this growth, but its aging fleet was resulting in losses. Increasing numbers of flights were either delayed or canceled as a result of maintenance problems. Although a larger and larger proportion of the population was traveling by air, given the choice of taking a PIA or foreign carrier, passenger traffic was opting for the latter. It was imperative that PIA modernize its fleet.

In addition to PIA's traditional passenger and cargo services, a growing proportion of sales was arising from the yearly Islamic Haj (pilgrimage) traffic to Mecca and Medina in Saudia Arabia. Demand had always been strong, but increasing numbers of Pakistani citizens were obtaining visas for the pilgrimage, as Saudi Arabia had recently shuffled the allocation of Haj visas among nations and Pakistan had benefited. PIA was a direct beneficiary of the increased visa allocation.

PIA had originally planned to purchase new commercial aircraft to replace and add to their existing fleet. The fleet modernization program, however, was put on hold due to higher priorities within the Pakistan government in Islamabad. These priorities were established after a review by the IMF of the government's spending plan. Much to PIA's discomfort, the austerity plan proposed by the IMF did not include funds for modernization. PIA had been counting on this fleet modernization and had postponed the incorporation of some Federal Aviation Administration (FAA) safety directives. With the cancellation of the fleet modernization program, PIA now had to move fast to ensure compliance with FAA safety mandates, or face being locked out of some of its most profitable gates. If PIA did not have some of these safety systems and quieter engines installed on their aircraft by June 30, 1998, they would be barred from U.S. airspace.

PIA was in a predicament. It knew exactly what should be done, but government control—especially in these times of crisis—left it no choice. Once PIA agreed to putting the fleet *modernization program* on hold, the managing board decided to pursue a fleet *renovation program* which would require much less hard currency. This plan called for extensively refurbishing PIA's existing aircraft at their new heavy maintenance facility in Karachi. For example, instead of the new quieter engines which new aircraft possessed, PIA would have to make do with the use of *hush kits* for the older engines. It would also require completely new cockpit avionics to take advantage of not only FAA mandates, but recent improvements in the Air Traffic Network (ATN) infrastructure. The first aircraft to be modified would be those utilized on their long-haul flights to the United States, primarily the *B747 classics* (Boeing). Aircraft engine suppliers were approached first and negotiations concluded.

What remained on the table was the cockpit avionics integration supplier. A cockpit retrofit program would require contracts both with the appropriate original equipment manufacturer (OEM), in this case Boeing, and a systems integrator, such as Avicular. Prior to the adoption of the economic austerity plan, Karachi had been the sight of an intense competition between the largest OEMs, Boeing, McDonnell Douglas, and Airbus, for new aircraft sales. It was only after the adoption of the austerity plan that Boeing was willing to discuss cockpit retrofits instead. Due to ACI's extensive experience with a variety of control systems for Boeing, its history with PIA, and its recent work on cockpit retrofit for McDonnell Douglas aircraft, ACI felt it was truly the preferred supplier for PIA. ACI believed that if any other vendor were selected, the added regulatory certification costs and delays would be prohibitively expensive. However, ACI had not undertaken Boeing cockpit retrofits to date (no one had), and looked to the PIA deal as an opportunity to build a new competitive base. But ACI's best and final bid had been too high. PIA's insistence on payment in local currency terms was now thought to be a tactic to extract better concessions from ACI and their agent, Makran.

The Pakistani Economy

Pakistan was divided from India in 1947 as a homeland for Muslims. Pakistan's relationship with India had, however, been under continuous strain since that time for a variety of reasons. The sources of friction included overlapping claims to Kashmir, India's involvement in the demise of East Pakistan, and the birth of Bangladesh in 1971, to name but a few. Because of these conflicts the military had always loomed large over politics in Pakistan. The country's persistence in continuing a nuclear rivalry with India, when neither nation was thought to be able to afford such a *luxury*, was one indication of this. The United States is frequently at odds with Pakistan regarding its nuclear weapons program. The U.S. has suspended military aid on several occasions, including a large F16 purchase in the early 1990s. However, Pakistan's proximity to Afghanistan and India make it strategically important to U.S. interests.

Pakistan practices Islamic Banking, which is based on the *shariah*. This code prohibits the payment of interest, and the suppliers of funds find themselves becoming *investors,* rather than *creditors.* Although financial profit in most forms was looked down upon under Islamic rule, there were 28 publicly traded equities in Pakistan in 1996. The trading of equity shares for profit was also somewhat inconsistent with the *shariah*.

Pakistan has relied upon the World Bank (WB), the IMF, and other multinational lenders (in addition to specific national foreign aid and investment providers) for much of its capital. The country's deteriorating trade gap in the mid-1990s had caused a sudden and significant drop in foreign currency reserves, from US$3 billion to less than US$1.5 billion in September of 1996. The IMF immediately interceded in the economy, imposing an austerity program in October. The government submitted to

EXHIBIT 1 Daily Exchange Rate: Pakistani Rupees per U.S. Dollar

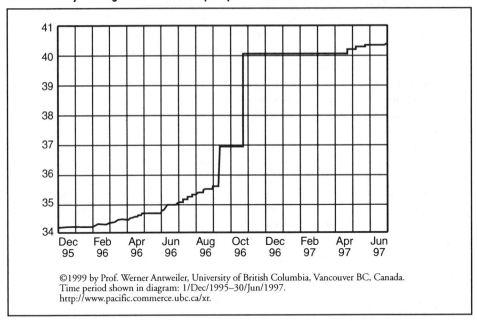

©1999 by Prof. Werner Antweiler, University of British Columbia, Vancouver BC, Canada.
Time period shown in diagram: 1/Dec/1995–30/Jun/1997.
http://www.pacific.commerce.ubc.ca/xr.

this austerity plan as a precondition of receiving a $600 million standby loan extended to cover balance of payments shortfalls. The political repercussions were swift and severe: the fall of the Benazir Bhutto administration.[1]

A central part of the IMF's austerity program was a devaluation of the Pakistan rupee by 7.86% against the U.S. dollar on October 22, 1996. Roughly six months later, there was renewed speculation that another devaluation was imminent in order to limit imports and help the export sector earn badly needed hard currency. Another recent economic setback had been the ruling by the European Union that Pakistan was guilty of dumping cotton, and had imposed anti-dumping fines of between 13.0% and 22.9% on Pakistani cotton. It was a painful blow to the export sector. The current exchange rate of 40.4795 Pakistan rupee (Rp) per dollar was maintained by the Pakistani Central Bank; all currency transactions were controlled by the Pakistani government, and were conducted at the official rate. The *black market rate* was approaching Rp50/US$, and as the spread between the black market rate and official rate increased, the probability of devaluation increased. There was no forward market for the Pakistani rupee.[2] Exhibit 1 illustrates the recent travails of the rupee.

---

[1] Benazir Bhutto is the daughter of the assassinated former Prime Minster Ali Bhutto and the first woman elected to lead a Muslim nation.

[2] Forward markets for currencies are contracts offered by financial institutions for exchanges of currency at future dates at predetermined exchange rates. These forward contracts are an extremely common and efficient method of managing currency risk on short-to-medium-term transactions. Unfortunately, forward contracts have in the past been typically limited in availability to the 10 or 15 most widely traded world currencies.

The Avicular/PIA Relationship

ACI had been the preferred avionics supplier to PIA for many years, and the retrofit segment of the business was thought to fit well with the overall strategy of the division. The group president was personally involved with the PIA proposal since this new retrofit market niche was central to the division's growth plan.

The avionics business was divided into two segments: Standard Furnished Equipment (SFE) and Buyer Furnished Equipment (BFE). OEMs such as Boeing, McDonnell Douglas, and Airbus purchased avionics equipment to be installed on new aircraft as SFE. The margins in selling to this segment were traditionally very low due to the competitive necessity of keeping competitors "off the aircraft." The low margins on OEM sales, however, were made up by higher margins in the sales of spare avionics packages to the same airlines. The purchase of BFE (also called *freedom of choice*) by the airlines is optional, and usually bid among three suppliers. BFE was purchased directly by the airline and installed by either the airline itself or the OEM. Each time an airline made a new aircraft purchase, a BFE proposal would be presented to the airline. The PIA B747 classic fleet retrofit fell into this category.

The major players in the global avionics business in 1996, in addition to Avicular (US), were Honeywell Incorporated (US), Rockwell Collins (US), Allied-Signal (US), and Sextant Avionique (France). To a lesser extent, Litton Industries (US) and Smiths Industries (UK) competed in small specialized segments. Of this competition, however, only Rockwell Collins and Honeywell had the capability to take on such a large cockpit retrofit job. Rockwell Collins was considered very competitive, and had extensive experience in dealing with the Pakistani government on several large military contracts completed under the U.S. Foreign Military Assistance program.

The global aerospace industry was historically a U.S. dollar business; a dollar-denominated industry. The large airframe manufacturers like Boeing had long taken the lead with the sheer size of their purchase deals. Recently, however, cracks were appearing in this business practice. Competition now focused on more than price. Other competitive elements included credit terms, credit risk, as well as currency of contract denomination.

Ibrahim Makran Pvt. LTD

In countries like Pakistan, the use of an agent is often considered a necessary evil. The agent can oftentimes help to bridge the two business cultures and provide invaluable information—at a cost. ACI's agent, Ibrahim Makran Pvt. LTD., based in Hyderabad, was considered one of the most reliable and well connected in Pakistan. Makran was also one of the largest import/export trading houses in Pakistan, giving it access to hard currency. It was 100% family-owned and managed.

Standard practice in the avionics business was to provide the agent with a 10% commission (10% of the total final sales price paid after payment is received). Typically, it was the agent who identified the business opportunity and submitted a Business Opportunity Request (BOR) to ACI Marketing. Sometimes this commission was negotiated, but due to the size and importance of this proposal, the commission was accepted without debate.

After PIA contacted ACI and Makran with their latest demand, Makran knew that ACI would want to maintain the deal in U.S. dollars. Makran had immediately inquired as to the availability of dollar funds from its own finance department for a deal of this size. The finance department confirmed that they had the necessary U.S. dollar funds to pay ACI, but noted that the standard fee was 5% of the invoiced amount.

Makran then advised ACI that it would be willing to purchase the receivable for the additional 5% (in addition to the 10% commission). The company's U.S. subsidiary based in Los Angeles would credit ACI within 30 days of ACI invoicing Makran. PIA advised Makran that if ACI accepted payment in Pakistan rupees, then local (Pakistan) payment terms would apply. This meant 180 days in principle, but often was much longer in practice. The agent also advised ACI that the Pakistan rupee was due for another devaluation soon. When pressed for more information, Makran simply replied that the company president, the elder Ibrahim Makran, had "good connections."

The ATS Finance Department

Philip Costa, the finance director for AvAC, had always wanted to be an engineer. His passion for exactness and numbers had, however, included the dollar sign, and he had moved up through the ranks at ACI quickly. The finance department he led was now in the midst of redesigning most of their processes and systems to reduce net working capital (NWC). One of these initiatives included a thorough review of existing payment terms and worldwide days sales receivable (DSR) rates. The department had a goal of reducing the worldwide DSR rate from 55 to 45 days in the current fiscal year. The *Pay for Performance* target for the current year (the annual performance bonus system at ACI) included NWC goals, and there was concern in the organization that the NWC goal might prove the obstacle to achieving a payout bonus despite excellent sales growth. And all cash flows, in and out, were to be evaluated in present value terms using a 12% discount rate. Philip started his assessment by reviewing the latest DSR report shown in Exhibit 2.

ACI payment terms were net 30 from date of invoice. However, payment terms and practices varied dramatically across country and region. ACI had not in the past enforced stringent credit terms on many customers; for example, neither contracts nor invoices stated any penalties for late payment. Many airlines did pay on time, but others availed themselves of ACI's low-cost financing.

A review of PIA's accounts receivable history indicated they consistently paid their invoices late. The current average DSR was 264 days. PIA had been repeatedly put on hold by the collections department, forcing marketing staff representatives to press the agent who in turn pressed PIA for payment. Philip's concern over the collection had driven him to search for guarantees of prompt payment. In the end, he had required the inclusion of a 20% advance payment clause in the contract as a means of self-insuring. Although marketing took the high DSR rate up with PIA and the agent, this deal was expected to be the same if not worse. One positive attribute of the contract was the fact that deliveries would not commence until one year after

EXHIBIT 2 Average Days Sales Receivables by Region and OEM, Aviation System Division

Region	Actual	Target	Amount
North America	44	40	$31 million
South America	129	70	$2.1 million
Europe	55	45	$5.7 million
Middle East	93	60	$3.2 million
Asia	75	55	$11 million
PIA	264	180	$0.7 million
Boeing		3930	$41 million
McDonnell Douglas	35	30	$18 million
Airbus Industrie	70	45	$13 million
Worldwide	55	45	

1. Many foreign carriers make purchases through U.S.-based trading companies, distorting the actual DSR practices by country.
2. The spread between individual customers within regions can be extremely large.
3. Disputed invoices are included. Amount is for all products, services, and exchanges.
4. Firms consistently meeting ACI's net 30-day terms were eligible for participation in ACI's preferred supplier program which entitled them to a 10% discount on future purchases. Only the largest customers had, to date, taken advantage of this discount. discount.

project start. If the expected improvements to the DSR were made in the meantime, maybe the high DSR rate on the PIA deal could be averaged with the rest of Asia. The 20% advance payment would be used to fund the front-end engineering work. Philip also insisted that it was the responsibility of his department to assess *credit risk* for the project. This typically required a detailed review of the buyer's financials. Unfortunately, the most recent published financial data for PIA was extremely sparse, and out of date (1990).

Meeting with Finance

Gabriel: "Good morning, Philip. I am sorry to trouble you yet again with this PIA deal, but we have a problem. Peter called me last night and advised me that PIA wanted to pay in local currency. If we don't agree, we risk losing the deal. I think it's fallout from the 20% advance payment clause. Our agent, Makran, said they could accept the risk and net 30 payment terms for 5% of the sales price. Although we're confident that we are the only competing company that can meet PIA's requirements, should this requirement be real and we refuse, it could derail the whole PIA project."

Philip: "Five percent is too steep! We simply cannot accept that. This is already one of the riskiest projects we have undertaken. The 20% advance payment is to help with the DSR since it is one of our primary goals. The DSR is being watched on a daily basis by division management. We already had to secure Group Level approval for this deal because it fell below our minimum 20% ROS [return on sales] target. Whose side is this agent on?"

Gabriel: "Why don't we accept the forex risk? After all, the rupee is fixed by the government."

Philip: "Gabriel, fixed exchanged rates are actually less stable than floating rates. If you consider the IMF and World Bank part of the Pakistani government, then you are right. However, the IMF and World Bank have far more influence over Pakistan's exchange rate than the Pakistani government. The recent currency devaluations in many emerging markets could keep spreading. In the last few days the Thai baht and Philippine peso were devalued, and this is likely to spill over to other Asian export-based countries. The Pakistan rupee was devalued late last year, and I would expect another late this year or early next year."

Gabriel: "I agree we would prefer not to accept this risk, but we need to make the sale so we don't create a hole in our strategic plan. If PIA certifies our latest B777 cockpit technology in their B747 classics, we have a tremendous opportunity worldwide with that workhorse jumbo. What about our other unit, the local Industrial Process Controls (AvIPC) unit in Pakistan? Didn't they recently score a big contract with the national Pakistani petrochemical company? Don't they need rupees?"

Philip: "True, they must. Unfortunately, the CMS system charges 1% transaction cost but still passes on the currency risk to us. Unless we pay substantially more. If we were to receive the rupee receivable in the next few weeks, I might be willing to pay the 1% and take the risk, but that's not the case here. The dollar is continuing to climb, and it looks like a lot of Asia is starting to fall."

Gabriel: "I need to get back to Peter. What should we do?"

ECUADORIAN DEBT FOR DEVELOPMENT

Jack was nervous. Jack Van de Water was the Director for International Education Programs at Oregon State University, and therefore responsible for managing the financing of all study-abroad programs. One of the causes of Jack's nervousness today was the need to decide whether or not the University was to take part in the *Debt for Development* (DFD) program in financing its study programs in the country of Ecuador. The DFD program was designed to aid not-for-profit entities like universities in increasing their spending capabilities abroad while contributing to the reduction of large foreign debt levels suffered by many developing countries. But Jack was nervous about committing institutional funds into a venture with obvious risks as well as returns.

Ecuador and Debt

Ecuador was another in the long line of Latin and Southern American countries attempting to deal with large levels of foreign debt. This debt was made up of loans taken out by the government of Ecuador and other semi-government institutions in Ecuador (like utilities, railroads, etc.) during the late 1970s and early 1980s when the prospects for economic development in that part of the world were quite strong. Ecuador, like Brazil and Mexico, went to the international capital markets to obtain large quantities of capital, to speed up the rate of industrialization. The debt was primarily in the form of actual U.S. dollars, a currency with wide international purchasing power at the time. The capital was intended to increase the internal infrastructure and manufacturing industries of Ecuador to allow it to generate increased earnings—particularly in export markets where it could be paid in U.S. dollars—so that the debt could be serviced and eventually completely repaid. Things, however, did not quite work out that smoothly.

The internal and external sectors of the Ecuadorian economy did not grow sufficiently to generate the large amounts of foreign currency earnings (primarily dollars) needed for debt service over the 1980s. By 1987, a large amount of Ecuadorian debt was classified as in arrears, and by 1988 a substantial secondary market had developed for the sale of dollar-debt owed by Ecuador to commercial banks throughout the world. Ecuador, like other heavily indebted countries, was faced with few alternatives to the servicing of dollar-denominated debt: 1. export (or run a net export surplus); 2. borrow additional dollars. The second alternative was not considered overly attractive by either the borrower or creditors. The export market was relatively stable, but not growing sufficiently to service the existing levels of debt. A third, but unspoken, alternative was to simply not make the debt service payments.

The term *debt* as normally used in reference to developing countries consists of large long-term borrowings by government or semi-government entities from the international capital markets. These international markets consist of governments, international aid and development organizations like the International Monetary Fund (IMF), and large commercial banks worldwide. Although the first two organizations do not operate on the basis of profit, the commercial banking sector does operate in an increasingly competitive profit-motivated industry.

As the debt crises of the early 1980s came and stayed, many of the commercial banks worked increasingly to either reschedule their loans to foreign borrowers (thus effectively redefining the loan as not being in arrears on servicing its obligations), or to rid themselves of their foreign debt assets completely. It was this dumping of debt, in which the commercial banks were willing to sell their loans to non-related third parties, which made up the growing secondary market for third world debt. Since the loans were often not currently being serviced by the borrowing country, and the prospects for payment in full are often poor, the banks were willing to sell the loans at a considerable discount at the face value of the actual loan. Exhibit 1 provides some examples of the actual discounts on these third-world loans current in the market in March 1991.

The Debt for Development Program

The DFD program was best described by the program's own introduction:[1]

> The Debt for Development Coalition, Inc. represents not-for-profit organizations committed to finding ways to turn the international debts of countries into economic development opportunities.
>
> If a portion of the external debt of developing nations can be converted—by donation or purchase—into local currencies, not-for-profit organizations can use the funds for development projects needed to help spur economic growth in Latin America, Africa, Asia, and the Pacific.
>
> Coalition members are U.S. colleges and universities, cooperatives, private voluntary organizations, and research institutes engaged in economic development programs overseas. The coalition also maintains close cooperation with various U.S. environmental organizations.
>
> The coalition works closely with non-government organizations in debtor nations to identify programs important to each country's economic priorities such as education, public health, nutrition, agriculture, small business enterprises, research, housing, credit, and natural resource management programs.

The DFD program arose from the growing activity in what was called *debt for equity swaps*. Many of the developing indebted countries wished to alter the nature of their obligations from debt to participating equity, where the holder would see returns tied to the profits (or losses) of the enterprises associated with the capital. The idea

---

[1] "Debt For Development," The Debt for Development Coalition, Inc., 1828 L Street, N.W., Suite 1111, Washington, D.C., 1989, page 1

	Friday (1/11/91)		Last Year	
Sovereign Debt	Bid	Offer	Bid	Offer
Brazil	23.00	23.50	24.25	25.00
Mexico	44.50	45.00	38.25	39.00
Argentina	20.00	25.00	11.00	11.75
Venezuela	50.37	51.00	34.75	35.50
Chile	74.75	75.75	63.75	64.50
Index[a]		35.3		31.6

[a]The index tracks resale value of debt of all five nations listed in table, plus Colombia, Ecuador, Peru, the Philippines, Poland, and Yugoslavia. The index is updated weekly.

Source: Barron's, January 14, 1991, p. 133. The data was drawn by *Barron's* from Lehman Brothers.

was to encourage actual long-term equity involvement in the country, rather than the debt repayment-at-any-cost posture of most debt holders.

The Debt for Development swap was something akin to a debt for equity swap, combining the alteration of straight debt to a form of liquid debt which was re-denominated from U.S. dollars to the domestic currency, in this case Ecuadorian sucre.[2] The first and foremost concern on the part of an indebted country like Ecuador was that the debt and debt service be in a foreign currency, in this case U.S. dollars. This swap program would allow Ecuador to exchange sucre debt for dollar debt.

Ecuadorian Debt for Development

The DFD program with Ecuador would work in the following way. Commercial banks holding Ecuadorian debt would sell their loans to the DFD program participant, in this case the Oregon State System of Higher Education (OSSHE) by way of the DFD Foundation. The debt would be purchased at a discount, the banks then receiving partial repayment in dollars, and writing the remainder of the loans off as bad debt obligations (loan losses) and happily exiting their predicament stage right. The U.S. government, as well as the governments of several other large industrial countries having banks with third-world debt, had provided a number of tax provisions to aid these commercial banking institutions in writing off these loans through advantaged loan loss reserves.

Ecuadorian debt had been quoted at 20 cents per dollar of face value debt in early 1991. Although this purchase price changes constantly, it was believed that it will fall between 15 and 25 cents per dollar at the time of the proposed debt conversion. Exhibit 1 provides sample secondary market prices for a number of Latin American countries at this time.

---

[2] Most debt holders have traditionally opposed debt re-denomination schemes due to the weakness and inconvertibility of many of the developing country currencies. A country heavily indebted in dollars could be seen to reissue all debt in its own currency, essentially printing money to repay the debt. This was commonly thought to be too dangerous for all parties, resulting in depreciated values in repayment and inducing the country to undertake inflationary policies not in its own best interest. The DFD program, however, altered this process substantially by limiting the actual sucre to be swapped, and by requiring a debt swap with a repayment schedule or maturity matching that of the initial debt obligation.

The OSSHE would then hold a substantial value (on the basis of face value) of Ecuadorian debt. The debt would then be swapped with the Ecuadorian government for Ecuadorian sucre. The Ecuadorian government would credit OSSHE with $0.50 for every dollar in face value debt. Ecuador would then exchange this discounted dollar value for the domestic currency, sucre (Su), at the official government exchange rate, currently Su970/$.[3] Ecuador would therefore succeed in reducing its dollar-denominated debt obligations to foreign banks and, just as importantly, insure that the proceeds of the conversion would be spent in the domestic economy (sucre do not buy anything anywhere else).

OSSHE would work with a local principal, in this case the Pontifica Universidad Catolica del Ecuador (PUCE), to funnel sucre cash proceeds in paying the ongoing expenses of the exchange programs. OSSHE would pay PUCE a negotiated fee, approximately 1.5% per annum, of the gain in sucre resulting from the debt conversion over that of the customary currency exchange.

There was, however, a final twist to the specific program. Ecuador, although anxious to retire or replace existing dollar-denominated debt with domestic currency, did not wish to add to inflationary pressures by pumping its money supply up by large amounts of sucre cash balances. The government of Ecuador therefore would swap the debt as described, but for *sucre-denominated bonds*, not cash. The bonds would have sucre-denominated cash flows (coupons) to be paid quarterly until maturity. The payment schedule and maturity would match the schedules of the original debt it was replacing.

This last feature posed a problem for Jack (he was to the point of facial ticks now, twitching). Given the limited resources a university possesses in conducting study-abroad programs, he needed all the sucre value possible for use in the current period. Jack inquired as to the liquidity of these government bonds, and was told that the market was thin, but the bonds would likely be able to be sold at discounts ranging from 10% to 30% depending on financial and inflationary conditions. Although inflation had been quite high throughout the 1980s, Ecuador's government believed it could keep the inflation rate to roughly 40% per annum in the coming years, with interest rates falling in the same range. Bonds of maturities and coupons thought to be comparable to those gained through the debt conversion program were being sold at discounts of only about 15% in March of 1991.

Jack's Dilemma

Jack was now running short of time. He had to decide whether to commit his resources and his study-abroad program financing, approximately $50,000 for the 1991-92 academic year, to the DFD program or not. Jack then summarized the major points which he needed to weigh in the pro and con columns of the dog-eared Big Chief tablet on his desk.

---

[3] Several other countries followed a slightly different procedure whereby the country would swap the debt at 100% face value, but then exchange the dollar debt to domestic currency at a significantly altered (overvalued) exchange rate. The indebted country thus gained one way or the other in the actual exchange of dollar-debt for domestic currency (cash or debt).

NOKIA CORPORATION

Nokia needs to make sure that its gold mine doesn't cave in.

After selling its TV-manufacturing business and reducing its share in the tire and cable company, this Finnish powerhouse now derives nearly 100% of its revenues from the wireless-telecommunications industry. It was in this sector that Nokia built its name in the 1990s. Almost out of nowhere, Nokia grabbed a 22% share of the cellular-handset market, second only to Motorola. And the prospects for further growth in handset and infrastructure sales are tremendous.

The sky seems to be the limit for Nokia, but it will encounter some turbulence along the way. The lucrative business has not escaped the notice of some of the world's largest electronics companies. Handsets are fast becoming a commodity business, just as margins are getting off the ground; firms such as Sony and Toshiba have entered the ring.

It's the decision-making issue that has rattled investor confidence in Nokia lately. In the first quarter, Nokia posted a 70% drop in pretax profits, and a loss in its mobile phone division due to 'poor organization and logistics.'

They trade at 12 times earnings before one-time charges—well below the company's revenue growth rate.

Reproduced with permission from Morningstar, Inc.

Karla Sibelius, Director of Research for a small Phoenix-based investment management firm specializing in U.S.-listed foreign securities, noted the positive review of Nokia written by Michael Porter in <u>International Stocks</u> (July 25, 1996). However, Karla became somewhat concerned as she looked at Nokia's recent stock price performance (see Exhibit 1). Nokia's shares began trading on the NYSE in July 1994 as American Depository Receipts (ADRs). One ADR represents one share of Nokia's common stock. Shares had traded as high as US$78 per share in September 1995, but by the end of July 1996, the stock price had dropped to around $US35 per share. Karla's confidence in Nokia was further eroded as she looked over the analyst's report highlighting the fact that Nokia's net profit had fallen by more than 43 percent from FIM3,939 million in 1994 to FIM2,232 million in 1995.[1] The analyst also noted that the decline would have been greater if Nokia had not benefited from a FIM485 million boost in net profit by changing its method of accounting for research and development (R&D).

---

[1]FIM refers to the Finnish markka, the currency of Finland. On December 31, 1995, the exchange rate was FIM4,359 per $US1.

The analyst's report also included a discussion of academic research on companies initiating voluntary accounting changes.[2] The study classified companies according to whether the accounting change had boosted (e.g., accelerated depreciation to straight-line depreciation) or reduced income (e.g., FIFO to LIFO). According to the report, firms adopting income-increasing (income-decreasing) accounting changes would have otherwise experienced a decrease (increase) in earnings. In addition, the research showed that firms undertaking income-increasing (income-decreasing) accounting changes experienced negative (positive) stock returns relative to comparable size firms for up to seven years subsequent to the change. Karla wondered whether Nokia's change in research and development accounting was an ominous sign about the company's future. Yet, the analyst's report also included a discussion of other academic research in which the authors estimated the relationship between R&D expenditures and subsequent earnings to determine the unrecorded book value of a firm's R&D assets.[3] According to the report, the research suggested that in determining equity values, the capital market adjusts reported earnings and R&D book values to reflect the capitalization and amortization of R&D expenditures. That is, the capital market apparently viewed R&D as an investment which should be capitalized on the balance sheet and then amortized against earnings because it generated future benefits.

Karla realized that since her firm's investment committee was likely to have many questions, she would have to carefully and thoroughly review Nokia's financial statements.

The Company

Nokia Corporation is a leading international telecommunications group which is now Europe's largest and the world's second largest manufacturer of mobile phones with sales in 120 countries. It is also a world leading supplier of GSM (Global System for Mobile Communications) / DCS (Digital Cellular System) cellular networks as well as a significant supplier of access networks, multimedia equipment and other telecom-related products. The company operates through three business groups—Nokia Telecommunications (digital exchanges, transmission systems), Nokia Mobile Phones (digital and analog cellular phones, pagers), and Nokia General Communications Products (satellite and cable TV products, PC and workstation monitors, car audio products, and mobile handset components). Nokia moved closer to having 100 percent of its operations in the telecommunications industry by divesting its tire and cable machinery businesses, announcing its intention to reduce its share in the cable business to under 50 percent, and withdrawing from the color television business.

Nokia was formed out of an alliance between a pulp mill, a rubber factory, and a cable manufacturer. The pulp mill had been situated on the Nokia river in

---

[2] B. Dharan and B. Lev. 1993. "The Valuation Consequences of Accounting Changes: A Multi-Year Examination." *Journal of Accounting Auditing and Finance*, 8 (4): 475-494.

[3] B. Dharan and B. Lev. 1993. "The Capitalization, Amortization, and Value-Relevance of R&D." *Journal of Accounting and Economics*, 21 (1): 107-138.

Finland and originally began operations in 1865. Just after the turn of the century, Finnish Rubber Works moved across the river and began operations. In the 1920s, Finnish Rubber Works took over a struggling metal manufacturer, Finnish Cable Works. Each of these companies functioned independently until 1967, when they merged to form the basis for the present telecommunications conglomerate. After the establishment of the new company, Nokia shifted its focus away from the domestic Finnish market as it pushed to become a regional power.

Many of Nokia's foreign dealings were with the Soviet Union in countertrade agreements. In 1973, the first international oil crisis adversely affected the entire Finnish economy, and consequently, had a substantial impact on Nokia's operations. Nokia began to reassess its operating strategy and heavy reliance on the Soviet Union. By this time, an electrical products business had grown up around the cable manufacturing operations. It was decided to extend the electrical goods product line and begin concentrating on manufacturing products with higher value added.

In 1975, Kari Kairamo, previously the head of Nokia's Pulp, Paper & Power Division, was promoted to Chief Executive Officer. Kairamo's main priorities were to improve Nokia's product line, its reputation for quality and production techniques, and to move the company from its low value-added focus on paper, chemicals, electricity, and heavy machinery. Out of these relatively low-tech product lines, Kairamo began to create core competencies in high-tech fields such as robotics, fiber optics, and telecommunications. In 1979, Nokia increased its interest in telecommunications and mobile telephones with the establishment of Mobira Oy (Nokia Mobile Phones), a venture jointly-owned with Salora, a Swedish consumer electronics manufacturer.

During the 1980s, Nokia increased its interests in the telecommunications industry by acquiring a majority interest in Finland's state-owned telecommunications company, which was subsequently named Telenokia. At the same time, Karaimo sought to make Nokia a household name in consumer electronics through aggressive acquisitions. By early 1988, Nokia was Europe's third-largest television manufacturer and Scandinavia's largest telecommunications company. However, incorporating the newly-acquired businesses under one roof did not occur without difficulties. The problems were exacerbated by heavy price competition in the consumer electronics field which slashed the value of the company's investments. In the face of these problems, Kairamo committed suicide in December 1988.

Nokia's problems were to continue into the early 1990s. Finland fell into a deep recession causing a steep decline in Nokia's stock price. Nokia attempted to survive by selling off businesses and focusing on the telecommunications sector. In 1991, the company acquired the British company Technophone, which had been the second largest manufacturer of mobile phones in Europe. The acquisition cemented Nokia's position in the worldwide cellular phone market and made the company the second largest producer of cellular phones behind Motorola.

Mr. Jorma Ollila, the new Chief Executive Officer appointed in 1992, increased Nokia's focus on the mobile telecommunications industry. In 1993, Nokia acquired manufacturing facilities in South Korea and Texas, and entered a joint venture agreement with Mitsui of Japan to become the first foreign firm to enter the Japanese cellular phone market.

Competitive Environment

The mobile phone industry moved from its introductory stages in the 1970s and 1980s to its consolidation stage in the 1990s. During this time, many small firms which had caught the initial wave of cellular phone technology, were consolidated into a few surviving firms. At present, Motorola of the U.S. is the number one maker of mobile phones in the world, followed by Nokia, and Ericsson of Sweden. Together, these firms make up roughly three-quarters of the mobile telecommunications market. Of the three companies, Motorola and Ericsson have the most experience—both of them have been involved in telecommunications for nearly a century. Ericsson was the first Swedish company to produce telephones after starting out as a telegraph company, whereas Motorola was one of America's first producers of wireless radios.

Within the past few years, both Nokia and Ericsson have made aggressive entries into the Far East. Ericsson is especially strong in China with a 40% market share. Nokia is especially strong in Japan and in South Korea, where it recently acquired a manufacturing facility. Motorola's attempts to enter the Japanese market have also been aggressive, though less successful than Nokia's. Motorola's strong position in the United States has been weakened by Nokia and Ericsson. In September 1996, Motorola announced its third quarter earnings would be significantly down due to weaknesses in international mobile phone sales during the preceding two months. Analysts attributed Motorola's weakness to a product line which relies on the older analog technology. Nokia and Ericsson have invested heavily in new Global System for Mobile Communications (GSM) and Personal Communications Services (PCS) markets based on digital technologies. By early 1996, Ericsson announced that it had succeeded in capturing a third of the digital mobile phone market in the United States. At the same time, both Motorola and Nokia have begun marketing ultra-small mobile phones which were well received. Ericsson had not yet developed a competing product and industry analysts believe Ericsson's product line to be one of the oldest in the industry.

In Nokia's 1995 annual report, Chairman Jorma Ollila, indicated that the company's goal was to become one of the leading companies focused on telecommunications. With operations in 120 countries, manufacturing facilities in four continents and with improved brand-recognition worldwide, Nokia's goal was becoming a reality. Ollila emphasized the importance of the company's strength in technology management and the challenge of achieving and maintaining world-class operational efficiencies through improved business processes.

Research and Development

Since the push by Kairamo to make Nokia known for high quality products, Nokia has made substantial investments in research and development. This has yielded many innovations, including the world's first portable NMT (Nordic Mobile Telephone) car phone in 1984 (see Exhibit 2).

R&D expenses totalled FIM2,531 million during 1995, an increase of 31% over the prior year. By year-end, more than 7,000 Nokia employees were dedicated to R&D. Nokia Research Center, the company's corporate R&D organization, grew rapidly in 1995 and increased its staff to 500, of which 15 percent hold post-graduate degrees. The unit, considered the technological pathfinder for the Nokia Group, covers the full range of activities from exploration of new technologies and product/systems concepts to exploitation in actual product development. It also interacts closely with the R&D units from all of Nokia's business groups.

Accounting for Research and Development

In the U.S., Financial Accounting Standard (FAS) No. 2 requires that companies expense R&D expenditures in the period in which they are incurred. The logic underlying this standard is captured by the following excerpts:

> Moreover, even if at some point in the process of an individual research and development project the expectation of future benefits becomes sufficiently high to indicate that an economic resource has been created, the question remains whether that resource should be recognized as an asset for financial accounting purposes. Although future benefits from a particular research and development project may be foreseen, they generally cannot be measured with a reasonable degree of certainty. [paragraph 45]
>
> "Because there is generally no direct or even indirect basis for relating costs to revenues, the Board believes that the principles of 'associating cause and effect' and 'systematic and rational allocation' cannot be applied to recognize research and development costs as expenses." [paragraph 49]

Although Nokia is a Finnish company, its financial statements are prepared according to International Accounting Standards (IAS). Under IAS 9 (Revised 1993), research expenditures are expensed in the period they are incurred, whereas development expenditures meeting certain criteria are permitted to be capitalized and amortized. IAS 9 (Revised 1993) specifies that the development costs of a project may be deferred to future periods if all of the following criteria are met:

(a) the product or process is clearly defined and the costs attributable to the product or process can be identified and measured reliably;

(b) the technical feasibility of the product or process can be demonstrated;

(c) the enterprise intends to produce and market, or use, the product or process;

(d) the existence of a market for the product or process or, if it is to used internally rather than sold, its usefulness to the enterprise, can be demonstrated; and

(e) adequate resources exist, or their availability can be demonstrated, to complete the project and market the product or process or use the product or process. [Paragraph 17]

Under IAS 9 (Revised 1993), development costs that are capitalized as assets are normally amortized over a period not exceeding five years (paragraph 23).[4] The accounting standard requires firms to conduct an impairment test at the end of each period so that when the criteria used to defer costs no longer apply, the unamortized balance should be charged as an expense immediately. When the criteria for deferral continue to be met, but the amount of deferred development costs that

EXHIBIT 1   Nokia Corporation—Monthly Stock Price and Trading Volume During the Period July 1992–July 1996*

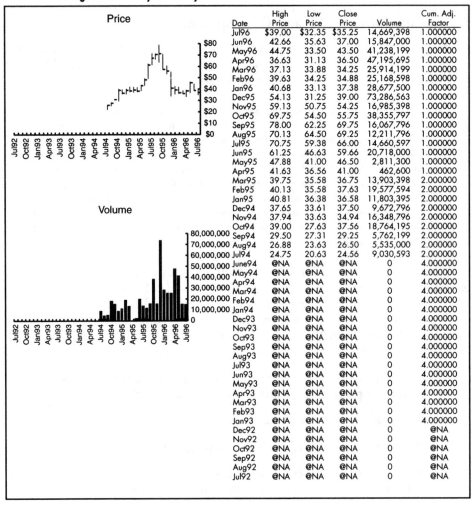

Date	High Price	Low Price	Close Price	Volume	Cum. Adj. Factor
Jul96	$39.00	$32.35	$35.25	14,669,398	1.000000
Jun96	42.66	35.63	37.00	15,847,000	1.000000
May96	44.75	33.50	43.50	41,238,199	1.000000
Apr96	36.63	31.13	36.50	47,195,695	1.000000
Mar96	37.13	33.88	34.25	25,914,199	1.000000
Feb96	39.63	34.25	34.88	25,168,598	1.000000
Jan96	40.68	33.13	37.38	28,677,500	1.000000
Dec95	54.13	31.25	39.00	73,286,563	1.000000
Nov95	59.13	50.75	54.25	16,985,398	1.000000
Oct95	69.75	54.50	55.75	38,355,797	1.000000
Sep95	78.00	62.25	69.75	16,067,796	1.000000
Aug95	70.13	64.50	69.25	12,211,796	1.000000
Jul95	70.75	59.38	66.00	14,660,597	1.000000
Jun95	61.25	46.63	59.66	20,718,000	1.000000
May95	47.88	41.00	46.50	2,811,300	1.000000
Apr95	41.63	36.56	41.00	462,600	1.000000
Mar95	39.75	35.58	36.75	13,903,398	2.000000
Feb95	40.13	35.58	37.63	19,577,594	2.000000
Jan95	40.81	36.38	36.58	11,803,395	2.000000
Dec94	37.65	33.61	37.50	9,672,796	2.000000
Nov94	37.94	33.63	34.94	16,348,796	2.000000
Oct94	39.00	27.63	37.56	18,764,195	2.000000
Sep94	29.50	27.31	29.25	5,762,199	2.000000
Aug94	26.88	23.63	26.50	5,535,000	2.000000
Jul94	24.75	20.63	24.56	9,030,593	2.000000
June94	@NA	@NA	@NA	0	4.000000
May94	@NA	@NA	@NA	0	4.000000
Apr94	@NA	@NA	@NA	0	4.000000
Mar94	@NA	@NA	@NA	0	4.000000
Feb94	@NA	@NA	@NA	0	4.000000
Jan94	@NA	@NA	@NA	0	4.000000
Dec93	@NA	@NA	@NA	0	4.000000
Nov93	@NA	@NA	@NA	0	4.000000
Oct93	@NA	@NA	@NA	0	4.000000
Sep93	@NA	@NA	@NA	0	4.000000
Aug93	@NA	@NA	@NA	0	4.000000
Jul93	@NA	@NA	@NA	0	4.000000
Jun93	@NA	@NA	@NA	0	4.000000
May93	@NA	@NA	@NA	0	4.000000
Apr93	@NA	@NA	@NA	0	4.000000
Mar93	@NA	@NA	@NA	0	4.000000
Feb93	@NA	@NA	@NA	0	4.000000
Jan93	@NA	@NA	@NA	0	4.000000
Dec92	@NA	@NA	@NA	0	@NA
Nov92	@NA	@NA	@NA	0	@NA
Oct92	@NA	@NA	@NA	0	@NA
Sep92	@NA	@NA	@NA	0	@NA
Aug92	@NA	@NA	@NA	0	@NA
Jul92	@NA	@NA	@NA	0	@NA

[4] The original version of IAS 9 specified that if development costs were deferred, "they should be allocated on a systematic basis to future accounting periods by reference either to the sale or use of a product or process or to the time period over which the product or process is expected to be sold or used." Thus, IAS 9 (Revised 1993) effectively changed the amortization period from an indefinite length of time to five years or less.

can reasonably be expected to be recovered from related future revenues is exceeded by the unamortized balance of the costs, the excess should also be charged as an expense immediately. The standard also requires that firms disclose the total of research and development costs, including amortization of deferred development costs charged to expense; the movement in and the balance of unamortized deferred development costs, and the basis, proposed or adopted, for the amortization of the unamortized balance.

The capitalization/amortization treatment permitted under IAS 9 (Revised 1993) with regard to development expenditures is similar to the treatment of software development expenditures in the U.S. Under FAS 86, software development expenditures which also generate uncertain future benefits, may be capitalized and amortized after the project becomes technologically feasible. Under this standard, capitalized software development costs are amortized either on the basis of current and future revenues for each product or using the straight-line method, which ever generates the greater amount of amortization.

EXHIBIT 2   Nokia Corporation–Chronological List of Nokia's Recent Technological and Product Developments

<u>Year</u>	<u>Technological and Product Development</u>
1986	Introduces an NMT cellular mobile exchange Introduces a low-radiation monitor
1987	Designs and manufactures nationwide pagers Introduces the world's first NMT pocket phone
1990	Introduces the world's first radio data system (RDS) pager
1991	Supplies equipment for world's first GSM
1992	Introduces its first GSM hand portable phone
1993	First manufacturer to launch hand portable phones for all existing cellular digital systems
1995	Introduces the world's smallest base station for GSM/DCS (Digital Cellular System) cellular mobile networks (Nokia Primesite)

EXHIBIT 3 Nokia Corporation—Abridged 1995 Annual Report

Prepared according to International Accounting Standards

Consolidated Profit and Loss Account

Financial year ended December 31	1995 MFIM	1994 MFIM
Net sales	36,810	30,177
Costs of goods sold	-25,518	-20,808
Research and development expenses	-2,531	-1,937
Selling, general and administrative expenses	3,749	-3,836
Operating profit	5,012	3,596
Share of results of associated companies	85	22
Financial income and expenses	-164	384
Profit before tax and minority interests	4,933	4,002
Tax	-769	-932
Minority interests	-77	-75
Profit from continuing operations	4,087	2,995
Discontinued operations	-2,340	-
Profit from ordinary activities before cumulative effect of change in accounting policies	1,747	2,995
Cumulative prior year effect (after tax) of change in accounting policies	485	-
Profit from ordinary activities	2,232	2,995
Extraordinary items	-	944
Net profit	2,232	3,939

Key Ratios

	1995	1994
Earnings per share, FIM:		
Continuing operations[1]	14.36	10.97
Ordinary activities before cumulative effect of change in accounting principles[2]	6.14	10.97
Dividend per share, FIM[3]	3.00	2.50
Shareholdersí equity per share, FIM[4]	48.55	43.65

[1] Profit from continuing operations divided by average of adjusted number of shares
[2] Profit from ordinary activities after discontinued operations out before cumulative effect of change in accounting policies divided by average of adjusted number of shares.
[3] The Board's proposed dividend for 1995.
[4] Adjusted number of shares at the end of the year.

Prepared according to International Accounting Standards

Consolidated Balance Sheet

December 31	1995 MFIM	1994 MFIM
ASSETS		
Fixed assets and other non-current assets		
Goodwill and other intangible assets	1,581	541
Property. plant and equipment	6,109	5,097
Investments	837	1,810
Long-term loan receivables	234	222
Other non-current assets	286	273
	9,047	7,943
Current assets		
Inventories	9,982	6,803
Accounts receivable, less allowances for doubtful accounts (31.12.1995 MFIM 155, 31.12.1994 MFIM 197)	9,518	7,835
Short-term investments	2,888	3,989
Bank and cash	1,326	1,279
	23,714	19,906
Total assets	32,761	27,849

December 31	1995 MFIM	1994 MFIM
SHAREHOLDERS' EQUITY AND LIABILITIES		
Shareholders' equity		
Share capital	1,498	1,498
Other restricted equity	5,455	5,494
Treasury shares	-470	-437
Untaxed reserves	1,873	1,727
Retained earnings	5,450	4,136
	13,806	12,418
Minority interests	422	555
Long-term liabilities		
Long-term debt	2,121	3,071
Other long-term liabilities	457	486
	2,578	3,557
Current liabilities		
Short-term borrowings	4,332	2,45
Current portion of long-term debt	187	278
Accounts payable and accrued liabilities	9,388	8,086
Advance payments	396	502
Provision for discontinued operations	1,652	-
	15,955	11,319
Total shareholders' equity and liabilities	32,761	27,849

Consolidated Cash Flow Statement	1995	1994
Financial year ended December 31	MFIM	MFIM
Cash flow from operating activities		
Profit before tax and minority interests	4,933	4,002
Adjustments, total	1,533	886
Operating profit before change in net working capital	6,466	4,888
Change in net working capital	-5,351	-1,450
Cash generated from operations	1,115	3,438
Interest received	508	349
Interest paid	-667	-568
Income taxes paid	-1,102	-326
Cash flow before extraordinary items	-146	2,893
Extraordinary expenses paid	-496	-350
Net cash used in/from operating activities	-642	2,543
Cash flow from investing activities		
Acquisition of Group companies, net of acquired cash	-27	-80
Treasury shares acquired	-	-78
Investments in other shares	-69	-351
Additions in capitalized R&D costs	-742	-
Capital expenditures	3,299	-1,967
Proceeds from disposal of shares in Group companies, net of disposed cash	876	45
Proceeds from sale of other shares	1,850	634
Proceeds from sale of fixed assets	396	24
Dividends received	75	142
Net cash used in investing activities	-940	-1,631
Cash flow from financing activities		
Proceeds from issuance of share capital	-	2,49
Capital investment by minority shareholders	37	23
Proceeds from (+), payments of (-) long-term liabilities	-754	-267
Proceeds from (+), payments of (-) short-term borrowings	1,976	-571
Proceeds from (f), payments of (-) long-term receivables	-41	29
Proceeds from (+), payments of (-) short-term receivables	186	-145
Dividends paid	-789	-211
Net cash from financing activities	615	1,348
Net decrease/increase in cash and cash equivalents	-967	2,260
Cash and cash equivalents at beginning of period	5,181	3,008
Cash and cash equivalents at end of period	4,214	5,268

The above figures cannot be directly traced from the balance sheet without additional information as a resultof acquisitions and disposals of subsidiaries and net foreign exchange differences arising on consolidation.The schedule shown below reconciles cash and cash equivalents at the end of the previously reported period to cash and cash equivalents reported for the beginning of the current period.

Reconciliation:		
As previously reported for 1994 and 1993, respectively	5,268	3,297
Foreign exchange adjustment	-87	-289
	5,181	3,00
Net decrease/increase in cash and cash equivalents	-967	2,260
As reported for 1995 and 1994	4,214	5,268

Selected Notes to the Financial Statements

1. Accounting principles

The consolidated financial statements of Nokia Corporation (Nokia or the Group) prepared in accordance with International Accounting Standards (IAS) are presented on pages 23-25, while financial statements prepared in accordance with Finnish Accounting Standards (FAS) are on pages 27-30 and 50-53.

Apart from the exceptions indicated in italic type in the following, the accounting principles adopted by Nokia are in compliance with IAS. A reconciliation between the financial statements under FAS and IAS is presented on page 26.

Changes in accounting principles

Effective from the beginning of 1995, the Group has adopted the revised IAS 9, Research and development costs, and capitalized the development expenses meeting the criteria stated in the standard. See note 2.

In 1995 the Group has recognized the revenue of large long-term contracts in accordance with the percentage of completion method. See note 4.

Accounting convention

The financial statements are presented in Finnish markkas and are prepared under the historical cost convention.

Principles of consolidation

The consolidated financial statements include the accounts of the parent company, Nokia Corporation, and each of those companies in which it owns, directly or indirectly through subsidiaries, over 50% of the voting rights. The accounts of certain companies in which Nokia has management control are also consolidated. Certain real estate and housing companies. as well as small companies which had no operations during the financial year, have, however, been left out of the consolidated financial statements. The effect of these companies on the Group's result and distributable reserves is immaterial. The companies acquired during the financial period have been consolidated from the date the responsibility for their operations was transferred to the Group. Similarly, the result of a Group company divested during an accounting period is included in the Group accounts only to the date of disposal.

All inter-company transactions are eliminated as part of the consolidation process. Minority interests are presented separately in arriving at the results before extraordinary items cut after taxes. They are also shown separately from shareholders' equity and liabilities in the consolidated balance sheet.

Acquisitions of companies are accounted for using the purchase method. Goodwill represents the excess of the purchase cost over the fair value of assets less liabilities of acquired companies, after provision for direct reorganization costs. Goodwill is amortised over a period not exceeding five years, unless a longer period not exceeding 20 years from the date of acquisition can be justified.

The Group's share of profits and losses of associated companies (voting rights between 20% and 50%) is included in the consolidated profit and loss account in accordance with the equity method of accounting. The Group's share of post acquisition reserves (retained earnings. untaxed reserves and other restricted equity) is added to the cost of associated company investments in the consolidated balance sheet.

Profits incurred in connection with the sale of fixed assets between the Group and associated companies are eliminated in the IAS financial statements in proportion to share ownership. Such profits are deducted from the Group's equity and fixed assets and released in Group accounts over the same period as depreciation is made. *Sales profits that arose before January 1, 1994, have not been eliminated in FAS financial statements.*

Investments in other companies (voting rights less than 20%) and also some joint ventures in start-up phase are stated at cost; provision is made where necessary to reduce the cost to estimated net realisable value.

Transactions in foreign currencies

Transactions in foreign currencies are recorded at the rates of exchange prevailing at the dates of the transactions. For practical reasons, a rate that approximates the actual rate at the date of the transaction is often used. At the end of the accounting period the unsettled balances on foreign currency receivables and liabilities are valued at the rates of exchange prevailing at the balance sheet date. Foreign exchange gains and losses related to normal business operations are treated as adjustments to cost of goods sold. Foreign exchange gains and losses associated with financing are entered as a net amount under financial income and expenses.

Foreign Group companies
In the consolidated accounts all items in the profit and loss accounts of foreign subsidiaries are translated into Finnish markka at the average exchange rates for the accounting period. The balance sheets of foreign Group companies are translated into Finnish markka at the rates of exchange ruling at the balance sheet date. Exchange differences arising from the application of the purchase method are treated as an adjustment affecting consolidated shareholders equity. Translation differences related to the restricted equity at the time of acquisition are treated as a part of restricted equity and exchange differences on the other reserves of foreign subsidiaries are credited or charged to retained earnings. Differences resulting from the translation of profit and loss account items at the average rate and the balance sheet items at the closing rate are taken to retained earnings. On the disposal of a foreign Group company, the cumulative amount of the translation difference is recognized as income or as expense in the same period in which the gain or loss on disposal is recognized.

The Group's policy is to hedge a portion of foreign subsidiaries' shareholders' equity and untaxed reserves to reduce the effects of exchange rate fluctuations on the Group's net investments in foreign Group companies. Exchange gains and losses resulting from the hedging transactions are offset against the translation differences arising from consolidation and recorded in the shareholders' equity.

Revenue recognition
Sales are recorded upon shipment of products and customer acceptance, if any, or performance of services, net of sales taxes and discounts. Revenues from large long-term contracts are recognized on the percentage of completion method. Provisions are made to cover anticipated losses on contracts.

Research and development
Research and development costs are expensed in the financial period during which they are incurred, except certain development costs which are capitalized when it is probable that a development project will be a success, and certain criteria, including commercial and technological feasibility, have been met. Capitalized development costs are amortized on a systematic basis over their expected useful lives. The amortisation period is between 3 and 5 years.

Maintenance, repairs and renewals
Maintenance, repairs and renewals are generally charged to expense during the financial period in which they are incurred. However, major renovations are capitalized and depreciated over their expected useful lives.

Property, plant and equipment
Property, plant and equipment are stated at cost less accumulated depreciation.

Depreciation is recorded on a straight-line basis over the expected useful lives of the assets, based on the following useful lives:

Buildings	20-40 years
Machinery and equipment	3-15 years

Land and water areas are not depreciated.

Gains and losses on the disposal of fixed assets are included in operating profit/loss.

Cash and cash equivalents
Cash and cash equivalents consist of cash on hand and balances with banks and liquid financial instruments.

Discontinued operations
A discontinued operation results from the sale or abandonment of an operation that represents a separate. major line of business of an enterprise and of which the assets, net profit or losses and activities can be distinguished physically, operationally and for financial reporting purposes. The profit effect of discontinued operations is separately disclosed.

Extraordinary items

In previous years certain income and expenses of abnormal nature, such as divestments of operations, were presented, net of tax, as extraordinary items in the consolidated profit and loss account. In accordance with the revised IAS 8 they would be classified as components of continuing or discontinued operations, as appropriate (see proforma result note 2.).

Appropriations

In Finland and certain other countries, companies are permitted to reduce or increase taxable income by net charges or by income representing adjustments to untaxed reserve accounts, provided that such amounts are reflected in the Group companies' financial statements.

In the consolidated IAS financial statements, accumulated appropriations are included in the balance sheet as part of shareholders' equity as "Untaxed reserves." Transfers to and from untaxed reserves are reflected through retained earnings.

Taxes

The consolidated financial statements include direct taxes, which are based on the results of the Group companies and are calculated according to local tax rules. Provision is made for deferred taxes at corporate income tax rates in effect at the end of the year, except in the case of any tax reduction that can reasonably be expected to continue in the foreseeable future.

2. Proforma profit in accordance with the revised IAS standards

	GROUP	
	1995	1994
Proforma profit from ordinary activities restated to reflect the new accounting policies (MFIM)		
Profit from continuing operations	4,087	2,982
Discontinued operations	-2,340	1,125
Profit from ordinary activities	1,747	4,107
Proforma earnings per share (FIM)		
From continuing operations	14.36	10.93
From ordinary activities	6.14	15.05

The Nokia Group has adopted the revised IAS accounting principles that came into effect at the beginning of 1995.

In accordance with the revised IAS 9, certain research and development costs are capitalized and amortized on a systematic basis over their expected useful lives. The amortization period is between 3 and 5 years. The cumulative prior year net effect (FIM 485 million) of R&D expenses has been included in the first four months' profit for 1995.

The revised IAS 8 requires that the profit effect of discontinued operations be presented separately. From the extraordinary items in Nokia's 1994 Financial Statements, the sale of Power division and the effect of the discontinued Picture Tubes unit would have been treated as discontinued operations. In 1995 the Financial Statements, discontinued operations include the financial impact of the decision to withdraw from the TV business.

The proforma result for year 1994 is presented above as if the revised IAS standards had already been adopted for 1994. The positive net profit effect of the capitalization of R&D expenses in 1994 would have been FIM 168 million.

3. Segment information

	Telecommu-nications	Mobile Phones	General Commu-nications Products	Other Operations	Eliminations	Group Total
Net sales						
1995, MFIM	10,341	16,052	10,837	458	-878	36,810
1994, MFIM	6,906	10,702	11,530	1,589	-550	30,177
Operating profit/loss, IAS						
1995, MFIM	2,722	1,753	584	47	-	5,012
1994, MFIM	1,700	1,745	210	-59	-	3,596
Capital expenditures						
1995, MFIM	1,106	1,606	482	105	-	3,299
1994, MFIM	506	971	381	109	-	1,967
Identifiable assets, IAS						
1995, MFIM	8,208	12,781	7,047	6,251	-1,526	32,761
1994, MFIM	4,448	6,772	7,765	9,584	-720	27,849

*Excluding acquisitions and R&D capitalization.

4. Percentage of completion method

Profit on large long-term contracts is recognized when sale is recorded on part-delivery of products or part performance of services, provided that the outcome of the contract can be assessed with reasonable certainty. This represents a change in accounting policy with effect from January 1,1995 in order to comply with the revised IAS.

Most of the Group's net sales arise from businesses other than those of a long-term project nature. Project deliveries occur in Cellular Systems, where part of its net sales (3.8 billion FIM) was of a long-term project nature. This change in accounting principle, which was due to the revised IAS 11, had a positive (76 MFIM) impact on operating profit in 1995. In 1994 the profit impact would have been immaterial.

7. Depreciation

	GROUP		PARENT COMPANY	
	1995 MFIM	1994 MFIM	1995 MFIM	1994 MFIM
Depreciation according to plan				
Goodwill and other intangible assets				
Capitalized R&D costs	435	-	-	-
Intangible rights	55	38	4	4
Goodwill	59	69	-	-
Other intangible assets	20	20	3	2
Property, plant and equipment				
Buildings and constructions	80	77	4	4
Machinery and equipment	1,046	691	12	9
Other tangible assets	130	114	-	-
Total	1,825	1,009	23	19

Change in accumulated depreciation in excess of plan
Goodwill and other intangible assets

Intangible rights	-15	-3	-	-
Other intangible assets	-3	-21	-	-
Property, plant and equipment				
Buildings and constructions	-187	-106	8	3
Machinery and equipment	-282	-224	1	4
Other tangible assets	6	-2	-	2
Total	**481**	**-356**	**9**	**9**
Depreciation by function				
Costs of goods sold	815	574	-	-
R&D	697	171	10	6
Selling, marketing and administration	177	156	13	13
Other operating expenses	77	39	-	-
Goodwill	59	69	-	-
Total	**1,825**	**1,009**	**23**	**19**

8. Financial income and expenses

	GROUP		PARENT COMPANY	
	1995	1994	1995	1994
	MFIM	MFIM	MFIM	MFIM
Dividend income	75	142	268	83
Interest income from long-term investments	29	26	108	147
Interest income from short-term investments	559	379	693	395
Other financial income	3	22	3	3
Exchange gains and losses	-10	450	-3	243
Interest expenses	-745	-580	-436	-426
Other financial expenses	-75	-55	-14	-28
Total	**-164**	**384**	**619**	**417**

10. Discontinued operations

In February 1996, Nokia announced its intention to exit the TV business. The Group anticipates that the exit plan will be completed during 1996.

The financial impact of this decision is reported in the 1995 accounts as discontinued operations. The estimated exit costs include the write-down of property, plant and equipment and other assets to estimated net realisable value, severance payments and the estimated operating loss through the date of discontinuance.

The 1995 operating loss of the TV business has been included as a component of discontinued operations in the consolidated profit and loss account. The 1994 operating loss was 136 MFIM. The net sales of the TV business were 3,229 MFIM in 1995 (3,841 MFIM in 1994).

	GROUP	
	1995	1994
	MFIM	MFIM
Operative loss 1995	-352	-
Discontinuation cost	-1,988	-
Total discontinuity cost	-2,340	-

11. Extraordinary items

	GROUP	
	1995 MFIM	1994 MFIM
Cumulative effect of change in accounting principles	485	-
Discontinued operations	-2,340	-
Valuation difference of shares	-	-134
Profits incurred in divesting operations	-	552
Gain on the sale of Tubes unit's fixed assets	-	318
Extraordinary items, FAS	-1,855	736
IAS adjustments and reclassifications	1,855	208
Extraordinary items, IAS	-	944

The parent company's extraordinary income is mainly profits on the sale of fixed assets. Extraordinary expenses principally include write-offs of Group company shares.

13. Goodwill and other intangible assets

	GROUP		PARENT COMPANY	
	1995 MFIM	1994 MFIM	1995 MFIM	1994 MFIM
Capitalized R&D costs				
Acquisition cost Jan. 1	1,115		-	
Additions	742	-		
Accumulated depreciation Dec. 31	-902	-		
Net carrying amount Dec. 31	955	-		
Intangible rights				
Acquisition cost Jan. 1	362	324	21	19
Additions	149	66	9	3
Disposals	-21	-28	-2	-1
Accumulated depreciation Dec. 31	-254	-226	-15	-13
Net carrying amount Dec. 31	236	136	13	8
Goodwill				
Acquisition cost Jan. 1	1,305	1,306	-	2
Additions	-	4	-	-
Disposals	-651	-5	-	-
Accumulated depreciation Dec. 31	-979	-972	-	-2
Net carrying amount Dec. 31	261	333	-	-
Other intangible assets				
Acquisition cost Jan. 1	255	239	137	137
Additions	80	26	2	2
Disposals	-136	-9	-105	-2
Translation differences	-	-1	-	-
Accumulated depreciation Dec. 31	-70	-183	-12	-114
Net carrying amount Dec. 31	129	72	22	23

Auditors' Report

To the shareholders of Nokia Corporation:

We have audited the accounting records, the accounts and the administration of Nokia Corporation for the year ended December 31, 1995. The accounts prepared by the Board of Directors and the President and Chief Executive Officer include the report of the Board of Directors, consolidated financial statements prepared in accordance with International Accounting Standards (IAS), consolidated and Parent company profit and loss accounts, balance sheets, cash flow statements and notes to the financial statements. Based on our audit we express an opinion on these accounts and the Parent company's administration.

We conducted our audit in accordance with Finnish Generally Accepted Auditing Standards. Those standards require that we plan and perform the audit in order to obtain reasonable assurance about whether the financial statements are free of material misstatement. An audit includes examining, on a test basis, evidence supporting the amounts and disclosures in the financial statements, assessing the accounting principles used and significant estimates made by the management, as well as evaluating the overall financial statement presentation. The purpose of our audit of the administration has been to examine that the Board of Directors and the President and Chief Executive Officer have complied with the rules of the Finnish Companies' Act.

In our opinion, the financial statements prepared in accordance with International Accounting Standards (IAS) present fairly, in all material respects, the financial position of Nokia Corporation and subsidiary companies at the end of the financial period and the consolidated results of their operations, for the year then ended in accordance with International Accounting Standards.

The accounts showing a consolidated profit of FIM 1 971 260 000 have been prepared in accordance with the Accounting Act and other rules and regulations governing the preparation of financial statements in Finland. The financial statements give a true and fair view, as defined in the Accounting Act, of both the consolidated and Parent company result of operations, as well as of the financial position. The accounts can be adopted and the members of the Board of Directors and the President and Chief Officer of the Parent company can be discharged from liability for the period audited by us. The proposal made by the Board of Directors concerning the disposition of the profit for the year is in compliance with the Companies' Act.

We have acquainted ourselves with the interim reports published by the company during the year. In our opinion, they have been prepared in accordance with the rules and regulations governing the preparation of such reports in Finland.

Helsinki, February 28, 1996

Prepared according to International Accounting Standards
Nokia 1991–1995, IAS

	1995	1994	1993	1992	1991
Profit and Loss Account, MFIM					
Net sales	36,810	30,177	23,697	18,168	15,457
Costs and expenses	-31,798	-26,581	-22,232	-17,880	-15,553
Operating profit/loss	5,012	3,596	1,465	288	-96
Share of results of associated companies	85	22	28	-5	9
Financial income and expenses	-164	384	-347	-441	-237
Profit/loss before tax and minority interests	4,933	4,002	1,146	-158	-324
Tax	-769	-932	-299	-167	-231
Minority interests	-77	-75	-80	-88	-49
Profit/loss from continuing operations	4,087	2,995	767	-413	-604
Discontinued operations	-2,340	-	-	-	-
Profit/loss from ordinary activities before cumulative effect of change in accounting policies	1,747	2,995	767	-413	-604
Cumulative prior year effect (after tax) of change in accounting policies	485	-	-	-	-
Profit/loss before extraordinary items	2,232	2,995	767	-413	-604
Extraordinary items	-	944	-1,917	-310	393
Net profit/loss	2,232	3,939	-1,150	-723	-211
Balance Sheet Items, MFIM					
Fixed assets and other non-current assets	9,047	7,943	7,994	7,630	8,263
Current assets	23,714	19,906	14,653	13,605	11,890
Inventories	9,982	6.803	5,129	3,840	3,409
Accounts receivable and prepaid expenses	9,518	7,835	6,227	6,650	2,754
Cash and cash equivalents	4,214	5,268	3,297	3,118	3,727
Shareholders' equity	13,806	12,418	6,511	6,727	7,393
Minority shareholders' interests	422	555	536	695	600
Long-term liabilities	2,578	3,557	4,080	3,705	4,373
Long-term debts	2,121	3,071	3,397	3,124	3,896
Other long-term liabilities	457	486	683	581	477
Current liabilities	15,955	11,319	11,520	10,111	7,787
Short-term borrowings	4,332	2,453	3,435	3,835	2,797
Current portion of long-term loans	187	278	139	1,221	1,086
Accounts payable and accrued liabilities	9,388	8,086	5,976	4,314	3,389
Advance payments	396	502	534	399	202
Discontinuity/restructuring provision	1,652	-	1,436	342	313
Total assets	32,761	27,849	22,647	21,238	20,153
Key Ratios					
Earnings per share, FIM	14.36	10.97	3.07	neg.	neg.
Dividend per share, FIM	3.00	2.50	0.70	0.50	0.50
Profit/loss before tax and minority interests, % of net sales	13.4	13.3	4.8	-0.9	-2.1

    A09-97-0019

PART II
FOREIGN EXCHANGE EXPOSURE

MULTIQUIMICA DO BRASIL 1999

"I'm really concerned about our position in Brazil. Our pharmaceutical products are being hurt by both local and foreign producers and our foreign exchange policies may well be to blame." So said Don Howard, controller of the foreign operations of the pharmaceutical group of Multichemical Industries, Inc. "Look at Levadol, for example; our sales are falling while those of Hoffman are up."

This conversation took place in January 1999 as Don was reviewing the preliminary 1998 results of the foreign operations of the pharmaceutical group with the group's general manager, Paul McConnell. The men were in the company's corporate offices in Houston, Texas.

Background

Multichemcial Industries, Inc. sold 75 different products in over 50 countries during 1998. Sales for the year were $3.1 billion (see Appendix 1 for financial data). The company's principal product groups were: pharmaceuticals, industrial chemicals, agricultural chemicals, and petrochemicals. Multichemical's overseas subsidiaries accounted for 35% of sales in 1998, with the majority of the activity taking place in Europe.

Multiquimica do Brasil (MB) was responsible for all sales and manufacturing which took place in Brazil. Thus, its managers had responsibility for products in several of the firm's product groups. Sales during the year were $65 million, 6% of foreign sales. This wholly owned subsidiary was formed in 1993 with the initial purpose of establishing manufacturing facilities for agricultural chemical, industrial chemical, and pharmaceutical products in Brazil. Prior to that, Multichemcial had been active in Brazil through export sales. In other words, products that were manufactured in the United States had been sold in Brazil through local, independent importers. Multichemical did not operate either manufacturing facilities or a division office in the country until 1993.

The new subsidiary began manufacturing and selling herbicides in 1993. MB did not show a profit until 1996. The losses that were incurred were primarily attributable to two factors: the larger startup costs associated with a new business and a weak economic period in Brazil. As a result of the losses sustained during the 1993 to 1996 period, MB was entitled to a substantial amount in tax loss carryforwards on its Brazilian Tax return. (The term "tax loss carryforward" refers to the fact that net operating losses, to the extent that they exceed taxable income of the preceding three years, can be carried forward, thus reducing future taxable income.)

In late 1995, the company installed a manufacturing plant to process Levadol, an aspirin-free pain reliever. Such facilities were included in the original operating plans for MB. They were scheduled, however, for the late 1990s. They went on stream sooner than originally planned due to an increase in the amount of duty on imports.

The manufacture of this product involved shipping the raw materials in bulk form from the United States. The raw materials were formulated, converted into tablet form, and packaged in the Brazilian plant, and then sold to distributors. MB sales of Levadol in 1998 were $6.8 million.

Product and Pricing Flow for Levadol

The raw materials for Levadol were shipped from a domestic subsidiary of Multichemical to MB. The invoiced price for the transferred goods during 1998 averaged $60/case equivalent (invoiced in U.S. dollars). The cost of goods sold on MB's books for Levadol averaged $131/case. This figure included the $60/case raw material cost, plus $31/case for import duty and $40/case to formulate, convert, and package.

The product was sold to wholesalers serving both drugstores and chain stores, usually on 90-day payment terms, for a price of approximately $218/case. The $87/case difference between the sales price and the cost of goods sold consisted of marketing costs (roughly 20% of sales), administration, distribution, and interest expenses, and approximately a 5% profit margin before taxes. The distributors, in turn, usually added a 10-20% margin. This was designed to both cover their costs and provide a profit margin.

Dollar Linkage Billing

Multichemical had recently instituted a management accounting system which worked to the benefit of the Brazilian subsidiary—a system known as *dollar linkage billing*. A statement on the invoice which was sent from the domestic (U.S.) subsidiary to MB said, "payable at the exchange rate in effect on the date of the receipt of goods." The exact amount of *real* payable to the parent was therefore set on the date on which the goods were received in Brazil, and not on the date of shipment by the U.S. business unit. (It typically took 30 days for goods to pass from the U.S. subsidiary to the Brazilian subsidiary.) The books used for management and control internal to the firm therefore recorded the intra-firm sales as if invoiced in local currency (Brazilian *real* in this case).

Customary Brazilian credit terms on imports were 180 days. Since the Brazilian *real* (R$) lost value in relation to the dollar on a more or less continuous basis, a foreign exchange loss would normally show up on a Brazilian firm's *real* denominated books. Given the above-mentioned system, however, the foreign exchange loss showed up on the U.S. tax books.

Even within the context of the Brazilian domestic market, MB's reported profit in dollar terms was affected by the more or less continuous change in the value of the *real.*[1] The major problem here was tied to the fact that competition had forced MB to offer 90-day payment terms to their customers. Given the fact that the *real* was formally devalued by a small amount on a continuous basis, any domestic subsidiary with terms of 90 days was faced with a currency loss—*translation loss*—whenever its books were translated back into dollar terms. This translation loss resulted from the *dollar value* of the original *real denominated* sale exceeding the *dollar value* of the actual *real denominated* settlement of the account receivable some 90 days later.

In an attempt to deal with the situation, MB put into place a method known as "forward pricing." Under the assumptions of this method, MB's management predicted the amount of *real* devaluation which would occur during the forthcoming 90 days. This estimate then served as the basis for raising the then-current sales price. In other words, they passed along the expected loss due to the devaluation of the *real* to the customers. As a result of this policy, product prices were revised monthly.

Hedging Policies

Although the Brazilian inflation rate had fallen from over 2700% in 1993 to 16% in 1996 and 7% in 1997, the exchange rate had not moved proportionally to the change in purchasing power.[2] The *real* had been regularly devalued by the government, but had clearly not changed completely in line with the rate of inflation. A future devaluation seemed inevitable. Many had expected a major devaluation in the fall of 1998 following the Russian economic crisis, but it had not happened. MB reacted by pushing up its prices, a policy which it continued to adhere to throughout 1998. Exhibit 1 illustrates the gradual devaluation policy implemented by the Brazilian government.

Beginning in late 1995, the corporate treasurer's office of Multichemical began to encourage MB to borrow locally. Such a policy was designed to match assets and liabilities in *real* terms and thus offset the translation loss on assets with a translation gain on liabilities. By having the subsidiaries borrow locally, the corporate treasurer was hoping to eliminate the risk of having to report large translation losses on the corporate income statement.[3] Local borrowing, in essence, helped to smooth the

---

[1] The *real* was introduced as Brazil's official currency on July 1, 1994, under then President Cardoso's *Real Plan*. The *Plan* combined the introduction of a new currency with renewed commitment to a tight monetary policy to drive inflation once and for all from the Brazilian economy. As illustrated in Appendix 2, inflation fell dramatically in 1995 and 1996, while the real was devalued only marginally from its initial value.

[2] For example, the *real* should have fallen much faster than it had according to the *theory of purchasing power parity* (PPP). PPP states that the exchange rate should change in proportion to relative inflation rates between the two currencies. With a 1994 end-of-year rate of R\$0.846/\$, and Brazilian and U.S. inflation rates of 66% and 3% for 1995, respectively, the *real* should have fallen to R\$1.364/\$ at end-of-year 1995, not R\$0.972/\$:

$$\text{Exchange Rate}_{1995} = \text{R\$0.846/\$} \times \frac{1 \quad .66}{1 + .66} = \text{R\$1.364/\$}$$

[3] Consolidation practices for foreign subsidiaries of U.S.-based companies are governed by Financial Accounting Standard 52. According to this standard, any foreign currency related gains and losses arising from the translation and consolidation of foreign affiliates would have to be passed through consolidated income for countries like Brazil which were experiencing hyper-inflationary conditions. Hyperinflation was defined as a cumulative inflation rate of 100% over a three-year period.

EXHIBIT 1   Daily Exchange Rates: Brazilian Reals per U.S. Dollar

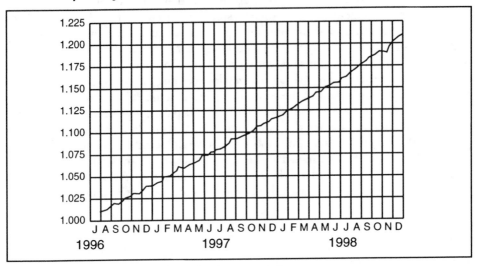

corporation's reported income stream by substituting a periodic interest expense for less frequent, but presumably larger, losses due to translation. There was a cost, however. Interest rates in Brazil in 1998 averaged 28%. (See Appendix 2 for exchange rate, interest rate, and inflation rate data.)

Performance Measurement Policies

Multichemical had recently changed its internal reporting system. Previous to the change, operating managers had been held responsible for the performance of their units as measured by the *operating income* figures. This meant that items such as other income, other expenses, interest expenses, and foreign exchange gains and losses were not focused upon in the quarterly business results review meetings. Over time, the senior management at the corporate level had come to feel that this system of performance measurement ignored the impact of some business decisions which could (or should) be taken by some of the operating managers in question.

After a thorough study of both the existing internal reporting system and a set of alternative systems, a new system was designed and introduced. *Full Responsibility Accounting*, as the new system was called, was made effective with the 1998 data. Under the terms of this new system, both individual product managers and product group managers were to be held responsible for the relationship between their profit-after-tax figures and the net assets under their control on both a worldwide and *major country* basis. The term *net assets* for a particular sub-unit of the overall corporate was defined as net property (gross property less accumulated depreciation) plus net working capital. Thus, both individual product managers and product group managers subsequently bore some of the responsibility for such items as interest expense and foreign exchange gains and losses.

The new system was designed with the intention that it would, among other things, force top management to delegate expansion and curtailment decisions to lower levels. The individual product managers and their superiors (the product group managers), sometimes in conjunction with an (geographic) area manager, were to have total responsibility for the assets which they employed in the process of producing, distributing, and selling their particular product. The firm's capital budgeting and operational budgeting systems were to be altered such that the full year's capital expenditures would be approved at once, and there would be agreement reached during the operational budgeting cycle as to the appropriate levels for inventories and receivables for the budget year in questions.

While the new system was very focused upon a return-on-assets figure, two other measures were to receive emphasis under the terms of the new program. Both net income and cash flow were to be measured and monitored. The former would be measured against a budgeted target and the latter would be assessed in respect to an understanding of the underlying strategy for the sub-unit. Thus, a sub-unit with a growth strategy might be expected to generate little or no cash (or indeed, even use cash) over a short- to medium-term time period. Of particular concern to product group managers, such as Paul McConnell, was the fact that they were now responsible for currency gains and losses and interest expense, the latter of which could be very high in the case of local borrowing.

Competition

MB had been able to successfully position Levadol such that a significant number of the population asked for Levadol when they wanted an aspirin-free pain reliever. This had become an important issue as the product became more widely stocked by the various grocery chains and cooperatives (with their open, freestanding shelves). Every year, MB sold a greater amount of Levadol through grocery stores than it had the year before. During 1998, it was estimated that 60% of the retail sales of all aspirin-free pain relievers in Brazil took place in grocery stores, while the remaining 40% were sold through some type of drug-related outlet.

During 1998, MB lost both volume and market share on Levadol. Over 36,000 cases of Levadol were sold in 1996. Less than 32,000 were sold in 1998 (see Exhibit 2 for volume and market share data). Although it was considered a premium product, an increasing number of distributors were reacting to the recession by substituting lower cost products.

EXHIBIT 2 Aspirin-Free Pain Relievers (percentage of market share by major competitors)

Year	MB	Hoffman	Generic	All Other	Total Volume (000s cases)
1993	3%	7%	31%	59%	125
1994	8	12	25	55	152
1995	9	17	21	53	202
1996	15	25	17	43	240
1997	13	32	13	42	287
1998	10	32	15	43	320

EXHIBIT 3   Average Wholesale Price of Aspirin-Free Pain Relievers (U.S. dollars per case)

Year	MB	Hoffman	Generic
1996	$182	$180	$172
1997	201	218	187
1998	218	212	200

MB's primary competition during 1998 was the Swiss firm Hoffman et Cie which sold a similar, but not identical, product. Hoffman's product was priced slightly lower than Levadol. The Swiss franc had depreciated versus the dollar in 1996 and 1997, and therefore had not appreciated against the *real* to the same degree as the dollar (see Appendix 2). Thus, the apparent incentive for Hoffman to raise its price to cover a translation loss was not as great as MB's. Also, Hoffman had been known to be somewhat more concerned with market share than with short-term reported profits.

Other reasons for Hoffman's strength had to do with the company's size in Brazil. In addition to having a large percentage of the pharmaceutical market, it also had a very large share of the market in agricultural chemicals. Its field sales force was about three to four times the size of MB's. Also, Hoffman gave somewhat longer payment terms. Hoffman's management apparently felt that they could squeeze the profit margin in pharmaceuticals a bit because of their strong position and high profits with agricultural chemicals.

In addition to Hoffman and other foreign-based firms, two local producers sold a generic substitute. The raw materials for the generic product were sourced in Brazil. The local patent covering this product had already expired. One result of this was that the industry was currently afflicted with an over-capacity of manufacturing facilities for product such as generic brand pain relievers. The price of the generic aspirin-free pain reliever had risen 16% in the preceding two years while the price of Levadol had risen 20%, making the price difference $18/case (see Exhibit 3).

"My greatest fear about Brazil is that we're being finessed by firms with a better knowledge of international business. Levadol should not be losing market share to Hoffman," said Paul McConnell. "I could understand some loss of market to the locals, but even there we should be able to sell the customer on our product superiority. Hoffman has a premium product. But it's not as good as ours."

Appendix 1 **Multiquimica do Brasil Financial Data: Consolidated Corporate Results (in millions of U.S. dollars)**

Income Statement	1998	1997
Sales		
Agricultural chemicals	$ 658	$ 600
Industrial chemicals	583	513
Petrochemicals	652	585
Pharmaceutical products	1,210	1,086
Subtotal	$3,103	$2,784
Cost of goods sold	$1,300	$1,169
Selling and administrative expenses	884	793
Depreciation	296	262
Research expense	292	250
Subtotal	$2,772	$2,474
Operating Income	$ 331	$ 310
Interest expense	45	42
Other income, net	41	30
Subtotal	$ 4	$ 12
Income before taxes	$ 327	$ 298
Income taxes	126	110
Net income	$ 201	$ 188

Balance Sheet	1998	1997
Current assets	$1,016	$1,001
Net property, plant and equipment	1,536	1,338
Other assets	241	139
Total Assets	$2,793	$2,478
Current liabilities	$ 363	$ 297
Long-term debt	394	309
Deferred income taxes	140	124
Stockholders' equity	1,896	1,748
Total Liabilities and Stockholders' Equity	$2,793	$2,478

Source: Multichemical Industries Inc., 1998 Annual Report (preliminary).

Foreign Exchange Rates and Interest Rates (end of year)

Year	Brazilian real (R$/$)	Brazilian Interest Rates (% per annum)	Swiss francs (SF/$)	Swiss Interest Rates (% per annum)	U.S. dollar Interest Rates (% per annum)
1992	—	nm	1.4560	7.80	6.25
1993	0.119	nm	1.4795	6.40	6.00
1994	0.846	nm	1.3115	5.51	7.14
1995	0.972	52.25	1.1505	5.48	8.83
1996	1.039	26.45	1.3464	4.97	8.27
1997	1.117	24.35	1.4553	4.47	8.44
1998	1.210	28.00	1.3765	4.07	8.35

nm = not meaningful. With inflation rates of over 2000% in the 1992-1994 period, nominal interest rates were artificially set by government at rates frequently below the rate of inflation. Officially, interest rates in Brazil in 1993 and 1994 were 3,293.5% and 5,175.24%, respectively. All interest rates are lending rates (prime rates).

Note on Brazilian exchange rate: On March 16, 1990, the *cruzeiro* replaced the *new cruzado* as the official currency at a 1 to 1 basis. On August 1, 1993, the *cruzeiro real* replaced the *cruzeiro* as the official exchange rate, with 1,000 *cruzeiros* equaling 1 *cruzeiro real*. On July 1, 1994, the *real* replaced the *cruzeiro real* as the official currency at a rate of 2,750 *cruzeiro real* per *real*.

Consumer Price Index Numbers and Yearly Percentage Changes

Year	Brazil Index	% Chg	Switzerland Index	% Chg	United States Index	% Chg
1992	0.1	94.3	92.1		94.8	3%
1993	2.8	2700%	97.4	3%	97.3	3%
1994	60.2	2050%	98.2	1%	100.0	3%
1995	100.0	66%	100.0	2%	102.9	3%
1996	115.8	16%	100.8	1%	105.3	3%
1997	123.8	7%	101.3	0%	105.3	2%
1998	127.7	3%	101.3	0%	107.0	2%

Source: *International Financial Statistics*, International Monetary Fund, monthly.

TCAS, Inc.

On May 16, 1995, Mr. John Christopher, the assistant treasurer of TCAS, Inc., pondered several foreign exchange hedging alternatives that had been outlined by the account manager from his lead bank. Mr. Christopher had called his account manager, Judy Wright, to ask for her advice regarding a Canadian dollar contract Mr. Christopher had negotiated with a Canadian company. Ms. Wright, after first evaluating macroeconomic fundamentals and determining what her bank's lending rates were likely to be based on this outlook, was now ready to advise Mr. Christopher of the various alternatives to hedge the foreign currency risk.

Company Background

TCAS (Transnational Corporate Advisory Services), Inc. was founded in 1982 as a financial training and consulting firm incorporated in Delaware. Its primary assets and products were the knowledge and skills of the three founding partners. All three had worked for the Continental Illinois National Bank for about twelve years but left the bank before its problems in 1984. The expertise of the three founders was multinational business management including the financial, production, and marketing aspects of doing business globally.

In 1988, TCAS merged with Computer Software and Systems Company to extend its products to include management information systems. TCAS, Inc. was involved in developing specialized software and building custom-designed, local area personal computer networks for small- and medium-sized companies. Because of the dramatic changes in computer technology and communication during the decade of the 1980s, the deregulation of financial markets, and the increased emphasis on globalization, TCAS, Inc. experienced rapid growth in net income and assets. However, beginning in 1993, TCAS began to face sharply increased competition from much larger corporations that began to sell very competitively priced services. As a result of these developments, TCAS's net income narrowed dramatically in 1993 and 1994. The company was heavily in debt and had only a few contracts in hand. TCAS was headquartered in Phoenix, Arizona, and its customer base to date had been comprised totally of US companies. TCAS decided that it was time to "go international."

John Christopher recognized that the submission of the bid in Canadian dollars to a Canadian customer was fundamentally a risky step for TCAS. He also realized

TCAS, Inc.
Sales and Income Statement

Year Ended Dec. 31	Sales (US$ 000)	Net Income (US$ 000)
1987	1250.0	550.0
1988	1930.0	850.0
1989	2200.0	1120.0
1990	2270.0	1050.0
1991	2940.0	1640.0
1992	3150.0	1700.0
1993	2870.0	550.0
1994	2650.0	-250.0

1994 Balance Sheet

ASSETS

	(US$ 000)
Current assets:	
Cash and securities	250.0
Accounts receivable	620.0
Inventories	80.0
Total current assets	950.0
Property, plant and equipment	
Cost	2240.0
less Accumulated depreciation	(330.0)
Goodwill and intangibles	520.0
TOTAL ASSETS	3380.0
LIABILITIES	
Current liabilities	
Bank loans	810.0
Accounts payable	480.0
Notes payable	120.0
Long-term liabilities	
Debt	620.0
TOTAL LIABILITIES	2030.0
Equity and retained earnings	1350.0
TOTAL LIABILITIES AND EQUITY	3380.0

that, in order to survive, the company had to expand its traditional customer base. John Christopher was surprised when TCAS was awarded the bid. He knew that his foreign exchange worries had just begun and he was in need of expert help.

A06-98-0021

The Bid

TCAS had bid Canadian dollar C$2,900,00 for the delivery and the installation of a new management information software system and an extensive local area network (LAN) computer system. The bid had been put together by the accounting department and accurately reflected costs. The bid was tendered on March 21 by FAX and was accepted on May 15. In accordance with the terms of the contract, the Canadian government agency (Canadian Crown Corporation) had telexed a letter of acceptance of the bid and wired 10% of the purchase price as a deposit on the morning of May 16. Also under the terms of the contract, TCAS would have to secure a performance bond from a third-party vender if awarded the bid. The performance bond would cost .75% of the outstanding contract value.

The remainder of the purchase price was due at the time the system was to be delivered and installed, which under the terms of the contract was to be within 90 days (the Canadian company had insisted on the 90 days and TCAS needed the extra time over the normal 45-day credit period) after the bid was accepted. The TCAS production manager had assured Mr. Christopher that there would be no problems in meeting this delivery schedule for the hardware, although the product was not currently in inventory. The software was already developed and available. Consequently, Mr. Christopher expected to receive a certified check for C$2,610,000 on August 16.

In preparing the bid, TCAS allowed for a tight mark-up of only 5% (see Exhibit 2) to improve the chances of winning the bid. Through past experience, TCAS knew that once it made the first sale, the quality of its product usually ensured additional purchases by the same company. Since the Canadian government agency had stipulated that the bid be in Canadian dollars, TCAS had used the opening spot rate existing on March 21, which was 1US$ = Canadian $1.4096.

The US Dollar and the Canadian Dollar

On May 16, 1995, the day after the bid was accepted, the value of the US dollar closed at 1US$ = C$1.3594. The Canadian$/US$ exchange rate had moved erratically

EXHIBIT 2 Bid Preparation (US$)

Design	300,000
Materials	779,287
Labor & installation	724,500
Shipping	32,466
Direct overhead	84,000
Allocation of indirect overhead	39,100
Sub-total	1,959,353
Mark-up (5%)	97,967
TOTAL BID	US$ 2,057,320
Conversion to C$ at March 21 spot rate of 1US$ = Canadian $1.4096	C$2,900,000

within a relatively narrow range over the past several months as reflected in the following table:

Month	Avg. C$/1US$
January 3	1.4027
February 7	1.3978
March 7	1.4168
April 4	1.4005
May 2	1.3553

The Canadian dollar had remained relatively stable against the US$ until mid-April 1995. It declined to the low registered on May 2 and recovered slightly by mid-May. Mr. Christopher was concerned that the Canadian dollar might depreciate against the US$ during the next 90 days before he received his final payment from the Canadian government agency. Mr. Christopher wanted to know what alternatives were available to him to reduce the foreign exchange risk associated with the outstanding Canadian dollar contract.

Foreign Currency Exposure Management

Judy Wright explained to Mr. Christopher the alternatives available to manage the foreign exchange risk brought about by the Canadian dollar contract. First, Mr. Christopher could do nothing. Over the 55 days since the bid was tendered, the US$ had depreciated by Canadian $0.0502 from Canadian dollar 1.4096 to Canadian dollar 1.3594, or 3.6% in absolute terms. This exchange rate change, if it held steady for the 90 days, would improve TCAS's mark-up from 5% to 8.6% when the Canadian dollars were converted into US dollars. Further depreciation of the US dollar could not be ensured, Judy explained, based on her review of macroeconomic fundamentals.

Foreign Currency Exposure Management Alternatives

The evaluation of expected macroeconomic developments confirmed Mr. Christopher's concerns about a possible depreciation of the Canadian dollar. Ms. Wright explained that a foreign currency hedge would be an appropriate response to the foreign exchange risk faced by TCAS, Inc. Since TCAS had an outstanding Canadian dollar contract, a hedge could be accomplished by any one of the following techniques:

1. *Forward contract*—This involved arranging to deliver Canadian $2,610,000 90 days in the future for conversion into US$ at a predetermined exchange rate. Thus, Mr. Christopher could contract today with Ms. Wright to deliver the Canadian dollar converted at today's quoted three-month forward rate of 1US$ = Canadian $1.3653.

2. ***Foreign currency loan***—This created a Canadian $ obligation 90 days hence. TCAS could borrow Canadian $ from Ms. Wright's bank for 90 days and then use the proceeds on completion of the contract to repay the principal and accrued interest. The loan proceeds would be converted immediately into US$ at the prevailing spot rate of exchange. Any gains or losses on the receivable due to a change in the value of the Canadian $/US$ exchange rate would be offset by equivalent losses or gains on the loan itself. Ms. Wright thought that such a loan could be made at 2.25% above the present Canadian prime rate of 10.25% plus an arrangement fee of 0.125%. The US prime rate was at 8.875%. TCAS paid a spread of 2.125% over prime in the US market and would pay a similar spread in Canada

3. ***Foreign currency options***—This instrument would give TCAS the right to either purchase (call) or sell (put) an asset at a specified price at a date in the future (European style) or anytime between the purchase date and a date in the future (American style). The buyer of an option has the right but not the obligation to exercise the option. The buyer of an option has a choice whether to exercise the option and either receive the asset (call) or deliver the asset (put) or to allow the option to expire unexercised. The seller (writer) of the option must stand ready to fulfill an option obligation and surrender an asset on demand (call) or receive an asset on demand (put). Since TCAS had a Canadian dollar contract, it could hedge this foreign currency exposure by buying a Canadian dollar put or writing a Canadian dollar call. Buying a Canadian dollar put option would protect TCAS from an unfavorable downward movement in the Canadian dollar exchange rate while allowing the company to benefit from any further appreciation in the Canadian dollar . The purchase of a currency option would require that Mr. Christopher pay Ms. Wright an option premium at the time the contract was entered into. At the time, the 90-day currency options premium rates on a strike of 1 Canadian dollar = US$ .7200 (or implied 1USdollar = Canadian dollar 1.3888) were: call premium—US dollar 0.0356/Canadian dollar; put premium = US dollar 0.0225/Canadian dollar. Note that the options are quoted as the US dollar price of one Canadian dollar which is the reciprocal of the Canadian dollar price of one US dollar. Writing a Canadian dollar call option would allow TCAS to benefit if there was little or no change in the value of the Canadian dollar. Instead of paying a premium, TCAS would receive the premium.

4. ***Foreign currency futures***—A standardized obligation to purchase or sell a specific amount of currency at a specified date. The buyer or seller of the contract is obliged to take delivery or make delivery of the currency; the position could only be eliminated if the futures position was offset. Most futures positions are offset prior to the last day of trading, leaving the seller with a profit or loss. Ms. Wright explained that a futures contract could be arranged through the International Monetary Market (IMM) of the Chicago Mercantile Exchange. The August futures price was 1C = US$ 0.735. The cost of a round turn per contract

(the purchase and subsequent sale of a futures contract) was US$ 50.00. Each Canadian dollar future contract represents Canadian $100,000.

5. *Pre-sale of foreign contract*—Ms. Wright explained that her bank had an export finance subsidiary that would purchase the short-term Canadian dollar contract from TCAS at a discount. The interest rate applicable was fixed for the term involved—90 days—at the cost of funding to the Export Finance Subsidiary, which was LIBOR currently at 7.375%, plus a premium based on normal credit criteria. At this time the credit spread for TCAS was 1.825% over LIBOR. TCAS would incur a flat up-front fee of 0.5%. The US dollar 90-day libor rate was 6.125%.

6. *Tunnel forwards*—A contractual agreement between the two parties which designates a specific exchange rate band within which TCAS would have to exchange currencies on a specific future date. It works like a forward exchange contract that fully protects the downside with no up-front premium paid, but the settlement rate falls within a range instead of at a specific rate. The upper and lower limits of the range act as contract settlement rates if the exchange rate exceed the limits of the range of the tunnel. Ms. Wright indicated that at the present time a zero cost tunnel or range forward (where the premium paid on the put is equal to the premium received) could be created with the strike on the Canadian dollar put set at US dollar .7133 and the strike on the Canadian dollar call set at US$ .7533.

Canadian Economic Performance

After finally gaining momentum in 1994, the economic recovery faltered in early 1995. After growing by more than 5-1/2% in 1994, real GDP increased only moderately in the first quarter of 1995 and was expected to decline in the second quarter, before rebounding in the third quarter of 1995. The economic slowdown in the United States dampened the demand for Canadian exports and the tighter monetary conditions moderated domestic demand in Canada. Fortunately, the economic slowdown also resulted in a significant drop in Canadian imports. The short-term interest spreads between Canada and the United States had increased from virtually zero in November 1994 to 2% in early April 1995. However, all indications were that the Canadian Central Bank would soon reverse policy direction and push interest rates lower in order to stimulate employment.

In its February 1995 budget, the federal government in Ottawa, Canada adopted drastic expenditure restraint in order to convince financial markets that deficit reduction targets would be met in spite of higher-than-expected hikes in short-term interest rates. The budget included proposals for major cuts in government employment, subsidies to business and agriculture, and transfers to the provinces.

The most interest-sensitive components of the domestic economy, durable goods and construction, declined markedly in the first quarter of 1995. The recent run-up in interest rates aborted the revival of residential investment. The impact

EXHIBIT 3 Macroeconomic Data

	1989	1990	1991	1992	1993	1994	1995 Est
Real GDP Growth % Canada	2.4	-.2	-1.8	.8	2.2	4.6	2.4
Real GDP Growth % US	2.5	1.2	-.6	2.3	3.1	4.1	3.3
Inflation CPI % Canada	5.0	4.8	5.6	1.5	1.8	.2	1.9
Inflation CPI % US	4.8	5.4	4.2	3.0	3.0	2.6	2.8
Unemployment Rate % Canada	7.5	8.1	10.4	11.3	11.2	10.4	9.6
Unemployment Rate % US	5.3	5.5	6.7	7.4	6.8	6.1	5.6
Gov. Deficit as % GDP Canada	1.4	0.7	-2.0	-2.9	-2.6	-0.5	1.0
Current Account as % of GDP Canada	-3.9	-3.4	-3.7	-3.6	-3.9	-2.7	-0.5
Gross Savings as % of GDP Canada	19.4	16.4	14.3	13.2	13.7	15.4	
Investment as % of GDP Canada	21.9	19.1	20.0	19.7	20.2	18.6	
Current Account C$ dollar (billions)	-22.8	-21.6	-23.6	-21.4	-22.3	-16.3	-10.1
Capital Account C$ (billions)	24.1	23.2	22.1	16.8	22.9	12.3	9.9
Short-term Interest Rates Canada	12.2	13.0	9.0	6.7	5.0	5.4	7.1
Short-term Interest Rates US	8.1	7.5	5.4	3.4	3.0	4.2	5.5
Long-term Interest Rates Canada	9.9	10.8	9.8	8.8	7.9	8.6	8.3
Long-term Interest Rates US	8.5	8.6	7.9	7.0	5.9	7.1	6.6
C$/US$ Exchange Rate	1.184	1.167	1.146	1.209	1.290	1.366	1.370
Gov. Deficit as % GDP US	-1.5	-2.5	-3.2	-4.3	-3.4	-2.0	-1.6

Source: OECD Economic Outlook (June 1998).

of this weakening of final demand on the Canadian GDP was offset somewhat by a substantial accumulation of inventories.

The Canadian unemployment rate remained broadly stable in the 9-1/2% range. Persistent labor-market slack kept wage increases low, and unit labor costs hardly rose. Slower output growth has been associated with smaller productivity gains. Overall, the rate of inflation had begun to ease.

The Banker's Role

Judy Wright knew that she would need to assist John Christopher in the selection of the appropriate hedging alternative. She also knew that she should be able to talk intelligently about the likely movements in the Canadian dollar over the next three months. Judy Wright asked her bank's economic department to pull together a set of numbers that would help her explain the outlook for the Canadian dollar to Mr. Christopher.

What economic and financial data would she request from the economic department? What analytical framework would she use to interpret the data? How should she best explain the economic data to Mr. Christopher, and what would be her recommendation for the appropriate hedging strategy?

LUFTHANSA

If Karl Marx could see what the foreign exchange market is doing to the world's captains of industry, he would surely be laughing. Not only do they put up with labor problems, competition, deregulation, and rapid changes in technology—no, that is not enough. Add currency volatility to that list in the last few years. And it's so bad that a successful corporate executive of one of the world's prestige airlines can put on a multimillion dollar currency speculation, and win—and still get lambasted by his critics. It's enough to make a capitalist cry.

— Intermarket, 1985

It was February 14, 1986, and Herr Heinz Ruhnau, Chairman of Lufthansa (Germany) was summoned to meet with Lufthansa's board. The board's task was to determine if Herr Ruhnau's term of office should be terminated. Herr Ruhnau had already been summoned by Germany's transportation minister to explain his supposed speculative management of Lufthansa's exposure in the purchase of Boeing aircraft.

In January 1985 Lufthansa, under the chairmanship of Herr Heinz Ruhnau, purchased twenty 737 jets from Boeing (U.S.). The agreed upon price was $500,000,000, payable in U.S. dollars on delivery of the aircraft in one year, in January 1986. The U.S. dollar had been rising steadily and rapidly since 1980, and was approximately DM3.2/$ in January 1985. If the dollar were to continue to rise, the cost of the jet aircraft to Lufthansa would rise substantially by the time payment was due.

Herr Ruhnau had his own *view* or expectations regarding the direction of the exchange rate. Like many others at the time, he believed the dollar had risen about as far as it was going to go, and would probably fall by the time January 1986 rolled around. But then again, it really wasn't his money to gamble with. He compromised. He sold half the exposure ($250,000,000) at a rate of DM3.2/$, and left the remaining half ($250,000,000) uncovered.

Evaluation of the Hedging Alternatives

Lufthansa and Herr Ruhnau had the same basic hedging alternatives available to all firms:

1. Remain uncovered,
2. Cover the entire exposure with forward contracts,
3. Cover some proportion of the exposure, leaving the balance uncovered,
4. Cover the exposure with foreign currency options,
5. Obtain U.S. dollars now and hold them until payment is due.

EXHIBIT 1 Lufthansa's Net Cost by Hedging Alternative

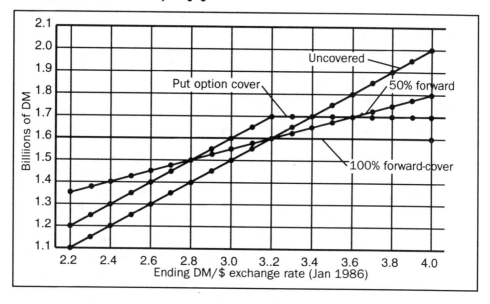

Although the final expense of each alternative could not be known beforehand, each alternative's outcome could be simulated over a range of potential ending exchange rates. Exhibit 1 illustrates the final net cost of the first four alternatives over a range of potential end-of-period spot exchange rates.

Of course one of the common methods of covering a foreign currency exposure for firms, which involves no use of financial contracts like forwards or options, is the matching of currency cash flows. Lufthansa did have inflows of U.S. dollars on a regular basis as a result of airline ticket purchases in the United States. Although Herr Ruhnau thought briefly about matching these U.S. dollar-denominated cash inflows against the dollar outflows to Boeing, the magnitude of the mismatch was obvious. Lufthansa simply did not receive anything close to $500 million a year in dollar-earnings, or even over several years for that matter.

1. Remain Uncovered. Remaining uncovered is the maximum risk approach. It therefore represents the greatest potential benefits (if the dollar weakens versus the Deutschemark), and the greatest potential cost (if the dollar continues to strengthen versus the Deutschemark). If the exchange rate were to drop to DM2.2/$ by January 1986, the purchase of the Boeing 737s would be only DM1.1 billion. Of course if the dollar continued to appreciate, rising to perhaps DM4.0/$ by 1986, the total cost would be DM2.0 billion. The uncovered position's risk is therefore shown as that value-line which has the steepest slope (covers the widest vertical distance) in Exhibit 1. This is obviously a sizeable level of risk for any firm to carry. Many firms believe the decision to leave a large exposure uncovered for a long period of time to be nothing other than currency speculation.

2. Full Forward Cover. If Lufthansa were very risk averse and wished to eliminate fully its currency exposure, it could buy forward contracts for the purchase of U.S. dollars for the entire amount. This would have locked-in an exchange rate of DM3.2/$, with a known final cost of DM1.6 billion. This alternative is represented by the horizontal value-line in Exhibit 1; the total cost of the Boeing 737s no longer has any risk or sensitivity to the ending spot exchange rate. Most firms believe they should accept or tolerate risk in their line of business, not in the process of payment. The 100% forward cover alternative is often used by firms as their benchmark, their comparison measure for actual currency costs when all is said and done.

3. Partial Forward Cover. This alternative would cover only part of the total exposure leaving the remaining exposure uncovered. Herr Ruhnau's expectations were for the dollar to fall, so he expected Lufthansa would benefit from leaving more of the position uncovered (as in alternative #1 above). This strategy is somewhat arbitrary, however, in that there are few objective methods available for determining the proper balance (20/80, 40/60, 50/50, etc.) between covered/uncovered should be. Exhibit 1 illustrates the total ending cost of this alternative for a partial cover of 50/50; $250 million purchased with forward contracts of DM3.2/$, and the $250 million remaining purchased at the end-of-period spot rate. Note that this value line's slope is simply half that of the 100% uncovered position. Any other partial cover strategy would similarly fall between the unhedged and 100% cover lines.

Two principal points can be made regarding partial forward cover strategies such as this. First, Herr Ruhnau's total potential exposure is still unlimited. The possibility that the dollar would appreciate to astronomical levels still exists, and $250 million could translate into an infinite amount of Deutschemarks. The second point is that the first point is highly unlikely to occur. Therefore, for the immediate ranges of potential exchange rates on either side of the current spot rate of DM3.2/$, Herr Ruhnau has reduced the risk (vertical distance in Exhibit 1) of the final Deutschemark outlay over a range of ending values and the benchmark value of DM3.2/$.

4. Foreign Currency Options. The foreign currency option is unique among the hedging alternatives due to its kinked-shape value-line. If Herr Ruhnau had purchased a put option on marks at DM3.2/$, he could have obtained what many people believe is the best of both worlds. If the dollar had continued to strengthen above DM3.2/$, the total cost of obtaining $500 million could be locked-in at DM1.6 billion plus the cost of the option premium, as illustrated by the flat portion of the option alternative to the right of DM3.2/$. If, however, the dollar fell as Herr Ruhnau had expected, Lufthansa would be free to let the option expire and purchase the dollars at lower cost on the spot market. This alternative is shown by the falling value-line to the left of DM3.2/$. Note that the put option line falls at the same rate (same slope) as the uncovered position, but is higher by the cost of purchasing the option.

In this instance Herr Ruhnau would have had to buy put options for DM1.6 billion given an exercise price of DM3.2/$. In January 1985 when Herr Heinz Ruhnau was mulling over these alternatives, the option premium on Deutshemark

EXHIBIT 2 What Herr Ruhnau Could See: The Rise

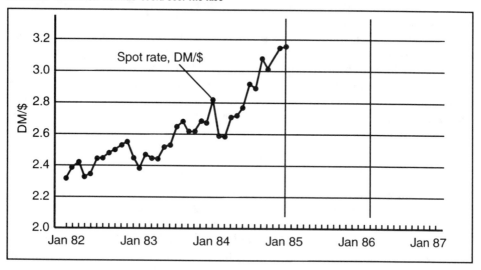

put options was about 6%, equal to DM96,000,000 or $30,000,000. The total cost of the purchase in the event the put option was exercised would be DM1,696,000,000 (exercise plus premium).

It is important to understand what Herr Ruhnau would be hoping to happen if he had decided to purchase the put options. He would be expecting the dollar to weaken (ending up to the left of DM3.2/$ in Exhibit 1), therefore he would expect the option to expire without value. In the eyes of many corporate treasurers, DM96,000,000 is a lot of money for the purchase of an instrument which the hedger expects or hopes not to use!

5. Buy Dollars Now. The fifth alternative is a money-market hedge for an account payable: Obtain the $500 million now and hold those funds in an interest-bearing account or asset until payment was due. Although this would eliminate the currency exposure, it required that Lufthansa have all the capital in-hand now. The purchase of the Boeing jets had been made in conjunction with the on-going financing plans of Lufthansa, and these did not call for the capital to be available until January 1986. An added concern (and what ultimately eliminated this alternative from consideration) was that Lufthansa had several relatively strict covenants in place which limited the types, amounts, and currencies of denomination of the debt it could carry on its balance sheet.

Herr Ruhnau's Decision

Although Herr Ruhnau truly expected the dollar to weaken over the coming year, he believed remaining completely uncovered was too risky for Lufthansa. Few would argue this, particularly given the strong upward trend of the DM/$ exchange rate as seen in Exhibit 2. The dollar had shown a consistent three year trend of appreciation versus the Deutschemark, and that trend seemed to be accelerating over the most recent year.

Because he personally felt so strongly that the dollar would weaken, Herr Ruhnau chose to go with partial cover. He chose to cover 50% of the exposure ($250 million) with forward contracts (the one year forward rate was DM3.2/$) and to leave the remaining 50% ($250 million) uncovered. Because foreign currency options were as yet a relatively new tool for exposure management by many firms, and because of the sheer magnitude of the up-front premium required, the foreign currency option was not chosen. Time would tell if this was a wise decision.

How It Came Out

Herr Ruhnau was both right and wrong. He was definitely right in his expectations. The dollar appreciated for one more month, and then weakened over the coming year. In fact, it did not simply *weaken*, it plummeted. By January 1986 when payment was due to Boeing, the spot rate had fallen to DM2.3/$ from the previous year's DM3.2/$ as shown in Exhibit 3. This was a spot exchange rate movement in Lufthansa's favor.

The bad news was that the total Deutschemark cost with the partial forward cover was DM1.375 billion, a full DM225,000,000 more than if no hedging had been implemented at all! This was also DM129,000,000 more than what the foreign currency option hedge would have cost in total. The total cost of obtaining the needed $500 million for each alternative at the actual ending spot rate of DM2.3/$ would have been:

EXHIBIT 3 What Herr Ruhnau Couldn't See: The Fall

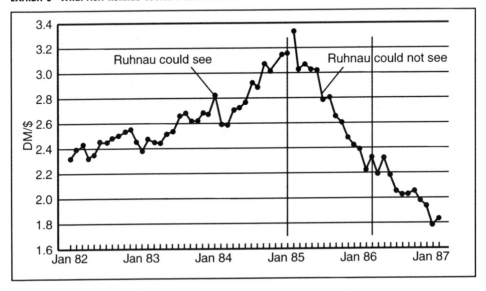

A07-99-0028

Alternative	Relevant Rate	Total DM Cost
1: Uncovered	DM 2.3/$	1,150,000,000
2: Full Forward Cover (100%)	DM 3.2/$	1,600,000,000
3: Partial Forward Cover	1/2(DM2.3) + 2(DM3.2)	1,375,000,000
4: DM Put Options	DM 3.2/$ strike	1,246,000,000

Herr Heinz's political rivals, both inside and outside of Lufthansa, were not so happy. Ruhnau was accused of recklessly speculating with Lufthansa's money, but the speculation was seen as the forward contract, not the amount of the dollar exposure left uncovered for the full year.

Case Questions

Herr Ruhnau was accused of making the following four mistakes:

1. Purchasing the Boeing aircraft at the wrong time. The U.S. dollar was at an all-time high at the time of the purchase, in January of 1985.

2. Choosing to hedge half the exposure when he expected the dollar to fall. If he had gone through with his instincts or expectations, he would have left the whole amount unhedged (which some critics have termed "whole hog").

3. Choosing to use forward contracts as his hedging tool instead of options. The purchase of put options would have allowed Herr Ruhnau to protect himself against adverse exchange rate movements while preserving the flexibility of exchanging DM for dollars spot if preferred.

4. Purchasing Boeing aircraft at all. Germany, as well as the other major European Economic Community countries, has a vested interest in the conglomerate Airbus. Airbus's chief rival was Boeing in the manufacture of large long-distance civil aircraft.

Given these criticisms, should the Board of Lufthansa retain Herr Heinz Ruhnau as Chairman? How should Ruhnau justify his actions and so justify his further employment?

CROSSWELL INTERNATIONAL

It is August 4, 1995, and the Mathieux brothers, Doug and Geoff, were concluding a summer-long effort of developing the Brazilian market for Crosswell International (U.S.). Crosswell's president and CEO, Hector Lans, is convinced that *Precious Ultra Thin Baby Diapers* will be a big seller in Brazil. In their role as brokers for Crosswell, the Mathieuxs have been exploring a number of different distribution channels in the Brazilian market. To date, the distributor response to *Precious* diapers has been enthusiastic, particularly in light of *Precious diapers'* superior quality compared to locally manufactured alternatives. The problem, however, is the price.

Brazilians base many purchasing decisions — at least in regard to disposable diapers — on cost, not on quality. The Mathieuxs find that distributors do not believe they can compete in the market with the relatively high prices offered by Crosswell, even with higher quality diapers. After much debate over how to improve the price competitiveness of *Precious* diapers, the Mathieuxs believe they may have found a solution. Their proposal is to combine extended credit terms to local distributors with Brazil's high domestic interest rates to effectively lower the diapers' price to Brazilian consumers.

The Brazilian Diaper Market

Until the latter part of the 1980s, most Brazilians had never heard of a disposable diaper, and not surprisingly, the disposable hygiene market in Brazil was virtually non-existent. By 1995, however, the personal care market was booming. This growth was largely a result of new-found economic stability and a growing middle class. As both the middle class and educational levels about hygiene expand, the personal care market should also expand.

Disposable diapers were first introduced in Brazil in the mid-1980s by U.S.-based multinational Johnson and Johnson (J&J). As J&J promoted its new diapers, Brazilians discovered the advantages of disposable diapers and sales grew steadily in the small upper-class market segment. The diapers were initially very expensive; retailers sold them at a Brazilian currency equivalent price of $1.50 - $2.00 per diaper (depending on size). J&J increased its diaper sales and in the mid-1980s set up manufacturing operations in São Paulo.

Eventually, J&J's large profit margins attracted competitors, so that by 1990 several other players had entered the game. Between 1990 and 1995 the market expanded dramatically, with U.S.-based Procter and Gamble (P&G) and several other major new entrants now manufacturing and distributing in Brazil. The good news

EXHIBIT 1 Baby Diaper Prices and Qualities in the Brazilian Market, 1995

Company (Country)	Brand	Quality	Prices per Diaper by Size Small	Medium	Large	No. in Package
Bebito (ARG)	Bebito	Low	R$0.198	R$0.232	R$0.302	24 / 20 / 16
Panales Duffy (ARG)	Duffy	Low	0.204	0.230	0.312	24 / 20 / 16
Cora Products (BRZ)	Pipita Anatomica	Low	0.248	0.290	0.380	24 / 20 / 16
Pom Pom (BRZ)	Pom Pom	Low	0.244	0.289	0.415	12 / 10 / 8
Chansommes (BRZ)	Puppet	Mid	0.279	0.332	0.463	12 / 10 / 8
Julie Joy (BRZ)	Julie Joy	Mid	0.265	0.301	0.437	24 / 20 / 16
Kenko (JAP)	Monica Plus	Mid	0.273	0.340	0.469	24 / 20 / 16
Kenko (JAP)	Tippy	Mid	0.363	0.425	0.544	24 / 20 / 16
Procter & Gamble (USA)	Pampers Uni	Mid	0.261	0.317	0.429	24 / 20 / 16
Johnson & Johnson (USA)	Sempre Seca Plus	Mid to High	0.396	0.451	0.594	24 / 20 / 16
French, Italian, Israeli, Japanese and U.S. firms	Various	High	Similar to Johnson & Johnson			Varies

Source: Authors, 1995. Average exchange rate of R$0.94/US$.

for Crosswell is that these diapers are still largely inferior in quality to *Precious* due to technological and capital constraints on domestic producers.

By early 1995 the Brazilian disposable diaper market was growing rapidly as the Brazilian middle class expanded and its purchasing power increased. Competition, however, quickly reduced profit margins as competitors began cutting prices. J&J's leadership position eroded as it's market share dropped from 78% in 1990 to less than 15% in 1995. In an effort to keep its remaining market share, but maintain higher prices in an effort to recover its investment in local manufacturing facilities, J&J has spent freely to promote its premium product image. Exhibit 1 provides an overview of the major players, products, and prices in the Brazilian disposable diaper market in 1995.

The Competitors

There were four main groups of competitors in the diaper market in Brazil. The first group, comprised of foreign multinational corporations producing in Brazil included J&J, P&G, and Kenko do Brasil. These companies commanded 40% of the market. J&J had the highest quality diaper produced in Brazil and commands the highest prices. P&G was viewed as the most efficient manufacturer, producing the mid-quality *Pampers*. Kenko do Brasil, a Japanese company, entered Brazil by acquiring several local Brazilian diaper producers. The company's brands, *Monica* and *Tippy*, were popular and held a substantial portion of the market. Kenko's quality and price were similar to P&G's *Pampers*.

The second group of competitors consisted of Brazilian companies that produced in-country. These companies generally used simpler manufacturing techniques due to limited financial backing and served the lower quality, lower-price market segment. Some brands, however, such as *Puppet* and *Julie Joy*, competed in the mid-price segment. These national brands had captured a 30% share of the market by 1995.

The third group of competitors consisted of Argentinian companies with brands such as *Duffy* and *Bebito*. These large diaper producers were taking advantage of the lower import tariffs resulting from the creation of *Mercosur* (as well as favorable exchange rates) by producing in Argentina and selling into Brazil.[1] The production costs of the Argentinians were low, and in the two years prior to 1995 they had captured a 20% market share in Brazil by offering low quality, low cost diapers.

The final group of competitors includes foreign companies from countries such as France, Italy, Israel, Japan and the United States. These companies are entering the market with imports of high quality diapers (at least higher in quality than the majority in the existing Brazilian market). However, they are priced at the high end of the market with prices close to those of J&J, and have garnered only a ten percent share to date. This is the market segment which Crosswell wanted.

Prices for large-size disposable baby diapers in Brazil range from R$0.30 to R$0.60 per diaper (R$ is the symbol for the Brazilian currency, the *Real*). Argentinian companies are at the low end of the range while J&J commands the highest prices.

In spite of the entry of more and more competitors and increasing production capacity, the Brazilian market was still seen as a high-growth market with excess demand. Brazilian President Fernando Henrique Cardoso's economic recovery plan, the *Real Plan*, is drastically restructuring the Brazilian economy and, in the opinion of most, for the better.[2] Consumers have gained confidence in the economy and consumer spending is rising. If the plan continues to be a success, the middle class will continue to grow in size and income, resulting in an expanding market for disposable diapers.

Hospital Specialty Company

Hospital Specialty Company (Hospeco) was the personal care products division of The Tranzonic Companies, a Cleveland, Ohio based manufacturer and distributor of a wide variety of paper, cloth and vinyl products. Tranzonic had sales of $131 million in 1994 and was listed on the New York Stock Exchange (symbol TRNZ). Appendix A provides a brief summary of Tranzonic's financial performance in the

---

[1] *Mercosur* is a regional common market including Argentina, Brazil, Paraguay, and Uruguay. It was implemented on January 1, 1995. This trading agreement set common external tariffs for the four members while reducing trade barriers and import tariffs for trade within the common market.

[2] The *Real Plan*, an economic program combining a new currency with new economic stabilization measures, is described in detail in a following section.

1990s. Tranzonic was composed of four major operating divisions, the personal care division (Hospeco), the industrial textiles division, the housewares division, and the industrial packaging division. Hospeco was the largest operating unit within the company, manufacturing and distributing a full line of feminine hygiene products, infant's disposable diapers, adult incontinence products, obstetrical pads, toilet seat covers, and related disposable hygiene products. Hospeco brand names included SAFE & SOFT®, EVERYDAY®, SOFT & THIN®, MAXITHINS®, PRECIOUS®, HEALTH GARDS®, FRESH GARDS®, and AT EASE®. Production facilities were located in Cleveland, Ohio; Lexington, Kentucky; and Phoenix, Arizona.[3]

Although Hospeco faced margin pressures in 1994 (brand product manufacturers had been reducing prices to draw market share from the private label sector), the firm increased its sales and earnings over the 1995 fiscal year. In response to increased competition, the parent company made significant new investments to insure cost competitive manufacturing of high quality products. The goal of Tranzonic and Hospeco, was to develop and maintain the capacity to offer customers a broad line of products that were equivalent to international brands in terms of quality and performance. Hospeco proved itself adept at leveraging strong customer relationships and introducing new product lines. For example, its adult incontinence product lines and sales continued growing with the "graying of America" and the associated expansion of the elder-care market.

Hospeco and Crosswell International

Hospeco did not begin to explore market potential outside the United States until 1994. In 1993, Hospeco's president was approached by Hector Lans, a Cuban-born Miami-based businessman, who promised big results if he was allowed to direct a new international sales subsidiary, and given the resources to pursue large untapped international markets. Mr. Lans managed to convince Hospeco's directors of the international market potential — particularly in Latin America — for their line of personal care products, and Crosswell International was born. The subsidiary was placed in Miami, Florida to focus specifically on Latin America.

By May 1995, in a little over 18 months, Hector Lans had begun developing several Latin American markets, with the glaring omission of Brazil. The lack of any real activity in the Brazilian market was largely a result of the language barrier — Brazil is primarily Portuguese-speaking — and a general lack of familiarity with the market. But Brazil offered enormous potential. Lans sought out two brothers, Doug and Geoff Mathieux, who possessed not only business experience in the Brazilian market but, just as importantly, the language skills necessary to be penetrate it (both were fluent in Spanish, French, and most importantly for Brazil, Portuguese). The Mathieux brothers agreed to act as brokers on behalf of Crosswell International in Brazil and focus on the development of the *Precious Ultra Thin Baby Diaper* product line.

---

[3] *The Tranzonic Companies, Annual Report, 1994.*

Economic Situation in Brazil

The economic situation in Brazil improved dramatically after the implementation of President Cardoso's *Real Plan* on July 1, 1994. There were two key elements of the *Real Plan*: 1) the establishment of a new currency, the *Real (R$)*, and 2) a commitment to a tight monetary policy which would, once and for all, drive inflation from the Brazilian economic and social fabric. Success to date had been promising. Inflation dropped from a pre-plan level of 50% per month to 2% per month, and was expected to stay at that rate throughout 1995. The new currency, the *Real*, was stable against the dollar and the Brazilian government was committed to maintaining its value.

Interest rates were, however, still high at 3-4% per month (not per year) for corporate deposit rates, and 8% to 10% per month for loan rates, as a result of the tight monetary policy under the *Real Plan* (see Exhibit 2). These rates were expected to remain stable for the next several months, with hope that interest rates may slowly decline over the coming one to two years as inflationary pressures subsided. A continuing influx of foreign capital was also expected to aid in this process of stabilization as inflows would hopefully buoy the Real and prevent the currency itself from depreciating and adding to inflationary pressures.

The Brazilian trade balance enjoyed a modest monthly surplus after several months of deficits during the beginning of 1995. Thanks to a large capital account surplus, Brazil was able to increase its volume of foreign reserves to over US$45 billion.[4] Foreign investment once again began flowing into Brazil, indicating that the *Tequila Effect* was wearing off.[5]

The stock market performed quite well during the last quarter, after several difficult months following Mexico's devaluation. These strong results were thought to be indicative of the new consumer and institutional confidence in the economy. After a year of strong growth, consumer spending and retail sales have leveled. Gross domestic product (GDP) growth was expected to reach 6.4% in 1995.

EXHIBIT 2 Brazilian Exchange & Money Rates, August 4, 1995

Real/US$ Exchange Rates	*Bid*	*Ask*
Commercial	0.9343	0.9357
Parallel	0.9070	0.9220
Tourist	0.9040	0.9270

Deposit Interest Rates	*Loan Interest Rates*
3.69% per month	30 days: 8.25% per month
	60 days: 8.75% per month
	90 days: 9.25% per month

Source: *Brasil FaxLetter*, Gilbert o L. DiPierro, August 4, 1995, Miami , Florida.

---

[4] *Brazil Outlook*, Number 9, September 1995, Editora Tama, Ltda., Rio de Janeiro, Brazil.

[5] The Tequila Effect refers to the spreading of negative economic impacts to all of Latin America's markets following the devaluation of the Mexican peso in December 1994. Although the devaluation was confined to Mexico alone, international investors withdrew from many Latin American markets in fear that the devaluation might spread. It took over half a year to soothe the anxieties of international investors regarding the stability of the other countries in the region.

A06-97-0002

EXHIBIT 3 Brazilian Real/U.S. Dollar Exchange Rate Under the Real Plan (Feb. 1994–Aug. 1995)

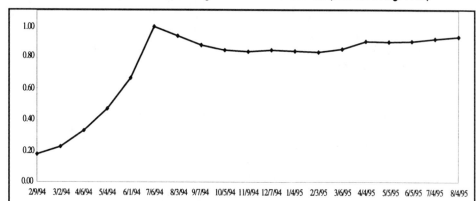

Note: The Real replaced the Cruzeiro as the Brazilian currency on June 30, 1994. The exchange rate on that date, Crz2750/US$, is used to index the currency rate prior to June 30, resulting in the "falling value" of the Real from February to July 1994 illustrated here. For financial valuation purposes, the exchangerate prior to June 30, 1994 is not directly comparable to the rate in effect after revaluation.

With the implementation of the Real Plan on June 30, 1994, the Brazilian *Cruzeiro (Crz)* was replaced with the *Real (R$)*, with the official exchange rate changing from approximately Crz2750/US$ to R$1.00/US$. Given the relatively high inflation rates experienced by Brazil after that time, the Real should have depreciated against the dollar — but it didn't. The influx of foreign investment became substantial, with benefits to the Real itself. In fact, as illustrated in Exhibit 3, the Real appreciated slightly during the first year after the plan, and remained stable through most of 1995.[6] Simultaneously, monthly deposit interest rates dropped precipitously under the Plan, stabilizing at three to four percent per month.[7] Given the apparent health of the economy, the positive trade balance, and a central bank which was adding significantly to its foreign exchange reserves, the outlook for maintaining the Real's value looked promising.

Developing the Brazilian Market

When the Mathieux brothers arrived in Brazil in May 1995, they conducted an in-depth analysis of the disposable diaper market. Their primary interest was to isolate what price they believed the market could sustain for Crosswell's *Precious*.

---

[6] The Brazilian government had actually intervened in the currency markets to keep the Real from appreciating further and making Brazilian exports increasingly expensive and uncompetitive on world markets.

[7] Monthly deposit rates averaged between 40% and 47% for the first six months of 1994, the period just prior to the *Real Plan*.

The Mathieuxs then completed a detailed import and distribution price analysis for *Precious*. Pricing was constructed in five stages (see Exhibit 4 for the detailed calculation), beginning with Crosswell's price to the Mathieuxs of $32.57 per case, and adding $1.50 per case commission for the Mathieuxs as brokers. The FOB price per case, Miami, was $34.07.[8]

Local freight, loading, documentation and insurance expenses were incurred in the second stage, resulting in a CIF price to the distributor of $39.25 per case.[9] Although a number of larger firms were increasingly foregoing export insurance expenses — in this case 2.25% of CFR price — Doug and Geoff viewed the potential liabilities of a start-up business line such as this as too large, forcing them to incur the added expense. The price to the distributor was invoiced in U.S. dollars. Given the current spot rate of R$0.935/US$, this translated into a price of R$36.70 per case to the Brazilian distributor. The distributor would carry the currency risk, while the U.S. exporter (and broker in this case) were guaranteed their margins on the transfer price without risk of currency movements.

The third stage, the actual logistics of getting the diapers from Miami and through Brazilian customs to the local distributor, was not trivial in either cost or complexity. Given the various fees, tariffs, currency and brokerage fees, the price in Brazilian Real rose rapidly from a CIF price of R$36.70 to R$40.44 per case, an added 10%.

The Brazilian distributor's role, the fourth stage in the pricing saga, added storage costs, inventory financing expenses, and distributor's margin. The price to retailers was now R$52.27 per case. In the fifth and final stage, the retailer paid industrial and merchandise taxes (15% and 18%, respectively), and added a customary 30% markup, resulting in a final price to the consumer of R$92.21. This was a price roughly 2.5 times the price of the diaper prior to hitting the docks of the Brazilian port. Brazilian *Precious* consumers would pay R$0.480 per large, and R$0.524 per extra-large baby diaper. This placed *Precious* in the upper third of the baby diaper price range in Brazil.

The brothers then proceeded to meet with importers, distributors, local representatives of chambers of commerce, and even trade representatives of the American Embassy offices in Brazil. Several useful contacts were established in trade shows in both Rio de Janeiro and São Paulo. Initial discussions with a number of potential distributors were encouraging as a number of distributors displayed strong interest in the diaper product line. Distributors were impressed with the quality of the product, acknowledging the superiority to that of locally-manufactured brands.

The objection that the brothers ran into time and time again, however, was the price. Although all distributors were impressed by the quality, they insisted that *Precious* diapers could not effectively penetrate the Brazilian market at the

---

[8] FOB, "free on board," is an international trade term in which the exporter's quoted price includes the cost of loading goods into transport vessels at a named point.

[9] CIF, cost, insurance, and freight, is the exporter's quoted price including the cost of packaging, freight or carriage, insurance premium, and other charges paid respecting the goods from the time of loading in the country of export to their arrival at the named port of destination or place of trans-shipment.

EXHIBIT 4 Precious Ultra-Thin Pricing

	Price / case	Rate	Applied
Cases per container		968	
Price/case to Mathieux bros (US$)	$32.57		
Commission (Mathieux)	1.50	1.50	US$ per case
FOB price per case (US$)	$34.07		
Freight, loading, & documentation	4.32	4180	$4180 per container
CFR price	$38.39		
Export insurance	0.86	2.250%	% of CFR
CIF/case to distributor (US$)	$39.25		
Exchange rate (R$/US$)	0.935	0.935	Average of bid/ask spread
CIF price/case to distributor (R$)	36.70		
Import duties (ID)	0.73	2.000%	% of CIF
Industrial product tax (IPI)	-	0.000%	% of CIF
Merchant marine renovation fee (MMRF)	1.01	25.00%	% of freight
Port storage	0.48	1.300%	% of CIF
Port handling fees	0.01	10.84	R$10.84 per container
Additional handling tax	0.10	20.000%	% of storage & handling
Indemnity for port employees	0.00	0.0407	R$0.0407 per container
Bank currency exchange fees	0.07	0.200%	% of CIF
Customs brokerage fees	0.73	2.000%	% of CIF
Tax on merc circulation services (ICMS)	-	0.000%	% of CIF+ ID+IPT+MMRF
Import license	0.05	50.00	R$50.0 per container
Local transportation	0.55	1.500%	% of CIF
Total cost to distributor (R$)	40.44		
Storage cost	0.55	1.500%	% of CIF * months
Cost of financing diaper inventory	2.57	7.000%	% of CIF * months
Distributor's margin	8.71	20.000%	% of Price + storage + cc
Price to retailer (R$)	52.27		
Industrial product tax (IPT-2)	7.84	15.000%	% of price to retailer
Tax on merc circulation services (ICMS-2)	10.82	18.000%	% of price + IPT2
Retailer costs and markup	21.28	30.000%	% of price + IPT2 + ICMS2
Price per case to consumer (R$)	92.21		

DIAPER PRICES	Bags of 8 per case	Diapers per case	Price to Consumer (R$/diaper)
Small	44	352	0.262
Medium	32	256	0.360
Large	24	192	0.480
Extra Large	22	176	0.524

proposed price (as developed in Exhibit 4). Although the Mathieuxs attempted to impress upon the distributors the changing structure of the Brazilian marketplace, and the opportunity they saw for a high-end high quality product at a premium price, distributors insisted that — at least at the time — success would only follow from a price which fell into the mid-priced segment of the diaper market. They also commented that "although the Americans saw the Real as stable, only time will convince us."

Material Hospitalar, Ltd.

In June 1995 the Mathieux brothers were referred to Leonardo Sousa by the local American chamber of commerce. Leonardo Sousa was the president of Material Hospitalar, a distributor of health care products with contacts in the hospital and disposable hygiene markets, and one of the largest distributors of hospital supplies in Brazil. Mr. Sousa expressed a strong interest in distributing *Precious* after a demonstration of their superior absorbency, and wished to proceed with the development of a business plan in which he would work with the Mathieuxs in importing and distributing Hospeco's baby diaper products on behalf of Crosswell International.

Mr. Sousa believed that the time was right to enter the baby diaper market, even though competition was intense. The market was currently experiencing growth rates of 25% a year, and he was confident that *Precious* could capture one half percent of the potential baby diaper market in Brazil within a year. That represented imports of 15 containers a month with a value of almost $33,000 per container.[10] The Mathieux brothers provided Leonardo with a price list and outline of a potential representation agreement with payment and credit terms. Payment had to be made in cash in advance or with a confirmed, irrevocable documentary letter of credit with a sight draft. In return they requested financial statements, banking references, foreign commercial references, descriptions of regional sales forces, and sales forecasts. Mr. Sousa was interested in obtaining exclusive distributor rights to all of Brazil, and Crosswell was willing to grant it to the right distributor.

Negotiations between Leonardo Sousa and the Mathieux brothers progressed. Numerous meetings were held throughout the summer of 1995. The brothers visited Material Hospitalar's warehouse in Rio and met three of Leonardo's business associates. They were impressed. The only remaining issue was price. Sousa and his associates insisted that the FOB Miami price offered to Material Hospitalar was prohibitively high, and would prevent successful market penetration. Sousa was not willing to take the chance of entry failure due to the high price.

Like other distributors, Sousa explained that thrifty Brazilians would not purchase unknown, expensive diapers even if they were higher quality. He wanted Crosswell to cut its diaper prices and fund an advertising campaign to promote the *Precious* name. When the Mathieuxs approached Hector Lans about obtaining funding for promotional efforts, they were told that given Tranzonic/ Hospeco's recent

---

[10] Each container held 968 cases of diapers and each case cost $34.07 to Leonardo Sousa (968 * $34.07 = $32,980).

financial performance, an ad campaign was out of the question. More specifically, Hector Lans had a limited budget and his superiors at Hospeco were pressuring him to show results for the expenditures related to the establishment of Crosswell. The Mathieuxs concluded that a lower price was the only way to reach an agreement with Sousa. "Once the *Precious* brand is known," he explained, "then you will be able to raise the price of the diaper. But remember, time is of the essence."

Sousa believed that Crosswell's price would have to drop by ten percent or more — the large size diaper needed to be priced at the consumer level at about R$0.43 to R$0.44 per diaper. This would place *Precious* in direct competition with the Brazilian-owned domestic producers, the *Chansommes* and *Julie Joy* brands. Sousa felt that the market shares held by these firms were particularly vulnerable given their inferior quality to that of *Precious*.

As a result, the brothers renewed negotiations with Hector Lans in Miami, explaining that a lower FOB price was necessary for successful market penetration. One suggestion made by the Mathieuxs was for Hospital Specialty to manufacture a cheaper, lower-quality diaper which could more easily fit into the target price range. Although Hector agreed to a small discount — down to $32.07 per case (before commission) — he insisted that Hospeco would not change its manufacturing process for sales to Brazil. The Mathieuxs agreed to cut their commission to three percent ($1 per case). Unfortunately, these changes still only dropped the price to R$89.87 per case, when it needed — in the eyes of Leonardo Sousa — to reach R$83 per case. The Mathieuxs still needed to cut about R$7 out of the price.

Exploring Alternatives

The Mathieuxs were determined to find a solution to the impasse. They knew that they could not reduce their price further without shrinking their commission to unacceptable levels, and even that would not be enough. One potential solution for substantial gains was to find a way to reduce the financing costs of Material Hospitalar. This would enable Sousa to increase his margins and pass the savings on to the retailers.

They first looked into the Foreign Credit Insurance Association (FCIA) and the US Eximbank (Export-Import Bank). They knew that these organizations existed to encourage and facilitate exports from the United States by providing loan guarantees to help finance trade. But the brothers needed to start moving goods immediately. The conditions for entry into the personal care market in Brazil were excellent. Sales were growing and the brothers had identified an excellent potential distributor who was ready to attack the market with Hospeco's premium diapers. These organizations required time to evaluate the loan and verify the background of the companies involved. Obtaining loan guarantees from the FCIA or Eximbank would take too much time (a minimum of three months), and a mountain of paperwork. This was particularly true for a small Brazilian distributorship that had never imported from the United States. Moreover, Crosswell International was unfamiliar with the loan guarantee programs. The Mathieuxs decided that this option was only viable for the long run. Once Crosswell and Material Hospitalar had successfully established the business line, they could consider this as an option for import/export financing.

Another possibility that the Mathieux brothers considered was importing through Uruguay. The import tariffs there were about half as high as Brazilian tariffs. A distributor could import goods into Uruguay, pay the lower import tariffs, and truck the goods into Brazil. Additional tariffs at the Brazilian border would be minimal, thanks to the *Mercosur* regional trade agreement. This option offered the possibility of reduced prices in Brazil but would be very time-consuming, and would require the Mathieuxs to establish an intermediary distributor in Uruguay itself. This would involve either finding an importer or distributor in Uruguay or investing capital there to create an import/export corporation. The latter option did not fit Crosswell's strategy, while the former could take a few months of research and negotiation in Uruguay. Importing through Uruguay would also slow the flow of goods into Brazil, as trucking goods from Montevideo to Rio de Janeiro would add an additional two weeks to delivery time. To add to the list, Leonardo Sousa was adamantly against this option because he did not want to lose control of the flow of goods. In addition, some of the gains earned through lower import tariffs would be offset by the higher financing costs (due to the longer delivery time) and inland transportation costs. Finally, this option would be resented by the Brazilian government which would effectively lose tariff revenues due to the 'round-tripping' of Crosswell's goods. The proposal did not look promising.

A third alternative was suggested by Sousa himself. Brazilian regulations required all imports to be pre-approved via an import license. To obtain the license, importers had to present a pro forma invoice to the appropriate regulatory agency. It was common practice for exporters to under-invoice merchandise on pro forma invoices to Brazil, and therefore pay significantly lower import tariffs. An importer might typically pay for 50% of the purchase price in cash up front (the payment being made to a bank account somewhere outside of Brazil such as Miami). The remaining 50% would be paid with a letter of credit, upon which the tariff charges would be levied. And because the layers of tariffs in Brazil were compounded, under-invoicing resulted in substantial savings to the importer. The amount that was saved could then be passed on to the consumer in the form of lower prices. Tranzonic was a publicly traded firm, and under-invoicing for tax evasion purposes in Brazil would violate U.S.-SEC regulations. Under-invoicing was clearly not a justifiable option from either an ethical or legal standpoint.

Interest Rate Differentials

During a business lunch with the owner of an import-export firm in Rio de Janeiro, the Mathieuxs learned that foreign corporations (i.e., European automobile manufacturers and Chinese textile firms) were successfully undercutting national companies' prices by taking advantage of Brazil's high interest rates. Borrowing rates in the U.S. were substantially lower than deposit rates in Brazil, and given the stable exchange rate, this created an opportunity for uncovered interest rate arbitrage gains.

The basic strategy was premised on the ability to get extended terms from the seller (Crosswell International) and get paid for the goods quickly from the local

Brazilian distributor (Leonardo Sousa). If Material Hospitalar could obtain 180-day credit terms, or a standard 180-day letter of credit from Crosswell, the firm could sell the goods into the local market for cash within 30 days of receiving the diapers at port. The cash proceeds from the resale could then be invested in the relatively "high-yielding" Real-denominated deposit rates. At the end of the following four to five months when the payment on the goods to Crosswell was due, the deposits could be closed and the profits taken to offset the cost of financing the purchase. This would reduce the R$2.57 per case financing cost of the distributor as described in the baseline analysis in Exhibit 4. Of course, this was only true if the Real/dollar exchange rate was stable over the period.

The Mathieux brothers were well aware that these interest rate differentials could not persist over the long-run. Eventually, interest rates in Brazil would fall (assuming inflation was not reignited). However, in the short run, many international firms were taking advantage of the situation to lower their effective prices and gain market share in Brazil. The Mathieux brothers returned to the U.S. intent on exploring payment methods and financing with Crosswell.

Methods of Payment

A contract between an importer and exporter specifies a number of critical transaction details, including the method of payment.[11] There are four methods by which an exporter can sell to a foreign buyer: 1) advanced payment or prepayment; 2) documentary collections; 3) letter of credit (L/C); and 4) open account. The critical differences in the methods primarily involved who assumes the commercial risk and who provides the financing, the importer or exporter.

1. **Advanced payment.** If the importer pays for the goods up front, *prepayment*, the importer assumes all of the risks of non-performance on the part of the seller. Because the buyer is paying for the goods prior to shipment, the buyer is financing the transaction. This is essentially a cash payment for goods like that of a retail sale.

2. **Documentary collection.** A documentary collection means that payment is due from the buyer upon presentation of certain documents (and explicitly not necessarily upon receipt of the actual goods). Also termed *collection of drafts*, the exporter issues an order to the importer for payment. This order, the *draft*, may require payment upon demand, a *sight draft*, or may require payment within a set

---

[11] The common items in a sales contract include: description of merchandise, specifying standards, grade or quality; exact quantity in units, specific weight, or volume; unit price expressed in a specified currency for payment; trade terms expressed as FOB or CIF, naming of specific ports of exit and entry, individual liabilities associated with individual costs and risks; packing; identifying markings; extent of insurance coverage and who is to provide it; shipping instructions including method of transportation and consignment, the documents required for shipping, and timing; type of payment method to be used (e.g., L/C).

number of days, a *time draft*.[12] A time draft therefore allows a delay in payment by the buyer, and is a form of financing provided by the exporter.[13]

Another subcategory of documentary collection is whether the draft is *clean* or *documentary*. A *clean draft* is very simple and straightforward: the control of the merchandise is turned over to the buyer regardless of the importer's payment or acceptance, very similar to an open account transaction. Multinational firms shipping merchandise to their own foreign affiliates often use clean drafts to effect payment (they trust their own affiliates to make timely payment). A *documentary draft* requires that a number of other shipping documents be attached to the draft, and the buyer must either make payment (sight draft) or acceptance (time draft) in order to obtain possession of the documents needed to take possession of the goods. There is obviously a little less trust involved in a documentary draft transaction.

3. **Documentary letter of credit.** A letter of credit (L/C) is a type of guarantee of payment provided by a bank upon the buyer's request. The issuing bank promises to pay the seller, the exporter, upon presentation of key documents specified in the terms of the credit. The promise to pay by the bank reduces the commercial risk to the exporter. The letter of credit may be confirmed or unconfirmed by the exporter's bank, depending on the contract between importer and exporter. A letter of credit is in many ways a documentary draft with the added safeguard of a bank's guarantee of payment. Although on the surface the cycle appears complex, the process simply involves the exchange of documents and money through intermediaries — normally commercial banks.

4. **Open account.** This is the form of most domestic business transactions where goods are shipped by the seller and a bill or invoice issued requesting payment within a set number of days. Credit terms associated with an open account method of payment may state a discount if paid within a set number of days and the final date on which payment is due (for example a 2% discount if paid within 10 days, with the payment due no later than 30 days, termed "2/10 net 30"). Credit terms internationally vary considerably across borders, and often reflect traditional business habits within a country-market.

The Proposal

The decision was made to use extended financing as the main selling point to bring Leonardo Sousa on board. The task facing the Mathieuxs was to be clear, yet convincing, when describing the potential benefits and associated risks of their

---

[12] There are two major varieties of time drafts, the *bill of lading draft* and the *fixed maturity draft*. A *bill of lading draft* requires that payment be made a fixed number of days after the bill of lading date. The *fixed maturity draft* requires payment on a date specified in the draft.

[13] When a time draft is presented to the importer, the buyer stamps a notice of acceptance on its face. Once "accepted," it becomes a promise to pay a specified amount of money on a future date like a note or bond. If the draft is drawn upon and accepted by a bank, it becomes a "bankers acceptance."

proposed solution. Leonardo Sousa must understand that the success of the strategy was dependent on a stable Real/dollar exchange rate, and his ability to collect as quickly as possible for the diapers. Any significant depreciation of the Real against the dollar would increase the size of Material Hospitalar's obligations to Crosswell, as well as threaten the competitiveness of *Precious* diapers in the Brazilian market.

Doug and Geoff reviewed the financial cycle involved in exporting to Brazil with a 180-day letter of credit.[14] Crosswell would — at least for the first year — require a confirmed letter of credit from the Brazilian's bank in U.S. dollars. The cycle they were currently analyzing was for an order placed August 4, 1995, by Leonardo Sousa. Exhibit 5 details the steps involved if Leonardo Sousa placed the order. Unfortunately, there were no foreign currency futures or forwards available to hedge dollar-denominated accounts payable in the event that the Real did begin to depreciate.[15] The Mathieux brothers grew silent as they both wondered if their proposal would fly.

Case Questions

1. What actions would you recommend to Crosswell and to Leonardo Sousa that would enable them to hit the target of R$83.00 per case of diapers?

2. What are the benefits and risks to Mr. Sousa if he uses a U.S. dollar-denominated 180 day letter of credit to finance the import of 15 containers of *Precious Ultra Thin Baby Diapers*? What are the potential benefits and risks to Crosswell?

3. How much added profit can Mr. Sousa earn from taking advantage of the 180 day letter of credit? (Use the sequence of events and dates described in Exhibit 5. Assume the exchange rate and deposit rates of interest are stable.) Can this be used to reduce the price that Mr. Sousa charges the retailers? Would it be enough?

4. How important is the exchange rate and the exchange rate risk to this product's success in the Brazilian market? Would your answer change if the economy was experiencing hyperinflation as opposed to relative price stability? Would your answer differ if Crosswell had chosen to invoice in Brazilian Reals instead of U.S. dollars?

---

[14] Crosswell International could currently borrow short term in the U.S. dollar market at the following rates: 30 days - 8.40%, 60 days - 8.44%, 90 days - 8.50%, 120 days - 8.51%, 180 days - 8.60% (all rates per annum).

[15] The Chicago Mercantile Exchange was currently studying the possibility of trading a Brazilian Real/U.S. dollar futures contract, but it was as yet unavailable.

EXHIBIT 5 Proposed Process of Financing with the Letter of Credit

Aug 1	Importer requests a price from Crosswell
Aug 2	Crosswell responds, via fax, with an FOB price Miami of $34.07
Aug 5	Importer agrees to terms and faxes a purchase order to Crosswell
Aug 6	Crosswell faxes a *pro forma* invoice to the importer agreeing to price and terms
Aug 7	Importer makes an application to its bank for a letter of credit (L/C)
Aug 8	Importer's bank issues L/C and sends advice to Crosswell's bank in Miami that a L/C has been opened in its behalf, with instruction as to what documents are required for payment under the L/C. The L/C guarantees payment in U.S. dollars in 180 days upon presentation of specified documents. (The distributor could also request 30, 60, 90, or 120 day credit terms, depending on what is negotiated with Crosswell International at the time of the sale.)
Aug 9	Crosswell's bank confirms the L/C
Aug 12	Crosswell turns the goods over to a freight forwarder for shipment and consigns the goods to the order of the shipper. Crosswell keeps large stocks of diapers in its warehouse so that orders can be shipped immediately upon request.) Crosswell prefers to be paid up front rather than wait 180 days for the total amount. It is standard for the company to add any discount fee to the total amount appearing on the importer's invoice.
Aug 13	Shipping company issues the bill of lading. Crosswell issues a time draft in the name of its bank (since its bank confirmed the L/C) and presents documents to the bank. Crosswell's bank "accepts" the time draft creating a *bankers acceptance*. Crosswell can at this point choose to wait to be paid in 180 days, or present the 180-day letter of credit to its bank for payment now. If requesting payment now, the company receives the stated amount less a discount fee set by its bank. The discount rate is equal to the company's short-term borrowing rate in the U.S. on August 4, 1995. The rates vary according to the number of days in the terms of the letter of credit.
Aug 14	The documents are forwarded from the exporter's bank to the importer's bank
Sept 6	Importer receives the goods
Sept 10	Importer sells goods to retailer and is paid cash by the retailer. Importer deposits amount due to Crosswell in a savings account for five months.
Feb 10	Importer pays the Brazilian bank, which then pays Crosswell's bank (180 days after shipment of the goods).

Appendix A   Selected Financial Data for The Tranzonic Companies (years ended February 28/29)

	1994	1993	1992	1991	1990
Sales	131,182,128	119,951,373	110,717,585	107,333,543	96,705,806
Operating earnings	4,858,423	6,816,888	7,193,019	6,714,882	5,541,952
Earnings before income taxes					
and cum effect	4,599,265	6,785,982	7,411,281	6,953,690	5,914,428
Income taxes	1,800,000	2,572,000	2,835,000	2,635,000	1,746,000
Earnings before cumulative					
effect of change in acctg	2,799,265	4,213,982	4,576,281	4,318,690	4,168,428
Cum effect of change in acctg	—	—	—	—	701,500
Net earnings	2,799,265	4,213,982	4,576,281	4,318,690	4,869,928
Per share amounts:					
Earnings before cum effect	.80	1.19	1.29	1.23	1.15
Cum effect of chg in actg	—	—	—	—	.19
Net earnings per common share	.80	1.19	1.29	1.23	1.34
Cash dividends:					
Per Class A Common Share	.18	.165	.16	.16	.16
Per Class B Common Share	.34	.325	.32	.28	.28
Total assets	73,537,946	63,675,545	58,015,061	52,515,283	49,498,159
Long-term debt	9,000,000	2,900,000	195,000	195,000	1,022,770
Shareholders' equity	47,479,072	46,328,637	42,743,659	38,848,871	36,103,517
Shareholders equity per					
common share	13.75	13.21	12.32	11.24	10.31
Common shares outstanding	3,452,038	3,507,838	3,468,128	3,456,934	3,500,149

Fiscal year 1994 includes a $1,300,000 charge to operating earnings ($792,000 after-tax or 22 cents per share) for costs associated with restructuring the Housewares Division. Fiscal year 1990 includes the cumulative effect of a change in accounting for income taxes.

	1994	*1993*	*1992*
Sales	$131,182,128	119,951,373	110,717,585
Costs and expenses:			
Cost of goods sold	87,493,123	78,470,393	71,604,322
Selling, general and administrative expenses	37,530,582	34,664,092	31,920,244
Restructuring cost	1,300,000	—	—
Operating earnings	126,323,705	113,134,485	103,524,566
Interest income	4,858,423	6,816,888	7,193,019
Interest expense	54,369	96,304	280,853
Earnings before income taxes	(313,527)	(127,210)	(62,591)
Income taxes	4,599,265	6,785,982	7,411,281
Net earnings	1,800,000	2,572,000	2,835,000
Net earnings per common share	$ 2,799,265	4,213,982	4,576,281
	$ .80	1.19	1.29

THUNDERBIRD
THE AMERICAN GRADUATE SCHOOL
OF INTERNATIONAL MANAGEMENT

ZAPA CHEMICAL AND BuBa

"...there is a tendency in Europe to treat the exchange rate as a type of virility symbol. I, myself, have never felt the need for such a symbol."

- British Prime Minister Margaret Thatcher

Stephanie Mayo, currency analyst for ZAPA Chemical of Cleveland, stared at her Reuters screen, her option pricing screen, and then out the window. It was Monday, September 21, 1992, and the markets seemed much calmer this morning. The French had voted oui by 50.95% to non of 49.05% to approve the Maastricht treaty the previous day. Stephanie was now debating what to do about her put option on Deutschemarks she had been holding for the last month.

The Original Exposure and Rate View

Stephanie had originally been given the exposure for management in mid-August. ZAPA Chemical had sold a specialty chemical distributorship in Stuttgart, Germany. The proceeds of the sale, approximately DM7.6 million, would be brought back to the United States sometime in November. Because of special tax and sales document filings in Germany, it could not yet be determined when exactly the funds would be available for repatriation.

The U.S. dollar had been falling like a rock since late March. The central bank of Germany, the Bundesbank, or as it is affectionately known — "BuBa," had added momentum to the drop when it had increased the German base lending rate by 75 basis points (3/4 of a percent) to 9.75% on July 16th. By August 17th, when Steph was given the exposure, the DM/$ rate looked as if it had settled down to a historically weak dollar of DM1.4649/$ (see Exhibit 1). At that time Steph had debated whether the dollar was as low as it was going to go, or just hesitating before sliding further. Steph felt there were a number of forces which could drive the dollar still lower.

♦ **The Bundesbank.** The Bundesbank had become very high profile in the last month as German interest rates continued to rise. The Bundesbank was slowing monetary growth to a crawl and driving interest rates up, all in an effort to stop the inflationary forces resulting from reunification. Of the many rumors emanating from the central bank, the ones about further interest rate hikes were the loudest.

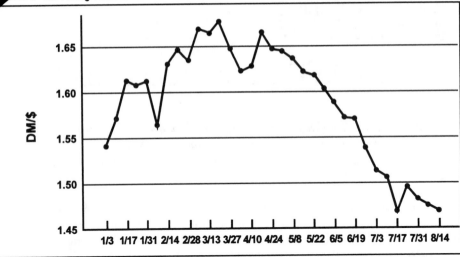

- **Dollar-DM Interest Differentials.** The anemic growth of the U.S. economy continued. The U.S. Federal Reserve was attempting to provide needed stimulus through lower interest rates. The United States was now enjoying the lowest interest rates in twenty years. The high interest rates in Germany and the low interest rates in the U.S., an unusual scenario by any account, was resulting in a massive capital flow from dollar-denominated assets into Deutschemarks.

  Three-month Eurodollar deposits were paying 3.3125%, while similar Euro-Deutschemark deposits were paying 9.750%. And there were no signs of either rate moving toward the other.

- **The French Vote on the Maastricht Treaty.** The European Community had now painted itself into a corner with the escalating debate on the willingness of individual countries to actually pursue true European economic integration. The Maastricht Treaty had been signed by the Council of Ministers in December 1991, but had to be ratified by each country. The Treaty had formalized the steps and timetable for the adoption of a single European banking system and currency by the end of the decade. But the Danes had voted no in June 1992, when the French vote was pending. The outcome had been impossible to call. The vote was September 20th.

- **Stress in the European Monetary System (EMS).** Not only were the high German interest rates causing a strengthening of the DM versus the dollar, but for the same reasons, they were putting pressure on all EMS currencies as they tried to maintain their parities with the Deutschemark. The Italian lira and the British pound were both trading at the bottom of their allowable ranges (according to the agreed ranges within the Exchange Rate Mechanism (ERM) of the EMS) versus the Deutschemark.

To top it all off, 1992 was an election year in the United States. In mid-August President George Bush was 18 to 20 percentage points behind Democratic presidential candidate Bill Clinton in the polls. The markets had historically favored and rewarded Republican economic policies as opposed to the policies of the Democrats.

The Risk Tolerance of ZAPA

ZAPA was a rather unusual firm in its approach to currency risk management. Although the parent corporation, ZAPA Oil, did not use foreign currency options for risk management, ZAPA Chemical used them exclusively. Because of losses caused by forward contracts in the previous year, Zapa's Treasury now used foreign exchange options whenever possible. If needed, synthetic forwards were created by simply buying calls and selling puts for the same strike prices and maturities (or vice versa).

ZAPA Chemical considered Treasury a cost-center. Treasury therefore saw its primary responsibility as conservative management of exposures. Profit through currency speculation was not its purpose. In addition to an in-house aversion to forwards, the group could not write uncovered options (with their corresponding unlimited loss potential). The fiasco in 1991 at Allied-Lyons, the British food conglomerate, had sparked an internal review of all activities of international treasury at ZAPA Chemical. Allied-Lyons had suffered losses of $150 million as a result of unwise and uncontrolled currency speculation. Although ZAPA did not in any way mirror Allied-Lyons, the review had resulted in the exclusion of writing uncovered call options, as well as the requirement that the use of new instruments be allowed only after approval of the operating committee. But, all things considered, management was appreciative when the expenses of running the cost-center were lower.

Hedge Decision: August 17th

On August 17th the Deutschemark had traded around the DM1.4649/$ point all day. After discussion with her risk manager, Steph had decided that a safety net was called for. Her logic was relatively simple. First, she believed that the dollar would fall further. Most currency forecasters felt the dollar was already at bottom, but then again, they had said the same thing at the magic DM1.50/$ level. She believed the DM would move in her favor. Secondly, although she held the directional view of dollar-down, she also felt there were too many unknowns to feel secure. Currency volatility would by all guesses increase in the coming 4 to 6 weeks, with uncertainty over Bundesbank policies rising and the French vote on Maastricht forthcoming.

Before making her decision, Steph had reviewed an alternative which was not considered by ZAPA to be a true alternative: the forward. The coming volatility of the markets —and Stephanie felt sure that things would be heating up — posed many uncertainties. Selling the entire DM exposure forward would at least allow her to sleep nights. But there were two distinctly negative characteristics of the forward at this time. First, the huge interest differentials between U.S. dollar and Deutschemark assets resulted in forward rates which were extremely unattractive. The 120-day forward on August 17 was DM1.4957/$. Given the spot rate of DM1.4649/$, this was an annual discount of nearly 6.2%, — expensive protection. By selling the Deutschemarks forward she would be locking in a rate which she sincerely felt was in the wrong direction from that which the spot rate would move. The forward was quite unattractive.

The safety net Steph had chosen was an out-of-the-money (OTM) put option (bank option) on Deutschemarks. Gotham Bank (NY) was willing to sell ZAPA a December put on the DM7.6 million for a premium of 1.40 cents per DM ($0.0140/DM) for a strike of 66 ($0.66/DM or DM1.5152/$). This was a total outlay of $106,400 for the DM December put option. Although seemingly a lot of money, the option price was a paltry 2.1% premium ($0.0140 ÷ $0.6600/DM) for a substantial amount of protection against a dollar rebound.

Steph, as she did with all her major stand-alone exposures, took a look at her option position versus the totally unhedged and total forward cover alternatives. Exhibit 2 reproduces her exposure valuation analysis. The put option's value would parallel the uncovered position, but with the added benefit of a safety net if the spot rate were to actually move in the opposite direction.

EXHIBIT 2 Hedge Alternatives for ZAPA Chemical's DM Exposure (millions of US$)

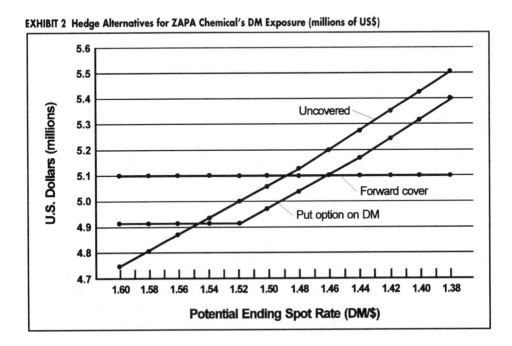

Daily Position Monitoring

Given the size of the position and the tension in the markets, Steph had watched the markets and the DM put option position daily. The next two weeks yielded good news and bad news. The good news was that Steph's intuition had been right on target. The dollar had declined rapidly in the days following her put option purchase, so that the prospective dollar value of the DM7.6 million was rising by the minute. The bad news, however, was that the December 66 put option was also falling, falling in value. As the put option had moved further and further out-of-the-money, the market value of the option (the premium) had fallen.

By September 1st the U.S. dollar was at an all-time low of DM1.39/$, and the option's premium was approximately 0.50 cents per DM. The potential loss on the option was $68,400.

$$(\$.0050/DM - \$.0140/DM) \times DM7,600,000 = (\$68,400)$$

Although it was a bit unsettling when expressed in this manner, Steph recognized that this was what the corporate hedger wanted to happen when purchasing an OTM put option for protection. The U.S. dollar declined to approximately DM1.40/$ and stayed there for the first two workweeks of September. Stephanie watched and waited.

September Turbulence

The week of September 14th had been a literal nightmare. The dollar had fallen, risen, and fallen again. The British pound had been withdrawn from the ERM. The Italian lira had been first devalued by over 7%, then finally withdrawn from the ERM as it came under further pressure. The Spanish peseta had been devalued 5% in the ERM. Other currencies had come under speculative attacks on Friday. The high interest rates in Germany had continued to bleed capital out of the other major European capital markets. Exhibit 3 reviews the roller coaster of events in these turbulent times.

In Great Britain the events of the previous weeks continued to have substantial news value. With the pound still floating freely against the Deutschemark, the long-standing critics of Britain's participation in the EMS were once more making a lot of noise. The leading critic, former British Prime Minister Lady Margaret Thatcher (often known as the "iron-maiden" for her tough political stands), commented in a speech on September 20th that "...there is a tendency in Europe to treat the exchange rate as a type of virility symbol. I, myself, have never felt the need for such a symbol."

The cynics still seemed to have carried the day. Many EC analysts saw the Maastricht Treaty and the idea of economic integration as something of a dead issue. The fundamental economic pressures which had led to the currency events of the first weeks of September were still present: extremely high interest differentials

EXHIBIT 3 EMS in Crisis: The Events of September 1992

Sept 1	The U.S. dollar falls below DM1.39/$.
Sept 4	The Italian lira trades below the ERM floor. Italian central bank raises discount rate from 13.25% to 15% to protect the lira.
Sept 6	EC finance ministers and central bank governors reaffirm their unwillingness to realign the EMS and promise massive intervention to protect the status quo.
Sept 8	Finland announces that it will no longer fix the markka to the ECU following a week of increasing speculation against the markka. The markka immediately falls against the DM and the dollar. The Swedish krona is hit by speculation as capital flows accelerate out of the Nordic countries into Deutschemark-denominated assets; Swedish monetary authorities begin raising interest rates to protect the krona.
Sept 9	Swedish central bank raises interest rates from 24% to 75% and plans to raise up to ECU 31 billion to protect the krona. Bundesbank is quoted as believing the Italian lira, Spanish peseta, and British pound should be devalued.
Sept 13	The Bundesbank cuts the Lombard borrowing rate, the base bank borrowing rate, by 25 basis points, from 9.75% to 9.50%. It is the first interest rate cut by the Bundesbank in five years. Italy/EMS announce that the Italian lira will be devalued by 7.6%. The Netherlands, Belgium, Austria, and Switzerland announce that their interest rates will be allowed to fall. Sweden announces that it will lower its marginal lending rate, the rate of interest which governs overnight interest rates between banks, to 20%.
Sept 14	The currency markets react favorably, the dollar rising from Friday's close of DM1.44/$ to DM1.49/$, a 2.4% appreciation. The markets wait for more interest rate cuts from the Bundesbank.
Sept 15	Bundesbank president Helmut Schlesinger makes it clear in an interview that the German monetary authority has not changed course towards expansionary policy. The Italian lira finds itself once more under attack as no interest rate cuts follow Sunday's devaluation. Rumors abound that Giuliano Amato, the Italian Prime Minister, is about to resign. The British pound comes under increasing speculative pressure as it falls below the allowed floor value against the Deutschemark.
Sept 16	The Bank of England raises its base lending rate to defend the falling British pound. By afternoon the Bank considers a further rate increase, but instead withdraws from the Exchange Rate Mechanism (ERM) of the EMS. Sweden raises the base lending rate from 75% to 500% to stop speculators from shorting the krona. Currency volatilities and option premiums skyrocket as crisis continues.
Sept 17	The Bundesbank refuses all pressure to cut German interest rates. The Spanish peseta is devalued 5% in the European Monetary System grid. The Italian lira withdraws from the exchange rate mechanism of the EMS. Official trading in the lira is suspended until the following Tuesday. The U.S. dollar falls from the previous day's high against the Deutschemark in response to rumors that the Bundesbank may be waiting to cut interest rates until after Sunday's French vote on Maastricht.
Sept 18	Sweden announces that it will cut the bank borrowing rate from 500% to 50%. The markets remain tense as all is put on hold awaiting the results of the French referendum on Sunday the 20th.
Sept 20	The French vote on the Maastricht Treaty and its proposed monetary unification of the EC.

between Germany and the United States; extreme devaluation pressures on most of the currencies of the EMS versus the Deutschemark.

Steph now wished to reevaluate her put option hedge position on the DM exposure. She knew that the DM7.6 million would be repatriated to the American parent on December 15th. This would match the maturity of the DM put option's expiration. But the massive volatility in the markets in the week before the September 20th vote had sent option values straight up. Steph was wondering whether it would be better to sell her put option and either cover the position with a forward or wait a few days until the markets calmed to replace the put position.

Steph quickly downloaded data on the daily spot rate and the December put option premium value. The graphic results of the comparison are shown in Exhibit 4. The put option premium had closed at 1.95 cents per DM on Friday (September 18th), while the spot and 90-day forward rates were DM1.5015/$ and DM1.5255/$, respectively. 90-day Eurocurrency interest rates had not changed since August. Steph thought she would have to move fast if — and it was a big if — she wished to sell her option while values (and volatilities) were still high.

Case Questions

1. Should Stephanie Mayo sell the put option protection already in place? Use the current market rates and prices to defend your logic.

2. How have the events of September altered Stephanie's view of the DM/$ exchange rate

EXHIBIT 4 EMS in Crisis: The Events of September 1992

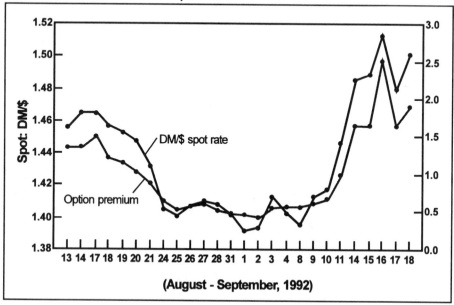

3. How has the volatility of the put option changed between August and September?

4. If you were the Vice President for Treasury at Zapa, what *benchmarks* would you use to measure Stephanie's hedging effectiveness? How would this alter Stephanie's hedging?

PART III
FINANCING THE
GLOBAL FIRM

THUNDERBIRD
THE AMERICAN GRADUATE SCHOOL
OF INTERNATIONAL MANAGEMENT

TREFICA OF HONDURAS

In the spring of 1998, Juan Antonio Vente, newly appointed president of his family's Honduran business, Trefica (Trefiladora Centroamericana, S.A. de C.V.), pondered his future course of action. He was fully aware that this decision would not only determine the future of the company, but also his family's investment future. Juan Antonio had never imagined that he would be given so much responsibility so quickly, but his father's rapidly deteriorating health had hastened things.

After only a few months on the job, Juan Antonio had already participated in the final stages of negotiations with the company's main supplier, Latin American Export & Import (LAEI). LAEI had agreed to acquire a 45% equity stake in the company. While this much-needed capital injection had improved Trefica's financial position, more capital would still be needed if the company were to stay afloat. The aggressive expansion and retooling of Trefica in recent years had put severe financial strains on the company. Time was running short. The problems had to be addressed now.

Honduras

Honduras is the second largest of the Central American republics and one of the most thinly populated, with a population of slightly over 5.7 million people, growing at 2.6% per annum. It extends 43,266 square miles, making it slightly larger than the state of Tennessee in the United States. Located east of Guatemala and northeast of El Salvador, Honduras is bordered on the south by Nicaragua and the Pacific Ocean, and on the north by the Caribbean Sea.

Honduras was one of the poorest countries in the Western Hemisphere, with annual per capita income estimated at US$750. It was also a classic example of a *Banana Republic*, a tropical country with a small upper class, almost no middle class, and a very large low-income population base. As opposed to some of its country-neighbors, Honduras had enjoyed 15 years of political stability, a democratic government, with regular and trouble-free elections.

The Honduran economy was also one of the least developed and least diversified in the Americas. Based largely on agriculture, more than 60% of the Honduran labor force was employed either in or around the production, distribution, and export of agricultural products. The most profitable exports were bananas and coffee, accounting for well over 40% of the country's total export earnings.

Company Profile and History

Trefica was founded in 1969 by Bekaert (Belgium), and specialized in the production and commercialization of wire-related products. The product line consisted of high-resistance rebar, chain-link fencing, nails, traditional metal wire and barbed wire, and wire mesh. The firm's annual wire-drawing capacity exceeded 72,000 metric tons. The company galvanized over 36,000 metric tons, and processed 8,400 metric tons in barbed wire and 18,000 metric tons of wire rod and rebar annually. Annual revenues had topped 483 million Honduran lempiras (US$35.8 million at Lps13.5/US$) in 1997. With its leading brands TREFICA, PANTERA, and BRAHMAM, Trefica thought itself well-positioned against all competitors.

Trefica was located in the city of Choluteca in southern Honduras. As the company was originally designed to service the Honduran and neighboring markets, its site was chosen for its strategic location. It was within 150 miles of all major markets in Honduras as well as those in neighboring El Salvador and Nicaragua. In addition, Trefica was within 10 miles of the port of Henecan in the Gulf of Fonseca on the Pacific coast, and 230 miles by rail from Puerto Cortes, the dominant port on Honduras' Atlantic coast.

As a result of the Marxist *Sandinista* movement in neighboring Nicaragua in mid-1979, the continued civil strife in El Salvador, and the United States' stepped-up military aid to the Contra forces based along the Honduran border in the early 1980s, Bekaert had concluded that the Central American political climate was simply too unstable. In 1984 Bekaert sold its interest in Trefica to Juan Antonio's father, Antonio Vargas Vente, a well-known and successful businessman in the Central American region.

Market Dominance, 1984-1992

Throughout the 1980s Trefica enjoyed continued success despite regional political turmoil. The lack of competition, particularly in Honduras, El Salvador, and Nicaragua, where 80% of sales were generated, assured Trefica of a virtual monopoly. The presence of high tariffs and import duties prevented any significant competition from abroad. Trefica enjoyed a seller's market where the consumer had few choices.

During the 1980s the Honduran government stubbornly fought devaluing the lempira from its fixed rate of Lmps2.0/US$. Instead, it chose to use foreign exchange and trade controls in an attempt to limit the inevitable imbalances resulting from an overvalued currency. By the late 1980s, however, Honduras' total external debt exceeded US$3.3 billion, more than doubling in size since 1980, forcing a devaluation of the currency (see Exhibit 1). In January 1990 President Rafael Leonardo Callejas took office and his new government immediately implemented measures designed to deal with the macroeconomic imbalances and reorient the economy towards export competitiveness. The package rationalized the import tariff structure, reducing the tariff ceiling gradually. Later reforms included the abolition in January 1993 of a

Year	Exchange Rate (Lps/US$)	Government Bond Yield (percent)	Bank Loan Rate (percent)	Consumer Inflation (percent)
1988	2.0000	10.4	15.4	4.53
1989	2.0000	10.4	15.4	9.89
1990	4.1120	10.4	17.1	23.30
1991	5.3167	10.4	21.9	34.00
1992	5.4979	10.4	21.7	8.73
1993	6.4716	10.4	22.1	10.78
1994	8.4088	23.1	24.7	21.69
1995	9.4710	27.2	27.0	29.48
1996	11.7053	35.6	29.7	23.83
1997	13.4670	29.6	32.1	20.20

Source: International Monetary Fund, *International Financial Statistics Yearbook*, 1998.

5% surcharge on imports from other Central American countries. Exports grew as the lempira continued to depreciate.

The maintenance of the fixed exchange rate and other counter-inflationary policies had been successful in holding inflation in Honduras to single digits in the 1980s. The devaluation of the lempira in the 1990s, however, brought about a sharp acceleration in inflation. The inflation rate for 1991 was 36%. Although renewed efforts to fight inflation succeeded in reducing the rate to 8.7% in 1992, it soon renewed its upward trend. Price liberalization, combined with the depreciation of the lempira and sharp rises in the prices of fuel, electricity, and public transport, resulted in double-digit inflation rates in the following years. Despite this, the Honduran real gross domestic product (GDP) grew at an annual rate of 3% or better in the early 1990s. As President Callejas continued to shake up the Honduran economy throughout his presidency, Trefica benefited as business continued to improve.

Global Transition, 1993-1996

Trefica's regional market dominance was now under some pressure. Although it offered products considered high quality by regional standards, they were sub-par when measured against international standards. Because of the lack of regional competition, Trefica had felt little pressure to improve its quality or service. The company did, however, need additional capacity, as it continually sold out production and was now beginning to lose orders as a result of lengthy backlog. As a result, Trefica undertook capacity expansion and modernization of its physical plant in mid-1992. The company purchased a used production line from a firm in the United

States at a substantial discount. Once the new line was operational, Trefica's basic wire-drawing capacity would nearly double.

Unfortunately, Honduras's anemic economy and illiquid financial sector limited Trefica's sources for financing. Long-term debt was nearly impossible to acquire locally. Many Honduran banks were obtaining significantly better returns in the short-term loan markets, and therefore opted to concentrate on those opportunities. Foreign banks were also unwilling to lend on a long-term basis, primarily as a result of their assessment of the regional political risks. Honduras, although more politically stable than its Central American neighbors, was considered too high a risk for such a small potential market. Trefica had no choice but to borrow heavily on a short-term basis.

Exporting beyond the Central American region had been sporadic over the years. By 1993, however, Trefica was exporting approximately 25% of its products outside the region, primarily to the United States. Although margins on export sales were thin, management felt that the real advantage to these sales were their dollar-denomination. Management believed that any further lempira depreciation would work in the company's favor.

Despite the reforms of the Callejas administration, even after renegotiating a significant portion of the country's foreign debt (and obtaining forgiveness on US$450 million in 1991), the country's external debt and foreign debt service were burdensome. In the 1994/95 fiscal year, debt service absorbed more than 80% of government revenue, about 15% of GDP. A foreign aid package arranged with the International Monetary Fund (IMF) required a strong anti-inflationary tight monetary policy. The result was ever-higher interest rates. The Honduran government, however, continued upon its course towards market liberalization.

Juan Antonio's father now realized that globalization would reach Honduras whether its industries were ready or not. His original plan of slowly modernizing his manufacturing facilities now became a race against time to bring Trefica's technology and capabilities up to global standards. Trefica was in no position to compete head-to-head in the global marketplace. Even after the modest modernization attempts, the majority of the machines and equipment were on the verge of obsolescence, at least by international standards. For Trefica to be a contender in the global arena, it would have to undertake an aggressive expansion that would double the plant's size and triple its output capacity.

This new more aggressive expansion was set to begin in the spring of 1994 and finish by the end of 1995. In addition to having to determine the size of the investment needed to compete in this new arena, there was also the question of where to obtain the funds to finance it. While its competitors in the United States, Mexico, and even Venezuela could consider several options, Trefica had few alternatives. Mr. Vente spent most of 1993 evaluating alternatives. His final list was relatively straightforward. (Since there was no Honduran stock market, a public equity offering was ruled out).

Private Placement. Trefica could find an investor to take a substantial equity position in the firm. The illiquidity in the system and generally negative economic outlook in the near future made most investors, however, wary of making such an investment. Many investors were uncertain as to the impact the liberalization of the Honduran market would have in the industrial sector. Their general attitude was to wait and see what would develop.

Foreign Bank Loans. By this time, several foreign banks had reevaluated their position on Central America and were beginning to enter. Particularly strong in Honduras were Hamilton Bank of Miami and the Deutsche Sudamerikanische Bank. Although these banks were active in the Honduran market, they were still not willing to provide long-term loans.

Local Bank Loans. The difficulties Mr. Vente ran into in 1991 trying to secure funds for the original modernization were still present. Long-term loans were not an option. Short-term bank loans were available only at extremely high floating-rate interest rates.

Government Assistance. As an industry leader and one of the most important players in the Honduran economy, Trefica was in a position to request special loans from the government to undertake the expansion. After several meetings with Central Bank officials and the Ministries of Industry and Finance, Trefica was assured that it would be given the possibility to secure long-term financing. Through an initiative of the Central Bank, Trefica was promised that it would be able to secure the funds it needed to complete the entire expansion.

The assurances given to him by the government, combined with his own sense of urgency, had prompted him to begin the first phase of his expansion with short-term loans from local banks. He felt that if he waited much longer, he ran the risk of not being fully prepared to compete for his market as competitors entered.

The Unexpected

What started as a project that would give Trefica a stronger competitive position to maintain its market leadership quickly turned into a series of potentially terminal problems. The first problem was with the machinery which had been purchased secondhand from a large U.S. steel conglomerate during Trefica's expansion. Although Trefica's engineers and production managers had inspected the machinery before making the purchase and agreed to its acceptability, they experienced continued setbacks when attempting to reassemble it in Choluteca. They had grossly underestimated the work and complexity of aligning the new machines to operate alongside those already in place.

Another challenge to Trefica was the creation and development of a market that would be able to absorb the additional capacity. After the expansion, Trefica would be able to supply the entire Central American market twice over and still have additional capacity. Reacting to its sense of urgency, Trefica had expanded the plant prior to evaluating the market. Management was faced with the daunting task, once the expansion was under way, of trying to form a marketing plan to more than double sales over the next three years.

The situation worsened considerably when the government reneged on its promise to aid in securing long-term debt. The Minister of Finance told Mr. Vente in the early summer of 1995 that all government investment plans and aid were on indefinite hold. Trefica was already halfway through its expansion and could not rationally turn back. Mr. Vente had little choice but to continue financing the expansion with short-term loans from the local banks, now at even higher interest rates. By 1995 Trefica was paying, on average, an annual interest rate of 29% on Lmp40.8 million in debt. While the setbacks in the installation of the machinery had been solved, the sales and marketing departments were still struggling to grow the market.

The LAEI Deal

The work of the sales and marketing departments begun in 1995 finally began to pay off in early 1997 as Trefica began the year with record sales in consecutive months. Unfortunately, although Trefica was on track to more than double sales in 1997, interest expenses had ballooned to such a size that even if the company met its aggressive sales projections for the year, income from operations would still be insufficient to cover debt-service obligations. In addition to the existing debt-service burdens, the firm had not anticipated the working capital needs of rapid sales growth. In order to sustain such aggressive growth, Trefica would have to borrow even more, something that did not sit well with either Mr. Vente or his bankers.

Throughout the expansion, Mr. Vente met with his biggest supplier, Latin American Export & Import of Panama (LAEI), to discuss Trefica's current and future situation. LAEI supplied 70% of all the steel that Trefica processed, down from its exclusive (100%) supplier role in the late 1980s. Although the meetings had been originally planned to discuss rising raw material needs, they quickly evolved into something more. After several meetings over an 18-month period, Antonio Vargas and son Juan Antonio managed to convince the owners of LAEI that Trefica's main problem was with its financing and not with its operations. Should Trefica be able to lower its interest expense, it would turn a profit. LAEI agreed to acquire 45% of Trefica for US$3 million cash plus an additional US$1 million paid to Mr. Vente directly. They agreed to increase the capital base by the US$3 million (Lmp40,000,000), diluting Mr. Vente's ownership from 100% to 55%.

Both sides benefited from the deal. LAEI's equity stake in Trefica solidified its relationship with its biggest customer in the region, while Trefica received a much-needed capital injection. It was also expected that Trefica would now be able to forego the use of letters of credit (L/Cs) used for all purchases from LAEI. (In addition to the banking charges incurred for the use of L/Cs, Trefica's banks required the company to hold bank deposits of roughly 3% of outstanding L/C balances.) LAEI also agreed to help Trefica secure loans with its U.S. bankers at more competitive rates than what Trefica was currently paying. Unfortunately,

EXHIBIT 2 Percent of Sales Comparison of Trefica's and Publicly Traded International Competitors' Income Statements

	Benchmark	*Trefica*
Net sales	100.0%	100.0%
Cost of goods sold	89.4	79.7
Gross profit	10.6	20.3
Selling expenses	1.3	8.8
General & administrative expenses	5.1	3.6
Operating income	4.2	7.9
Interest expense	2.2	10.8
Currency fluctuations	0.0	0.4
Income before taxes	4.8	-3.3
Provision for income taxes	1.3	0.0
Net income	3.5	-3.3

within six months of signing the agreement, LAEI began to have second thoughts on its involvement with Trefica.

LAEI's capital injection proved only a temporary respite from debt service pressures. Further steps were needed. On a more positive note, the company's operations were increasingly efficient and the quality of its product was now in line with international standards. Export sales were also up, now making up nearly 35% of total sales. Juan Antonio had confirmed this via two recent benchmarking evaluations. As part of the benchmarking study, Juan Antonio had constructed a percent of sales comparison between Trefica and its publicly traded competitors in the United States and Mexico (financial data was available only for these). Exhibit 2 presents the results of the percent of sales comparison for the income statement for 1997, once again confirming Juan Antonio's fears that Trefica's financial structure was its greatest threat to survival. Appendices 4 and 5 present the results of Juan Antonio's pro forma financial analysis for Trefica for the coming five-year period, including a recommended restructuring of its debt.

Soon after the LAEI/Trefica deal, one of LAEI's biggest competitors, The Soto Group of Mexico, acquired majority control of Tubac of Guatemala, the strongest steel tube manufacturer in the region. Tubac and Trefica were the biggest players in their respective industries and consumed a significant amount of steel on a monthly basis. Tubac had previously been a big buyer of LAEI's product. The Soto Group now posed a significant threat to LAEI's market dominance; the Soto Group appeared determined to buy its way into LAEI's market.

Alternatives

Juan Antonio's problems were considerable. An added complexity stemmed from the fact that when deciding what steps to take, he had to consider the future of the company, his family's investment, and to some degree his own professional future. He reviewed once again the four options he had identified:

1. **Stay the course.** Although the firm was not making an accounting profit, it was privately held and it still generated significant cash flow. If the debt structure could be paid down, the family could maintain its ownership and control and wait for better times.

2. **Find a U.S. partner.** Juan Antonio was in contact with a leading U.S. wire manufacturer that was willing to invest in Trefica by taking a 20% equity position. The partner would in turn give Trefica access to its distribution channels in the U.S. and U.S. financial markets. Additional plans included rationalizing production between the U.S. and Honduras plants as deemed necessary. Juan Antonio would remain as company president. The company was willing to invest approximately US$1.9 million, raising the capital base of the company to US$8.6 million.

3. **Sell control to a Mexican supplier.** The success of the Soto Group had peaked the interest of yet another major Mexican supplier. The Vente family's 55% ownership would fall to 34%, but of a much larger company. The Mexican company was willing to invest US$4 million in Trefica and buy LAEI out. The capital base of the company would be US$10.7 million. Juan Antonio would remain president of the company until 1999, at which time the board would review his position.

4. **Sell control to LAEI.** Juan Antonio informed LAEI regarding his negotiations with the new Mexican supplier. He could give them the option of buying him out completely. In return for selling their interest in the company, Juan Antonio's family would be expecting a premium for their shares, something Juan Antonio felt was manageable. The sale price LAEI proposed was US$5 million dollars for the Vente family equity stake. This amount included the US$1 million LAEI had paid to Mr. Vente when LAEI first took an equity position only a few months before.

Consultant Report

A consultant study commissioned by the Ventes on the future prospects of the wire milling and manufacturing industry had concluded that an expected worldwide overcapacity, coupled with depressed steel prices, would squeeze profit margins and depress potential revenues in the business for several years. Mexican competitors were expected to pose ever-greater threats as Mexico and other Central American countries moved toward a free trade pact in the not-too-distant future. Cost advantages of Trefica might come under heavier attack as most Mexican competitors paid roughly 1/4 the electricity costs Trefica did on a per-kilowatt hour basis. Other major energy costs and needs were also subsidized heavily by the Mexican government, including natural gas used to fire many of their furnaces. Trefica did not have access to natural gas. Mexican firms were typically vertically integrated; Trefica was not. Mexican firms had also been gaining greater acceptance in the international capital markets, giving them access to new and cheaper sources of capital. In all, the report painted a bleak picture for the future of the industry as a whole, and the Honduran company in particular.

Conclusion

There was a knock on the door. Juan Antonio was told the family members had all arrived for the board meeting and were waiting for him in the boardroom. Although he planned to present the various options and their implications, he hoped family members might be able to offer some other ideas—or at least opinions. He knew a decision could not be postponed any longer.

Appendix 1 Trefiladora Centroamericana, S.A. deC.V., Balance Sheet (Honduran lempiras)

ASSETS	1986	1987	1988	1989	1990	1991	1992	1993	1994	1995	1996	1997	Average
Cash	945,868	2,161,597	1,309,732	1,744,497	2,154,963	4,181,789	2,355,362	5,339,825	4,206,915	4,523,437	1,966,389	9,084,430	
Deposits (L/Cs)	392,307	442,025	1,407,778	1,233,246	8,571,186	6,941,832	5,905,820	4,559,707	4,767,718	2,828,935	8,274,030	23,096,099	
Accounts receivable, net	3,434,038	4,074,678	6,939,758	10,377,832	15,716,953	9,586,698	17,242,597	24,196,755	24,365,810	30,417,959	44,243,048	70,383,597	
Inventory	7,372,216	6,067,252	11,746,048	10,187,163	14,216,210	14,069,816	26,570,868	23,524,874	37,830,277	38,017,143	78,881,311	151,137,100	
Prepaid expenses	53,413	170,044	55,265	55,309	52,983	123,993	187,455	236,642	299,403	875,461	2,075,512	1,848,523	
Current assets	12,197,842	12,915,596	21,458,581	23,598,047	40,712,295	34,904,128	52,262,102	57,857,803	71,470,123	76,662,935	135,440,290	255,549,749	
Long-term receivables	8,275	8,275											
Investments	1,129,359	1,629,359	1,629,359	2,519,059	2,519,059	3,519,059	3,719,059	4,442,300	4,660,583	5,191,583	5,258,751	1,829,300	
Property, plant & equipment	8,430,984	9,065,494	9,494,400	9,699,621	10,492,663	18,892,163							
Accumulated depreciation	(5,060,064)	(5,561,936)	(6,018,689)	(6,400,088)	(6,870,932)	(7,393,299)							
PP&E, net	3,370,920	3,503,558	3,475,711	3,299,533	3,621,731	11,498,864	17,145,939	31,895,925	47,944,952	75,242,481	106,526,372	113,622,890	
Leasing	30,000	30,000	30,000	30,000									
Other assets	32,139	28,322	65,346	53,548	99,732	121,318	265,197	394,347	916,590	315,722	552,886	470,454	
Total assets	16,768,535	18,115,110	26,658,997	29,500,187	46,952,817	50,043,369	73,392,297	94,590,375	124,992,248	157,412,721	247,778,299	371,472,393	
LIABILITIES & SHAREHOLDERS' EQUITY													
Notes Payable	6,926,025	6,178,589	10,311,028	10,615,055	17,152,180	23,481,767	27,638,962	19,568,825	21,246,792	34,086,688	74,506,745	154,171,794	
Account payable	1,254,649	1,780,008	3,848,640	4,302,918	8,555,636	8,050,204	19,696,831	32,669,951	60,242,138	65,668,780	86,103,254	93,727,534	
Taxes payable	518,557	621,880	992,886	689,178	1,250,869			798,402	460,005				
Current liabilities	8,699,231	8,580,477	15,152,554	15,607,151	26,958,685	31,531,971	47,335,793	53,037,178	81,948,935	99,755,468	160,609,999	247,899,328	
Contingencies	165,808	201,208	236,608	272,008	307,409	354,808	402,808						
Long-term debt					1,738,000		6,147,953	5,445,610	6,396,454	6,708,312	20,076,600	16,930,243	
Common shares	5,076,000	5,076,000	5,910,000	7,318,000	8,000,000	8,794,000	10,552,500	12,663,000	13,929,000	34,888,500	43,598,000	85,000,000	
Retained earnings	2,827,496	4,257,425	5,359,835	6,303,028	9,948,723	9,362,590	8,953,245	22,576,165	22,717,859	16,060,441	23,493,700	21,642,822	
Total liabilities & shareholders' equity	16,768,535	18,115,110	26,658,997	29,500,187	46,952,817	50,043,369	73,392,299	93,721,953	124,992,248	157,412,721	247,778,299	371,472,393	
Selected Ratios													
Current assets/Total assets	0.73	0.71	0.80	0.80	0.87	0.70	0.71	0.61	0.57	0.49	0.55	0.69	
Total debt/Total assets	0.42	0.35	0.40	0.37	0.41	0.48	0.47	0.26	0.22	0.26	0.38	0.46	
Total debt/Equity	0.90	0.68	0.94	0.80	1.07	1.31	1.75	0.71	0.75	0.80	1.41	1.60	
Selected Items as Percent of Sales:													Average
Accounts receivable	20%	23%	31%	33%	34%	21%	29%	25%	18%	23%	20%	15%	24%
Inventory	43%	34%	52%	33%	31%	31%	45%	24%	29%	29%	36%	31%	35%
Prepaid expenses	0%	1%	0%	0%	0%	0%	0%	0%	0%	1%	1%	0%	0%
Notes payable	41%	35%	46%	34%	37%	51%	46%	20%	16%	26%	34%	32%	35%
Accounts payable	9%	10%	17%	14%	18%	17%	33%	34%	46%	50%	40%	19%	25%
Selected Items as Days Sales Outstanding:													Average
Accounts receivable	73	83	113	122	123	76	106	92	67	84	75	53	89
Inventory	157	124	191	120	112	112	163	89	105	105	133	114	127
Prepaid expenses	1	3	1	1	0	1	1	1	1	2	3	1	1
Notes payable	148	126	168	125	135	186	169	74	59	94	125	116	1127
Accounts payable	27	36	63	51	67	64	121	124	166	181	145	71	93

Appendix 2 Trefiladora Centroamericana, S.A. de C.V., Income Statement (Honduran lempiras)

	1986	1987	1988	1989	1990	1991	1992	1993	1994	1995	1996	1997
Revenues	17,091,942	17,859,386	22,466,324	31,099,847	46,488,162	46,001,466	59,577,511	96,141,521	132,078,015	132,071,386	216,739,933	483,032,059
Cost of goods sold	(11,221,648)	(11,675,084)	(13,624,136)	(21,004,072)	(32,565,160)	(29,882,874)	(47,035,781)	(78,763,796)	(108,791,301)	(101,738,769)	(177,254,911)	(384,937,617)
Gross margin	5,870,294	6,184,302	8,842,188	10,095,775	13,923,002	16,118,592	12,541,730	17,377,725	23,286,714	30,332,617	39,485,022	98,094,442
Gross margin (%)	34%	35%	39%	32%	30%	35%	21%	18%	18%	23%	18%	20%
Selling, G&A expenses	(1,800,904)	(2,300,665)	(3,405,305)	(4,513,392)	(6,491,422)	(8,612,210)	(5,556,964)	(8,617,307)	(10,705,875)	(11,144,615)	(16,860,165)	(46,754,763)
Operating profit	4,069,390	3,883,637	5,436,883	5,582,383	7,431,580	7,506,382	6,984,766	8,760,418	12,580,839	19,188,002	22,624,857	51,339,679
Operating margin (%)	24%	22%	24%	18%	16%	16%	12%	9%	10%	15%	10%	11%
Depreciation & amortization	(493,159)	(527,326)	(527,008)	(500,919)	(506,285)	(576,041)	(1,079,620)	(2,344,556)	(3,279,395)	(4,066,916)	(8,663,433)	(12,992,000)
EBITDA	3,576,231	3,356,311	4,909,875	5,081,464	6,925,295	6,930,341	5,905,146	6,415,862	9,301,444	15,121,086	13,961,424	38,347,679
EBITDA/sales (%)	21%	19%	22%	16%	15%	15%	10%	7%	7%	11%	6%	8%
Other revenues	981,423	552,156	683,440	2,491,900	3,556,150	1,923,290	2,107,635	2,560,784	2,505,175	30,720	1,420,336	5,980,328
Interest expense	(599,243)	(600,358)	(1,209,180)	(2,264,842)	(3,286,178)	(7,597,809)	(5,504,250)	(5,670,574)	(6,871,329)	(11,759,307)	(27,564,550)	(52,297,868)
Other expenses	(184,727)	(67,978)	(247,814)	(1,177,975)	(38,105)	(202,133)	(948,474)	-	(1,560,576)	(945,290)	-	(1,824,329)
Earnings before taxes	3,773,684	3,240,131	4,136,321	4,130,547	7,157,162	1,053,689	1,560,057	3,306,072	3,374,714	2,447,209	(12,182,790)	(9,794,190)
EBT of sales (%)	22%	18%	18%	13%	15%	2%	3%	3%	3%	2%	-6%	-2%
Taxes	(1,442,372)	(1,302,602)	(1,691,911)	(1,779,354)	(2,047,867)	(39,822)	(210,602)	(958,078)	(918,703)	(625,627)		
Participation in affiliates								113,000	218,283	531,000	67,168	-
Net income	2,331,312	1,937,529	2,444,410	2,351,193	5,109,295	1,013,867	1,349,455	2,460,994	2,674,294	2,352,582	(12,115,622)	(9,794,190)
Return on sales	14%	11%	11%	8%	11%	2%	2%	3%	2%	2%	-6%	-2%
Selected Performance Ratios												
Sales growth per year		4.5%	25.8%	38.4%	49.5%	-1.0%	29.5%	61.4%	37.4%	0.0%	64.1%	122.9%
Cost of goods/sales	65.7%	65.4%	60.6%	67.5%	70.1%	65.0%	78.9%	81.9%	82.4%	77.0%	81.8%	79.7%
Return on assets	13.9%	10.7%	9.2%	8.0%	10.9%	2.0%	1.8%	2.6%	2.1%	1.5%	-4.9%	-2.6%

Note: EBITDA = earnings before interest, taxes, depreciation and amortization.

Appendix 3 Trefiladora Centroamericana, S.A. de C.V., Statement of Cash Flows (Honduran lempiras)

	1986	1987	1988	1989	1990	1991	1992	1993	1994	1995	1996	1997
Cash flow from operations:												
Net income	2,331,312	1,937,529	2,444,410	2,351,193	5,109,295	1,013,867	1,349,455	2,460,994	2,407,187	2,352,582	(12,115,622)	(9,794,190)
Adjustments:												
Depreciation and amortization	493,159	527,326	527,008	500,919	506,285	576,041	1,079,620	2,344,556	3,279,395	4,066,916	8,663,433	12,992,000
Participation in affiliates									218,283	(531,000)	(67,168)	-
Profit in sale of assets	-	(5,820)	(5,405)	(26,125)	-	(9,669)	(29,015)	(22,630)	(60,597)	-	-	-
Increase (decrease) in accts receivable	(2,489,665)	(640,640)	(2,856,805)	(3,438,074)	(5,339,121)	3,202,170	(7,655,899)	(6,954,158)	(169,055)	(6,052,149)	(5,115,589)	(59,111,565)
Decrease (increase) in inventory	(1,162,548)	1,304,964	(5,678,796)	1,558,885	(4,029,047)	146,394	(12,501,052)	3,045,994	(14,305,403)	(186,866)	(40,864,168)	(54,448,181)
Increase in prepaid expenses	32,610	(81,231)	(55,265)	(44)	2,326	(71,010)	(63,462)	(49,187)	(62,761)	(576,058)	(1,200,051)	171,329
Increase (decrease) in other assets	(1,821)	(3,817)	(37,024)	11,798	(46,184)	(21,586)	(143,879)	(129,150)	(522,243)	600,868	(237,164)	253,386
Increase in accounts payable	985,417	(118,754)	1,693,129	150,570	4,814,369	171,784	11,644,280	4,314,638	26,365,371	7,114,362	20,434,474	18,393,174
Decrease (increase) in deposits	1,349,279	(49,718)		854,532	(3,380,940)	3,575,307	(2,590,058)	1,346,113	(208,011)	1,938,783	(5,445,095)	-
Net CF from operations	1,537,743	2,869,839	(3,968,748)	1,963,654	(2,363,017)	8,583,298	(8,910,010)	6,357,170	16,942,166	8,727,438	(35,946,950)	(91,544,047)
Cash flow from investing activities:												
Proceeds from sale of fixed assets		6,000	11,850	32,970	-	22,976	30,000	298,501	317,725	-	595,770	-
Purchase of shares / Deposits	(253,095)	(500,000)		(889,700)	(1,310,000)	(5,272,953)	3,474,070	(723,241)				(4,065,171)
Purchase of fixed assets	(657,941)	(652,510)	(470,206)	(296,186)	(763,042)	(8,419,082)	(6,725,335)	(4,097,987)	(19,735,231)	(21,562,670)	(11,296,840)	(10,507,544)
Net CF from investments	(911,036)	(1,146,510)	(458,356)	(1,152,916)	(2,073,042)	(13,669,059)	(3,221,265)	(4,522,727)	(19,417,506)	(21,562,670)	(10,701,070)	(14,572,715)
Cash flow from financing activities:												
Borrowings	-	-	17,016,814	18,661,000	30,808,249	32,407,728	49,009,758	44,412,359	33,866,580	42,040,114	108,981,170	208,871,833
Payment of loans	-	-	(12,933,575)	(18,356,973)	(22,533,124)	(27,816,141)	(38,704,610)	(43,262,339)	(31,257,550)	(28,888,360)	(64,890,198)	(138,241,880)
Increase in capital												40,000,000
Payment of cash dividends	-	(507,600)	(508,000)	-	(781,600)	(806,000)	(300)	-	(1,266,600)	-	-	-
Net CF from financing	-	(507,600)	3,575,239	304,027	7,493,525	3,785,587	10,304,848	1,150,020	1,342,430	13,151,754	44,090,972	110,629,953
Increase (decrease) in cash	626,707	1,215,729	(851,865)	1,114,765	3,057,466	(1,300,174)	(1,826,427)	2,984,463	(1,132,910)	316,522	(2,557,048)	4,513,191

Appendix 4 Trefiladora Centroamericana, S.A. de C.V.
Income Statement (in Honduran lempires) Pro Forma 1998–2002

	1997	1998	1999	2000	2001	2002
Revenues	483,032,059	579,638,471	695,566,165	834,679,398	1,001,615,278	1,201,938,333
Cost of goods sold	(384,937,617)	(457,914,392)	(549,497,270)	(659,396,724)	(791,276,069)	(949,531,283)
Gross profit	98,094,442	121,724,079	146,068,895	175,282,674	210,339,208	252,407,050
Gross margin (%)	20.3%	21.0%	21.0%	21.0%	21.0%	21.0%
Selling, general & admin expenses	(46,754,763)	(52,167,462)	(62,600,955)	(75,121,146)	(90,145,375)	(108,174,450)
Operating profit	51,339,679	69,556,617	83,467,940	100,161,528	120,193,834	144,232,600
Operating margin (%)	10.6%	12.0%	12.0%	12.0%	12.0%	12.0%
Depreciation & amortization	(12,992,000)	(14,490,962)	(17,389,154)	(20,866,985)	(25,040,382)	(30,048,458)
EBITDA	38,347,679	55,065,655	66,078,786	79,294,543	95,153,452	114,184,142
EBITDA/Revenues (%)	7.9%	9.5%	9.5%	9.5%	9.5%	9.5%
Other revenues	5,980,328	6,877,377	7,908,984	9,095,331	10,459,631	12,028,576
Interest Expense	(52,297,868)	(41,328,874)	(21,948,980)	(21,124,785)	(19,664,549)	(17,428,100)
Other expenses	(1,824,329)	(2,097,978)	(2,412,675)	(2,774,576)	(3,190,763)	(3,669,377)
Earnings before taxes (EBT)	28,553,490	33,007,141	67,015,269	85,357,498	107,798,153	135,163,699
Taxes	0	(13,202,857)	(26,806,108)	(34,142,999)	(43,119,261)	(54,065,480)
Net income	28,553,490	19,804,285	40,209,161	51,214,499	64,678,892	81,098,219
Return on sales (%)	5.9%	3.4%	5.8%	6.1%	6.5%	6.7%
Return on assets (%)	7.7%	5.1%	9.0%	10.0%	10.8%	11.6%

Pro Forma Assumptions	1997 Actual	1998-2002
Sales growth per year	122.9%	20.00%
Cost of goods sold (% of sales)	79.69%	79.00%
Selling, G&A (% of sales)	9.68%	9.00%
Depreciation as % of sales	2.69%	2.50%
Other expenses/revenues growth	not meaningful	15.00%
Effective tax rate	0.00%	40.00%

Appendix 5 Trefiladora Centroamericana, S.A. de C.V.
Balance Sheet (in Honduran lempiras) Pro Forma 1998–2002

	1997	1998	1999	2000	2001	2002
ASSETS						
Cash	9,084,430	5,796,385	6,955,662	8,346,794	10,016,153	12,019,383
Deposits (L/Cs)	23,096,099	17,389,154	20,866,985	25,040,382	30,048,458	36,058,150
Accounts receivable, net	70,383,597	95,283,036	114,339,644	137,207,572	164,649,087	197,578,904
Inventory	151,137,100	144,909,618	173,891,541	208,669,849	250,403,819	300,484,583
Prepaid expenses	1,848,523	2,318,554	2,782,265	3,338,718	4,006,461	4,807,753
Total current	255,549,749	265,696,747	318,836,096	382,603,315	459,123,978	550,948,774
Investments	1,829,300					
PP&E, net	113,622,890	119,304,035	125,269,236	131,532,698	138,109,333	145,014,800
Other assets	470,454	470,454	470,454	470,454	470,454	470,454
Total assets	371,472,393	385,471,235	444,575,786	514,606,467	597,703,765	696,434,028
LIABILITIES & SHAREHOLDERS' EQUITY						
Accounts payable	93,727,534	111,163,542	133,396,251	160,075,501	192,090,601	230,508,721
Short term debt in lempiras	101,746,784	33,638,283	32,879,043	31,090,195	27,996,948	23,268,115
Short term debt in US$	52,415,010	18,112,922	17,704,100	16,740,874	15,075,279	12,528,985
Short term debt, total	154,161,794	51,751,205	50,583,144	47,831,070	43,072,227	35,797,100
Total Current	247,889,328	162,914,747	183,979,394	207,906,571	235,162,828	266,305,821
Long term debt (US$ debt)	16,930,243	96,109,381	93,940,124	88,829,130	79,991,279	66,480,328
Total debt (short + long)	118,677,027	147,860,586	144,523,267	136,660,200	123,063,506	102,277,428
Common shares	85,000,000	85,000,000	85,000,000	85,000,000	85,000,000	85,000,000
Retained earnings	21,642,822	41,447,107	81,656,268	132,870,767	197,549,658	278,647,878
Total liab's & Shareholders'equity	371,472,393	385,471,235	444,575,786	514,606,467	597,703,765	696,434,028

Appendix 5 Trefiladora Centroamericana, S.A. de C.V.
Balance Sheet (in Honduran lempiras) Pro Forma 1998-2002 (Continued)

	1997	1998	1999	2000	2001	2002
Debt Structure Assumptions:						
Short term debt (in lempiras)	90%	35%	35%	35%	35%	35%
Percent lempira	66%	65%	65%	65%	65%	65%
Percent US$	34%	35%	35%	35%	35%	35%
Long term debt (in lempiras)	10%	65%	65%	65%	65%	65%
Total debt	100%	100%	100%	100%	100%	100%
Interest Rates & Exchange Rates:						
Short term lempira debt	32.10%	30.00%	29.00%	28.00%	27.00%	26.00%
Short term US$ debt	12.50%	9.75%	9.75%	9.75%	9.75%	9.75%
Long term US$ debt	12.50%	10.50%	10.50%	10.50%	10.50%	10.50%
Lempiras/US$	13.50	13.50	13.50	13.50	13.50	13.50
Actual US$ debt principals and interest payments (in US$):						
Short term debt principal	$ 3,882,593	$ 1,341,698	$ 1,311,415	$ 1,240,065	$ 1,116,687	$ 928,073
Interest payments(US$)		$ (485,324)	$ (130,816)	$ (127,863)	$ (120,906)	$ (108,877)
Interest payments (lempiras)		(6,551,876)	(1,766,010)	(1,726,150)	(1,632,235)	(1,469,840)
Long term debt principal	$ 1,254,092	$ 7,119,213	$ 6,958,528	$ 6,579,936	$ 5,925,280	$ 4,924,469
Interest payments(US$)		$ (156,762)	$ (747,517)	$ (730,645)	$ (690,893)	$ (622,154)
Interest payments (lempiras)		(2,116,280)	(10,091,485)	(9,863,713)	(9,327,059)	(8,399,084)

*Note: Interest payments are calculated on previous year's debt principals to prevent circular reference.

Pro Forma Assumptions: Operating Activities

Cash (% of sales)	1.0%	Prepaid expenses (% of sales)	0.4%
L/C Deposits (% of sales)	3.0%	A/P days sales outstanding	70
A/R days sales outstanding	60	Dividend payout rate	0.0%
Inventory (% of sales)	25.0%	Net PP&E growth	5.0%

THE FAR EAST TRADING COMPANY

"We have worked 30 to 40 years to develop our countries to this level, but along comes a man with a few billion dollars, and who in a period of just two weeks, has undone most of the work we have done. As a result, the people of our countries suffer. You talk about human rights and protecting people. But they must be protected from people like Soros who has so much money and so much power and totally thoughtless because he is not only hurting the people of Myanmar, but the poor people in Indonesia, Malaysia, the Philippines and Thailand."

Prime Minister Datuk Seri Dr. Mahathir Mohamad of Malaysia
New Straits Times, Kuala Lumpur, July 27, 1997

For Thailand to blame Mr Soros for its plight is rather like condemning an undertaker for burying a suicide.

The Economist, August 2, 1997, p. 57.

Jan Karl Karlsen, CFO of The Far East Trading Company Ltd. A/B, hurried down the Kuala Lumpur hotel corridor to his meeting with the financial controllers of many of the company's regional operating units. His task this morning was to explain personally the profit warning reported by the company in a press release the previous Friday, November 21, 1997, in Stockholm. This had been the second official profit warning of the year, and FETC's shares on the Stockholm Stock Exchange had once again fallen. The questions from shareholders, creditors, and analysts were increasingly numerous and pointed.

Karlsen's thoughts on the flight from Stockholm to Kuala Lumpur had been dominated by what he considered the three critical factors facing FETC's management: *cash flow, confidence,* and *control.* FETC was expected to suffer significant losses from the current Asian currency crisis. Operating units throughout East Asia were already reeling from currency exposures, working capital financing shortfalls, and the general economic slowdown spreading out from the currency crisis which had begun in July in Thailand. These growing losses were now causing downward revisions in forecasted cash flows for the second half of 1997 and would most certainly continue into 1998. This in turn caused declining confidence in management as FETC was once again in the headlines of the business press in Sweden, FETC's home country. With losses came increasing criticism of management and increasing influence of the company's creditors. Ultimately, control of the company could be at stake if management did not take action.

The Company

The Far East Trading Company Ltd. A/B was incorporated in Stockholm, Sweden, on March 27, 1897, by H.N. Johansson. Johansson, an experienced sea captain, had established a trading house in Bangkok, Thailand, in 1884 and wished to establish a trading company in Sweden which could serve as a financial base for continuous trade between the Far East and Europe. In the early years, the Far East Company made markets in rice, oilseed, spice, and timber. As the company expanded with the turn of the century, FETC opened trade routes to Africa, the Indies, North America, and Australia, eventually making shipping itself a major part of its business.

What differentiated the Far East Trading Company in 1897 was still significant in 1997. FETC was a global trading company which had no real domestic business base but, instead, served to provide a cultural and corporate center for the conduct of global trade. For the next century, no matter what market or business it was involved in, the continuity of Swedish management was the only constant. Throughout the Twentieth Century, the company prospered and faltered, like so many others, but persevered and maintained its corporate charter in Stockholm. Due to the immense distances in time and space for the conduct of trade, the firm was a loosely knit collection of independent country units from its very beginnings. The individual

EXHIBIT 1 The Far East Trading Company, 1997

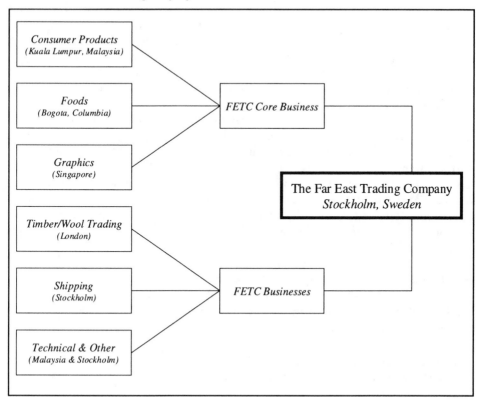

business lines conducted by FETC were under the direct and active management of the country manager assigned from the Swedish home office, and the decentralized organizational structure produced what many came to call *country kingdoms*. The individual country-based operating units were inherently entrepreneurial, entering into any area of trading or distribution which offered profit potential. The result was an amazingly diverse set of global businesses.

The recent history of FETC had been dominated by a major reorganization and management change in 1992. After sustaining growing losses throughout its European and Asian country businesses, a new management group took control in 1992 headed by the new Managing Director, Jesper Erickson, and the new CFO, Jan Karl Karlsen. Although FETC was a Swedish corporation, Erickson focused on the fact that nearly 75% of its earnings were in the Far East. Erickson immediately moved to assert central control over the loosely linked worldwide operations, sell off much of the Group's remaining European business units, and reorganize the FETC Group along two different lines, *FETC Core Businesses* and *FETC Businesses* (Exhibit 1). Erickson's long-term strategy was to concentrate FETC's activities in fewer business areas in order to pursue growth prospects in line with FETC's expertise.

FETC Core Businesses

FETC's strength—and future prospects in the eyes of management—was in three core areas of identified competence: *Consumer Products*, *Foods*, and *Graphics*. These three areas were expected to make up over 70% of FETC's turnover in the coming decade. The company's plan was to organize activities around these business areas across countries, rather than by country as under the historical organizational structure. Each of the core businesses would be managed independently from an identified business center of its activities: *Consumer Products*—Kuala Lumpur, Malaysia; *Graphics*—Singapore; *Foods*—Caracas, Venezuela.

The *Consumer Products* segment was made up of two major sub-segments: marketing services and nutritional products. The Marketing Services Group provided marketing, sales, distribution, and merchandising services to consumer product firms without significant in-country operations in the ASEAN[1] countries and Greater China. Name-brand clients utilizing the marketing services segment included Philip Morris, Lego, and Sara Lee. The *Nutritions Group* was largely composed of a newly operational state-of-the-art dairy plant in Shanghai, China. The Shanghai plant produced dry and liquid infant and baby nutritional products, but was not yet operating at full capacity.

The second core business, the *Foods* segment, was the newest of the three core business segments. Unique for FETC, Foods was purely South American in composition, and headquartered in Bogotá, Columbia. Serving the Andean Region, the Foods Group focused on meats and meat products, including manufacture of concentrated animal feed, pig farming, slaughterhouses, meat-processing plants,

---

[1] ASEAN, the Association of Southeast Asian Nations, is a regional economic and trade organization with original membership including Brunei, Indonesia, Malaysia, Philippines, Singapore, and Thailand.

and their associated distribution networks. It had been quite successful to date. Foods made up only 9% of FETC Core Business sales in 1996, but created over 30% of operating profits.

The *Graphics* business segment, the third of the FETC core businesses, provided material and service solutions to the graphic arts industry in East Asia. This included the importation and distribution of equipment, services, and solution consumables to this rapidly growing sector of the Asian economy. Although historically the unit had served as the local representative of a number of major European manufacturers of graphic arts equipment, the product line had received a significant boost in 1996 with the signing of an agreement to represent Eastman Kodak's graphic arts products throughout its service region. Operations in the region had been recently reorganized under one management roof in Singapore.

FETC Businesses

When Jesper Erickson reorganized much of FETC in 1992, all of those Group interests which did not fall into the three *FETC Core Businesses* were collected under *FETC Businesses*. Erickson believed these businesses were the leftovers of the earlier era in which country managers were allowed to follow entrepreneurial instincts, not the proven competency of the organization. The result was a steady liquidation of non-core businesses.

FETC Businesses included timber (procured in Southeast Asia, Ghana, and Brazil, and traded through a central trading unit in London); wool under the trading

EXHIBIT 2 FETC Turnover & Operating Profit Margins, 1995–1996 (millions of Swedish krona)

FETC Core Businesses	1996 Sales	%	1996 Profits	%	1995 Sales	%	1995 Profits	%
Consumer Products	6,809	60%	7	3%	5,113	45%	65	20%
Marketing Services	6,085		(26)		4,504		24	
Nutrition	724		33		609		41	
Logistics	–				–			
Foods	966	9%	84	30%	1,217	11%	116	35%
Graphics	3,574	31%	187	67%	3,085	27%	151	45%
Total Core	11,349	100%	278	100%	9,415	100%	332	100%
FETC Businesses								
Timber	979	19%	26	8%	900	18%	16	5%
Wool	803	16%	19	6%	816	17%	(27)	-9%
Shipping	737	14%	(8)	-3%	778	16%	12	4%
Technical	825	16%	71	23%	702	14%	85	28%
Other activities	1,761	34%	202	65%	1,744	35%	217	72%
Total Businesses	5,105	100%	310	100%	4,940	100%	303	100%
Core Businesses	11,349	69%	278	47%	9,415	66%	332	52%
Businesses	5,105	31%	310	53%	4,940	34%	303	48%
Total FETC Group	16,454	100%	588	100%	14,355	100%	635	100%

name Stanford & Wilson (a buyer, processor, and seller of combed-wool products in Europe); shipping and technical services. All shipping unit businesses were scheduled for divestment and liquidation. The Chemicals Group, part of Technical Services, was a marketer and distributor of specialty chemicals to a variety of manufacturing industries. In addition to distributing third-party products, Chemicals produced and distributed via a number of joint ventures in Thailand. The long-standing success of Chemicals in Thailand had built a base for expansion of the segment to a number of other Asian country markets, with entries into Vietnam, Myanmar, and most recently, Indonesia.

Other activities included in FETC Businesses' results included plantations in Malaysia which were recently liquidated, and unallocated expenses related to the Corporate Center in Stockholm and other regional centers in Asia.

1997 Half-Year Results

With FETC's half-year report (for the January-June period) published in August (Exhibit 3), problems were apparent. Although sales were up by 12% in Swedish krona terms, operating income was down by a full 26%. Sales were up in all three Core Businesses and four of the seven FETC Businesses, but the operating results of Consumer Products (-144%), Foods (-77%), Wool (-82%), and Other Activities

EXHIBIT 3 FETC Net Sales and Operating Results, Half-Year Report, 1997 (millions of Swedish krona)

	Net Sales			Operating Result		
	Actual	Actual	Chg	Actual	Actual	Chg
Segment	1997	1996	in %	1997	1996	in %
Graphics	1,747	1,618	8%	78	67	16%
Consumer Products	3,949	3,169	25%	-15	34	-144%
Foods	554	464	19%	9	39	-77%
Total Core Business	6,250	5,251	19%	72	140	-49%
Chemicals	342	323	6%	52	54	-4%
Technical Business	509	349	46%	34	34	0%
Timber	592	471	26%	20	9	122%
Wool	277	428	-35%	3	17	-82%
Shipping	121	402	-70%	17	-19	189%
Foods/Germany	325	–	– %	-6	–	– %
Other Activities	270	529	-49%	28	40	-30%
Total FETC Businesses	2,436	2,502	3%	148	135	10%
Total FETC	8,686	7,753	12%	220	275	-20%
Administrative Expenses*	–	–	–	-85	-93	-9%
Total	8,686	7,753	12%	135	182	-26%

·Administrative expenses are predominantly composed of unallocated overheads of corporate centers.

A06-99-0003

(-30%) were down. The causes, as best as Jan Karlsen could determine, combined both operating and financing cost problems.

Operations. The report noted specifically that cost control and utilization issues in Asian market segments were largely to blame. The core business units in Thailand had experienced significant inventory pilferage and accounting fraud (postponed orders had continued to be booked as current sales) since the first of the year. Unit management had been quickly replaced, but the declining Thai market continued to put pressure on management performance. Days sales outstanding on receivables were stretching out, and many suppliers had simultaneously begun drawing in their credit terms. Both sales and costs had grown.

The Chinese powdered milk plant, a major capital project, was still operating at less than 70% capacity, adding to the continuing operating burden on the Chinese subsidiary. This state-of-the-art factory, recently brought online in Shanghai for the production of infant nutritional products, was continuing to suffer high per-unit costs. A recent stockholder briefing had summarized management's outlook on the Chinese investment:

> It is our strong belief that these commitments to and investments in China, despite the difficulties and risks in the near term, will provide attractive future profits and worthwhile long term returns. It must be underlined, however, that China will require prolonged nurturing, and that substantial expenses and investments will be required in 1997 and 1998.

Financing. Financing expenses were significantly higher than in the previous year. The individual subsidiaries were largely responsible for their own funding. The parent company had provided minimal equity investment in the beginning, and additional funding needs were supplied over time through retained earnings and debt. The majority of the debt acquired by individual units was from outside the organization, typically from local and regional banks, not from the parent company. As opposed to many multinational firms which had only recently entered Asia, FETC's long history in the region had allowed it to build bank relations over time. The reliance on debt had risen throughout the 1990s as profits had declined.

In 1995 and 1996 many of the Asian units had moved to reduce financing expenses by financing both long-term debt and short-term working capital financing needs offshore in U.S. dollars. The stable currencies of the region allowed the firm to borrow dollars offshore at an average interest rate of 9% in 1996, as opposed to 14% for Malaysian ringgit or 18% for Thai baht. The parent company had also encouraged the individual units to decrease capital needs through improved inventory turns and reduced cycle times, as well as capital costs through more aggressive financial management. But in June 1997 the dollar had strengthened, leading to rising debt service expenses and foreign exchange losses.

FETC had concluded its half-year report to stockholders in August with a profit warning that "... it is expected that 1997 full-year operating profits will be lower than in 1996." FETC's share price suffered another setback, and Jan Karlsen was spending more and more of his time meeting with both institutional investors and the major creditors of the company.

The Asian Currency Crisis

The roots of the Asian currency crisis extended from a fundamental change in the economics of the region, the transition of many Asian nations from net exporters to net importers. Starting as early as 1990 in Thailand, the rapidly expanding economies of the Far East began importing more than they exported, requiring major net capital inflows to support their currencies. As long as the capital continued to flow in—capital for manufacturing plants, dam projects, infrastructure development, and even real estate speculation—the pegged exchange rates of the region could be maintained. When the investment capital inflows stopped, however, crisis was inevitable.

The most visible roots of the crisis were in the excesses in capital flows into Thailand in 1996 and early 1997. With rapid economic growth and rising profits forming the backdrop, Thai firms, banks, and finance companies found they had ready access to capital on the international markets, finding U.S. dollar debt cheap offshore. Thai banks continued to raise capital internationally, extending credits to a variety of domestic investments and enterprises beyond that which the Thai economy could support. As capital flows into the Thai market hit record rates, financial flows poured into investments of all kinds, including manufacturing, real estate, and even equity market margin-lending. As the investment *bubble* expanded, some participants raised questions about the economy's ability to repay the rising debt. The baht came under sudden and severe pressure.

As the Thai government and central bank intervened in the foreign exchange markets directly (using up precious hard currency reserves) and indirectly (by raising interest rates to attempt to stop the continual outflow), the Thai investment markets ground to a halt. This caused massive currency losses and bank failures. On July 2, 1997, the Thai central bank, which had been expending massive amounts of its limited foreign exchange reserves to defend the baht's value, finally allowed the baht to float (or sink in this case). The baht fell 17% against the U.S. dollar and over 12% against the Japanese yen in a matter of hours. By November, the baht had fallen from Baht25/US$ to Baht40/US$, a fall of about 38%. In the aftermath, the international speculator and philanthropist George Soros was the object of much criticism, primarily by the Prime Minister of Malaysia, Dr Mahathir Mohamad, for being the cause of the crisis. Soros, however, was likely only the messenger.

Within days, in Asia's own version of the *tequila effect*, a number of neighboring Asian nations, some with and some without similar characteristics to Thailand, came under speculative attack by currency traders and capital markets.[2] The Philippine peso, the Malaysian ringgit, and the Indonesian rupiah all fell within months (see Exhibit 4). In late October, Taiwan caught the markets off-balance with a surprise competitive devaluation of 15%. The Taiwanese devaluation only seemed to renew the momentum of the crisis. Although the Hong Kong dollar survived (at great expense to the central bank's foreign exchange reserves), the Korean won was not so

---

[2] The *tequila effect* is the term used to describe how the Mexican peso crisis of December 1994 quickly spread to other Latin American currency and equity markets, a form of financial panic termed *contagion*.

EXHIBIT 4 The Economies and Currencies of Asia, July–November 1997

Weaker Econmies	1996 Current Acct (bil US$)	Liabilities to Foreign Banks (bil US$)	Exchange Rate		
			July (per US$)	November (per US$)	% Change
Indonesia (rupiah)	-9.0	29.7	2400	3600	- 33.3 %
Korea (won)	-23.1	36.5	900	1100	- 18.2 %
Malaysia (ringgit)	-8.0	27.0	2.5	3.5	- 28.6 %
Philippines (peso)	-3.0	2.8	27	34	- 20.6 %
Thailand (baht)	-14.7	48.0	25	40	- 37.5 %
Stronger Economies					
China (renminbi)	47.2	56.0	8.4	8.4	+ 0.0 %
Hong Kong (dollar)	0.0	28.8	7.75	7.73	+ 0.0 %
Singapore (dollar)	14.3	55.3	1.43	1.60	- 10.6 %
Taiwan (dollar)	11.0	17.6	27.8	32.7	- 15.0 %

Source: International Monetary Fund, *International Financial Statistics*, October–November, 1997.

lucky. In November the historically stable Korean won also fell victim, falling from Won900/US$ to more than Won1100/US$. By the end of November the Korean government was in the process of negotiating a US$50 billion bailout of its financial sector with the International Monetary Fund (IMF). The only currency which had not fallen besides the Hong Kong dollar was the Chinese renminbi (Rmb), which was not freely convertible. Although the renminbi had not been devalued, there was rising speculation that the Chinese government would devalue soon for competitiven reasons.

Asian Crisis Impact

The falling value of Asian currencies was reflected in a series of impacts on the FETC Group's financial results. First, business units across Asia individually suffered currency *transaction losses* associated with exposures to non-domestic currencies (most frequently, either accounts payable or debt obligations in U.S. dollars). Local management in these business units, however, argued that although their Swedish krona value was diminished, these units were in many instances continuing to make significant progress and take growing market shares in local currency terms—which was what mattered.

Secondly, the FETC Group would suffer currency *translation losses* in both earnings and asset values on a consolidated basis. These translation losses would include not only the reduced Swedish krona value of Asian currency financial results, but also the reduced equity value of the Asian businesses themselves. This was the reduced Swedish krona value of the firm's original equity investments in its Asian businesses as recorded in consolidated equity. (In anticipation of the potential fall of the Thai baht, FETC had declared dividends from Thai units in 1996 which surpassed their total income for the period.)

FETC had pursued a relatively common practice of hedging its (corporate) net equity investment in its subsidiaries (an asset) by borrowing in the currency of the subsidiary (a liability). But FETC had borrowed U.S. dollars, not Thai baht or Malaysian ringgit, in the belief that these currencies would maintain their pegs to the U.S. dollar. However, with the devaluations of the Asian currencies, FETC was now realizing substantial equity losses with no corresponding fall in the value of the dollar liabilities.

Third, the *operating exposure* of the firm, the firm's changing long-term competitiveness as a result of the currency changes, was yet to be determined. The currency crisis had already caused the World Bank and IMF to intervene in the region in the hopes of preventing a general recession as a result of failing financial institutions and general economic collapse. Regardless, it appeared East Asia was headed for an extended recession. The consumer product and graphics units were already finding themselves squeezed as a result of importing increasingly expensive dollar-denominated merchandise requiring higher retail prices than the market would support. And local competitors were gaining lost market share.

Of immediate need in the eyes of Karlsen was the firming-up of the Group's many working capital lines with banks. The banks were repeatedly denying expanded working capital lines, even for units with growing sales. The Kuala Lumpur and Singapore units had both recently begun lagging intra-firm payments, including debt service, due to capital shortfalls. Currency charges were also rising as all intra-firm payments were required to be in U.S. dollars. More and more scheduled payments were not occurring as promised.

FETC's Second Profit Warning: November 21, 1997

Jan Karlsen concluded that with the continually declining earnings in the Core Business segments, there was little choice but to go public with a second profit warning.

> FETC's Management and Supervisory Board have evaluated the consequences of the crisis in a number of Asian financial markets, and the impact the recession in several Asian countries has on FETC's businesses and earnings. On the assumption that conditions in our main markets are unchanged for the balance of the year, FETC expects a loss after tax of about SKK 300 million in 1997 after a number of non-recurring costs and provisions ...

It now appeared that management had no choice but to take rather drastic measures if FETC was to have hopes of returning to profitability within the near term. Erickson and Karlsen returned to a topic of constant debate between them: the potential liquidation of FETC's non-core businesses. Erickson wanted to liquidate them immediately, at any price. This would generate additional capital for the reduction of corporate debt loads and signal shareholders that management was taking positive actions in the crisis. Karlsen was more reluctant to sell off these other units quite yet, arguing that if they waited they would be able to find buyers who would pay at least 20% more. In the meantime, the businesses would continue to generate cash flows which were critically needed.

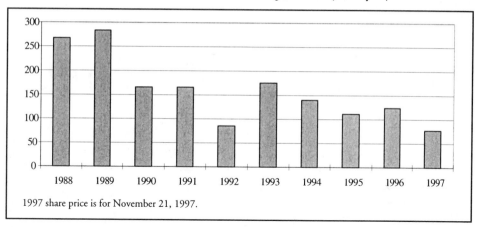

1997 share price is for November 21, 1997.

An emergency meeting between the senior management team and institutional investors had concluded with the agreed expectation that the Group would return positive results by the second half of 1998. The first profit warning of the year had left the share price at about SKK80. It was still unclear what this second profit warning would do to it.

As Jan Karl Karlsen entered the Singapore hotel meeting room, still focusing on the three C's of *cash flow, confidence,* and *control,* he consciously changed his thoughts from Swedish to English. He knew there were two sets of questions he had to answer: (1) what FETC's corporate outlook was from the Stockholm perspective; and (2) what actions were needed immediately in the regional business units.

THE STRATEGIC ALLIANCE OF
BANG & OLUFSEN AND PHILIPS N.V.

During September 1991, Anders Knutsen, President, and Povl U. Skifter, Chief Financial Officer, the top management team of Bang & Olufsen A/S (B&O), were reviewing the performance of Denmark's premier consumer electronics company and contemplating its future strategy. During the period 1978 to mid-1991, under the dynamic leadership of Vagn Andersen, B&O had survived with good future prospects, even though many observers had expected the company would die. Intense global competition had caused a host of other companies to drop out or merge, leaving a relatively few large multinational firms to dominate the worldwide consumer electronics industry in the 1990s.

During the past four years, two unexpected external shocks had a very negative impact on B&O's sales and financial results. The worldwide stock market crash of October, 1987 and the Gulf War crisis of August 1990-March 1991 had each caused consumers to cut back on their purchases. This was especially true for the consumer electronics industry as a whole and for B&O's market niche in particular.

Mainly as a result of the Gulf War crisis, B&O had just reported a DKK 74 million loss after taxes and minority interests for the fiscal year ending May 31, 1991. Although the operating loss was painful to report, it did not seriously endanger B&O's financial health. B&O's liquidity was adequate and its debt burden manageable due in part to an equity infusion from the Dutch concern, Philips Consumer Electronics (Philips), as part of a strategic alliance in 1990.

Unfortunately, more serious problems existed that could impact the long-run health of B&O. Most of the problems were structural and could be traced to B&O's small size relative to its large multinational competitors. Anders Knutsen and Povl Skifter could identify at least eight problems of major concern.

- **Niche Strategy.** Because of its small size, B&O did not compete across the board in consumer electronics, but rather followed a niche strategy. This emphasized outstanding design, systems solutions, and rapid response to changing customer tastes. Despite heavy emphasis on research and development, it was becoming increasingly difficult to get new products to market in a timely manner.

- **Economies of Scale.** Although B&O designed and produced some proprietary components for its own use, it lacked economies of scale relative to its competitors. B&O purchased the rest of its components from others but lacked the buying power to get the best volume discounts.

- **Dependence on Competition for Supply.** Most of the purchased components were bought from Philips, and to a lesser extent from other possible competitors. This left B&O potentially vulnerable to delivery schedules over which it had no control. If component shipments were delayed for even a few months, it would seriously impair B&O's strategy of timely introduction of a constant stream of new products. On the other hand, B&O's long-time purchasing experience with Philips had always been highly satisfactory.

- **Economies of Scope.** Following a niche strategy meant that B&O could not offer its sales outlets a complete line of products. Thus, the products of competitors were nearly always displayed side-by-side with B&O's products, competing for floor space and the sales force's attention.

- **Price.** Since B&O needed to cover heavy investments in research and development with relatively modest sales volume, its products were always high-priced compared to the competition.

- **Sensitivity to Business Cycles.** B&O's sales were extremely sensitive to business cycles. On the other hand, its cost structure was not flexible enough to adjust quickly to variable sales volume. The result was periodic losses with even modest swings in sales.

- **Foreign Exchange Exposure.** Since B&O produced nearly all of its products in Denmark but sold 77% outside of Denmark, it was potentially very sensitive to foreign exchange economic and transaction exposures. For example, when foreign currencies strengthened relative to the Danish krone, B&O's exported products could become more price competitive. This would be only partially offset by the higher foreign exchange costs of imported components. The reverse was also true. If foreign currencies weakened, B&O could face a negative foreign exchange effect. With respect to transaction exposure, B&O hedged most exposures with forward contracts.

- **Shareholder Strength.** Although B&O's B-shares were listed on the Copenhagen Stock Exchange, the controlling A-shares were held by foundations, representing descendants of the founders, and a group of five Danish institutional investors.[1] An investment agreement among the A-shareholders ensured that no unfriendly takeover could occur. However, the family members, in particular, did not have outside funds that could be used to finance additional A- or B-share issues. B&O's modest financial results during the 1980s also precluded significant internal financing for growth and would make it difficult to attract new investors if a public equity issue should be attempted.

The Consumer Electronics Industry

The worldwide consumer electronics industry was characterized by rapid technological development and obsolescence, significant economies of scale and scope, a high degree of capital intensity, declining unit prices, and fierce global competition among multinational firms. The main audio/video product lines in the 1990s were derivatives of the old television, video recorder, phonograph, and radio industries. About 80% of B&O's sales were of products first introduced in the two preceding fiscal years. This was typical of the industry worldwide. Thus, the technological pace placed a heavy emphasis on timely research and development, which necessitated heavy capital investment costs.

The Competition B&O's main competitors included six large Japanese and three large European companies. Notably absent were any significant U.S. competitors since they had been mostly eliminated by intense Japanese competition during the 1980s. The main Japanese competitors were Sony, Sanyo, Hitachi, Toshiba, Yamaha, and Matsushita.

The three main European competitors were survivors of an ongoing consolidation process in Europe. Philips, Thomson CSF, and Nokia were the survivors of 16 European companies in the television sector of consumer electronics.[2] In addition, the two principal British competitors, GEC and Rank, had been taken over by Hitachi and Toshiba, respectively.

The nature of consumer electronics products lends itself to mass production and mass distribution methods. Gaining economics of scale and scope, while denying these to competitors, is a critical determinant of competitive advantage. However, a few niche companies, such as B&O, managed to survive despite lacking such economies.

Ownership and Control

B&O was founded in 1925 by Peter Bang and Svend Olufsen. It remained a privately-owned company until 1977, when B-shares were sold to the public and B&O listed on the Copenhagen Stock Exchange. In the following years, public ownership was gradually increased with a participating preferred share issue sold to institutional investors in 1981, and a public B-share issue in 1983. In 1988 the family heirs and institutional investors signed an investment agreement which gave the right of first refusal to each other on A-share transfers. An important objective of both the heirs and institutional investors was to maintain control in order to ensure that B&O could continue to pursue its long-range strategy while remaining a Danish-owned company.

Finance

B&O's historical financial results prior to the strategic alliance were typified by extreme volatility both in operating results and share price development. The cumulative returns to stockholders were also quite modest. Exhibit 1 shows the key financial results for the period 1986-1991. Exhibit 2 shows the share price development during the period 1983-1991. Cumulatively, Exhibits 1 and 2 capture the financial situation before and after the strategic alliance (June 1990).

EXHIBIT 1 B&O Financial Highlights for the Group (million DKK)

	_1986/87_	_1987/88_	_1988/89_	_1989/90_	_1990/91_
TURNOVER					
Turnover	1,902.1	1,955.7	2,098.8	2,279.5	2,180.1
Turnover outside Denmark	1,451.9	1,472.9	1,591.1	1,729.4	1,677.8
as % of total	76.3	75.3	75.8	75.9	77.0
EARNINGS					
Operating earnings	137.8	39.5	85.3	91.1	(47.1)
Earnings before extraordinary items	81.1	(19.5)	47.6	28.5	(115.5)
Earnings before tax	81.1	(19.5)	48.8	68.0	(135.5)
Earnings after tax & minority interests	53.1	(8.6)	32.3	55.3	(74.4)
TOTAL ASSETS					
Total assets	1,332.9	1,337.2	1,459.4	1,715.6	1,685.2
Shareholdersí funds	478.3	477.9	505.3	603.5	656.5
Minority shareholders	–	–	–	–	183.4
Asset cover, %	35.9	35.7	34.6	35.2	49.8
Return on investment on 1/16/90, %	18.4	(4.1)	10.2	13.5	(22.5)
SHARE CAPITAL					
Share capital	100.0	124.0	124.0	124.0	124.0
Earnings after tax per 100 shares (kroner)*	43	(/)	26	45	(60)
Dividend, % of nominal value	10	0	10	10	0
Quoted share price at May 31	432	432	277	402	530
EMPLOYMENT					
Number of employees at year end	3,177	2,856	3,357	3,200	3,301

*Adjusted for share capital increases under market price. Asset cover includes shares held by minority share-holders.

Marketing

B&O produced a line of audio/video products, such as televisions, video recorders, and stereo systems, which could be easily connected into a coordinated household entertainment system. B&O products had a worldwide reputation for advanced design, ease of use, and systems integration. In addition to excellent technical qualities, B&O products were designed to appear as ultramodern furniture pieces.

B&O marketed its products worldwide through its own sales subsidiaries and independent distributors. In the United States it experimented with franchised outlets selling exclusively B&O products. About 77% of B&O's sales were outside of Denmark. Although it had a respectable share of the Danish audio/video market, it had a relatively small share of each of its other geographic markets.

B&O products appealed to those who placed a high value on lifestyle. Its customers were willing to pay a premium price for high-quality, user-friendly products featuring a futuristic design. B&O had a rather large global share of this narrow product market niche.

EXHIBIT 2   Share Price Development 1983–1991

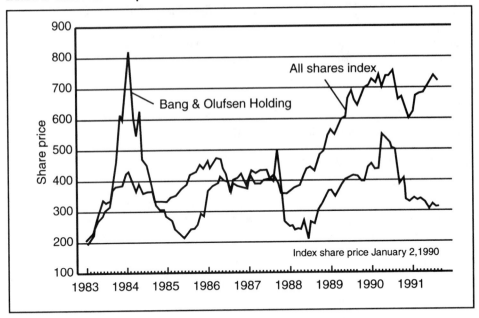

Production

Most of B&O's production was located in Jutland, Denmark, in the towns of Struer, Lemvig, and Skive. B&O employed about 3,300 persons, of which about 85% were located in Denmark. The rest were located in numerous sales and service subsidiaries abroad. About 10% of the Danish employees were engaged in product development.

B&O produced a significant share of the components it needed. Some of these were proprietary products based on B&O's own research and development. The rest were standard items but were self-produced in order to guarantee quality and assurance of delivery. The balance of components were sourced outside. Philips was a major European supplier. Some of the Japanese electronic firms were also suppliers.

B&O assembled all of its products at its manufacturing locations in Jutland. Although labor was relatively costly in Denmark, its reliability and productivity were also high. The direct labor content of most of B&O's products is modest, but the research and development overhead was quite significant because of the relatively small production runs of each product.

Restructuring the Corporate Organization

In anticipation of future cooperative agreements, during 1989 B&O, in cooperation with its financial advisors, Gudme Raaschou Investment Bank, devised a creative reorganization plan which became effective on June 1, 1990. B&O A/S changed its name to B&O Holding A/S continued as the listed company. A new company was established by B&O Holding A/S as a 100%-owned subsidiary. It was called

B&O A/S and took over the audio/video activities, comprising about 85% of the group's activities. Exhibit 3 shows B&O's corporate organization before and after the change.

The new corporate organization had several advantages over the old one:

- B&O's fundamental image, product concepts, management situation, and strategies were preserved.

- B&O Holding remained controlled by the existing shareholders and had the same Board of Directors as B&O A/S.

- In the future, new subsidiaries of B&O Holding could be easily established to exploit new technologies or products unrelated to the existing product line.

EXHIBIT 3 Bang & Olufsen's Corporate Reorganization of June 1, 1990

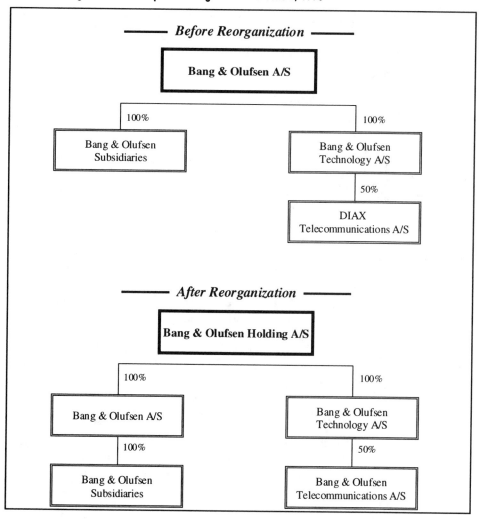

These new subsidiaries could then form alliances or joint ventures with whatever companies were appropriate for their activities.

- The terms of equity participation in the new subsidiaries could vary with market conditions and their synergistic value to specific partners without reference to the share price of B&O Holding or its other subsidiaries.

- Potential partners could buy into just those activities that were valuable to them and not be forced to invest in less suitable activities.

- In the future, B&O Holding could sell off subsidiaries that it no longer wanted, perhaps to its partner, or to another company acceptable to its partner.

Joint Venture with L. M. Ericsson

During the 1980s, B&O had received numerous feelers from companies attracted by its upscale market niche. Some were interested in acquiring B&O. Some wanted to conduct cooperative activities, while others proposed joint ventures or strategic alliances. Among the most interesting of these possibilities were proposals from L. M. Ericsson (Sweden) and Philips.

During 1989 a joint venture to develop and market products in the telecommunications industry was proposed by L. M. Ericsson, one of the leading multinational firms in the world in the industry. L. M. Ericsson was particularly interested in a small digital telephone concentrator which had been developed by B&O. This product was complementary to the telephone exchanges for which L. M. Ericsson was famous. Although the B&O digital telephone concentrator was not fully developed, it represented potential future competition for L. M. Ericsson, particularly if B&O could find another strong partner.

The proposed joint venture was attractive to B&O because it would have had difficulties financing further development and improvement of the digital telephone concentrator. Moreover, this product would be sold through different marketing channels and to a different type of customer than B&O's existing audio/video product line.

The proposal was that B&O provide the technology and product, while L.M. Ericsson would provide access to its worldwide marketing network. L.M. Ericsson would invest DKK 50 million in return for 50% of a newly formed corporate joint venture, Diax. Agreement was reached and Diax began operations January 1, 1990. B&O's interest was placed under B&O Technology A/S, a subsidiary of B&O Holding, as part of the June 1990 reorganization.

Strategic Alliance with Philips

As a major supplier of components to B&O for nearly 60 years, Philips was very comfortable with B&O and its management. Several times Philips had approached B&O about acquiring an equity interest or cooperating in various activities. Both companies were ripe for something positive to happen when negotiations were opened in 1989.

Philips was eager to join forces with B&O in the upscale consumer electronics market. Philips had a product designed for this market but it did not possess the high-quality image of B&O's products. Philips was also worried that if financial pressure continued, B&O might choose a competitor as a partner. A Japanese competitor would be very damaging. Philips had always been supported politically by B&O in its efforts to gain national and EU support to make the remaining European companies more competitive vis-à-vis Japanese competitors. Philips was also interested in cementing relations with B&O as a major customer for Philips' components.

B&O was interested in Philips because a closer relationship could partially solve some of B&O's long-run problems. In particular, Philips could give B&O the following advantages:

- More rapid access to new technology,

- Assistance in converting Philips' technology into B&O product applications,

- Assurance of component supplies at large volume discounts from Philips itself, as well as from its large network of suppliers,

- Equity financing from Philips.

During the course of 1989-1990 a strategic alliance between B&O and Philips was agreed upon. It went into effect on June 1, 1990, simultaneously with B&O's corporate reorganization. The main features of the alliance were:

- Philips would provide B&O with instant access to its new technology, but not vice-versa.

- Philips would give B&O access to its supplier network to take advantage of the discounts and delivery terms that Philips enjoyed. However, B&O was not forced to buy from Philips or its suppliers.

- Philips invested DKK342 million in an equity increase for B&O A/S in return for a 25% ownership of the expanded company.

- Philips agreed not to be represented on the Board of Directors of B&O A/S or B&O Holding but was given the right to veto the choice for President of B&O A/S. However, it could not choose the President.

- Philips was given the right to buy another 25% of the equity in B&O A/S for net book value if the B&O Holding A-shares should in the future be sold to investors outside of the present group. This protected Philips from having a competitor overseeing its activities with B&O A/S.

- B&O was given the right to buy back its shares from Philips at net book value if the alliance did not live up to expectations.

When B&O's strategic alliance with Philips was announced to the public on May 3, 1990, the reaction was instantaneously favorable both in the press and in the stock market. B&O's share price jumped by 35% during the next two days and remained at the new level until the Gulf War crisis depressed the share price once again. Exhibit 4 shows B&O's share price development before and after the announcement.

EXHIBIT 4 Bang & Olufsen's Share Price Development, April–May 1990

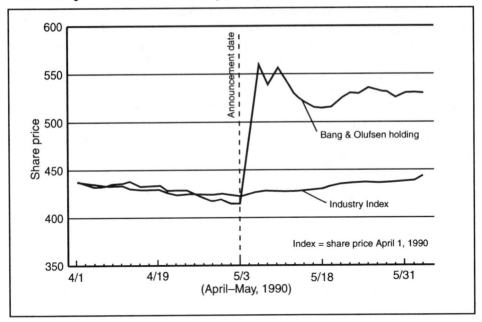

The Future   As Anders Knutsen and Povl Skifter contemplated the future from the perspective of September 1991, they could look back with satisfaction on the steps taken during the last two years to solve some of B&O's long-run problems. In particular:

- The equity base was considerably strengthened by the Philips investment.

- B&O had gained more rapid access to new technology.

- B&O had improved its access to components at a better price.

- B&O's organization had been rationalized to encourage more joint ventures of the type illustrated by DIAX with L.M. Ericsson and the Philips alliance.

On the other hand, the DKK 74 million loss, which had just been announced, reminded them that certain long-run problems remained. Indeed, even in the short run, B&O had not yet taken full advantage of the possibilities opened up by the Philips alliance and the new organization structure.

At the time of the strategic alliance, Franz Timmer, Managing Director of Philips Electronics (subsidiary of Philips N.V.), had made several suggestions to B&O's management about the future strategic path for B&O A/S. They were:

- Focus on design and systems integration, where B&O A/S had a comparative advantage.

- Outsource more of B&O A/S's component production, where it did not have economies of scale.

Case Questions

1. Analyze the steps that should be taken by B&O A/S and Philips to gain the synergies that were expected.

2. Given your answer to Question 1, over how long a time period do you anticipate these steps will take before the results become recognized in B&O's share price?

3. Many strategic alliances are unstable. Do you believe that this one will probably end in a voluntary sale of the rest of B&O A/S to Philips, continue as a viable alliance, or split up?

4. How can B&O Holding raise funds in the future to maintain its share of the equity if B&O A/S grows significantly?

BRITISH COLUMBIA HYDRO

"Treasury cannot be seen as a passive activity," Bell says. "Once we isolated treasury as a separate subset of our business and set some goals for it, it helped our people view problems in a fresh way. If you think of it in terms of opportunities, it may be the biggest profit centre you have got in your company, particularly if you are capital intensive."

Larry Bell, CEO, British Columbia Hydro
Intermarket, September 1989.

British Columbia Hydroelectric and Power Authority (BC Hydro) is a Provincial Crown Corporation, a wholly owned subsidiary of the Province of British Columbia. BC Hydro is the fifth largest Canadian utility, generating, transmitting, and distributing electricity to more than one million customers in British Columbia. The fact that it is a government-owned utility does not change its need to manage treasury operations against financial risks.

BC Hydro has substantial exposure to financial risk. Larry Bell, as Chairman of BC Hydro, was determined to do something about the financial price risks—the movements of exchange rates, interest rates, and commodity prices—facing the firm. It was now March 1988, and the time for discussion had ended and the time for decisions had come.

Financial Exposures

Upon taking over as Chairman of BC Hydro in late 1987, Larry Bell started at the ground up in his analysis of the firm's financial exposures. Bell was formerly British Columbia's Deputy Minister of Finance, and therefore not a newcomer to issues in financial management. His first step was to isolate those major business and financial forces driving net income (revenues and operating costs) and the balance sheet (asset and liability component values).

BC Hydro was—at least by financial standards—relatively simple in financial structure. The firm's revenues came from power sales. Power sales were in turn divisible into residential and small business (60%), and transmission sales (40%). Residential power use was extremely stable, so that 60% of all revenues of BC Hydro were easily predictable. However, the same could not be said of transmission sales. This was power sold to large industrial users, user's who numbered only 80 at that time. The power use of these 80 industrial users was determined by their business needs, and needs were highly cyclical. BC Hydro's sales were predominantly domestic, with only about 5% of all revenues generated from power sales to utilities across the border in the United States.

EXHIBIT 1 Currency Composition and Exchange Rate Impacts on British Colubia Hydro's Liabilities and Net Worth

Debt and Equity by Currency of Denomination	*Initial Values (Canadian Dollars)*	*March 1988 (Canadian Dollars)*
Debt Canadian dollar-denominated	4,000,000,000	4,000,000,000
U.S. dollar-denominated	3,250,000,000	4,000,000,000
Equity	540,000,000	540,000,000
Total liabilities and net worth	7,790,000,000	8,540,000,000
Exchange rate related gains (losses)		(750,000,000)

Source: BC Hydro and Moodys Canada. Initial values debt are Canadian dollar equivalents, regardless of original currency of denomination, on original date of issuance.

The cost structure of BC Hydro was also relatively simple—debt service. Debt service dominated operating expenses, averaging 55% of operating expenses over the mid-1980s. (Debt service rarely constitutes more than 15% of operating expenses in typical corporate financial structures.) Power generation, however, is extremely capital intensive. The requirements for capital are met primarily by debt.

In 1987 BC Hydro had approximately C$8 billion in debt outstanding. Unfortunately, BC Hydro was a victim of its own attractiveness. It had been a direct beneficiary of the need for U.S.-based investors to diversity their exposures in the late 1970s and early 1980s. It had tapped the U.S. dollar debt markets at extremely attractive rates for the time. But now it was faced with the servicing of this U.S. dollar-denominated debt, a full-half of its total debt portfolio. Much of the U.S. dollar debt had been acquired when the U.S. dollar was weaker (approximately C$1/US$) and both U.S. and Canadian interest rates were higher. As shown in Exhibit 1, the appreciation of the U.S. dollar had resulted in an increase in the Canadian dollar debt equivalent of C$750 million. Equity amounted to approximately C$540 million. BC Hydro was highly leveraged to say the least.

BC Hydro had followed the general principles of conservative capital structure management. It had financed long-term assets with long-term debt. The match of asset and liability maturities was quite good, but the currency of denomination was not. This currency mismatch constituted an enormous potential exposure to the financial viability of the firm.

Isolating the Issues

In early 1988 Chairman Larry Bell called in Bridgewater Associates, a Connecticut financial consulting firm, for help. Bob Prince and Ray Dalio (president) of Bridgewater, along with senior management of BC Hydro and representatives of the BC Ministry of Finance met at Whistler Mountain, British Columbia. The purpose of the retreat was to first identify the primary financial risk issues facing BC Hydro, and secondly purpose preliminary solutions. Chairman Bell encouraged an open exchange of ideas.[1]

---

[1] *Intermarket*, September 1989, p. 26.

We have to do what makes sense economically. We'll deal with the accounting and regulatory hurdles after they've been resolved. If someone wanted to point out that our legislation wouldn't allow us to trade in futures, that's fine. The legislature sits every year.

Bell felt that consideration of institutional or legal constraints would prevent the analysis from getting to the core issues. The group proceeded to isolate two basic questions that had to be addressed prior to moving forward:

1. Does BC Hydro want to eliminate all financial risk, or only manage it?

2. BC Hydro is in the business of providing power. Is it also in the business of trading or speculating in the financial markets?

Discussion was heated on these points and ended with no clear agreement initially. Ray Dalio of Bridgewater pushed the discussion by arguing that the interest rate and foreign exchange problems the firm was saddled with were the direct result of a simple basic problem: the lack of a plan.

BC Hydro hadn't thought through its financial activities strategically. They were thinking about running their business, not asset-liability management. You can't take that approach in a volatile economic environment.

The participants agreed to move on to a detailed discussion and analysis of the BC Hydro's financial exposures without resolving these first two issues.

Financial Price Risks

Financial risk management focuses on how the movement of financial prices (interest rates, exchange rates, and commodity prices) affect the value of the firm. Isolating these impacts on any individual firm requires the evaluation of how revenues and costs, both operational and financial, change with movements in these prices. Bridgewater Associates and BC Hydro's staff conducted a number of statistical studies to find what economic forces were at work in the costs and revenues of the firm.

Revenues. The results were quite clear. The 60% of power sales going to the 1.25 million small business and residential consumers was extremely stable, and was therefore insensitive to movements in interest rates, or other business cycle indicators such as unemployment or inflation. In fact residential power use was sensitive primarily to population size. The 40% of power sales to the large industrial users was, however, very cyclical. Closer analysis of the industrial users indicated that these users were sensitive to basic commodity prices (pulp, paper, chemicals mining, etc.). Statistically speaking, transmission sales were found to be heavily dependent on movements in commodity prices (positively related) and industrial production (positively related).

Costs. A closer look at the cost structure of BC Hydro also revealed a number of clear economic forces at work. Operating expenses were dominated by debt service, over 55% of the total. The remaining 45% of operating costs possessed little variable content. Although business conditions for industrial users could decline, the nature of the utility industry still required that operations continue with little change in operating expenses achievable.

Secondly, since 55% of operating expenses were debt service, costs could potentially move directly with interest rates. But BC Hydro's practice over the past decade had been to finance long-term assets with long-term debt, and long-term debt at fixed rates obviously did not move with shorter-cycle interest rate movements. Long-term interest rates were locked in. And interest rates (short-term and long-term rates) had in general been falling in both the United States and Canada since the early 1980s.

Short-term interest rates move with commodity prices. Because increases in commodity prices frequently lead to more inflation, and interest rates and bond yields must in turn move with changes in inflation, significant commodity price increases translated directly into rising interest rates.

It was now clear that if BC Hydro's revenues and cost structures were to be managed against underlying economic or financial forces, protection would be needed against commodity prices. Exhibit 2 illustrates how power sales moved positively with commodity price changes. At the same time, it also shows how short-term interest rates moved with commodity price changes, but long-term interest rates did not. Since BC Hydro was financed nearly exclusively with long-term debt, its present debt structure was not enjoying the fruits of these correlated movements (lower commodity prices and interest rates).

Currency Exposure. BC Hydro was facing an enormous foreign currency exposure. The fact that revenues were 95% Canadian dollar-denominated, while C$4 billion

EXHIBIT 2   British Columbia Hydro's Revenue and Cost Sensitivity to Commodity Price Changes

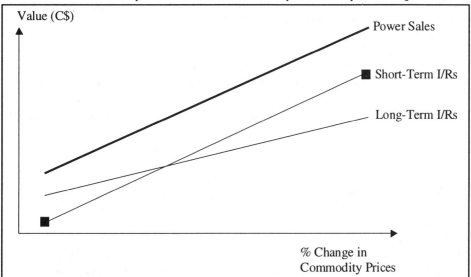

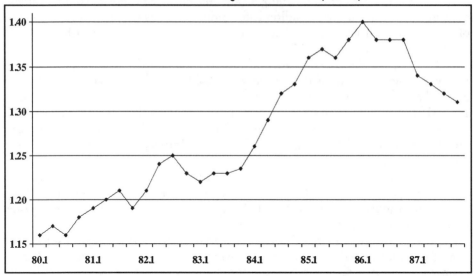

of total long-term debt was a U.S. dollar-denominated, meant that debt-service was completely exposed to currency risk. The firm earned only 5% of its revenues in U.S. dollars, and therefore had no "natural way" of obtaining the foreign currency it needed to service debt. As Exhibit 3 illustrates, although the U.S. dollar had risen versus the Canadian dollar steadily between 1980 and 1986, the Canadian dollar had regained some ground in the past two years.

By 1988 Larry Bell estimated that BC Hydro had realized C$350 million in foreign currency losses on its U.S. dollar debt, all of which passed through current income. The remaining exposure still approached C$400 million depending on the direction of the exchange rate movement. Something had to be done quickly. The urgency of the issue was particularly acute given that the total equity of BC Hydro amounted to only C$540 million!

The outstanding U.S. dollar debt was to be repaid in single "balloon" payments upon maturity. BC Hydro therefore had an enormous amount of cash flowing into a sinking fund for debt principal repayment. The funds were presently being reinvested in Canadian bonds, yielding short-term current rates on Canadian debt instruments.

Proposed Risk Management Strategies

Several alternative solutions were put forward for both the revenue-cost risks and the foreign currency risks. It seemed the solutions would have to be independently constructed.

The basic revenue-cost mismatch, the fact that BC Hydro held little short-term debt which would parallel the movement of revenues with commodity prices, was attacked first. The obvious solution was to increase the proportion of short-term debt. Although this approach would clearly increase the matching of commodity price cycles, it would do the opposite with regard to asset-liability maturity matching. It was argued that 60% of all power revenues were still very stable, and that the debt structure of the entire utility should not be reworked in order to pursue risk management goals. The critics of the short-term debt approach also emphasized that historical correlations might not hold up in the future. Movements of revenues and short-term interest rates correlated with commodity price movements may not hold true. The debate was heated.

The foreign currency exposure problem was at first glance, simple. The easiest and most risk-averse approach would simply be to buy U.S. dollars forward. There was little risk in that the debt-service schedule was known exactly in terms of amounts and timing, and the resulting forward cover would eliminate the currently risk.

Several senior finance ministry officials suggested a currency-interest rate swap instead. All agreed that both would work equally well. However, they were not certain that as a Crown Corporation they would be allowed to enter into a swap agreement. Late in the afternoon of the weekend retreat an additional detail was also recognized, that the signing of a forward contact (or series of forward contracts) to cover the U.S. dollar debt-service would require BC Hydro to recognize and realize (pass through the income statement) the total currency loss remaining, approximately C$500 million. This was obviously unacceptable.

A second alternative put forward by Ray Dalio of Bridgewater Associates was to move all sinking-fund capital out of Canadian dollar bonds into a similar risk category of U.S. dollar-denominated securities. This would result in the security values moving in the opposite direction of the U.S. dollar debt, thus offsetting adverse (or favorable) exchange rate changes; a natural hedge. But, this also meant that BC Hydro, a Crown Corporation, would be intentionally constructing an enormous uncovered foreign currency position. This met with considerable opposition by representatives of the British Columbia Ministry of Finance.

The participants returned from the quiet wilderness setting of Whistler Mountain to the hustle and bustle of Vancouver. It was now March 1988; Larry Bell needed a decision soon.

> "When I came to BC Hydro, because half our costs are associated with debt servicing, there were significant opportunities that could be shaken loose in a proactive treasury operation," he recalls. "As a manager, I shouldn't run this company unless I exploited all of those opportunities."

PART IV
FOREIGN INVESTMENT
DECISIONS

PERRIER, NESTLÉ, AND THE AGNELLIS

The outcome of one of the fiercest takeover battles in Europe could be decided in the French courtrooms. Nestlé, the Swiss-based food giant, needed to reassess its tactics to win the fight with the Agnelli family of Italy over Perrier, the French mineral water company. The chances seemed slim, with the Agnellis and their allies now controlling 49.3% of Perrier.

The court battle would initially involve two other parties, not the Agnellis themselves: Exor, a French holding company that owned 28.8% of Perrier (with 35.5% of the voting control), and Saint Louis, a conglomerate that had recently purchased 13.8% of Perrier's treasury stock (Exhibit 1). The Agnellis were aligned with both these groups and owned shares in them.

On January 21, 1992, Nestlé launched two lawsuits: one in Nimes to challenge Exor's right to exercise its 35.5% vote, and another in Paris to annul Saint Louis's purchase of 13.8% of Perrier's treasury stock. If Nestlé did not win both cases, it would lose the battle. The stakes were high. On the previous day, Nestlé, along with its ally Banque Indosuez, had made a full bid for Perrier at FF1,475 a share, for a total value of FF13.25 bn ($2.35 bn). Nestlé knew that the bid would not go uncontested. It had to assess the possibility of counterbids, their sources, timing, and success probabilities. The company also had to decide how high a price it was willing to pay if the bidding war escalated.

Background

The events could be traced back to Perrier S.A.'s problems with the benzene contamination in 1990 of its flagship Perrier mineral water that resulted in a highly publicized worldwide recall. Even before the scandal, Perrier S.A., the world's largest mineral water producer, had been rumored to be under siege by several suitors, notably Paris-based Exor S.A., a diversified holding company with interests in wine and real estate. Exor had accumulated control of 35.5% of Perrier by the end of 1989. The Agnellis, Italy's premier business dynasty who control Fiat S.p.A., became involved when they launched a friendly bid for Exor with the intent to take control of Perrier.

Nestlé then entered the picture, and what followed was one of the most complex takeover contests in Europe involving a web of cross-shareholdings, alliances, personalities, and nationalities. The *Financial Times*, March 26, 1992, observed:

> Rarely since the early days of oil wild-catting has the ownership of holes in the ground excited as much high passion and low intrigue as during the tortuous

four-month-old battle for France's Source Perrier, the world's largest mineral water company. Nor has any recent takeover struggle exposed more clearly the complex forces at work in a Europe where long-established continental models of capitalism, with their tribal loyalties and interlocking networks of power, are forced to confront the rude imperatives of international markets.

Source Perrier S.A.

Perrier S.A. is the world's largest mineral water company. The company owns strong brands such as Perrier, Contrex, Volvic, Vichy St. Yorre and a 35% stake in Italian San Pellegrino. In the US, Perrier owns Arrowhead, Great Bear, Calistoga, and Poland Springs.

Perrier derives about two-thirds of its sales from mineral water and the rest from cheese (Roquefort and Sorrento, accounting for about 26%), and other miscellaneous items (7%). It had FF13.2 bn in sales in 1991 and operating income of FF1.1 bn, generating a net income per share of about FF36 (see Exhibits 2a, 2b and 3). Its top mineral water brands included Contrex, Volvic, Arrowhead, and Perrier, accounting for about 65% of the company's water sales by volume (Exhibit 4a). For nearly half a century the company was run by the now 76-year-old Frenchman Gustave Leven, the son of a stockbroker. *Forbes* wrote in May 1989:

> Leven does not tell stockholders what Perrier owns; the miscellaneous assets are hidden through affiliates whose holdings are undisclosed. Listed simply as another affiliate, Soplacin, for example, held the Canal Plus [a French TV station] stake. Who is Gustave Leven and what is he up to? Son of a French stockbroker, he bought the Perrier springs in Vergeze in 1947. At that time Perrier was a prestigious but tiny business; it sold 18 million bottles a year of the spring's sparkling water. Today Perrier sells 1 billion bottles a year from the Perrier spring alone.
>
> But more recently Leven was unable to build upon his own marketing success. His efforts to diversify have not been successful, and now competition and exchange rates have crimped his basic business. But bubbles aren't what interest the speculators who have pushed up the price of Perrier's shares. Nor are they all that concerned about the quality of earnings. In France, as in the U.S., earning power is becoming less important in pricing shares than prospects for takeover and breakup. And, in France even more than in the U.S., the individual small stockholder is in the dark about asset value because he doesn't have the same knowledge the insiders do about what these assets are worth. It's a cozy game Gustave Leven's playing."

Without any clear successor in mind, Leven, whose family also owned 18% of Perrier, ran the company as his personal fiefdom and investment vehicle with complex shareholdings in products ranging from glass containers and paper products, to TV channels.

Perrier S.A.'s stock was one of the best performing on the Paris stock exchange in 1988 and the first half of 1989 (Exhibit 5).

The Benzene Affair On January 19, 1990, laboratory workers at the Mecklenburg County Environmental Protection Department in Charlotte, N.C. discovered traces of benzene in Perrier bottles. Though the traces were minute (between 12.3 and

19.9 parts per billion, less than in a cup of decaffeinated coffee and completely harmless), the company's mismanagement of the ensuing public outrage damaged Perrier severely. Prior to the benzene affair, the Perrier brand accounted for 14% of Perrier's sales (by value) in 1990.

Chairman Gustave Leven failed to recognize the severity of the problem when he downplayed the importance of the contamination at a February 14, 1990 press conference. Even though the company recalled all 160 mn bottles worldwide (at a cost of $200 mn) and Perrier water was unavailable for six weeks, the conflicting and incomplete explanations of the source of the contamination shook consumer confidence (it turned out that a filter that was supposed to sieve out naturally-occurring benzene had not been replaced). The revelation hurt an image that was built on purity, resulting in sales declines of 18% and a profit reduction of 21% worldwide. In America, Perrier's market share declined from 13% to 9%. In June 1990, in the wake of the benzene scandal, Leven was ousted by Exor chairman Jaques Vincent.

In December 1991, Perrier was still struggling to recover from its benzene scandal and its overall sales had declined for a second year in a row (see Exhibit 4a). Its stock price was languishing in the mid-FF1200 range, down from a high of nearly FF2000 per share prior to the benzene affair (see Exhibit 5).

Nestlé S.A.

Founded 126 years ago and still headquartered in Vevey, Switzerland, Nestlé is the world's largest food manufacturer. Ever since Helmut Maucher (the first German to run Nestlé) took over as CEO in 1981, the once-sleepy giant embarked on an aggressive expansion strategy, acquiring food-related businesses all over the globe (Carnation in the US, $3 bn; Rowntree in the UK, $4.5 bn; and Buitoni in Italy, $1.4 bn). Although unusual for Europe, Nestlé did not shy away from hostile bids to acquire what it believed were strategically important target companies.

Nestlé operates 423 factories in 62 countries and employs about 200,000 people. In 1991, it earned Sfr2.5 bn ($1.6 bn) on sales of Sfr50.5 bn ($33.6 bn). (See Exhibits 5A and 5B, for 1989-1991 financial data, and Exhibit 7 for comparative industry data.) Geographically, its most important markets are Europe (46% of sales), USA (21%), Latin America (17%), Asia (8%) and Africa (5%). The most important products are instant beverages, milk and dairy products, culinary products, frozen food, infant and dietary products, chocolate and candy, beverages and some non-food businesses such as cosmetics and pharmaceuticals. The company has well-established brands such as the flagship Nescafe. In the US, Nestlé owns brands such as Nescafe, Taster's Choice, Carnation, Quick, Stouffer frozen foods, Contadina, Beringer wines, and several chocolate and candy brands. It also owns 25% of the French cosmetics firm L'Oreal.

It is Nestlé's stated goal to double its sales worldwide within the next decade. The company wants to maintain a high-quality food image with brands that are in the top three in their respective markets. Furthermore, it aims to develop new products for changing consumer tastes that take advantage of changing lifestyles. The company felt that this necessitated expanding its position as the world's leader in food related technologies and R&D.

Nestlé generates large cash flows from mature businesses to fund growth in new markets and build new brands. Though one of the most international companies in terms of markets and composition of employees, Nestlé is still largely Swiss-owned. Until 1989, foreigners where almost completely excluded from owning Nestlé shares. Due to increasing protectionist pressures and given Nestlé's aggressive acquisitions, ownership restrictions were abolished. Further, for a firm that derives 98% of its sales outside Switzerland and has a market value of $31 bn, Switzerland was seen as too limited as a source of equity capital.

Nestlé appears to be skilled in transferring successful brands and products internationally by keeping key, proven characteristics of the product but adapting the offering to local market tastes. Nescafe, for example, is available in 200 different varieties from mild for the US to very strong for Latin America. Successful brands are difficult and expensive to develop from scratch. The company reaps significant economies of scale in product development, marketing, purchasing (e.g., the company purchases 15% of world coffee production), and in production (all chocolate production was consolidated after Nestlé bought Rowntree). As the largest food company in the world, Nestlé possesses the necessary clout in distribution to secure shelf-space and has nurtured relationships with host countries to develop new markets.

Decision-making is highly decentralized, and the company adopts a multidomestic strategy worldwide. Most local business units operate independently of the corporate headquarters, the regional manager, or the country manager. This strategy allows the subsidiaries considerable flexibility in serving local tastes. Nestlé relies on local managers with in-depth market knowledge, and believes in promoting from within.

Nestlé's Mineral Water Business   Nestlé entered the mineral water business in 1969 when it acquired Vittel (France), and subsequently Blaue Quellen (Germany) and Ashbourne (UK) in the 1970s. Nestlé strives to be a dominant global player in the mineral water market. In this business, the product itself can hardly be physically differentiated, and much depends on the strength of the brand name.

The Agnelli Family

The Agnellis of Italy are one of Europe's most prominent and influential families. The family controls the car and engineering company, Fiat S.p.A. Giovanni Agnelli, possibly Europe's best known businessman, has sought to diversify the family's holdings in recent years. Fiat's profitability has deteriorated in the face of stiff Japanese competition. In 1991, Fiat's operating profits were only $500 mn, down 70%. Fiat depends on Italy for 2/3 of its sales, but its market share there has shrunk from 60% to 45% over the last four years. Today, Fiat represents only 50% of the Agnellis' revenues. If the European Union (EU) adopts a common policy towards Japanese car imports by the late 1990s, it is likely that Italy will no longer be able to restrict Japanese market share in Italy and the competitive environment for Fiat will become even more intense.

The Agnellis' diversification strategy was effected through two Luxembourg holding companies, Ifil (chairman, Umberto Agnelli) with $2.2 bn in assets, and

Ifint (chairman, Giovanni Agnelli) with $1.5 bn in assets. Ifint is the more aggressive and opportunistic holding, whereas Umberto Agnelli and Ifil are more interested in long-term investments. In France, Ifil has stakes in BSN (5.8%), Worms & Cie (7.4%) and Saint Louis (6.5%). The Agnellis have been the largest foreign investor in France, controlling enterprises with estimated sales of FF44 bn. *The Economist*, March 28, 1992, observed:

> The Agnellis' desire to enter new industries has grown as the performance of Fiat, their core car and engineering business, has deteriorated. No wonder, then, that the Agnelli family has been diversifying fast. It has done so via two holding companies, IFIL and IFINT.
>
> IFINT, with $1.5 billion of assets, is an opportunistic investor in a variety of fields including car components, engineering and property. Its main aim is to diversify geographically. Some 40% of its assets are in America, and another 30% in Europe.
>
> Until the Perrier spat, the Agnellis had always worked closely with leading bankers and industrialists in other countries, especially France. And they were content to take small stakes in companies on a friendly basis. Indeed, Umberto Agnelli, Giovanni's younger brother and the chairman of IFIL, is said to want to create a form of Japanese-style keiretsu group in which European companies co-operate closely without having to buy large stakes in one another.
>
> The snag, according to one French industrialist close to the Agnellis, is that IFINT, which is chaired by Giovanni Agnelli and managed by Gianluigi Gabetti, has a more aggressive, short-term strategy which can conflict with IFIL's long-term view. Mr. Gabetti admits that the two units may compete, particularly in France, but says that "what {the Agnellis} don't want is for competition to become conflict." Yet by bidding for Exor, the holding company which controls 29% of Perrier's shares, IFINT sparked off a row whose repercussions will make it harder for IFIL to forge long-term alliances in France, which had looked like a promising market.

The Agnellis sought to diversify further into the French food market by gaining control of Perrier. With the blessings of the Franco-Greek Mentzelopoulos family who owns 16% of Exor, they wanted to take over Exor, thus gaining control of Perrier more cheaply than via an outright bid. In November 1991, Ifint launched a FF1,320 per share friendly bid for 2/3 of Exor, with the intent to acquire control of Perrier. However, this alienated the Suez group, a 10% minority shareholder in Exor. The role of the Leven family who owned 18% of Perrier was unclear, but it seemed they would have sold to the highest bidder. The Levens were also not believed to be one monolithic block, and had not voted together on some occasions.

Exor S.A.

Exor is a holding company that owns the famous Chateaux Margaux Vineyards, Paris real estate, plus 28.8% of Perrier directly and another 6.7% jointly with Societe Generale. Jaques Vincent has been chairman of Exor S.A. since 1980. Jaques Vincent and Exor had humble beginnings—Exor began as a grocery concern, but, over the years, Vincent began diversifying the company and in 1983, he bought a 13% share in Perrier. Although this put him nominally in the big leagues of the French business establishment, he is considered a corporate maverick who doesn't get on too well with business leaders in France.

Perrier considered Exor an ally against a possible foreign buyer. Over the years, Exor built up its share through outright purchases and through an investment vehicle, OMNICO (which is 49% owned by Exor and 51% owned by Societe Generale, the French bank). In 1989, by increasing Exor's control to 35.5% of Perrier (prior to this increase, Exor had owned 23.7%), Vincent took control of the board and became its vice chairman. Gustave Leven's poor handling of the benzene scandal finally enabled Vincent to push him out and become chairman of Perrier in June 1990.

Other Key Players

Suez Group Indosuez is a French merchant bank and part of the Suez group of France, a financial firm with FF800 bn ($150 bn) in assets. Suez is a 10% shareholder in Exor and Exor, in turn, owns 2.4% of Suez stock. As long as the other shares were widely distributed, Suez's 10% share would give it substantial influence. If the Agnellis owned 2/3, Suez's share would carry less effective voting power. Indosuez thus decided to turn against the Agnellis, and teamed up with Nestlé. The two began buying shares in Exor and Perrier in the open market. Finally, on January 20, 1992, Nestlé and Indosuez jointly launched a FF1,475 per share full takeover bid, through their takeover vehicle, Demilac.

Lazard Freres Lazard Freres is an international investment bank that is considered to be particularly influential in France. The firm is privately held, and run by Michel David-Weill, who embodies the path to power in France—a top academic record from the elite schools, extensive networking, and (as some observers suggest), a strong dose of political patronage.

The Agnellis historically had forged close ties with Lazard Freres. Lazard helped the Agnellis acquire a 5.8% stake in BSN and Giovanni Agnelli himself sits on Lazard's board. Michel David-Weill, the chairman of Lazard, serves as a director on several Agnelli-controlled companies. While the Agnellis have worked with Lazard on their previous French investments, they did not inform Lazard of their Exor intentions. Lazard has historically had even stronger ties with BSN, and now felt spurned by the Agnellis. When Umberto Agnelli hinted that even BSN might itself be an eventual takeover target of the Agnellis, Lazard had to support BSN. They teamed up with Nestlé and Indosuez, and turned against the Agnellis.

BSN BSN is Europe's fourth largest packaged food concern with FF53 bn ($10 bn) in sales in 1990. The company has strong market positions in dairy products and mineral water, with its sales concentrated in France and Europe. Its major brands include Danon (yogurt), Gervais (cheese) and Badoit/Evian (mineral water). The company is run by 78-year old Antoine Riboud, who has been chairman since 1965.

Umberto Agnelli is a director of BSN. The Agnellis had helped BSN to expand in Italy. BSN and the Agnellis struck a deal in 1987, where the Agnellis were to help BSN expand in Italy and BSN, in return, would help the Agnellis diversify into the food business. After the Agnellis' ambitions became obvious, Riboud was afraid that the Agnellis might challenge BSN's position in mineral water in France. BSN agreed to buy Perrier's Volvic brand from Nestlé, should Nestlé's bid succeed.

Saint Louis The sugar, paper, and packaging concern, Saint Louis, is controlled by Worms et Cie. a French family-controlled bank that owns 36% of Saint Louis. The Agnellis have a 6.5% stake in Saint Louis, and also own 7.4% in the Worms holding company.

Saint Louis entered the takeover battle on January 3, 1992, when it bought a 13.8% stake (FF 1.5 bn, $266 mn or FF1,200 per share) of Perrier treasury stock from Perrier in an off-market transaction. It was unclear whether, under French takeover laws (see Exhibit 9), the authorities would consider this a new capital infusion into the company. Saint Louis was alleged to have known of the impending Nestlé bid when it bought the shares. Worse still, Exor chairman Vincent was accused of having forged the date on the sales order of Perrier stock to Saint Louis. The sale of this stake combined with the Agnellis' alliance with Saint Louis would have given the Agnelli camp almost full control of Perrier.

The Mentzelopoulos Family The Franco-Greek family, Mentzelopoulos, controlled a 16% share of Exor. Greek born Mr. Mentzelopoulos made his first fortune in Pakistan after World War II as an agent for grain merchants. He then bought control of the ailing Felix Potin chain of Parisian grocery stores, which Mr. Jacques Vincent subsequently restored to prosperity.

Since his death in 1980, his estate has been managed by his daughter Corrine, who married Gustave Leven's nephew, Hubert. Corrine Mentzelopoulos has been a friend of the Agnellis for two decades. Corrine Mentzelopoulos, a director of Exor, had been chairman of Exor earlier and would not have sold any Exor shares to anyone except the Agnellis. Although well-known in French corporate circles, the Franco-Greek family was considered by many to be outside the corporate establishment in France.

Credit Agricole Credit Agricole, a French bank, one of the largest in Europe with $303 bn in assets, owned 5% of Exor and 8.5% of Perrier. Credit Agricole supported Nestlé's bid.

Societe Generale Another French bank, Societe Generale, supported the Agnellis. Exor and Societe Generale jointly owned the investment vehicle OMNICO that had a 6.7% stake in Perrier. (See Exhibit 8 for an overview of allies and adversaries.)

The Mineral Water Business

Mineral water is a highly profitable business with margins typically around 15-20% for large producers. It had been growing worldwide rapidly during the 1980s, at about 10% per year. In Germany, for example, per capita consumption increased from 41.4 liters in 1980 to 89.2 liters in 1991, constituting the fastest growing beverage group. The annual consumption per capita was 105 liters in Italy and 77 liters in France, compared to 33 liters in the US and 6 liters in the UK. If more health-conscious consumers in the US and the UK developed an appetite similar to that of the French, growth in that market could be dramatic. Nestlé clearly wanted to position itself as a dominant player in these markets.

Since Perrier's share price and its sales were still depressed following the benzene scandal, Nestlé felt that Perrier made an attractive target, particularly since its market share was slowly starting to recover and its other major brands were not affected by the scandal.

The Takeover Bid for Exor

On November 28, 1991, Ifint, the Agnelli investment company, made a FF1,320 per share friendly bid for 2/3 of Exor S.A. Partial bids are still legal under an August 1989 French law (Exhibit 9). The law also required that a bidder who holds between 33 1/3 and 50% of a company must make an offer for 2/3 of the company (however, the French finance ministry has plans to make full bids mandatory in the future). The Conseil des Bourses de Valeus (CBV, the agency regulating stock markets) cleared the 2/3 bid on December 5. It was unclear how large Ifint's stake was at that point, but according to some sources, Ifint controlled about 35% of Exor when it made the bid, and was allied with the Mentzelopoulos family who owned another 16%.

The partial bid enraged the Suez group, and although Ifint quickly extended the offer to all shareholders, this apparently prompted Suez to approach Nestlé.

The COB Investigation

On December 12, 1991, the French stock exchange supervisory office, Conseil des Operations de Bourses (COB) began an investigation into investments in Perrier, but Ifint denied any intent to acquire Perrier shares. The COB investigation discovered that Exor had acted in concert with Societe Generale to acquire Perrier shares and that they controlled 35% as of May 1990. Under French takeover legislation, failure to disclose a stake exceeding 1/3 could result in loss of voting rights for two years or more.

The CBV ruled on December 19, 1991, that Exor must bid for 2/3 of Perrier or request an exemption under the law (the exemption was requested and turned down by the CBV on January 16; Exor appealed in the Paris court on January 27, 1992). The CBV also put Ifint's bid for Exor on hold until the Perrier question was resolved. Four days later, the CBV allowed Ifint to continue its bid because Exor's purchase of Perrier shares predated the 1989 law. However, Exor's failure to disclose its 35% stake in Perrier in 1990 could still lead to a loss of voting rights on the excess over the original share they owned.

The Saint Louis Deal

In a strange turn of events that later led to criminal investigations of Perrier's management, Perrier sold treasury stock representing a 13.8% stake to Saint Louis, an ally of the Agnellis. The sale supposedly occurred on January 3, 1992, ten days before

Nestlé announced that it might be interested in buying Perrier. However, Perrier and Exor chairman Vincent were suspected of forging the date on the sales order, and it was believed that the sale may have actually taken place after Nestlé's announcement. Vincent became the object of a criminal investigation by the French police. The Saint Louis transaction meant that Exor with its allies now controlled 49.3% of Perrier. The COB launched an investigation into the treasury stock sale on January 16, 1992.

Nestlé's Bid for Perrier

Nestlé indicated for the first time that it had considered buying Perrier on January 13, 1992. Two days later, BSN refused to comment on a press report that it was going to back Nestlé's bid. On January 20, Nestlé and Indosuez made a full bid for Perrier at FF1,475 a share. The bid was conditional on Nestlé obtaining at least 50% of the voting rights. BSN announced that it would buy the Volvic brand if the bid succeeded. In addition to Suez and BSN, Nestlé had the support of two other powerful French allies: Lazard Freres and Credit Agricole. The *Financial Times* wrote on March 25, 1992:

> The Agnellis, meanwhile, compounded their error by alienating BSN and Lazard, which has long used its formidable network of government and business contacts to dominate the French merger scene.
>
> Riboud was uneasy that the Exor bid would prompt the Agnellis to challenge BSN's position in mineral water. He grew still more alarmed when the Agnellis hinted that their longer-term target was BSN itself, where the 73-year-old Riboud has no clear successor.
>
> That prompted Riboud to co-operate closely with Nestlé and Lazard to thwart the Agnellis' designs on Perrier.
>
> Although Lazard had advised the Agnellis on earlier French investments, they did not involve it in their overtures to Exor, apparently believing that they were well-enough established not to need help.
>
> Spurned by the Agnellis and confronted with a threat to the interests of BSN, with which Lazard has intimate ties, the bank aligned itself with the Nestlé-Suez camp.

At the same time, Nestlé and Indosuez initiated court proceedings in two French courts: one in the Nimes commercial court to temporarily freeze Exor's and Saint Louis's voting rights in Perrier until the investigation was over, and another one in a Paris trade court to annul the share transfer from Perrier to Saint Louis.

The next day, on January 21, 1992, Perrier rejected Nestlé's bid. On January 22, 1992, both courts placed temporary orders on Exor to prevent the selling of Perrier shares except for the best public offer. On February 4, the European Commission (EC) opened a merger investigation into Ifint's bid for Exor. Ten days later, the French Finance Ministry cleared the Nestlé offer for Perrier. On March 2, the EC cleared Ifint's bid on the condition that Ifint (Ifil owns at least 5.8% of BSN) does not participate in board discussions involving BSN's mineral water activities.

Bids and Counterbids

BSN made a hostile bid for Exor on February 21, offering FF1,420 per share. The offer was quickly rejected by Exor on the 26th. The CBV approved BSN's bid. BSN was acting in concert with Nestlé and Indosuez to put pressure on the Agnelli camp.

The Paris appellate court rejected Exor's request for an exemption (from having to bid for Perrier) on February 26. Exor was forced to either launch a full bid for Perrier or a 2/3 bid at 2% premium over Nestlé's offer. The following day, Exor made an FF1,475 unconditional offer for 100% of Perrier shares.

Other Concerns

Even if Nestlé's bid succeeded, it had to keep in mind the competition laws adopted by the EC in 1990. EC competition authorities would take a close look at any merger involving participants whose worldwide sales exceeded Ecu5 bn and whose EC-wide sales exceeded Ecu250 mn. The basic purpose, under Article 86 of the law, is to prevent "abuse of dominant position," where a dominant position is said to arise when a company has a market share of 40% or more. Article 86 applies to any mergers between two firms whether or not they are EC companies, as long as they produce effects within the EU.

Should Nestlé's bid succeed, it would control 56% of the mineral water sales in France. In order to preempt EC action on anticompetitive grounds, Nestlé had agreed to sell the Volvic mineral water business to BSN for FF3.05 bn. However, there was some concern here as well, since these two allies in the bidding contest for Perrier would *together* control 82% of the mineral water market in France.

The nature and application of the law was still evolving. One thing was clear: under Commissioner Leon Brittan, the competition authorities were becoming increasingly vigorous in the enforcement of Article 86.

EXHIBIT 1 Ownership and Control Structure as of February 1992

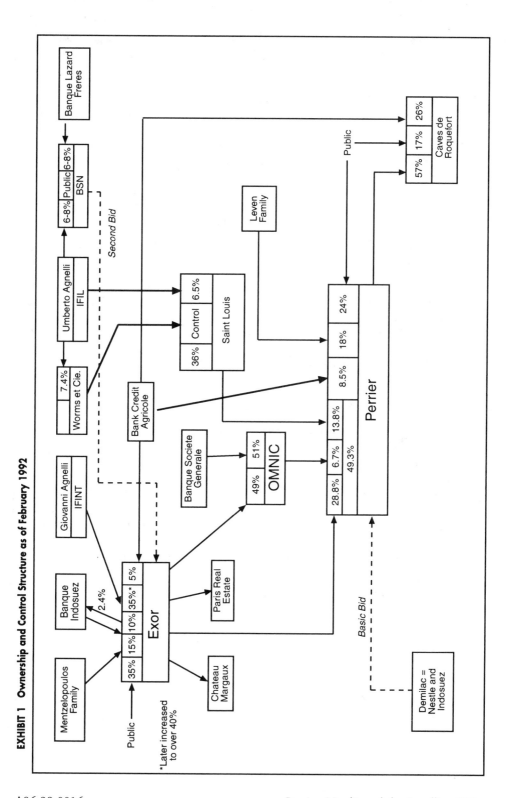

	1989	1990	1991
Sales	16,671,912	13,628,407	13,190,807
Other Revenue	513,489	864,648	456,036
Expenses			
Materials	7,461,282	5,740,712	4,773,252
Personnel	3,395,110	3,186,030	3,227,974
Other	3,548,717	3,389,020	3,459,398
Local Taxes	428,751	367,501	367,868
Depreciation and Amortization	938,923	695,590	740,244
Other	-3,140	13	-124
Operating Income	1,415,758	1,114,189	1,078,231
Financial Income and Expenses			
Financial Income	182,792	231,561	590,420
Financial Expenses	796,978	891,076	813,912
Exceptional Items			
Exceptional Income	1,034,114	3,258,926	1,019,360
Exceptional Charges	1,250,205	2,881,360	1,314,137
Pretax Income inc. Exceptional Items	585,481	832,240	559,962
Profit Sharing Plan	-34,528	-22,253	-18,514
Income Taxes	295,327	362,641	232,162
Consolidated Net Income	255,626	447,346	309,286
Share of Net Income of Unconsolidated Subs.	45,640	49,819	47,205
Discontinued Operations		-162,859	0
Consolidated Net Income	301,266	334,306	356,491
Minority Interest	-29,427	24,584	-30,959
Net Income	271,839	358,890	325,532
Number of Shares Outstanding ('000)	8,983	8,983	8,983
Earnings Per Share (FF)	30.26	39.95	36.24
Dividend Payout Ratio (%)	66%	58%	63%

EXHIBIT 2b Perrier Financial Data: Balance Sheet (1989–1991) (in FF '000, except per share data)

	1989	1990	1991
Fixed Assets			
Intangibles	1,671,389	1,438,545	1,456,025
Goodwill	1,316,794	934,515	1,483,330
PPE	4,237,265	4,208,671	4,795,841
Financial Assets	709,346	564,186	649,524
Equity Securities	321,748	763,345	326,526
	8,256,542	7,909,262	8,711,246
Current Assets			
Cash	711,349	546,541	364,188
Securities	404,116	344,119	42,501
Other Receivables	1,262,962	1,006,889	980,148
Receivables	2,145,428	1,632,082	1,571,414
Inventories	1,417,539	1,387,600	1,419,140
	5,941,394	4,917,231	4,377,391
Prepaid Expenses	82,645	142,764	65,901
TOTAL ASSETS	14,280,581	12,969,257	13,154,538
Shareholders Equity			
Capital	449,153	449,153	449,153
Capital Surplus	291,648	304,947	304,947
Reserves	1,640,533	1,678,328	1,772,549
Treasury Stock	(96,219)	(96,219)	(96,219)
Other	9,900	8,145	10,258
	2,295,015	2,344,354	2,440,688
Minority Interest	894,118	928,948	1,114,030
Provisions for Risk and Charges	950,272	535,993	538,667
Consignations	663,049	622,483	627,366
Deferred Expenses	6,299	8,445	21,776
Liabilities			
Accounts Payable	1,484,419	1,144,478	931,402
Short Term Debt	1,940,059	1,799,503	1,485,290
Loans and Long-Term Debt	6,047,350	5,585,053	5,995,319
	9,471,828	8,529,034	8,412,011
TOTAL LIABILITIES	14,280,581	12,969,257	13,154,538

EXHIBIT 3 Product and Geographic Segment Data for Perrier (1991 data, in millions)

| Product* | Value of Sales* | | | | % Change from 1990 | | | |
	Total (FF)	France (FF)	Europe (Ecu)	R.O.W. (US$)	Total (FF)	France (FF)	Europe (Ecu)	R.O.W. (US$)
Perrier	1919.4	1118.6	46.2	83.1	1.5%	1.0%	2.9%	-2.6%
Other Mineral Water	6883.7	3056.3	80.2	581.3	6.6%	6.3%	17.3%	1.4%
Soft Drinks	230.7	229.2	0.2	0.0	-20.0%	-20.1%		
Roquefort Cheese	1599.4	1162.3	48.1	18.0	2.1%	1.8%	0.1%	4.1%
Sorrento Cheese (USA)	1845.1	0.0	0.0	328.3	-0.2%			-3.6%
Services	872.5	825.8	5.5	1.5	2.5%	5.5%		
Total	13350.8				3.7%			

EXHIBIT 4a   Perrier 1991 Mineral Water Sales (Volume) Data (millions of liters)

Mineral Water Brand	Country	Million Liters	% Growth from 1990
Contrex	France	829	-6.2%
Volvic	France	784	22.7%
Arrowhead	USA	576	-1.7%
Perrier	France	335	-7.7%
Poland Spring	USA	338	6.3%
Vichy St. Yorre	France	176	-6.4%
Oasis/Ozarka	USA	172	-6.0%
Great Bear	USA	141	-2.8%
Zephyrhills	USA	119	5.3%
Other French	France	126	37.0%
Other North American	USA	79	-11.2%
Other Spanish	Spain	66	-25.0%
Vichy Celestins	France	64	-1.5%
Brazil	Brazil	47	27.0%
Buxton	UK	35	6.1%
Total Water		3887	1.7%
French Brands		2314	3.7%
North American Brands		1425	-0.6%
Rest of the World		148	-6.3%

EXHIBIT 4b   Volume Changes for Leading Non-Perrier Mineral Water Brands (1990/91)

Brand	Volume (in mn. liters)	% Change (90/91)
Evian	1304	1.0%
Vittel	853	-6.0%
Badoit	274	11.0%
Vittel-Hepar	106	17.4%

EXHIBIT 5 Share Prices for Perrier, Nestlé, and the French Stock Market (End of Month prices adjusted for stock splits, in FF)

Year	Month	Perrier	Nestle	French Stock Market
1988	January	481	3934	465
	February	604	4205	502
	March	552	4067	510
	April	675	4220	524
	May	812	4141	546
	June	912	4151	610
	July	882	4053	632
	August	933	4171	619
	September	1206	4181	636
	October	1270	4314	683
	November	1296	5896	698
	December	1479	6597	747
1989	January	1735	6695	800
	February	1630	6306	815
	March	1695	6527	811
	April	1754	6636	839
	May	1659	6281	847
	June	1518	7340	885
	July	1643	8090	891
	August	1741	8085	904
	September	1895	8375	934
	October	1976	8430	902
	November	1775	8430	856
	December	1875	8680	910
1990	January	1718	8480	900
	February	1482	8570	856
	March	1555	8550	872
	April	1695	7975	938
	May	1699	8725	950
	June	1582	8375	932
	July	1483	8280	900
	August	1332	7500	797
	September	1050	6640	715
	October	1095	7440	727
	November	1239	7000	714
	December	1060	6960	719
1991	January	1222	7070	695
	February	1409	7680	740
	March	1498	8300	823
	April	1452	8390	820
	May	1490	8800	841
	June	1388	8400	810
	July	1336	8610	810
	August	1342	8420	833
	September	1366	8000	872
	October	1300	8310	862
	November	1242	8150	857
	December	1221	8600	810

1) The yield on long term government bonds in France is 8%, and in Switzerland, 6%, in December 1991.
2) The current exchange rate is FF3.704 per SFr., and SFr1.488 per US$.

EXHIBIT 6a   Nestlé Financial Data: Income Statements (1989–1991) (SFr millions)

	1989	1990	1991
Sales	48,036	46,369	50,486
Cost of Goods Sold*	27,149	25,678	27,498
Gross Margin	20,887	20,691	22,988
Distribution Expenses	2,542	2,537	2,793
Marketing and Administrative	13,070	12,932	14,482
Research and Development	539	566	627
Total Operating Expenses	16,151	16,035	17,902
Operating Income	4,736	4,656	5,086
Net Interest Expenses	753	679	530
Other Expenses, net	71	248	504
Pretax Income	3,912	3,729	4,052
Income Taxes	1,538	1,404	1,605
Translation Adjustment (-)	51	132	49
Minority Interest (-)	85	84	139
Equity in Earnings (+)	174	163	211
Net Income	2,412	2,272	2,470
Number of Shares Outstanding (mn)	3.67	3.68	3.60
Earnings Per Share (SFr)	656.33	618.23	619.23

Includes depreciation charges. Nestle's depreciation for the years 1989, 1990, and 1991 are, respectively, Sfr2.57 bn., Sfr2.15 bn., and Sfr2.53 bn.

EXHIBIT 6b   Nestlé Financial Data: Balance Sheets (1989–91) (SFr Millions)

	1989	1990	1991
Current Assets			
Liquid Assets	4,231	5,528	4,888
Trade and Other Debt	7,503	7,305	8,034
Inventories	6,251	5,627	6,273
	17,985	18,460	19,195
Fixed Assets			
Tangible Fixed Assets	15,112	14,867	17,162
Investments	1,976	1,641	2,002
Other Assets	333	608	631
	17,421	17,116	19,795
Total Assets	35,406	35,576	38,990
Short-Term Liabilities			
Trade Creditors	6,554	6,375	7,576
Financial Creditors	6,799	7,254	6,577
Provisions for Taxes	628	752	736
	13,981	14,381	14,889
Long-Term Liabilities			
Financial Creditors	2,628	2,262	2,788
Provisions and Trade Creditors	4,170	4,920	5,282
	6,798	7,182	8,070
Total Liabilities	20,779	21,563	22,959
Minority Interests	688	599	661
Shareholders Equity			
Equity Capital	347	347	364
Participation Capital	24	24	24
Addl Capital and Ret. Earnings	13,568	13,043	14,982
	13,939	13,414	15,370
	35,406	35,576	38,990

EXHIBIT 7 Food Industry Comparisons

Company	Price/Book	Price/Cash Flow	Price/Earnings	Div. Yield	Mkt. Value ($ mn)
BSN	2.6	9.8	19.1	1.9	11,533
Cadbury Schweppes	3.7	10.9	16.8	3.6	5,622
Campbell Soup	5.3	13.3	19.5	2.3	9,307
General Mills	9.5	14.5	20.8	2.3	10,773
Heinz	4.2	n/a	15.2	3.0	9,753
Hershey Foods	2.8	12.3	16.2	2.4	3,619
Kellogg	6.3	15.4	20.6	2.0	13,857
Nestle	2.9	8.8	14.6	2.2	23,184
Procter & Gamble	6.1	13.0	20.0	2.1	34,570
Quaker Oats	4.3	9.3	15.7	3.4	n/a

Source: Morgan Stanley Capital International Perspective.

EXHIBIT 8 Overview of Allies and Adversaries

	Agnelli Family	Perrier	Mentze-lopoulos	Exor	Saint Louis	Societe Geníl	Nestle	Lazard	Suez Group	BSN	Credit Agrcíle
Agnelli Family		☺	☺	☺	☺	☺	💣	💣	💣	💣	💣
Perrier			☺	☺	☺	☺	💣	💣	💣	💣	💣
Mentze-lopoulos				☺	☺	☺	💣	💣	💣	💣	💣
Exor					☺	☺	💣	💣	💣	💣	💣
Saint Louis						☺	💣	💣	💣	💣	💣
Societe Geníl							💣	💣	💣	💣	💣
Nestle								☺	☺	☺	☺
Lazard									☺	☺	☺
Suez Group										☺	☺
BSN											☺
Credit Agrcíle											

1) Subject to a few exceptions, when thresholds of 33 1/3% or 50% are passed or when 2% increments occur over aone year periodóif bidder holds between 33 1/3% and 50%ómandatory offer leading to 66 2/3% must be made toall shareholders.

2) For listed shares, disclosure is required when thresholds of 5%, 10%, 20%, 33 1/3%, 50%, and 66 2/3% are reached,within 15 days to the target, and 5 days to the Council of Stock Exchanges. Failing this, shares over the thresholdsbecome non-voting in the bidderís hands for a two-year

3) Takeover bids are regulated by a law of August 2, 1989 and the regulation of the Stock Exchange Council (Conseildes Bourses de Valeur) and the COB as approved by the Ministry of the Economy

4) The same price must be paid to all shareholders; however, a lower price may be paid under certain conditions tominority acceptors for dealings in controlling interest.

5) Bidder shareholder approval is generally not required.

6) Various obstacles prevent the use of poison pills and other defenses as now used in the US. However, some poisonpills can be implemented if they are initiated prior to the announcement of the offer. Some defenses, e.g.,limitation of voting rights exercisable by a single shareholder, double voting rights for longstanding shareholders,issue of options to purchase securities to a friendly shareholder, require shareholder approval with two-

7) During the offer period, the target may not increase its share capital except if the Board of Directors has beenauthorized to so by a shareholder general meeting held less than a year before. Also, such capital increases cannotbe reserved for certain shareholders or third parties.

8) In general, there are no nationality restrictions for investments in

9) Limited companies (SAs) may have a Board of Directors or a Board of Management controlled by a SupervisoryBoard which must approve some major decisions. Companies may also be in the form of limited partnerships(Societe en Commandite par actions) which are managed by managers who may be limited companies and oftenappointed on such terms as to make their

10) French labor law provides that a bidder must inform and consult with its unions prior to launching an offer. TheChairman of the target company must similarly inform and consult with his unions once he becomes aware of theoffer. The targetís union can invite the bidder to explain his intentions.

11) Litigation defenses are often useful only as stalling tactics in France. Contesting the legality of bids is generally notlikely, given that bids are made only with the approval of the stock exchange authorities.

Source: "Constraints on Cross-Border Takeovers and Mergers: A Catalogue of Disharmony," *International BusinessLawyer*, February 1991.

P.T. SEMEN GRESIK

Mismanagement, poor regulation or simple inertia had left more than half of state-owned enterprises "unhealthy." State-appointed managers ran companies like fiefdoms; bloated, failing industries were kept alive more from national pride than economic sense. As 1997 came to a close, 164 state firms were reporting a combined pre-tax profit of just $1.2 billion. Yet state enterprises employed more than 700,000 Indonesians and were worth some $60 billion. They were overseen by touchy ministers and entrenched managers. They were wrapped in a mythology of development. Slimming down or selling off these sacred cows meant playing with fire.

"Anatomy of a Deal," by Jose Manuel Tesoro, *AsiaWeek*, January 22, 1999.

On July 6, 1998, the Indonesian government announced that Cementos Mexicanos (Cemex) was the *preferred bidder* for the largest government-owned cement company—PT Semen Gresik. The first round of bidding had pitted Cemex against Holderbank of Switzerland and Heidelberger of Germany, two of the largest cement manufacturing firms in the world. And a mere seven weeks had passed since the resignation of President Suharto, a turning-point in Indonesia's politics and economics.

In a surprise announcement on August 20, Cemex was informed that its first-round bid would have to be restructured, the primary change being a maximum of 14% of ownership passing from the government to Cemex. Then, as *preferred bidder*, Cemex would wait for the other first-round bidders to submit second bids no later than September 28. If their second bids were superior to that of Cemex's first bid, Cemex would have the right to match theirs if it wished. In the event the second bids did not match that of Cemex, Cemex would automatically be declared the winner. Cemex was also required to bid in the second round. The vice president for finance of Cemex, Hector Medina, and his acquisition staff now had only a few weeks to finalize their position.

Indonesian Privatization

The entire process of selling-off Indonesian state firms was directed by Mr. Tanri Abeng, a former deal-maker in Indonesia's private sector and thought to be well-suited for the position as a result of his lack of ties with politicians. Abeng's background encouraged foreign investors to believe that Indonesia's government was serious about its privatization program. Abeng had previously held positions as the head

State-Owned Company	Industry	Financial Adviser
1. Telekomunikasi Indonesia	Telecommunications	Merrill Lynch, Lehman Brothers
2. Indonesia Satellite (Indosat)	Telecommunications	Goldman Sachs
3. Semen Gresik	Cement	Goldman Sachs
4. Tambang Timah	Tin mining	Morgan Stanley, Banque Paribas
5. Aneka Tambang	Gold mining	Morgan Stanley Banque Paribas
6. Tambang Batubara Bukit Asam	Gold mining	Morgan Stanley, Banque Paribas
7. Jasa Marga	Toll road operator	Lehman Brothers
8. Pelabuhan II (Pelindo II)	Port operator	Goldman Sachs
9. Pelabuhan III (Pelindo III)	Port operator	Credit Suisse First Boston
10. Angkasa Pura II	Airport manager	UBS/SBC Warburg Dillon Read
11. Perkebunan Nusantra IV	Plantation	Jardine Fleming
12. Krakatoa Steel	Steel	Salomon Smith Barney

of Indonesian operations for Union Carbide (United States), Heineken (the Netherlands), and finally the Bakrie Group, a diversified Indonesian conglomerate. After being named State Enterprises Minister in 1997 by then President Suharto, he was given a very ambitious revenue target: raise $1.5 billion from the sale of stakes in selected Indonesian state-owned enterprises.

Abeng moved quickly, placing 12 government-owned companies up for sale. The 12 included port-operator *Pelindo*, highway and airport operators, mining companies, agricultural plantations, and telecommunications companies—including *Indosat*. These 12 possessed assets of 461 trillion rupiah (Rp), or $50.6 billion. By early June of 1998 Abeng had arranged for nine different investment banking firms to act as financial advisors and agents to the 12 companies on the auction block.

Goldman Sachs's Indonesian partner, Bahana, was hired to represent the Indonesian cement producer Semen Gresik. In May Abeng appointed Goldman Sachs and Lehman Brothers senior advisors to the Indonesian government in its privatization drive. Exhibit 1 summarizes the firms.

The Indonesian privatization drive was the direct result of the economic crisis in which Indonesia was currently mired, and the subsequent promises made by President Suharto to the International Monetary Fund (IMF) in order to obtain economic and financial assistance. The structural reform program agreement signed with the IMF required Indonesia and President Suharto to open the Indonesian economy to outside investors and market forces. Under the terms of the agreement, Indonesia would sell stakes in four firms by the end of 1998, all 12 companies by the end of 1999.

The World Bank would supervise the privatization process implemented by the government. In stage one, each bidder—upon the completion of due diligence—would submit a binding offer for shares in the company based on directives given by the government (typically on how much of the government's share was actually up for sale). The winning bid would combine financial, social (employment guarantees), and environmental dimensions. The winning bidder of stage one would then enter into a provisional sales agreement with the government. Third parties were then allowed to submit bids in a second stage to improve upon the winning bidder's offer.

EXHIBIT 2   Selected Consolidated Financial Results of Cemex SA (December 31, millions of constant pesos)

	1993	1994	1995	1996	1997
Net sales	25,759	27,687	33,924	35,540	38,464
Operating income	6,269	7,431	8,100	8,482	9,088
Majority net income	4,637	4,951	10,045	10,319	7,725
Earnings per share (EPS)	4.39	4.60	7.81	7.95	6.01
Operating margin (%)	24.4	26.8	23.9	23.8	23.6
EBITDA	8,120	9,471	10,786	11,483	12,116
EBITDA margin (%)	31.6	34.2	31.8	32.3	31.5

EBITDA = earnings before interest, taxes, depreciation and amortization.

Source: Cemex, http://www.cemex.com.

The winning bidder of stage one was then given the right to match the better offer, if it wished, in order to win the bid.

Many of these state-owned enterprises were already publicly traded (minority shares), so that market values did exist for these firms. However, these market capitalizations had been severely degraded following the onslaught of the Asian economic crisis. Markets, in addition to the individual equities traded in these markets, had fallen across Asia. For example, official forecasts for the Indonesian economy expected a 10% fall in total gross domestic product (GDP) for 1998. (The magnitude of this depression and economic collapse is seen when this 10% fall is compared with the deepest recessions in recent U.S. economic history—when GDP fell by a mere 2% during the 1930s.)

Cemex S.A. de C.V.   Founded in 1906, Cementos Mexicanos S.A. (Cemex) is the largest cement manufacturer in the Americas and the third largest cement producer in the world, just behind Holderbank of Switzerland and Lafarge of France. Based in Monterey, Mexico, Cemex has operations in 22 countries and trade relations with over 60 countries worldwide. Cemex is the market leader in Mexico, Spain, Venezuela, Panama, and the Dominican Republic, with a rapidly expanding presence in Colombia, the Caribbean, the southwestern portion of the United States, and most recently the Philippines. Exhibit 2 provides an overview of Cemex's recent financial results. (Appendix 1 provides additional Cemex results.)

Cemex has a corporate strategy which provides much of the impetus for its Asian expansion: 1) to leverage its core cement and ready-mix concrete franchise; 2) to concentrate on developing markets; and 3) to maintain high growth by applying free cash flow toward selective investments that further its geographic diversification. This strategy was focused on repositioning the company from being a dominant regional producer to a true global player in the cement industry.

Most notable regarding Cemex's performance had been its ability to maintain its operating and EBITDA margins over the tumultuous 1990s. Consistently higher than all of its European-based global competitors, the source of its efficiencies rested with a capable combination of relatively new vintage capital facilities, pricing-power and market dominance in its primary markets, and a progressive management group and strategy which focused on customer satisfaction and service (a rare concept in cement markets). The bottom line in all commodity-based industries, however, was operating excellence. Cemex consistently attained margins, even in new acquisitions, which competitors could not match. Operating margins expanded by 18% in Spain after Cemex acquired Valenciana and Sanson, and 19% in Venezuela after acquiring Vencemos.

Cemex had little experience in Asia, but it did possess significant experience of its own in surviving an economic crisis. The devaluation of the Mexican peso in December 1994 and the resulting Mexican economic crisis of 1995 had provided Cemex with some in-house insights into enterprise value. Cemex's own price-to-book value had plunged to 1.16 in March 1995 following the fall of the peso, yet Cemex was able to recover remarkably quickly from this discounting by the equity markets. It hoped to use some of these insights into market valuation in expanding its presence in Asia when Asian cement stocks were themselves trading at significant discounts to what their true values likely were.

> This is most definitely the right time to buy in Asia. The current crisis in Asia has resulted in a fall in value per tonne of capacity for cement companies to US$100 per tonne from US$500 per tonne.
>
> Lorenzo Zambrano, Chairman, Cemex[1]

Cemex's first direct operating activities in Asia commenced with its acquisition of a 30% stake in Rizal Cement of the Philippines in September 1997 for US$100 million. Although Cemex itself had aspirations of expanding across Asia, and the Asian economic crisis had made many firms throughout the Far East relatively cheap, many analysts had grave concerns over the ability of Cemex to digest more acquisitions in the region rapidly. Nonetheless, Cemex continued to pour over the possibilities in the region, paying significant attention to the movements of its major global competitors.[2] In early 1998 Cemex directed Goldman Sachs to find a company in Indonesia in which the firm might acquire a strategic stake. Exhibit 3 provides an overview of the major cement manufacturing firms across the region, their recent earnings and share price performance, and several measures of cement producer valuation.

Valuation

> Value, in our opinion, should be the guiding principle in such turbulent times. While stock prices in efficient markets naturally respond to day-to-day changes in life, this should not cloud the fact that the underlying assets possess an intrinsic economic value. When the market price falls below that value, a profit opportunity arises. . . . Is there value in the Indonesian cement sector and, if there is, when is it going to be realised?[3]

---

[1] *The Financial Times,* November 7, 1997.

[2] Within months of the start of the Asian crisis Holderbank (Switzerland) and Blue Circle (United Kingdom) were both moving on properties in Malaysia and the Philippines, while LaFarge (France) moved to expand into the Philippines and India.

[3] "On the Brink of Value Realization," Indosuez W.I. Carr Securities Limited, June 22, 1998, p. 5.

EXHIBIT 1 Indonesial Enterprises Slated for Privatization and Their Financial Partners

Firm (Country)	Market Cap (US$ million)	EV/ Capacity	EV/ EBITDA	Price/ FCF	Price/ Earnings	Earnings Per Share (EPS) 1997	1998E	Share Price Performance Change	12 mo.	Relative
INDIA										
Associated Cement	460.0	77	12.4	22.1	142.4	56.2	9.2	-84%	3%	6%
Gujarat Ambuja Cement	433.5	128	8.0	11.5	12.4	18.0	18.6	3%	-10%	-8%
India Cement	97.8	64	4.3	4.3	4.9	12.8	12.0	-6%	-8%	-6%
Madras Cement	102.7	73	4.2	3.8	5.8	642.7	572.2	-11%	-59%	-58%
Average		86	7.2	10.4	41.4			-19%	-17%	
INDONESIA										
Indocement	957.9	39	12.6	15.8	(27.9)	(371.1)	(123.8)	improved	38%	82%
Semen Gesik	461.9	53	8.5	11.4	56.0	(90.2)	121.0	improved	-14%	14%
Semen Cibinong	49.5	65	5.5	0.5	(1.1)	2.0	(334.0)	-16800%	-61%	-48%
Average		52	8.9	9.2	9.0			-12%	61%	
THAILAND										
Siam Cement	926.6	190	7.2	4.1	(1.5)	(440.3)	(37.5)	improved	-48%	-23%
Siam City Cement	338.3	97	9.8	10.0	(3.7)	(96.0)	(36.6)	improved	-2%	44%
TPI Polene	71.7	150	15.2	(1.3)	(1.3)	(53.4)	(28.4)	improved	-79%	-68%
Average		146	10.7	4.3	(2.2)			-43%	-16%	
MALAYSIA										
Cement Industries	69.6	26	9.3	11.5	(91.3)	52.7	(2.3)	-104%	-70%	-44%
Kedah Cement	109.4	93	5.1	2.7	4.0	28.3	26.5	-6%	-76%	-55%
Malayan Cement	238.9	45	20.1	11.0	6.7	29.8	10.0	-66%	-56%	-17%
Average		55	11.5	84	(26.9)			-67%	-38%	
PHILIPPINES										
Alsons	54.0	40	4.0	4.6	4.4	0.6	0.5	-17%	-74%	-56%
Davao Union Cement	19.3	56	3.0	2.0	1.9	0.4	0.3	-25%	-89%	-81%
Fortune Cement	120.6	96	6.2	7.2	10.0	0.4	0.4	0%	-66%	-44%
Hi Cement	60.3	39	3.1	3.1	5.8	0.7	0.5	-29%	-68%	-47%
Average		58	4.1	4.2	5.5			-74%	-57%	
TAIWAN										
Asia Cement	1,716.2	228	10.1	8.9	13.9	2.3	2.4	4%	-23%	-33%
Taiwan Cement	1,343.7	147	14.1	14.1	25.4	1.2	1.4	17%	-38%	-46%
Average		188	12.1	11.5	19.7			-30%	-40%	
SOUTH KOREA										
Hanil Cement	65.4	25	4.2	3.0	11.5	2,186.5	2,031.0	-7%	-48%	-29%
Ssaangyong Cement	84.8	70	8.0	2.1	11.5	529.2	392.3	-26%	-60%	-45%
Tong Yang Cement	35.5	62	6.0	1.5	6.8	1,151.0	1,061.7	-8%	-59%	-45%
Average		52	6.1	2	9.9			-56%	-40%	

All values are estimates for 1998 unless otherwise stated. Market capitalization as of March 2, 1998. Enterprise Value (EV) calculated as total market capitalization plus net debt.

Source: Constructed by author from Paribas Asia Equity and other sources.

In addition to most of the traditional valuation techniques (price to earnings, price to free cash flow, earnings per share growth) there are typically additional techniques useful in specific industries. Two such techniques widely used in the cement industry are *enterprise value to capacity* and *enterprise value to EBITDA* (earnings before interest, taxes, depreciation and amortization).

Enterprise value to capacity is a frequently used method of valuation in the cement industry, and is calculated by dividing *enterprise value* (the total of market capitalization and net debt) by the existing installed capacity of the cement producer. Because of standardized technology across countries, EV/capacity provides a very clear indicator of how different companies may be described as under- or over-valued. Industry experts estimated the *set-up costs* (*replacement cost*) in Asia to be roughly US$160/tonne for a standard 1.5 million metric tons per year (mmt/y) production facility.

Enterprise value to EBITDA is a more common measure of value used across all industries, and focuses on the market's current market capitalization to the current pre-financing and tax based operating earnings of the firm. Similarly, *price to free cash flow* (P/FCF) and *price-to-earnings* (PE) ratios also provide market values to firm cash flows and earnings by more standard methodologies.

As illustrated in Exhibit 3, the lowest EV/capacity in Asia in 1998 were the producers in Indonesia (52), South Korea (52), and Malaysia (55). The lowest EV/EBITDA values were found in a different subset of countries, with the lowest being the Philippines (4.1), South Korea (6.1), and India (7.2). The cement producers of Indonesia and Thailand had suffered negative earnings in 1997 and 1998, although the expectations for 1998 were for significant improvement (but still negative for these two countries). The other manufacturers across the region were still sliding, at least in regard to expected earnings for 1998. Share price performance for cement manufacturers since the inception of the crisis in June 1997 was, however, unambiguously disastrous.

The prospects of the Indonesian cement industry were not clear. In March the Indonesian government announced it would deregulate the local guideline price system (HPS), and the Indonesian Cement Association (ASI) would assume responsibility for supervision of cement distribution and control of cement prices. This was expected to result in price wars as excess supply of cement was expected to continue through the year 2002. Prices could fall by 10% to Rp139,500 per tonne. Because cement is a bulk commodity with high transportation costs, markets are typically geographically defined. Prices therefore vary significantly from one region or country to another.

The Asian currency crisis had led to a significant differentiation—some would say *distortion*—of relative costs and prices across the Asian cement industry. As seen in Exhibit 4, cash costs ranged from a low of $10/tonne in Indonesia to $30/tonne in Taiwan. At the same time, prices were also the lowest in Indonesia, currently falling to $16/tonne, while Pakistan and Taiwan earned $55 and $54/tonne, respectively. The result was an Indonesian industry which was the lowest cost, but also relatively low in gross margin.

The large discrepancies in costs and prices had led many of the world's largest cement producers to consider something long forgotten, large scale low-cost production and international distribution through exports. For example, the Taiwanese cement

EXHIBIT 4 Bagged Cement Prices and Cash Costs Across Asia, June 1998

Country	Ex-Factory Price (US$/tonne)	Cash Costs (US$/tonne)	Margin (US$/tonne)	Gross Margin (per tonne)
Pakistan	55	29	26	47%
Malaysia	40	26	14	35%
India	46	27	19	41%
Philippines	39	23	16	41%
Korea	39	28	11	28%
Taiwan	54	30	24	44%
Thailand	38	20	18	47%
Indonesia	16	10	6	38%
Average	41	24	17	40%

Source: Indosua W.I. Carr Securities, June 12, 1998.

market may be quite vulnerable to Indonesian exports. Assuming cash production costs in Indonesia of $10/tonne, loading costs (on both ends) of $2/tonne, and shipping costs to Kaohsiung (Taiwan) from East Java (Indonesia) of $10/tonne, Indonesian exports could severely undercut domestic Taiwanese producers.[4] Several analysts argued that even the United States cement markets may be vulnerable to Indonesian exports if shipping costs between Indonesia and the U.S. could be kept at $35 to $40/tonne. Cement prices in the U.S. hovered just below $75/tonne. Semen Gresik was currently in the process of a significant upgrading of its port facilities to increase its export capabilities. (Appendix 2 provides a discounted cash flow valuation of PT Semen Gresik.)

PT Semen Gresik

> We believe that Gresik would be on the top of the list of acquisition targets for foreign cement players. The partial sell-down of the government's 65% stake will represent a unique opportunity for the foreign players to take a meaningful stake in the Indonesian cement industry (previously closed). However, in our view this foreign interest is dependent on, at a minimum, gaining management control.[5]

Semen Gresik began producing cement in 1957 by exploiting large and readily accessible limestone deposits in East Java, and was the first government-owned cement producer in Indonesia to go public, issuing 35% of its shares on the Jakarta exchange in July 1991. The ownership structure had not changed since 1991, with 65% of the shares held by the Indonesian government and 35% free float on the Jakarta exchange. The 1998 Indonesian privatization program was focused on maximizing the revenues per share received by the government for some proportion of the 65% held by the government.

Semen Gresik had become the largest Indonesian cement producer in September 1995 when it had purchased Semen Padang (West Sumatra) and Semen Tonasa (South Sulawesi) for a total of $476 million. The three companies still operated

---

[4] Export cost estimates drawn primarily from Indosuez I.D. Carr Securities, June 12, 1998, p.11.

[5] Ibid, p.17.

EXHIBIT 5 Indonesia's Major Cement Manufacturers

	Semen Gresik	Semen Indocement	Semen Cibinong	Andalas
Installed capacity (mmt/y)	17.0	15.5	10.5	1.2
Market share	43%	35%	17%	5%
Dominant market in Indonesia	East Java	Jakarta	West Java	–
1997 sales (mmt)	11.7	9.5	4.6	1.4
1998e sales (mmt)	7.0	5.7	2.8	0.8
Change in sales, 1997 to 1998	-40%	-40%	-39%	-43%
1998e capacity utilization	41%	37%	27%	67%
Costs comparison:				
Production costs (Rp/tonne)	135,478	145,956	155,009	na
Production costs (US$/tonne)	13.6	14.6	15.5	na
Cash costs (Rp/tonne)	115,949	117,844	129,411	na
Cash costs (US$/tonne)	11.6	11.8	12.0	na
Debt in Rupiah (billion)	Rp1,792	Rp 391	Rp 40	na
Debt in U.S. dollars (million)	$226	$889	$903	na
Primary owner	Government	Private	Private	Government
Minority owner	Market	None	Holderbank	None
Status	Privatizing	Partner?	Stable	Privatizing

na=not available. e= estimated. Costs for Semen Gresik are numerical average of the three primary production facilities.

Source: Deutsche Bank Research, Mexican Special Report, July 6, 1998, p. 5.

separately, maintaining independent administrative structures. Although this added substantial capacity to Semen Gresik's resources, it was also an unpopular government-directed consolidation as fears arose over possibilities of layoffs and reorganizations away from the outer island/provinces.

The Indonesian market, however, like all cements markets around the globe, was regional in nature. The largest markets in Indonesia were Jakarta—dominated by Indocement—and West Java—dominated by Semen Cibinong. Regardless of which region the individual producer dominated, the Asian crisis had hit all the major producers. Indocement and Cibinong were expected to only reach 37% and 27% capacity utilization rates in 1998, respectively. All producers were expected to see 1998 annual sales volumes fall by roughly 40% from the previous year. Exhibit 5 provides an overview of the major Indonesian cement producers as of July 1998.

Semen Gresik's management of the Asian economic crisis had, however, been relatively successful. As a result of rising input costs (roughly 10% of Gresik's production costs were imported), the firm—all three operational units—had increased its ex-factory prices by over 40% in the spring of 1998, to an average of Rp 229,000 per tonne (US$23/tonne at the then current exchange rate of Rp 10,000/$). Appendices 3 and 4 provide recent and pro forma income statements, cash flows, and balance sheets for Semen Gresik.

Bidding for Semen Gresik

Tari Abeng believed that Semen Gresik was the proper choice to begin the state's privatization program. President Suharto agreed, and allowed Abeng to proceed without interference.[6] The firm was considered one of the best managed government-run enterprises, and had shown some resiliency in the declining business conditions suffered by most in the current crisis. Gresik was not only the largest Indonesian cement producer, it was generally regarded as potentially the most efficient, particularly with so much of its existing capacity using the latest technology, and being of such a recent vintage. Roughly 30% of Semen Gresik's installed capacity had come on-line in 1996 and 1997.

In the midst of rising political tension throughout Indonesia—focused primarily on the push for President Suharto's resignation—Abeng initiated negotiations on May 5 with three of the world's largest cement manufacturers: Holderbank, Heidelberger, and Cemex. Holderbank, fresh off the acquisition of Union Cement (Philippines) and Siam City (Thailand), appeared the most aggressive. Cemex's due diligence team of 30 professionals arrived in Indonesia six days later. On May 17, President Suharto resigned. After a temporary pause in the process, Abeng proceeded with the privatization process. Heidelberg withdrew at this stage, leaving only Cemex and Holderbank to pursue the allotted two-week period of due diligence. On June 19, both companies filed their bids. Holderbank offered $0.96/share, roughly $200 million. The Cemex bid was much higher—$1.38/share—a potential investment of $287 million (both bids were for 207.6 million shares).

At this point Tari Abeng's gamesmanship became apparent. Departing from the original privatization program outlined by the World Bank, Abeng invited both bidders to up their bids at this point without revealing the bids submitted by either party. While Cemex confirmed its existing bid, Holderbank increased its bid to $1.21/share, or $251 million. Cemex was officially declared the winner and the *preferred bidder* for the final stage two.

Cemex's winning stage one bid was actually a complex combination offer:

1. A bid of $1.38/share for 35% of Semen Gresik's shares held by the Indonesian government. Given a current share price of Rp 9,150 (about $0.63/share at the current exchange rate of Rp14,500/$), this represented nearly a 100% premium.

2. An announced intention to purchase an additional 16% of the company's shares on the open market, bringing its total constructed position to 51%.

3. A five-year put option to the Indonesian government to sell its remaining shares to Cemex at a base price of $1.38/share plus an 8.2% annual premium.

4. A one-off payment of $129 million to the Indonesian government in 2006 if Semen Gresik's performance surpassed specific expectations.

5. A contribution of approximately $50 million to the on-going port facilities upgrade and capacity expansion of Semen Gresik (bringing it up to 17.5 mmt/y capacity; see Appendix 5).

---

[6] Krakatoa Steel had actually been the first privatization subject, but had run into a variety of delays resulting in a still-borne privatization program.

This purchase of 207.6 million shares would reap the government approximately $287 million.[7] If the additional 16% were tendered at roughly the same price, the investment for control of Semen Gresik by Cemex would total $417.5 million. This was approximately one-quarter of what Indonesia had promised the IMF to raise through privatization—in just the first of the 12 firm sales.

Growing Opposition　　Meanwhile, social and political tensions were rising over the falling employment levels of the Indonesian economy. A number of prominent Indonesian government officials raised questions regarding the wisdom of selling valuable Indonesian assets to foreign interests, particularly in light of the control these powers would exert over the companies and their employees. The management of Semen Gresik itself had previously been under pressure to assure employment levels at its Tonasa and Padang subsidiaries (acquired in 1995), and now the prospect of this parent becoming further subordinated itself was not a popular one.

A second area of debate arose over the process itself. A number of prominent bankers in Jakarta were quoted in the press as questioning both the transparency of the process directed by Abeng, and the ethics of the process. At the center of the controversy was whether the investment banking firm—Goldman Sachs—was not actually playing both sides of the street. Goldman Sachs represented both the potential buyer (Cemex) and the seller (the Indonesian government). By mid-July the controversy reached its zenith, the pressure resulting in Goldman Sachs resigning as Cemex's advisor:

> Goldman Sachs decided to withdraw in the interest of transparency. We didn't think there was anything illegal in what Goldman Sachs was doing. The bank simply wanted to avoid further public debate over its role.
> Sofyan Djalil, Special Assistant to Minister of State Enterprises

Cemex immediately replaced Goldman with Jardine Fleming. Despite the resignation, Goldman Sachs' relationship with Bahana remained controversial. As described by Goldman Sachs, the relationship was "a joint operating agreement with no current cross-ownership." In principle, the problem was one of suspicion in an environment which could not at that time allow suspicion to arise.[8]

A third debate, one which erupted literally days after the culmination of the first stage, was the announcement by the Jakarta Stock Market's watchdog organization—*Bapepam*—of a probe into insider trading in Semen Gresik shares. Evidence put forward to suggest the possibility was that Gresik shares had risen 57% in the month of June while the general market fell. On the day of bid submission (June 19), a record 62 million shares of Gresik were traded, closing above Rp8,700/share for the first time. Bapepam announced that the investigation would focus on the trading activities at Jardine Fleming (now associated with

---

[7] Semen Gresik had 35% of its shares publicly issued, totaling 593,200,000 shares. 65% of Gresik's share ownership was held by the Indonesian government, totaling 1,101,700,000 shares.

[8] The sensitivity of this topic is summarized well by Michael Vatikiotis: "Indonesians cannot be accused of cynicism if they say that these investment banks are guilty of the same kind of collusion and nepotism which brought down the Suharto regime," from "Banking on Big Names," *Far Eastern Economic Review*, 11/19/98.

Cemex), Bahana (aligned with Goldman Sachs), and the state-controlled investment bank Danareksa Securities.

Although the bids submitted by the two companies were for shares held by the Indonesian government, and the actual bids submitted secretly, both companies had been quite public in their plans to acquire additional shares sold on the open market in combination with a winning bid. Both firms wished to acquire control of Gresik, and that would have to be done by combining government shares with free-floating shares. The investigation into insider trading continued for months with no violations ever substantiated. The bidding process would continue.

Indonesia Backs Off   For months rumors had been circulating in West Sumatra that the new owners of Semen Gresik would lay off nearly half the 3,000 employees of Semen Padang's operations. Cemex's acquisition team had, during the due diligence process in which the team had direct contact with present Gresik management and labor, guaranteed that no one would be laid off before the year 2000. Demonstrations intensified in West Sumatra and Jakarta, however, after the first round of bidding. Protests in Jakarta grew in size and fervor, and by late July were occurring nearly daily (eventually resulting in the posting of signs designating a "Demonstration Area"). Rumors that management at Semen Padang paid demonstrators in both West Sumatra and Jakarta were denied by employees.

The governor of West Sumatra then threatened to remove certain land rights and concessions provided to Semen Padang if control of Semen Gresik was allowed to pass to foreign investors. The opposition parties became more and more public with their demands and threats, promising they would occupy the properties of Semen Padang in the event of foreign acquisition. The final tide turned when Azwar Anas, a former army general, former West Sumatra governor, and former CEO of Semen Padang (prior to acquisition in 1995) took the unofficial lead in opposing the privatization. On August 11 Tanri Abeng was called to testify before the Economic Committee of Indonesia's Supreme Advisory Council. Here Abeng finally capitulated to the growing pressure.

> I was able to grasp that the real reason behind the resistance is purely emotional and cultural. Nothing to do with economics. From there on, I knew, no way. We are fighting a losing battle if we push so hard.
>
> Tanri Abeng, August 12th

Abeng informed Cemex that the sale of Semen Gresik would have to be restructured and the second round of bidding would be postponed. Speculation on the structure of the new sale intensified, and in a conference call with Morgan Stanley Dean Witter, the Managing Director of Semen Gresik stated that he believed the company would still be sold as one, and not broken up into the individual units (Semen Padang, Semen Tonasa, Semen Gresik). It was also rumored that the winning bidder would be required to make a tender offer to the public minority shareholders at the same price as the bid price, but only if taking more than a 20% position from the government.

Final Bids

On August 20 Tanri Abeng's Office of State Enterprises announced that the government would entertain bids for only 14% of Semen Gresik rather than the original 35% offered, assuring that the government would remain the controlling shareholder after the sale. Tanri Abeng's office informed Cemex that its stage one bid would have to be restructured, keeping its preferred bidder status, and then the second round bids would be accepted. It was now up to Cemex to determine what it wished to do in its restructured stage one bid. Competitor bids were due no later than September 28, a little more than five weeks from now.

Appendix 1   Selected Consolidated Financial Results of Cemex SA (millions of constant pesos)

Income Statement Information	1993	1994	1995	1996	1997	1998
Net sales	25,729	27,687	33,924	35,540	38,464	42,720
Cost of sales	15,512	15,968	20,689	21,550	23,571	24,701
Gross Profit	10,217	11,719	13,235	13,990	14,893	18,019
Operating Expenses	3,948	4,288	5,135	5,518	5,805	6,360
Operating Income	6,269	7,431	8,100	8,472	9,088	11,659
Comprehensive Financing Costs	221	(213)	7,498	5,588	1,611	(1,309)
Other Income (Expenses)	(895)	(1,754)	(2,142)	(1,801)	(1,396)	(1,506)
Income BeforeTaxes & Others	5,595	5,464	13,456	12,259	9,303	8,844
Minority Interest	861	595	1,440	1,256	1,083	391
Majority Net Income	4,637	4,951	10,045	10,319	7,725	7,952
Earnings Per Share (EPS)	4.39	4.60	7.81	7.95	6.01	6.30
Dividends Per Share (DPS)	0.81	0.83	0.87	na	na	1.18
Number of Shares Outstanding	1,056	1,077	1,286	1,303	1,268	1,258
Balance Sheet Information						
Cash andTemporary Investments	2,900	6,385	4,691	4,316	3,862	4,027
Net Working Capital	5,285	6,954	7,498	6,452	5,971	6,320
Property Plant & Equipment (net)	39,145	53,944	65,337	60,646	60,976	60,805
Total Assets	71,212	104,027	110,738	104,998	103,878	103,551
Short Term Debt	6,073	8,534	11,515	8,609	6,674	10,948
Long-Term Debt	25,455	41,059	40,135	41,757	40,213	31,049
Total Liabilities	35,723	56,546	60,901	59,197	56,198	52,682
Minority Interests	6,845	10,158	11,758	10,562	11,992	12,384
Stockholders Equity, ex Minority	28,644	37,323	38,079	35,239	35,689	38,484
Total Stockholders Equity	35,489	47,481	49,837	45,801	47,681	50,868
Book value per share	27.12	34.65	29.62	27.15	27.80	30.49
Other Financial Data						
Operating Margin	24.4%	26.8%	23.9%	23.8%	23.6%	27.3%
EBITDA Margin	31.6%	34.2%	31.8%	32.3%	31.5%	34.4%
EBITDA	8,120	9,471	10,786	11,483	12,116	14,697
Cash Earnings	4,950	5,873	3,020	4,993	7,316	10,263
Cash Earnings Per Share	4.69	5.45	2.35	3.85	5.70	8.13

Source: Cemex SA , http://www.cemex.com

Appendix 2   Discounted Cash Flow Valuation of the PT Semen Gresik Group

Assumptions	Value	Assumptions	Value
Cost of capital:		FX rate (Rp/$)	13,000
Risk-free rate	33.7%	Inflation	29.4%
Equity risk premium	6.0%	Tax rate	30.0%
Beta	1.20	Growth rate of operating CF	30.4%
After-tax cost of debt	23.6%	Terminal value growth rate	5.0%
Cost of equity	40.9%	Working capital to sales ratio	14.0%
Percentage debt	50%		
Percentage equity	50%		
Weighted cost of capital	32.2%		

Billions of Rp	1998	1999	2000	2001	2002
Assumed growth rate	*16%*	*27%*	*20%*	*20%*	*20%*
EBIT	458.0	614.0	736.8	884.2	1,061.0
Add depreciation & amortization	261.0	276.0	276.0	276.0	276.0
EBITDA	719.0	890.0	1,012.8	1,160.2	1,337.0
Less changes in net work capital	(19.0)	(21.8)	(17.2)	(20.6)	(24.8)
Less capex	(40.0)	(40.0)			
Terminal value					74,680.1
Total FCF	660.0	828.2	995.6	1,139.5	75,992.3
Present value factor	1.0000	0.7562	0.5718	0.4324	0.3270
Present value of cash flow	660.0	626.2	569.3	492.7	24,845.8
Cumulative present value					27,194.0

Enterprise value	27,194.0	Terminal value as % of total EV:	90%
Less net debt	(4,113.5)	Implied Price to FCF (1998):	58.9
Less minority interests	(23.1)		
Equity value, total	23,057.4		
Shares outstanding (millions)	593.2		
Fair value of equity per share	38,869		
In US dollars $	2.99		

Capital cost assumptions from Paribas Asia Equity, "Semen Gresik," August 1998, p.3.

Appendix 3 PT Semen Gresik's Historical & Pro Forma Income Cash Flows (billion rupiah)

Statement of Income	1996	1997	1998F	1999F
Sales by unit:				
Gresik	625	608	874	1,189
Tonasa	235	465	437	522
Padang	485	495	511	607
Non-cement	17	20	20	20
Total net sales	1,362	1,588	1,842	2,338
Growth in net sales (%)		17%	16%	27%
COGS Gresik	(365)	(377)	(534)	(734)
COGS Tonasa	(144)	(290)	(289)	(345)
COGS Padang	(273)	(286)	(277)	(317)
Total cost of goods sold	(782)	(953)	(1,100)	(1,396)
Gross profit	580	635	742	942
Gross margin (% of net sales)	43%	40%	40%	40%
Less selling, general & admin expenses	(259)	(313)	(284)	(328)
Operating profit	321	322	458	614
Less net interest	(43)	(101)	(279)	(535)
Contributions from subsidiaries	3	4	5	6
Others	5	9	10	10
Non-operating income	(35)	(89)	(264)	(519)
Pretax profit	286	234	194	95
Less Indonesian taxes	(65)	(44)	(29)	(11)
Minorities	(4)	(5)	(6)	(6)
Net profit	217	185	159	78
Return on sales (%)	16%	12%	9%	3%
Effective tax rate (%)	23%	19%	15%	12%

Cash Flow (billion rupiah)	1996	1997	1998e	1999e
Profit before interest & taxes	321	322	458	614
Depreciation & amortization	138	180	261	276
Associated adjustments	(3)	(4)	(5)	(6)
Change in net working capital	156	(466)	(96)	(144)
Operating Cash Flow	612	32	618	740
Taxes paid	(65)	(44)	(29)	(11)
Interest paid	(43)	(101)	(279)	(535)
Capitalized interest	(92)	(178)	(187)	(263)
Forex gains (losses)	-	(286)	(674)	-
Cash earnings	412	(577)	(551)	(69)
Dividends paid	(65)	(65)	(74)	-
Net capex (disposal)	(592)	(1,337)	(648)	(60)
Change in share capital	-	-	-	-
Others	(248)	-	-	-
Change in net debt	(493)	(1,979)	(1,273)	(129)
Ending cash (debt)	(1,003)	(2,982)	(4,255)	(4,384)

Source: Barings, March 3, 1998.

Appendix 4 PT Semen Gresik's Balance Sheet (billions of rupiah)

Assets	1992	1993	1994	1995	1996	1997
Cash & banks	336	140	52	275	220	461
Accounts receivable	14	5	17	145	179	238
Inventory	30	45	82	175	228	323
Other current	8	19	20	54	81	82
Total current assets	388	209	171	649	708	1,104
Fixed assets	108	109	769	1,471	2,090	2,282
Investments	14	3	6	45	14	14
Other assets	383	649	60	1,186	1,418	2,037
Total assets	893	970	1,006	3,351	4,230	5,437
Liabilities & Net Worth						
Trade payables	-	8	17	41	76	82
Accounts payable	6	21	17	62	309	414
Taxes payable	4	14	4	32	49	51
Other payables	17	4	18	70	47	-
Long-term debt (current)	-	40	79	287	227	93
Notes payable	-	-	-	-	136	-
Current liabilities	27	87	135	492	844	640
Long-term debt	182	181	139	532	900	2,339
Minorities	-	10	11	14	18	20
Share capital	148	148	148	593	593	593
Revaluation surplus	240	240	240	1,252	1,252	1,252
Reserves	293	302	333	468	622	600
Shareholders' funds	681	690	721	2,313	2,467	2,445
Total capital	863	881	871	2,859	3,385	4,804
Net assets	866	883	871	2,859	3,386	4,797
(Total assets - current liabilities)						

Source: Barings, March 3, 1998.

Appendix 5 Installed Capacity of the PT Semen Gresik Group (millions metric tons/year)

Semen Gresik (Java):	1994	1995	1996	1997	1998
Gresik I	500	500	500	208	208
Gresik II	1,300	1,300	1,300	1,300	1,300
Tuban I	575	2,300	2,300	2,300	2,300
Tuban II	-	-	-	2,300	2,300
Tuban III	-	-	-	-	2,400
Total	2,375	4,100	4,100	6,108	8,508
Semen Padang (Sumatra, acquired 1995):					
Indatung I	254	254	254	254	254
Indatung II	660	660	660	660	660
Indatung III	660	660	660	660	660
Indatung IV	1,620	1,620	1,620	1,620	1,620
Indatung V	-	-	-	-	2,300
Total	3,194	3,194	3,194	3,194	5,494
Semen Tonasa (Sulawesi, acquired 1995):					
Tonasa I	-	-	-	-	-
Tonasa II	590	590	590	590	590
Tonasa III	590	590	590	590	590
Tonasa IV	-	-	2,300	2,300	2,300
Total	1,180	1,180	3,480	3,480	3,480
Total under Gesik Ownership	2,375	8,474	10,774	12,782	17,482
Percent change (%)	32%	257%	27%	19%	37%

Source: Morgan Stanley Dean Witter, June 22, 1998, p. 4, and ING Barings, March 3, 1998, p. 2.

Appendix 6 PT Semen Gresik's Share Price and Market Capitalization for Selected Dates (1998)

Date	Share Price (Rp)	Exchange Rate (Rp/$)	Implied Price (US$)	Market Capitalization (Rp)	Market Capitalization (US$)
Feb 3	6775	9,750	$ 0.69	3,997,250	410
March 3	5,600	9,300	$ 0.60	3,304,000	355
June 19	9,150	14,500	$ 0.63	5,398,500	372
July 6	9,150	14,700	$ 0.62	5,398,500	367
July 10	9,150	14,600	$ 0.63	5,398,500	370
Aug 18	10,775	12,000	$ 0.90	6,357,250	530
Aug 21	8,750	12,000	$ 0.73	5,162,500	430
Aug 28	10,500	13,000	$ 0.81	6,195,000	477

Note: Market capitalization on the basis of the following shares outstanding: 593,200,000

Appendix 7 Daily Exchange Rates: Indonesian Rupiah per U.S. Dollar

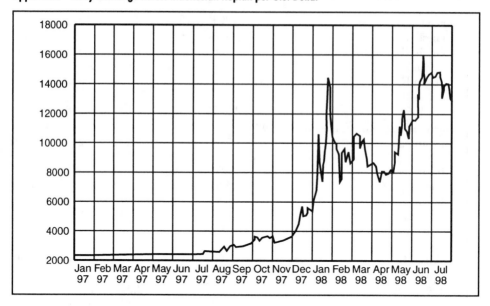

Appendix 8 PT Semen Gresik Share Price, April 1–August 24, 1998

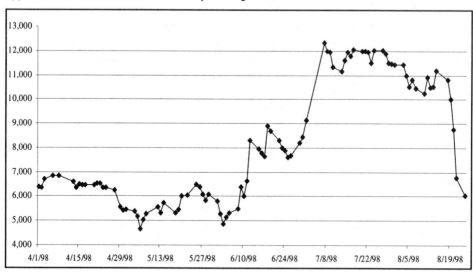

A06-99-0025

THUNDERBIRD
THE AMERICAN GRADUATE SCHOOL
OF INTERNATIONAL MANAGEMENT

TIANJIN PLASTICS (CHINA)

The surge in foreign direct investment spending is easing back from its 1994 highs as the authorities seek to channel funds into so-called priority areas—away from real estate and towards high-tech manufacturing production, infrastructure expenditure, energy and communications and, on a geographical basis, increasingly into the 18 inland provinces.

Recent guidelines, however, continue to fail to offer sufficient incentives for expanded participation in the infrastructure sector as far as foreign investors are concerned. Plans to attract US$20 billion into China's power sector by the year 2000, for example, are hampered by the ceiling of 15% put on investment rates of return.

"Struggling With Reform,"
Corporate Finance Foreign Exchange Yearbook 1995/96, p. viii.

It was May 1996, and Pat Johnson looked out the window at the seemingly perpetual New England winter. His recommendation regarding the financial viability of the Tianjin Plastics power plant project in China was due in two days. The recommendation would require a final evaluation of all financing options—project financing, as well as reaching contract closure with his joint venture partner, Tianjin Plastics/Chinese Ministry of Power Industry (MOPI). Pat was the project finance analyst for Maple Energy, a U.S.-based international power plant developer. The problems with the project as proposed were substantial. Pat was afraid that even if the basic financials could be structured to be acceptable to both Maple and MOPI, Maple would face substantial risks in getting its investment dollars back out of China. And it was snowing again.

Maple Energy

Maple Energy (US) was a wholly-owned subsidiary of Northern States Utilities. Since its inception in 1989, Maple has successfully completed power plant projects in Argentina, Costa Rica, the Dominican Republic, and the United Kingdom. Current project development focused on Asia, particularly India and the People's Republic of China (PRC).

Maple was truly a *developer* of power plant projects. Maple would structure the agreement for the construction of a power plant (usually a joint venture arrangement with a local partner), arrange the necessary financing, acquire and contract for all power sales once the project was fully operational, and subcontract to other firms the construction and actual operation. The power plant itself was a "turnkey EPC," an engineering procurement and construction contract in which the contractor designs, builds, and tests the power plant, so that the actual owners only have to turn the key to run it.

Most power plant projects like the one under consideration by Maple and Tianjin Plastics were undertaken as *project finance* ventures. Project financing is a method by which large stand-alone investments may be financed on the basis of their own assets and cash flows, with no substantial recourse to the assets of the equity holders themselves. Project financing is the primary method by which the massive infrastructure investment was taking place throughout southeast Asia, including China, Malaysia, Indonesia, the Philippines, India, Bangladesh, Pakistan, Laos, Thailand, Vietnam, and a host of other emerging economies. Pat, although well-versed in the intricacies of project finance (they were typically extremely detailed agreements requiring thousands of pages of documentation), was extremely uncomfortable with the problems posed by the Tianjin proposal.

Project Finance

Project finance was not new. Examples of project financing go back centuries, many of the earliest examples actually providing the financing of merchant trade with Asia. Trading companies such as the Dutch East India Company and the British East India Company financed their trade on a voyage-by-voyage basis. Each individual voyage's financing would be returned upon the return of the ship, from which the fruits of the Asian marketplace were sold at the docks to Mediterranean and European merchants, and the individual shareholders of the voyage paid in full.

In many ways little had changed about the financing needs of Asian investment. Although the investment was now for infrastructure such as electricity, water, railways, telecommunications networks, and resource-based industries like mining rather than for spices and silk, project finance was still the preferable approach. Pat knew that each individual project was different, but they all had a similar set of characteristics, listed in Exhibit 1, lending them (pun intended) to project finance.

In order to attract capital to a project, the lenders must feel secure that they will be repaid. Bankers are not by nature entrepreneurs, and they do not enjoy entrepreneurial returns from project finance. The banks are not providing venture capital and they do not accept risks that are more properly the responsibility of equity investors.[1] The problem presented by project financing lies in the balancing of the needs of the sponsor for total non-recourse financing with the needs of the banks, whose aim is to be assured of repayment either from the project, the sponsor, or some interested third party.

---

[1] The risks normally associated with project financing include: reserve or resource risk, operating risks, market risk, *force majeure* risk, political risk, foreign exchange risk, currency conversion risk, and completion risk. An essential element of the structuring of project financing is which party (bank, project sponsor, or offtake contractor) assumes the responsibility for each of the risks listed.

EXHIBIT 1 Characteristics of a Viable Project Financing

1.	The project must be backed by a strong credit; the sponsor should be financially healthy to assure lenders that the sponsor will be around to build it and operate over its lifespan.
2.	The risk involved relates to credit and not to equity or venture capital.
3.	The project itself must be financially viable.
4.	Supply contracts for the product must be in place at a cost consistent with the financial projections.
5.	A market for the product must be assured at a price consistent with the financial projections.
6.	The contractor who is to construct the project must be acceptable.
7.	Financial capability and technical expertise must be available to cover cost overruns and complete the project.
8.	The sponsor or the borrower must be capable of operating the project.
9.	The project must not represent new/unproven technology.
10.	There must be an appropriate equity contribution.
11.	Adequate insurance must be available, both during construction and operations.
12.	Any required government approvals must be available.

Qualitatively, the characteristics lead to a set of properties which are critical to the success of a *project financing*.

1. **Separability of the project from its investors.** The project is established as an individual legal entity, separate from the legal and financial responsibilities of its individual investors. This not only serves to protect the assets of equity investors, it provides a controlled platform upon which creditors can evaluate the risks associated with the singular project, the ability of the project's cash flows to service its debt, and assurance that the debt-service payments will be automatically allocated by the project, not by the complex decision making arising from the multinational firm.

2. **Long-lived capital intensive singular projects.** Not only must the individual project be separable and large in proportion to the financial resources of its owners, its business line must be singular, singular in its construction and operation at a set capacity. The capacity is set at inception, and is seldom, if ever, changed over the project's life.

   Examples of project finance have included some of the largest individual investments undertaken in the past three decades: British Petroleum's financing of its interests in the North Sea (totaling $972 million in 1972); the Trans-Alaska Pipeline, a joint venture between Standard Oil of Ohio, Atlantic Richfield, Exxon, British Petroleum, Mobil Oil, Phillips Petroleum, Union Oil, and Amerada Hess (1978). Each of these represent capital expenditures which no single firm would/could attempt to finance.[2] Yet, through a joint venture arrangement, the higher than normal risks absorbed by the capital employed could be managed.

3. **Cash flow predictability from third-party commitments.** An oil field or an electric power plant produced a homogeneous commodity product which would produce predictable cash flows if third party commitments to take and pay could be established. In addition to revenue predictability, non-financial costs of production needed to be controlled over time, usually through long-term supplier contracts with price adjustment clauses based on inflation. This predictability of net cash inflows through long-term contracts eliminated much of the individual project's business risk, allowing the financial structure to be heavily debt-financed (sometimes over 80% debt) but still 'safe' from financial distress.

The predictability of a project's revenue stream is essential in securing project financing. Typical contract provisions which are intended to assure adequate cash flow normally include the following issues: quantity and quality of the project's output; a pricing formula that enhances the predictability of an adequate margin to cover operating costs and debt service payments; a clear statement of the circumstances that permit significant changes in the contract such as force majeure or adverse business conditions.

4. **Finite projects with finite lives.** Even with a longer-term investment, it is critical that the project have a definite ending point at which all debt and equity has been repaid. Because the project is a stand-alone investment in which its cash flows go directly to the servicing of its capital structure, and not to reinvestment for growth or other investment alternatives, investors of all kinds need assurances that the project's returns will be attained in a finite period. There is no capital appreciation, there is only cash flow.

Pat's checklist indicated that Tianjin seemed to meet all of the basic requirements. But the basic law of project finance was his paramount concern: the debt-service payments of any project finance proposal must match as closely as possible the ability of the project to generate earnings. The devil was indeed in the details.

The Tianjin Plastics Joint Venture

Tianjin was an important industrial and port city in Northern China under the direct administration of the central government. The 9.2 million inhabitants of Tianjin were among the first to enjoy the benefits of increasing openness towards foreign investment when the Tianjin Economic and Technological Development Area was established in 1984. This new economic zone became one of the most favored among foreign

---

[2] Project finance has been employed in many other industries and applications as well. For example, R&D Limited Partnerships (RDLP) were common in the 1980s, such as Cummins Engine's $20 million financing of a new form of diesel engine. Other firms (Genetech, Nova Pharmaceuticals, and Amgen) have utilized similar financing forms in which a finite project was financed with

investors quickly. By 1995 over 156 foreign companies had established differing levels of activity in the economic zone, some of which were China's largest foreign investors such as Motorola (USA) and Samsung (Korea).

Tianjin Plastics was a government-owned enterprise which utilizes an extremely energy-intensive extrusion process for the production of a variety of raw industrial plastic products. The proposed power plant, a 140 megawatt coal-fired steam-electric plant, would provide all of Tianjin's power needs, with excess to spare—which would in turn be sold on the regional electrical power grid. Maple had already concluded the negotiation of the power purchasing agreement (PPA) with the Chinese Ministry of Power Industry (MOPI).[3] The most notable feature of the agreement was the provision for free coal feedstock for the life of the power plant (20 plus years).

The power plant construction and testing would require four years. If production could be started later, the power could start flowing to Tianjin Plastics by the summer of 2000, and the cash flows from operations could start flowing to Maple at the same time. The project was a build-operate-transfer (BOT) arrangement, where the Maple-Tianjin-MOPI joint venture would own and manage the plant for twenty years, at which time the plant would be turned over to the regional utility in Hebei province. So regardless of the productive life of the plant, the economic life of the project, from Maple's viewpoint, would end in the year 2020.

Project Economics

The *pro forma* financial statements on the project forecast an operating margin of 178,000,000 Chinese renminbi (Rmb) beginning in the year 2000, increasing 3% annually thereafter.[4] The project was to be granted a tax holiday for the first six years of operation, and would face a tax rate of 40% after that on corporate income. Interest and principal repayment would begin in the year 2000. The annual depreciation of plant and equipment was estimated to be Rmb98,000,000 per year for 10 years (which was already subtracted to arrive at the operating margin). The government of China required that 25% of annual depreciation charges be "reinvested" in operations. There would be no recapture of depreciation at the end of the investment. Operating losses incurred during the tax holiday could be carried forward seven years for tax purposes.

The joint venture would be split 49% Maple, 46% Tianjin Plastics, 5% MOPI, with Maple holding the controlling interest. This was the structure Maple generally preferred, so that it could maintain actual control of operations while its local partner could provide nearly equal financing and something more important than mere dollars or renminbi—local participation. The actual equity-stake in a project of this type ranged between 15 and 30% of total capital. In this case, equity would make up only 15% of the total $110 million in capital needed. The majority of the capitalization would come from bank financing—local banks, foreign banks, and international

---

[3] Most power purchasing agreements state the specific amounts of power to be provided for the life of the contract as well as the price to be paid, normally based on an inflation-adjusted

[4] The Chinese currency, the *Renminbi*, is Mandarin, with an English phonetic pronunciation of "run-mean-bee."

lending institutions with interests in economic development.[5] A diversified capital structure, both in equity and debt participation, was one of the keys to successfully developing a project finance venture. Lining up the bank financing, both public and private, however, was increasingly a problem.

But all was not well with some of the major lenders. The U.S. Export-Import Bank, a government-funded lender for the facilitation of U.S. exports to foreign buyers, had announced today that it would not participate in the funding of the Three Gorges Dam Project in China. The project, with an estimated cost between $24 and $40 billion, was already underway on the Yangtze River east of Wuhan. Several major U.S.-based firms (Caterpillar, Rotec Industries) had openly campaigned for Ex-Im Bank support. The Ex-Im Bank's refusal to participate was based on the environmental repercussions of the dam, which would flood the historic Three Gorges Region of central China.

Maple's part of the deal would be its 49% of the $16.5 million in equity. The project size was standard for a medium-sized player like Maple, its projects typically ranging from $10 to $200 million in total capital employed. The average payback from Maple's projects was about 6 years after commencement of power plant operations, also normal for the industry.[6] The company's required hurdle rate was 15%, but would have to be higher to compensate for the additional risks posed by the Chinese market.

Maple, however, wanted this project to happen. The market potential for similar power plant projects in China was enormous. It was estimated that the PRC would need 21 gigawatts of new capacity each year for the coming decade. This was equivalent to re-electrifying all of southern California each year, a truly promising market opportunity. But for all of the needs of power plant development, the capital resources of China were obviously inadequate to meeting the task, and there remained considerable impediments to foreign capital stepping in to fill the gap.

Financing Arrangements

Total construction financing of $93.5 million (Rmb786.8 million) was provided through a combination of loans from the equipment vendors ($22.0 million), Tianjin Plastics ($7.59 million), Maple Energy ($8.085 million) and a bridge loan from a West Coast U.S. bank ($55.0 million). Upon completion of the project, all three parties would convert their respective loans into equity. MOPI's and Tianjin Plastic's loans were in renminbi as was 10% of the equipment vendors loan.

---

[5] It is the participation of international institutions like the World Bank, the International Financing Corporation, the European Bank for Reconstruction and Development, etc., which reduces the risks associated with lending to emerging market countries, at least to a level at which private lending institutions are willing to participate.

[6] Unfortunately, as a result of the extended construction period often experienced in developing countries, this translated into a payback of between 10 and 12 years after much of Maple's equity capital was put at risk.

The bank required completion guarantees from both Tianjin Plastics and Maple Energy. Local currency construction loans carried a rate of 14% while the U.S. dollar loans carried a rate of 9.0%.

The construction plan called for the funds provided by the project sponsors to be drawn down at the beginning of the first year, the bank loan to be drawn down equally over years two and three, and the loans from the vendors to be drawn down at the beginning of year four. Interest on the loans would accrue for the four years. At the end of the four years the interest earned by Tianjin, Maple, and the vendors would be paid out by the banks and capitalized in the project financing loan. In the case of the vendors, the loan principal would be taken out by the new project financing loan as well.

The post-completion financing of $117.4 million ($93.5 million principal plus $23.9 million in accrued interest) was arranged through a club syndication consisting of three banks which had experience with project financing in China, and by the Bank of China. The three foreign banks were the U.S. West Coast bank that provided the bridge loan, a large Canadian bank, and a well positioned Japanese bank. All three banks also had an *indirect* interest in the project: Maple was a good customer of the West Coast bank; a number of the vendors to the project were Japanese; and the Canadian bank was actively pursuing business in the PRC. The Bank of China loan of Rmb90.7 million (the equivalent of $10.9 million) was provided at a fixed rate of 13% for 12 years. Repayments of loan principal on the Bank of China loan and on the club syndication loan were to be made in equal annual installments.

The syndication loan was structured into two tranches, for $33 million and $57 million, respectively. The first tranche was a *project-sponsored/supported limited recourse loan*, and the second tranche was a *project-supported non-recourse loan*. The first tranche was priced at .95% over six-month LIBOR for six years (the average payback period for Maple). The second tranche was for 10 years and priced at 1.75% over six-month LIBOR (currently 5.75%).[7] The club syndication loan was denominated in U.S. dollars. The three banks were willing to accept the currency convertibility risk on both tranches.

Currency Impediments

A major problem for all foreign investors was the Chinese currency, the renminbi (Rmb). The renminbi was not currently freely convertible, so that any cash flows for either profit repatriation or debt-service repatriation would have to go through a government approval process. Requests for hard currency exchange and the opening of foreign exchange accounts must be submitted to the State Administration of Exchange Control (SEAC). Even with a reduction in actual restrictions in recent years, foreign investors in China must still obtain SEAC approval to buy or sell foreign currencies, as

---

[7] Non-recourse loans tend to be at a higher rate than either balance sheet loans or limited recourse loans.

EXHIBIT 2 The Changing Value of the Chinese Renminbi

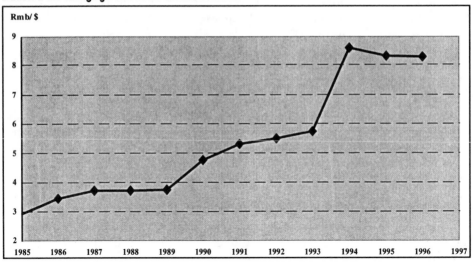

well as submit documentation evidence for each individual transaction.[8]

The renminbi had first depreciated with the abolishment of the dual currency system in 1994, but had stabilized since that time (although one must keep in mind that it was still a highly managed official currency value). The outlook for the value of the renminbi was uncertain; the Bank of China had set the year 2000 as the target date for full convertibility for currency transactions related to the current account (trade transactions), but no date was yet set for the more complex capital account (money and capital market transactions and investments). The Chinese government continued to control the amount of renminbi converted to hard currency with an iron fist in an attempt to manage the currency's value and the external impacts on the domestic financial economy through volatile exchange rates or imported inflation.[9]

As illustrated in Exhibit 2, however, the stabilization program for the renminbi's value was not always that successful. The renminbi was trading around Rmb8.32/$ in the first three months of 1996. Surprisingly it had actually appreciated slightly against the dollar in 1994 and 1995, but inflationary pressures were reigniting concern. Where it would be in one year, four years, or 20 years, was anyone's guess.[10]

---

[8] China utilized a dual exchange rate system up until January 1994, when it was abolished. The dual system was a result of the establishment of swap centres in 1988 to trade currencies outside the official exchange rate. Whereas the official rate was maintained at an overvalued official rate, the swap centre rates more closely followed the black market rates, reducing the degree of economic distortion for international payment settlements.

[9] In reality, even with governmental agreements or guarantees, international banks were not convinced that these agreements would be honored over the extended period of time a project

[10] The renminbi rate was allowed to float ± 0.3% from the official daily rate, which was itself fixed at the closing rate from the previous day's trade-weighted index value.

Barriers to Foreign Investors

The barriers to investing in China were substantial. First, the Chinese government was attempting to limit the return on investment (ROI) on projects of this type to 12%. After most power plant developers like Maple balked at such low rates of return, the Chinese government revised the target ROI to between 15% and 17% if the plant demonstrated outstanding efficiency.[11] Many analysts still considered that to be low, estimating that at least 18% was needed as adequate compensation for projects of this type.

Secondly, the Chinese government often refused to guarantee fulfillment of a contract such as this one, even though Tianjin Plastics was a state-owned-enterprise. This increased the level of risk as perceived by the bank lenders, and certainly was not helping the cause at the moment.[12] The fact that MOPI was a partner might have little impact on the performance of the Chinese government.

Finally, the Chinese government did not allow *registered capital*, the equity capital initially invested under the agreements of the project, to be repatriated. This meant that Maple would not be able to return to the parent company anything other than the profits, the dividends, which might or might not in actuality arise over the life of the project. There would be no re-payment of equity participation.

Repatriation of Equity Investment

It was in fact the last point which had bothered Maple's project evaluation team the most. Maple had always been able to repatriate, in one way or another, a large part if not all of its capital invested in a power plant project. A number of different proposals had been evaluated in order to find a way out. Proposals varied from back-to-back loans to dollar-indexed rate adjustment clauses to Rmb swaps.

The simplest solution from Maple's perspective was to have the power price paid by Tianjin Plastics indexed to the dollar. Given the relatively dependable revenue stream and the minor role of costs of production (remembering that the primary variable cost was coal, which was free, and the majority of fixed costs arising from capitalization) this would essentially guarantee earnings in the joint venture which would maintain their U.S. dollar value as repatriated. This would obviously please both the foreign creditors and Maple, but the Chinese pricing bureau of MOPI had ruled this out immediately as the revenue structure of Tianjin itself was purely domestic (renminbi based). MOPI was also opposed to this scheme because of the negative impact it might have on the returns on their invested capital in the project.

---

[11] The Chinese government revised its expectations only after a clear indication that power plant and other infrastructure capital investment was literally flowing away from China towards India as a result of the restrictions on investment returns.

[12] Many pro-Chinese developers argued that this was not a legitimate concern, pointing to the fact that most of the loans which eventually were either re-scheduled or actually defaulted upon by the Latin American debtors in the early 1980s were, with few exceptions, all guaranteed by the host government. The comparison, however, did not serve to make many of the potential lenders feel much better.

EXHIBIT 3 Back-to-Back Loan Proposal Between Maple Energy and Wintel

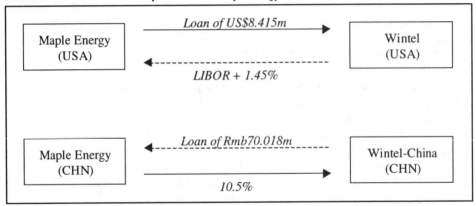

A method employed in China on several occasions in the last three years was the *back-to-back loan* (illustrated in Exhibit 3). Maple had identified another Western firm, Wintel (US), who already had an investment in China. Wintel had generated profits in renminbi but could not repatriate the earnings. Maple and Wintel had discussed a back-to-back loan agreement in which Wintel would loan the equivalent of Rmb70.018 million to Maple for six years at 10.5%, and Maple would in turn lend to Wintel $8.415 million at LIBOR plus 1.45% for the same six years. At the prevailing exchange rate of Rmb8.32/$, the loan amounts were equal in value. Instead of converting the dollars and making the equity investment in China, Maple would *borrow* the renminbi for the investment (from Wintel). Both loans were structured with bullet principal repayment at maturity. The renminbi loan would be serviced by Maple's share of the local currency profits in excess of Rmb70.018 million. Wintel was willing to enter into this structure because its registered capital was locked into renminbi and it could only make 8% on its liquid funds in China. Additionally, if it were to borrow the funds back in the United States it would pay a higher rate—LIBOR plus 1.80%—for the same six years.

Currency Risk

A partially convertible currency posed special problems. Assuming governmental approval would be obtained for the conversion, the currency risk for such an extended period of time was unacceptable. Maple had worked with a number of the major multinational banks in evaluating a number of potential solutions. What made this currency risk different from any other long-term floating rate foreign currency denominated receivable was the lack of financial derivatives to hedge renminbi cash flows. All risk management derivative products relied upon access to money and capital market instruments in the subject currency, and those financial markets simply did not yet exist in China or in Chinese renminbi anywhere. This same principle applied to other suggested alternatives such as U.S. dollar—Chinese renminbi swaps.

The remaining solution of the greatest potential value was to finance the majority of the project in renminbi, that is, borrow locally. This would simply match the local

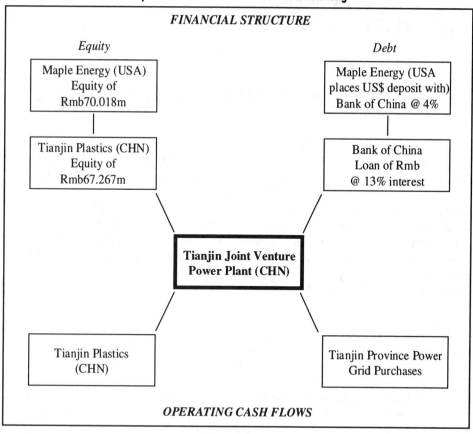

currency inflows with local currency outflows—financing outflows—insulating the majority of the firm's cash flows from currency risk. Discussions with officials of the Chinese banking industry indicated that, with the proper approvals, a 10 year loan agreement at approximately 13% would be possible. But there was one catch: the renminbi loan would require 100% dollar-denominated collateral: the lenders for the Tianjin power plant project would put up a $101.5 million deposit with the Bank of China.[13] Although the deposit would not be required until operation startup in 2000, this seemed to be a rather expensive alternative. For example, similar 10 year loans in the U.S. dollar markets at this time were roughly 8%. (The basic arrangements for this dollar-deposit collateralization proposal are illustrated in Exhibit 4.) Pat made an additional final note regarding the dollar deposit, that the profits earned and repatriated to Maple (US) would still be exposed to currency risk.

Time was running short, and Pat was running out of ideas.

---

[13] The dollar security deposit would be drawn-down over time (Maple would be able to draw dollars out) as the principal of the renminbi loan was amortized and repaid.

BWIP's Acquisition of Pacific Wietz

In early November 1993, Jack Worthing, Treasurer of BWIP Holding, Inc., sat in his office contemplating the alternatives available for structuring the acquisition of Pacific Wietz GmbH & Co. KG of Germany. The acquisition was scheduled to take place on January 5, 1994, and would give a significant boost to BWIP's continuing efforts to penetrate the global chemical industry. The acquisition of Pacific Wietz would also provide a strong foothold in the booming Continental European market. The structuring of the acquisition, however, was still unclear. Questions remained as to which unit of BWIP would actually make the purchase, what type of purchase it would be, how it was to be financed, and how the entire structure would fit within the confines of BWIP's global tax strategy.

The Company

BWIP Holding, Inc., the parent company of BWIP International, Inc. (BWIP), was incorporated in Delaware on March 12, 1987, with corporate headquarters in Long Beach, California. The company is a worldwide supplier of advanced technology fluid transfer and control equipment, systems and services. Its principal products are pumps and mechanical seals, primarily for the petroleum and electric power industries and increasingly for the chemical industry. The company manufactures, sells, distributes and services its products throughout the world. Net sales in 1992 were over $399 million and were expected to exceed $425 million by year-end 1993.

As of October 1993, BWIP was organized into two primary business segments—Pump/Seal and Fluid Controls. The Pump/Seal segment designed, manufactured, distributed and serviced both highly engineered and standard centrifugal pumps, primarily for use in the power and petroleum industries. BWIP was currently in the process of disposing of the Fluid Controls segment. Manufacturing facilities were located in eight different countries, including large plants in the United States, The Netherlands, Mexico, Argentina, and Belgium. The company also maintained after-market service centers in 17 countries.

BWIP's strength was in the international energy markets, typically constituting more than 80% of sales. Foreign operations in total accounted for approximately

41% of net sales in 1992, and were expected to be slightly higher in 1993. Export sales from the United States were expected to represent 34% of domestic sales in 1993, compared with 27% in 1992.

Roughly 19% of BWIP's sales in 1992 were to markets other than petroleum and power. The company manufactured equipment for chemical, military, mining, mineral and ore processing, pulp and paper, and municipal and agricultural water markets. These industries had been targeted for growth through new products, acquisitions and marketing programs. The Pacific Wietz acquisition was part of BWIP's strategic plan to expand its penetration into other industries.

Pacific Wietz

Pacific Wietz (PW) was one of the leading European manufacturers of mechanical seals and seal systems, particularly for the chemical industry. Its acquisition would bring important new technologies to BWIP, including an advanced GASPAC™ dry gas seal for the compressor market. Pacific Wietz operated manufacturing plants at Dortmund, Germany, and Oensingen, Switzerland, and had a network of 13 sales offices in Germany, Switzerland, and the Netherlands, employing about 250 people. It also had marketing and dealer relationships in an additional 10 countries in Europe and the Far East. BWIP expected considerable marketing and product development synergies from the acquisition.

Pacific Wietz was expected to close 1993 with pretax profits of about 10% on sales of approximately $25 million. BWIP considered Pacific Wietz's value as an operating entity to be greater than the fair market value of its net assets. After lengthy negotiations, $24 million was agreed upon as the purchase price.

October Briefings

Although the broad outline of the transaction had been established, there were a number of issues that needed to be settled. On Friday, October 1, 1993, Jack arranged meetings with BWIP's Tax Director, Mack Guffin, to discuss financing strategies, and with the corporate controller, Grøn Pincenez, to review some of the fundamental accounting and structuring issues related to the acquisition. He planned to meet with PW's owners in Germany the following week to clarify certain details of the transaction. He would then meet with Mack and Grøn again to finalize BWIP's acquisition structure.

Jack had several objectives that he wanted to achieve in structuring the acquisition. His choice among the various alternatives would have to consider the sources of capital as well as cost, potential currency exposure implications, and the burden on PW's cash flows and profitability. What sources of debt should be utilized and in which currencies? How much debt could PW be expected to bear, and how should the debt be structured? His strategy would also have to consider the tax management implications for the parent. Could the transaction be structured to avoid generating excess foreign tax credits or to utilize existing tax credits? Could tax losses from the transaction be charged directly to income?

The accounting issues were interrelated and also complex. Could the transaction meet the requirements for pooling-of-interests accounting, or would the purchase method have to be used? Would it be a *share purchase* or an *asset purchase*? Should the new entity be established as a subsidiary or a branch? What were the tax implications of these choices?

Meeting with Mack Guffin, Tax Director

Jack started quickly: "As you know, Mack, we need to raise funds to finance the Pacific Wietz acquisition. I've asked you to wait until our next meeting to provide specific cost estimates. Today I just want to discuss any other concerns—other than costs—you have about how to structure the acquisition."

Mack nodded and waited.

"First it would seem to me we need to consider from where we should execute the deal. PW is a German company, so we could set up a German subsidiary to handle the acquisition, or we could do it directly from the parent company here in the United States, or we could use our existing subsidiary in the Netherlands. What do you think?"

Mack looked pensive, but proceeded. "Well, as far as financing it goes, we could raise capital either here in the United States or in Europe. One possibility of course, is to issue equity—but that is likely to be expensive. We can also choose between borrowing via the parent company or arranging for the foreign subsidiary to borrow locally. If we borrow at the parent level, it will probably be in the form of an interest-bearing intercompany loan to the subsidiary. These choices will, of course, have different tax consequences."

Jack interjected. "But Pacific Wietz's cash flows are predominantly in Deutchemarks, so if we borrow in Deutschemarks from a German bank, couldn't we minimize our currency exposure? Or, why not have our subsidiary in the Netherlands [BWIP BV] borrow locally? A loan from the Netherlands, even in guilders, would also result in little currency risk because the mark and guilder are so closely linked."

"Good points, Jack, but remember that the choice of where to borrow is separate from the choice of what currency to borrow. We could make a loan in any currency we choose regardless of where the funds are raised, but then we would have to consider hedging the exposure. And no matter where we source the funds, we will have to think about how added debt and interest income will affect our financial condition."

Jack nodded his agreement. "As you noted, tax management is also a critical issue. As you know, Mack, we have been quite efficient in our utilization of foreign tax credits (FTCs) over the past few years. We're now paying an effective tax rate below the U.S. federal income tax rate (see Exhibit 1). However, as you also know, we are now sitting on a lot of excess FTCs here in the United States. Is there some way to structure the transaction so that we can use up our excess FTCs and not create more? Since Germany is a high-tax country, any profits generated by PW would be

EXHIBIT 1 Reconciliation of Effective Income Tax Rate (for the year ended December 31)

	1993	1992	1991
Federal income tax rate	35.0%	34.0%	34.0%
Foreign earnings taxed at different rates, including withholding taxes	5.3	5.6	3.4
State income taxes, net of federal income tax benefit	2.9	3.0	2.5
Alternate minimum tax (minimum tax credits utilized)	--	--	(3.5)
Utilization of tax credits	(10.2)	(4.0)	(2.1)
Other	(0.8)	(5.4)	0.8
Effective tax rate	32.2%	33.2%	35.1%

No taxes have been provided relating to the possible distribution of approximately $46 million of undistributed earnings considered to be permanently reinvested, primarily in the Netherlands. The amount of such additional taxes is estimated to be approximately $10 million.

In addition, during 1992 the Company adopted Statement of Financial Accounting Standards No. 109,"Accounting for Income Taxes." The adoption contributed to the Company's lower effective tax rate for 1992 and the cumulative effect of such change resulted in a $2.0 million gain ($0.08 per share) during 1992.

Source: BWIP Holding, Incorporated, *1993 Annual Report*, p.28.

subject to higher tax rates, and when—or, if—we bring that money home, we are just going to end up with more excess credits."

Mack nodded in understanding. "One strategy would be to extend a loan to PW in order to shift the tax effect of PW's earnings to a lower tax environment. Debt-service payments to the parent company would generate regular foreign-source income and deficit foreign tax credits in passive-income form."[1]

"That sounds like a good strategy, but we'll also have to consider the accounting issues involved. Do you think there would be any specific advantage in having interest payments made to the Dutch subsidiary instead? Would it be better to have the Dutch subsidiary or the U.S. parent carry the loan?"

"Aside from the currency exposure issue that I just mentioned, interest income paid to the Netherlands subsidiary from PW should increase its profitability." Mack hesitated, then continued. "Although corporate income tax rates in the Netherlands are low—similar to those in the U.S.—you might recall that we have already accumulated a significant amount of undistributed earnings there—about $46 million if I remember correctly—and we might not want to add to that. On the other hand, if we could raise money somewhere else and channel it through the Netherlands, then the subsidiary would have tax deductible interest payments of its own."

---

[1] The payment of interest would be foreign-source income to the parent for U.S. tax purposes. Since the interest payment would be an expense of PW, there would be no corporate income tax credits on the foreign-source income in the eyes of the U.S. tax authorities. The only foreign tax credits generated for U.S. tax purposes would arise from withholding taxes imposed by Germany on interest paid to the U.S.-based company. For a detailed explanation of U.S. international

EXHIBIT 2 Potential Funding of the Pacific Wietz Acquisition

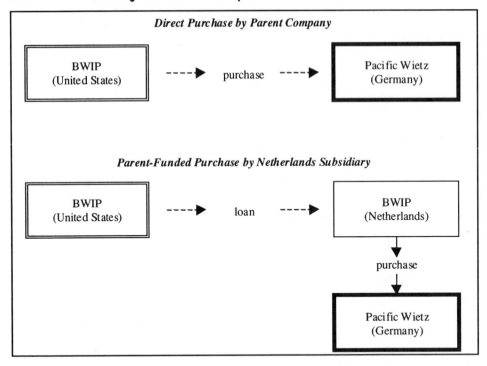

Jack and Mack concluded that there were two basic ownership alternatives, either a direct purchase by the parent or via the Netherlands subsidiary (see Exhibit 2). If the Netherlands subsidiary was the owner of record, the parent could still provide either part or full funding for the acquisition. After considerable debate, they also concluded that there were in all, four sources of funds worth considering: 1) borrow in Deutchemarks from a bank in Germany; 2) borrow in the Netherlands and use excess cash and unremitted profits still held by the Netherlands subsidiary; 3) have the parent company borrow U.S. dollars in the United States; or 4) use a combination of sources and channel funds through the Netherlands subsidiary.

Jack decided that his next information need was an overview of the costs of the alternative sources of debt. He asked Mack Guffin to prepare the figures and have them ready for the briefing that would take place after his return from Germany. In the meantime, BWIP's Controller, Grøn Pincenez, was waiting outside his office.

Meeting with Grøn Pincenez, BWIP Controller

"Please come in, Grøn. I'd like to review some of the fundamental accounting issues related to the acquisition." Jack waited for Grøn to take his chair and arrange his glasses. "If I remember correctly, there are two methods that may be used to account for a business combination—the *purchase method* and the *pooling-of-interests* method.[2]

I know that we have used purchase accounting for most of our acquisitions in the past. Perhaps you could go over the basic differences."

Grøn pushed his glasses back up on the bridge of his nose. "Of course. *Purchase accounting* is similar to the accounting treatment used in the acquisition of any asset group. The fair market value of the consideration (cash, stock, debt securities, etc.) given by the acquiring firm is used as the basis for valuing the acquired company. In essence, the assets and liabilities of the acquired company are *stepped-up* from their original book value to their respective fair market values at the time of the acquisition.[3] Any difference between the value of the consideration given and the fair market values of the net assets obtained is normally recorded on the consolidated balance sheet as *goodwill*.[4] The *pooling method* assumes a combining of stockholders' interests, and can only be used when the acquisition is executed by means of a share exchange. The valuation basis in this case is the historical book value of the net assets of the acquired company. It effectively ignores the fair market value of the acquired entity and the value of the consideration given to its shareholders. Therefore, there can be no goodwill or changes in asset valuations at the date of combination."

Jack nodded. "So basically the *pooling method* leaves the balance sheet of the acquisition as it is—or was, and the *purchase method* re-values the balance sheet and brings it up to date, including the creation of goodwill from our acquisition. Is that about it?"

"Yes, that's the result," Grøn confirmed, and pushed his glasses back up once again.

---

[2] Although both methods are acceptable in many countries, including the United States, the financial structure of the transaction dictates which accounting method must be used. For U.S.-based companies, Accounting Principles Board Opinion No. 16, "Accounting for Business Combinations," specifies twelve criteria which must be met before a combination may be accounted for as a pooling-of-interests. For example, the acquiring company must issue voting common shares in exchange for 90% or more of the voting common shares of the company being acquired. If even one of the twelve criteria is not met, the pooling method is disallowed and the purchase method must be used.

[3] Under purchase accounting, the assets and liabilities of the acquired company are normally *stepped-up* to their respective fair market values at the time of the acquisition. In most cases, the new values are recorded only in the consolidated accounts. It can be argued that the parent's cost of acquiring the subsidiary should be *pushed down* to the acquired company's balance sheets because the original historical cost values become irrelevant once the firm is under new ownership. In *push-down* accounting, the buyer's purchase price is *pushed down* to the target and used to restate the carrying value of the subsidiary's assets and liabilities. This issue becomes important from the perspective of evaluating the performance of the subsidiary's managers: should they be expected to earn an acceptable rate of return on the basis of the historical cost of the subsidiary's net worth or on the basis of the parent's acquisition cost? Push-down accounting assumes that the answer is the latter.

[4] For example, assume that $2 million of excess cost is due to an under valuation of property, plant and equipment (PP&E) owned by PW, and a remaining $6 million is attributable to above-average earnings prospects, i.e. a synergistic effect resulting from the combination of the two companies. When the accounts are consolidated, $2 million is added to the PP&E account; that is, the book value of PW's PP&E is stepped-up to its fair market value. The remaining $6 million is identified as *goodwill* on the consolidated balance sheet; and depending on the country in which the acquisition is executed, the goodwill is either amortized against earnings over its expected useful life or immediately

"Now I know that the most common form of acquisition involves purchasing the <u>shares</u> of the acquired company. However, an alternative is to purchase the target company's <u>assets</u>. If we do this, we can limit our acquisition to those parts of the business that coincide with our needs. What are the major distinctions here, and do we run into any serious accounting implications?"

"Well, from our perspective as the acquiring company, there really isn't much difference. It is an option worth considering, because we would end up buying only the assets that we really want, and maybe for less. If the asset acquisition involves *goodwill*, this kind of asset-purchase goodwill is tax-deductible, at least in the United States and the Netherlands."

Jack looked anxious. "Okay, I'm not sure I really understand goodwill. I was under the impression that the tax treatment of goodwill had changed quite a bit in several countries, but I haven't kept up. Can you give me a quick overview of what our choices are with goodwill, assuming we end up dealing with it?"

"Sure. Tax and accounting rules for goodwill amortization vary considerably across countries. In all countries, goodwill associated with a *share acquisition* is <u>not</u> tax-deductible. However, in some countries, like Germany, Japan, the Netherlands, and the United States, goodwill may be deductible for tax purposes if the acquisition is an *asset acquisition* as opposed to a share acquisition. In other countries, like the United Kingdom, while goodwill is not tax deductible, it needn't be amortized for financial accounting purposes either. In this case, reported income is higher each period than it would be in—say the United States—where goodwill is customarily amortized over long periods of time."

Grøn continued. "In Germany, for financial reporting purposes, goodwill can be either charged directly to equity reserves, or capitalized and amortized on a straight-line basis, generally over four years. However, for tax purposes, capitalization of goodwill is mandatory and the amortization period for goodwill is fixed at 15 years. In the UK and the Netherlands, the most common treatment of goodwill is to write it off in total against retained earnings or a similar equity reserve account at the date of acquisition. However, tax laws in the Netherlands allow goodwill to be written off over a five-year period."

The last point captured Jack's attention. "So if we were able to position the goodwill in the Netherlands, we could write it off much faster against taxes. That's something I want to look at more closely." Jack seemed to subtly shift gears. "Speaking of taxes, I just finished discussing the issue with Mack. We would like to structure the acquisition in a way that would reduce the negative impact of acquiring a profitable company in high-tax Germany. Perhaps we could extend a loan to PW for the full amount of the purchase price. The added burden of interest expense would effectively reduce its taxable income. In essence, we could use the interest charges as a means to transfer PW's profits from a high-tax environment to a lower tax one. How would this be accounted for?"

Grøn pondered the question as he cleaned his glasses with his handkerchief. "From an accounting viewpoint, BWIP would record the acquisition as before, and the loan would be entered in the books as a separate transaction. On a consolidated basis, the intercompany loan would be eliminated. I think it may be a strategy worth considering because we may be able to get the loan itself classified as a long-term investment. Under the right circumstances, this would mean that any loan-related foreign exchange gains or losses could be accumulated in a balance sheet account—a *translation adjustment account*—rather than flow through the income statement."

Jack looked puzzled. "I don't follow you on that. What difference does it make where the currency gains and losses go, if we still suffer them?"

"It can make quite a difference. If the loan is a standard loan for tax purposes, currency gains and losses on it would pass through current income. We would normally not like to take any hits—or gains if that be the case—in income from currency movements. But if we could get it classified as a foreign investment, and then suffered some currency gains and losses on its value, we might be able to simply push them into the translation adjustment account on the consolidated balance sheet. No real income impact in that case."

Grøn continued. "But there is also the tax angle to consider. As an international group of companies, we would of course prefer profits to accrue in the group company having the lowest tax rate and prefer that charges against income—such as interest—be incurred in a country having a high tax rate. But most countries have tax avoidance rules designed to prevent the blatant switching of profits through intergroup interest payments. We will have to set the interest rate on the loan so that it does not differ materially from current market rates. However, that may still leave us opportunity for some repositioning of profits and losses on the financing."

Grøn, finally finished polishing the lenses, replaced the glasses, gave them one final shove, and continued. "The choice of where to take the tax deduction for interest payments depends on more than just a simple comparison of nominal tax rates. Because a large amount of our activities are abroad, we may have insufficient profits taxable at the parent level to support major borrowings, in which case we should finance at the subsidiary level. In the United States, a certain proportion of interest expense deductions may have to be allocated against foreign source profits as a restriction on FTC relief. Some countries, such as the Netherlands, disallow interest paid on money borrowed from domestic or foreign sources if it is borrowed specifically to make a foreign acquisition. The Dutch argue that since income from overseas subsidiaries is normally exempt from Dutch tax, it is unreasonable for interest on the money borrowed to be charged against Dutch profits of the parent. However, the taxpayer will usually try to structure loans so that they appear to be allowable for domestic purposes."

Jack looked tired. "Thanks, Grøn, that's helpful. Let me try to summarize what we've said so far. We can structure the acquisition as a share purchase, as an asset purchase, or as an exchange of shares. If we use one of the first two options, we will have to use purchase accounting, and then the issue of goodwill accounting arises. However, if we opt for a stock swap, we may be entitled to use pooling, in which case goodwill is avoided. No matter which structure we decide on, we might still be able to extend a loan to PW as a vehicle to shift the tax effect of PW's earnings to a lower tax environment. But if we do, we will have to set the interest rate on the loan pretty close to prevailing market rates. And we also have to think carefully about where we might want interest payment deductions to occur. Am I close?"

Grøn nodded in affirmation, causing his glasses to slide back down his nose. "Yes, I would say that is fairly accurate. Do you think PW's shareholders would be willing to accept stock instead of cash? If so, we could preserve our cash and possibly use pooling-of-interests accounting."

Jack pursed his lips and considered the question. "I don't know. I will be meeting with PW's owners next week. After that I may have an answer to that question."

October 13 Meeting
Grøn Pincenez, Controller

"We now have more information to base our structuring decisions upon. First, PW is a partnership, and we will be buying the partnership interests directly from private owners.[5] We discussed paying the owners with stock but they prefer to receive cash, so that rules out a stock swap. On the question of a share purchase versus an asset purchase, the owners reminded me that in Germany the acquisition of partnership interests is considered to be an asset transaction, at least for tax purposes."

Grøn leaned forward in his chair, pushing his glasses back up the bridge of his nose. "Then we will need to use purchase accounting and deal with the issue of goodwill. We are also required by law to revalue any patents that we acquire. PW is now profitable, but it has no goodwill amortization expense, and the book value of its patents is relatively low. The creation of goodwill and the revaluation of patents will mean a substantial increase in intangible assets. These will probably have to be amortized and expensed. In addition, after the acquisition, PW will be paying interest expense from your proposed intercompany loan."

Jack leaned back in his chair. "But that will lower PW's pretax income, and with Germany's high tax rates, that should be to our advantage. Isn't that what we wanted?"

Grøn agreed. "Tax considerations are clearly important. A step-up in the basis of the assets could increase after-tax cash flows and, as you pointed out, leverage reduces taxes. A merger or acquisition may allow *net operating loss carry forwards* (NOLs) to be used faster. On the other hand, these tax advantages are counterbalanced to some extent by tax costs that are triggered by the acquisition itself. These might include an acceleration of capital gains taxes and tax from the recapture of depreciation."

Jack interrupted. "I'm not clear on that. Do you mean that after the acquisition has resulted in stepped-up asset values we will have larger depreciation charges as a result? Is that good or bad?"

---

[5] German law recognizes two types of limited liability companies as legal entities in their own right: the Aktiengesellschaft (AG) and the Gesellschaft mit beschränkter Haftung (GmbH). The AG is analogous to the publicly held corporation in the United States. It is the only business entity in Germany whose shares may be traded on a stock exchange. A GmbH is analogous to a privately held corporation in the United States. Its shares are not freely transferable, and the responsibility for managing it is usually assumed by one or more individual directors instead of a management board. A Kommanditgesellschaft (KG) is a limited partnership and a Kommanditgesellschaft auf Aktien

Grøn shoved his glasses up and nodded in affirmation. "Exactly. And, if I may go on, there are also restructuring costs and information-related costs incurred in connection with the merger. If these tax and information costs are netted against the tax gain, there may be no net tax advantage to the acquisition. It would be to our advantage if tax losses arising from the transaction itself could be written off against current income. We could write off such tax losses if we made PW into a branch instead of a subsidiary."

"I see. So we could actually establish PW as either a branch or a subsidiary. I hadn't considered the idea of making it a branch. What are the basic differences from an accounting viewpoint, and what do you see as the advantages and disadvantages of each form?"

"A subsidiary company is a separate, incorporated entity, that maintains separate accounting records, even though consolidated statements are usually prepared for financial reporting purposes to our public shareholders. In theory, transactions between a subsidiary and a parent should be accounted for on an *arms-length* basis. A branch, on the other hand, is not a separate entity. In accounting for branch operations, a *branch* account on the home office books is debited while a *home office* account on the branch books is simultaneously credited for the same amount and vice versa. Thus, for a domestic branch, the balances of these reciprocal accounts should be equal in dollar amounts, but the balances should be on opposite sides of the respective accounts. Of course for an international branch the currency of denomination of the account may cause differences. Does that answer your question concerning the basic differences?"

"Yes, it does. And the advantages and disadvantages?"

"Well, there are definite differences in the tax the treatment of a foreign subsidiary versus a foreign branch.[6] Corporations are required to withhold taxes on dividends, royalties, and other forms of payments to nonresident corporations. The rates are specified in the tax treaties in effect between the relevant countries.[7] In the United States, there is also branch profits tax to consider. All profits that cannot be demonstrated as having been reinvested in fixed hard assets are taxed as if they were dividends. However, there is no branch profits tax in either Germany or

---

[6] German business profits are subject to two taxes, corporation tax *(Körperschaftsteur)* and municipal trade tax *(Gewerbeertragsteuer)*. Corporation taxes, to which the income of a subsidiary would be subject, is levied under a split-rate, imputation system. Profits distributed to shareholders are taxed at a rate of 36% and undistributed profits are taxed at a rate of 50%. The effective municipal trade tax rate on income varies by location from just under 12% to just over 20%. Both corporation tax and municipal trade tax on income are also imposed on the taxable income of a foreign company's German branch. While the municipal trade tax rates are the same for branches and resident German companies, corporation tax in the case of a German branch is levied at flat rates, normally 46%, with no reduction for distributions.

[7] At this time (1993), Germany's dividend withholding tax on payments to a U.S. company (with holdings greater than 25%) is 10%. Dividends to European Community corporate shareholders on holdings of at least 25% were subject to a withholding tax of only 5%, regardless of the provisions of the treaty. The withholding tax on dividend distributions by German companies *is not imposed* on profits transferred by a German branch to its foreign head office.

the Netherlands. We could establish a separate subsidiary in Germany prior to the acquisition. If we did so, we would need to fund it with a combination of debt and equity. A balance of about three-to-one would probably be okay. Any higher level of debt and it might be seen as a *thin corporation*."

Jack frowned. "A *thin corporation*?"

"Let me explain. In cases where interest charges can be offset against overseas profits, the local tax burden could be reduced by setting up a subsidiary with a small equity capital base and funding the majority of the unit with interest-bearing debt. This would be quite attractive in cases where the subsidiary has or is likely to have for some years substantial taxable profits; the interest is deductible toward tax liabilities. The host country is unlikely to welcome this erosion of the tax base and might therefore have *thin capitalization* rules. Such rules disallow the deduction of interest and treat the interest payment as a distribution of taxed profits—a dividend—if certain ratios are not met. A finding that a debt claim is an equity interest would apply for all tax purposes and would result in interest being treated not as a deductible expense but as a dividend distribution out of taxed profits. The withholding tax rules on dividends would also apply. Although there are no formal rules, most countries view an acceptable structure as no more than a debt-equity ratio of three to one under these conditions."

"I see. Using a three-to-one ratio, we could, for example, contribute $18 million in debt using an intercompany loan, and $6 million in equity. This new subsidiary would then acquire the assets of PW for $24 million in cash."

"Yes—well, we could do it that way. However, setting up a new German subsidiary will unnecessarily add to the cost of the transaction, and as I said before, the tax loss could not be written off immediately against income. Any losses arising from the transaction would, in effect, be bottled-up within the new Germany subsidiary. If, on the other hand, either the parent company or our Netherlands subsidiary were to acquire PW, it would be considered a branch for tax purposes. This means that tax losses incurred in Germany as a result of the transaction would be immediately deductible against current income in the Netherlands. Of course, when the branch becomes profitable in the future we will have to add back the losses deducted, but in the meantime we will have benefited from timing differences."

"And what about goodwill?"

"Goodwill associated with an asset acquisition is tax deductible in all three countries, but the write-off period is only five years in the Netherlands versus 15 years in both Germany and the United States. This could be an important consideration. If the Netherlands subsidiary were to purchase PW's assets, after the acquisition PW would still be considered a separate entity by the German authorities for tax purposes, even though it is considered a branch of the Netherlands subsidiary for financial reporting purposes. Therefore, we could prepare a new tax balance sheet for PW, revaluing the assets to fair-market value and allocating the remainder of the purchase price to goodwill and patents. We should separate goodwill and patents because they can be amortized over different periods of time. The loan payments made by PW to the Netherlands subsidiary would also be tax deductible in Germany. At the same time, as I said before, in the Netherlands, PW will be considered a foreign

EXHIBIT 3 BWIP's Hypothetical German Subsidiary Balance Sheet

Before the acquisition[a]

Assets		Liabilities & Shareholders' Equity	
Cash	$24 million	Debt	$18 million
		Equity	6 million
Total	$24 million	Total	$24 million

After the acquisition[b]

Assets		Liabilities & Shareholders' Equity	
Assets (fair market value)	$18 million	Debt	$18 million
Patents	2 million	Equity	6 million
Goodwill	4 million		
Total	$24 million	Total	$24 million

Notes:
[a]BWIP would first form its own empty-shell subsidiary in Germany with a combination of $24 million in debt and equity. The subsidiary would have no assets other than cash.
[b]The German subsidiary would use the $24 million in cash to acquire the assets (asset purchase) of Pacific Wietz. Theassets purchased would include the current fair market value of the physical assets held by Pacific Wietz, plus the stepped-up values of patents and goodwill.

branch of our Dutch subsidiary for both financial reporting and tax purposes. Upon consolidation, the goodwill resulting from the acquisition of PW could be amortized and expensed by the Netherlands subsidiary. The loan payments made by PW to the Netherlands subsidiary might also be tax deductible in the Netherlands.

"Thanks Grøn, that helps. I think I understand the choices, and their implications, for structuring the deal. I am meeting this afternoon with Mack to see how the cost and availability of funds will affect our strategy. I will get back to you with what we come up with."

October 13 Meeting with Mack Guffin, Assistant International Treasurer

"Good afternoon, Jack. I trust you enjoyed your trip to Germany. You asked me to put together some figures on the cost and availability of debt financing. I know the company is not ready to issue any new equity at this time, so I have ruled out equity from the start. I have put together a short list of the debt alternatives available to us now."

"Fine. What do interest rates look like at this time?"

"Interest rates in Germany are, in fact, at record highs. The economic impact of German reunification has ignited inflationary pressures, resulting in a predictable anti-inflationary response by the German central bank, the Bundesbank. The prime lending rate is 9.5%, one of the reasons the Deutschemark is so strong at DM1.60/$. However, there would be little difficulty raising funds in the Netherlands. The commercial bank prime lending rate in the Netherlands is now 8.5%. However, our subsidiary there has a standing credit agreement totaling 50 million Dutch Guilders.[8] Borrowings under this agreement are at floating rates, usually set at a few basis points above the London interbank rate (LIBOR). Both the three and six month rates for LIBOR are now 3.3%. As I mentioned before, we have about $46 million in undistributed profits in our Dutch subsidiary; a lot considering its about 1.8 guilders per dollar."

"There would also be little difficulty raising funds in the United States. As you know, we have a U.S. credit agreement of $100 million already in place. This unsecured three-year facility extends through August 1996. Borrowings under the agreement are at floating rates, and are normally linked to the prime rate, which is 6%. Right now we have outstanding borrowings totaling $11 million and letters of credit totaling $14.9 million. We also have other uncommitted, unsecured revolving credit facilities totaling $35.7 million, which remain untouched."

Conclusion

After his meetings with Mack Guffin and Grøn Pincenez, Jack Worthing felt that he had a better understanding of the financial, accounting, and tax issues involved with the proposed acquisition. The challenge he now faced was to summarize and clarify these issues in writing his draft proposal for the Pacific Wietz acquisition.

Case Questions

1. How is the method of accounting employed for the acquisition related to the financing of the acquisition? Be specific.

2. What exactly is the significance of goodwill creation for BWIP's financing strategy?

3. How is the financing of the transaction (the source of the funds, the form of the funds, and the cost of the funds) related to the tax goals of BWIP?

4. Sketch out graphically, in a style similar to that shown in Exhibit 2, at least three different acquisition structures which could be used by BWIP. List the pros and cons of each, and take a position as to which you recommend.

---

[8] This was an unsecured revolving credit facility of which 35 million Dutch Guilders was restricted to the issuance of letters of credit and bank guarantees for the benefit of the

Appendix A   Calculation of U.S. Tax Liabilities on Foreign Source Income: A German Dividend Remittance

Foreign-source dividend income repatriation (hypothetical values from a German subsidiary):

Before tax foreign subsidiary income	DM10,000
Less local corporate income tax (40%)	- 4,000
Net income	DM 6,000
Retained earnings (50%)	DM 3,000
Distributed earnings (50%)	DM 3,000
Withholding tax on dividends (10%)	- 300
Net dividend repatriated to U.S. parent	DM 2,700

Gross-up procedure for US taxation purposes:

Exchange rate at time of remittance	DM 1.6000/$
Net dividend remitted to U.S. parent (US$)	$ 1,687.50
Add back all withholding taxes paid (DM300 ÷ DM1.60/$)	187.50
Add back distributed proportion of income taxes paid ((DM4,000x.5) ÷ DM1.60/$)	1,250.00
Grossed-up dividend income for U.S. taxes	$ 3,125.00
Theoretical U.S. corporate income taxes (35%)	$ 1,093.75
Foreign tax credits	1,437.50
Additional U.S. tax due	0
Excess foreign tax credits	$ 343.75

Notes:
1. Withholding taxes imposed by governments are intended to assure some minimal level of taxes are paid on income earned by foreign residents if they do not file tax returns in that country. If foreign residents did file, they may be entitled to a return of the withholding tax depending on their individual tax position.
2. Income categories (or baskets as they are termed in tax law) such as royalties, interest, license fees, and other non-dividend income, are tax-deductible expenses of the foreign subsidiary and therefore do not have German corporate income taxes withdrawn from them. Therefore when calculating U.S. foreign tax credits for these income baskets, no credit is given for any taxes paid other than for the full amount of withholding taxes applied by theGerman tax authorities.
3. Additional US taxes are due if the theoretical tax liability exceeds the amount of foreign tax credits. If U.S. taxliability is less than the amount of foreign tax credits, the firm owes no additional U.S. taxes and now possesses excess foreign tax credits.
4. Most US-based multinational firms attempt to manage worldwide tax liabilities on two levels: 1. to minimize the total tax burden (total taxes paid worldwide divided by total income earned worldwide); and 2. to minimize the level of excess foreign tax credits given the difficulty of ever using these credits.

SCHNEIDER S. A.
AND SQUARE D COMPANY

"Two-and-a-half years of talking, and I have just been taken for rides," fumed Didier Pineau-Valencienne, president and CEO of France's Schneider S. A. Negotiations for a long-term joint venture agreement—as a precursor to a friendly merger—with the U.S. company, Square D, had ground to a halt. DPV (as he is known in France) attributed this failure to a recent change in attitude on the part of Square D's CEO Jerre Stead.

Within the next week or so, DPV had to decide: Should he call off the negotiations and redirect his energies elsewhere, or should he make a tender offer for Square D?

By mid-February 1991, the U.S. economy finally entered the long-anticipated recession. The only real questions were how long would it last and how deep would it be. Further, in the aftermath of the recent Gulf War, markets worldwide were in turmoil, and no one was quite sure where the world economy was headed. Slowdowns appeared imminent elsewhere. Europe was running out of steam after years of growth propelled by moves toward integration. Declines in Japanese stock and property markets were leading to bearishness in that part of the world.

Schneider S. A.

Founded in 1782, Schneider is one of the largest and most prominent multinational enterprises in France. In 1990, with its 85,000 employees working in plants and sales outlets in more than 115 countries, the company had French Franc (FF) 49.7 billion ($9.7 billion) in sales, and a net income of FF 924 million ($180 million). (See Exhibits 1 and 2.) These were derived from a few core activities and four key subsidiaries: (1) electrical power equipment (*Merlin Gerin*); (2) industrial controls and automation equipment (*Telemecanique*); (3) nuclear power equipment and propulsion systems (*Jeumont-Schneider Industrie*); and (4) electrical engineering/ contracting (*Spie Batignolles*). (See Exhibit 3.)

After a drastic restructuring in the 1980s under the leadership of DPV, Schneider held strong market positions at the European and international levels in all of its main sectors (Exhibit 4). More than half the revenues are derived from France, the rest of Europe accounting for 21%, accounting North America 7%, Asia 6%, Africa 5% and South America 4%.

Until 1980, Schneider was largely under the control of the Belgian family, the Empains. Over the past two centuries, the company had become, in the words of Michel-Francois Poncet of the French bank, Banque Paribas (a board member of Schneider), "an antiquated department store of unrelated family activities." It had a substantial investment in such loss-making areas as shipbuilding and steel.

In addition, the owner Baron Empain diversified the company into non-related sectors such as sports equipment, publishing, real estate, advertising and packaging. This diversification strategy was worsened by weak financial and operating controls, and the fact that as the main shareholder, Baron Empain, was unable to meet the group's financial needs.

In 1981, Baron Empain asked DPV (previously an employee of Schneider and subsequently of the French chemicals giant Rhone-Poulenc) to take responsibility for turning the group around. *The Chicago Tribune* wrote in February 1991:

> "When Didier Pineau-Valencienne left Rhone-Poulenc to head the troubled steel maker Empain-Schneider ten years ago, colleagues gave him a telling going-away gift: a big movie poster for a spaghetti western with star Henry Fonda saying, I shoot first. Since then Pineau-Valencienne has lived up to the poster's image...in aggressively reshaping Group Schneider into a major player in the electrical equipment industry.

> Educated at Dartmouth College's Amos Tuck School of Business Administration, Pineau-Valencienne switched from an early career in publishing where this amateur poet made a mark by negotiating rights to publish Albert Camus' novel 'The Fall' in the U.S. to restructuring sick businesses. The first of those was Empain-Schneider in the late 60s, then came Rhone-Poulenc in the 70s, and finally a return to Empain-Schneider in the 80s. In the process he earned such unflattering names as Doctor Atilla and DPV the Destroyer."

Jean-Leon Vandoorne, the associate chief editor of the largest financial daily in France, *Les Echos,* doesn't agree: "DPV is one of the most modest and straightforward managers I know. He tells you what he means and doesn't give you the run-around."

DPV set out to restructure Schneider, and despite protests from the labor unions and the French government, sold businesses that did not fit his plan to refocus the company on its core electrical products and construction businesses. During the period from 1981 to 1988, Schneider built a strong base through a set of aggressive acquisitions in France and abroad. Between 1986 and 1990, Schneider invested FF 23 billion ($4.5 billion) in acquisitions, FF 8.3 billion ($1.62 billion) in capital expenditures and FF 7 billion ($1.36 billion) in R&D. As the company's 1990 *Annual Report* noted:

> "The Schneider group is dedicating a very considerable part of its resources to strengthening its position as a world leader in....electrical distribution and automation equipment, markets which are undergoing rapid globalization. Economies of scale are of critical importance....[and] research and development expenditures in the power distribution and automation spheres are substantial and fast growing, requiring significant market shares over which to spread these

expenses. Global integration is speeding up as national standards are rapidly being supplanted by international ones. From its solid European base, Schneider has in particular set goals to strengthen its presence in North America, which accounts for one-quarter of world sales...."

During this period, DPV was backed in his efforts by supportive and stable shareholders. Further, they have been ready and willing to provide the capital necessary for Schneider's expansion efforts. For example, in June 1990, Schneider issued FF 3 billion ($584.9 million) in convertible bonds with redeemable share purchase warrants, approximately half of which was bought by the group's principal shareholder.

Given Schneider's relatively feeble presence in North America, DPV had been contemplating a major investment in the U.S. market. The barrier to large-scale entry in the U.S. was distribution, which would be too costly to build *de novo*. Among the options under scrutiny, Square D, the last major independent producer of electrical distribution and automation equipment in the U.S., was regarded by DPV as an attractive potential target for a strategic alliance.

Square D Company

Square D, founded in 1903, is a publicly held electrical distribution and industrial control equipment producer with operations mainly in the U.S. Square D operates thirty-five domestic and eighteen international facilities with 18,500 employees (including 4,000 based abroad). The company has been profitable for the last fifty-nine years, and 1990 marked the fifth consecutive year of record sales ($1,653 million, compared to $1,598 million in 1989: Exhibit 5). The electrical distribution business segment accounted for 70% of sales and 83% of profits; operations in the U.S. market accounted for approximately 80% of sales and 92% of profits (see Exhibit 6 for information on its product range). However, the company has significant market positions in Mexico, Canada, the UK, Thailand and Australia.

In both commercial and residential electrical distribution equipment, Square D is the market leader in the U.S. (ahead of General Electric (GE) and Westinghouse). It is number three in industrial electrical distribution equipment (after Westinghouse and General Electric), and number two in electromechanical industrial control equipment (after Allen Bradley).

In 1990, Square D had a net income of $120.7 million ($101.9 million in 1989), although between 1985 and 1990, its operating margins declined from around 16% of sales to around 11%. The company attributed this decline to shifts in product mix (resulting in a lowered share of high margin products), increased efforts at internationalization (resulting in a higher share of low margin products), higher selling expenses (reaching 14% of sales), and losses of $30 million from some business segments.

In October 1990, Square D's stock was selling at a little over $35 on the New York Stock Exchange; by mid-February 1991, the price had risen to over $50, with the market anticipating some kind of move on Schneider's part. Square D has a beta of 1.02, measured against the U.S. market portfolio (the beta is a measure of the expected percentage movement in a firm's stock returns for each percentage movement in the expected returns on a well-diversified portfolio of stocks, known as the "market" portfolio).

The company sells its branded products at a premium compared to its competition. The company's logo (a capital D embedded in a square) has become a familiar symbol associated with circuit breakers found in the basements of millions of American homes. With over 1200 distributors—most of them independent, and not captive—located all over the U.S., Square D has one of the best selling networks in the industry. The company backs up its distribution network with a strong and well-trained sales force.

The current CEO, Jerre Stead, was recruited as president and COO in 1986, from Honeywell Inc., where he had spent 21 years. He was credited with the turnaround of Honeywell's residential products division in 1982-83, in the midst of a recession.

Stead planned to turn Square D into a major global player, and described the culture he wanted to foster in the company as one of being dedicated to growth and committed to quality, with strong cash flows and a conservative balance sheet. In 1990, Square D spent $94 million on capital expenditures and $55 million on R&D, on sales of $1,653 million. It had cash and cash equivalents of $245 million on its balance sheet, and the ratio of debt to year-end market value of equity was 22% (10% in 1989). Comparable financial data on Square D and its competitors are provided in Exhibit 7.

The Joint Venture Negotiations

By the late 1980s, the electrical distribution industry was globalizing rapidly, and most of Schneider's leading competitors—notably Asea Brown Boveri (ABB) of Sweden—were making significant resource commitments in the U.S. Given the relatively weak position that Schneider had in a market that accounted for a quarter of world sales and the intense competition for market share among the leading players, DPV had to think of ways to expand his presence in the U.S. Otherwise, Schneider could be left behind. DPV noted, ".....all my competitors came to the same conclusion; it is a rapidly changing market that is globalizing. The creation of ABB forced us to question our industry and its operations in a rather fundamental way."

In order to establish a foothold in the North American market, Schneider acquired the Canadian company Federal Pioneer for FF 1.4 billion ($273 million) in 1990. Earlier, in 1987, they acquired Federal Pacific in Mexico. However, given their relatively small size, these acquisitions were ineffective as platforms for U.S. entry. DPV then looked to GE and Westinghouse to examine prospects of joint venture agreements, but both these efforts fell through.

A 1988 study done for Schneider by the U.S. consulting firm McKinsey and Co. identified three firms as potential partners for Schneider in the U.S.: Cutler Hammer, Crouse Hinds, and Square D. Of the three, Square D appeared to be the firm that offered the greatest complementaries (see Exhibit 8). In September of 1988, Schneider hired the New York investment banking firm Dillon Read to help initiate a joint venture discussion with Square D.

From the start, Stead made it clear that it was crucial for Square D to remain independent. Anything that involved a loss of independence would be vetoed by his board. DPV agreed to this, and in a letter to Stead in 1989, committed himself to "...expressly exclude any hostile operation," and informed the directors of Square D that he would not pursue any transaction that was not approved by them. Further, he made a personal commitment to Stead that he would not purchase a single share of Square D stock in the open market.

However, negotiations broke down in September 1989 as the two firms could not agree on the terms of the joint venture. At this stage, DPV hired the services of the French investment banking firm, Lazard Freres. The Lazard advisory team, comprising general partners Robert Lovejoy in New York and Jean-Marie Messier in Paris, recommended that DPV offer an equity swap between Square D and Merlin Gerin, whereby each firm would own a significant portion of the other. Again, after numerous meetings (and presentations to Square D's board made by DPV), the talks broke down. Square D's board seemed convinced that the proposed transaction would give Schneider *de facto* control of Square D without paying a control premium. Further, some directors expressed open distrust of DPV's intentions, given his track record of hostile acquisitions.

By now, it was September 1990. DPV was getting frustrated. During the course of the negotiations, Square D's stock price had gone up quite substantially, and yet, DPV had made the personal commitment not to buy stock in the open market. Indeed, a year earlier, Schneider's pension fund acquired some stock without DPV's knowledge. As soon as he discovered the purchase, he ordered the pension fund to sell it. He noted, "I informed Stead immediately to show him that he should have no fear while we were in conversation. Even in November (1990) when I called him, when the stock was going up, up, up, I told him I didn't buy. I had been extremely correct during all that period."

Stead felt that it was DPV's insistence on the equity exchange, rather than on the manufacturing and licensing aspects of the joint venture that led to the breakdown: "...each time, we ran into a wall, and the wall was Schneider's desire for [the] equity exchange."

In DPV's mind, three factors led him to conclude that it was time to abandon the talks. One, mid-way through two days of a presentation to the Square D board where DPV laid out the details of the strategic merits of the combination (with the support of Stead), Stead cooled off yet again. Two, market anticipation of failure of joint venture talks had led to a run-up in Square D's stock price, and risk arbitragers on Wall Street now held a significant portion of the stock. Three, given the intensely competitive nature of the industry, DPV was concerned that a competitor could enter the picture, and a bidding war could ensue. (See Exhibit 9 for a brief description of Schneider's potential competitors.)

The Next Move

DPV moved quickly to arrange financing on a contingency basis. Should Schneider decide to go ahead with a tender offer, Banque Paribas and Societe Generale agreed to provide 50% of the financing. Further, both Lovejoy and Messier, his closest financial advisors, were of the view that DPV had tried everything he could on the joint venture front, and that it was time to make a move. The structure of financing agreed to was as follows: 50% would be in U.S. dollars, provided by a one-year bridge loan from Societe Generale and Banque Paribas. The other 50% would be in French francs, approximately 38% of which would, in turn, come through the issue of a financial instrument known as the TSDI (a perpetual subordinated floating rate note), and the rest from cash reserves within the Schneider group (see Exhibit 10 for financing details).

Valuation

As a base case, Lazard projected revenues to grow by 3.5% during 1991, and 7% per year thereafter. Earnings before depreciation, interest, and taxes (EBDIT) were estimated to be 15% to 16% of sales, and capital expenditures to grow at about 5% annually from the 1990 base. Net working capital requirements were projected at 11% to 13% of sales, and the marginal corporate tax rate at 37%. Depreciation was estimated to increase from 4% of sales in 1991 to 4.3% in 1997, and remain stable thereafter. Under these assumptions, Lazard's estimates of the base-case per-share value of Square D's equity (assuming different discount rates and different multiples of the fifth-year terminal EBIT: corporate valuations often use multiples of EBIT or cash flows or earnings, in order to calculate terminal values) were as follows:

Discount Rate	EBIT Multiple	Equity Value ($)
13%	8X	65
	9X	71
	10X	76
14%	8X	63
	9X	68
	10X	73
15%	8X	60
	9X	66
	10X	71

The yield on ten-year treasury bonds in the U.S. in 1991 is currently 7.5% and Square D's (equity) beta is 1.02. Lazard estimated that, if Square D were to go out and issue debt in US$ today, its all-in-cost of debt financing would be 10%.

Lazard also estimated that the present value of synergies from the proposed combination would add 34% to the base-case present value calculated above. These synergies were expected to come from: (1) rationalizations of R&D spending (for example, Schneider has already developed products that Square D had been spending R&D resources on); (2) rationalizations of manufacturing facilities (by merging facilities); (3) shared distribution channels in the U.S., Canada and Mexico; (4) increased productivity (for example, in the production of miniature circuit breakers (MCB), one of Square D's core products, Schneider is far more efficient: labor costs account for over 25% of Square D's cost of MCBs, while they account for less than 5% of Schneider's cost); (5) widened product offering (Merlin Gerin and Telemecanique would increase Square D's product range); and (6) profits from sales of unprofitable and unrelated parts of Square D's businesses (expected to generate about one-third of the total synergies).

The electrical products and automation industries had recently seen a spate of takeover activity, the largest of these being Black & Decker's acquisition of Emhart for $2.67 billion, and ABB's acquisition of Combustion Engineering for $1.46 billion. The P/Es in these acquisitions ranged from a low of 16.2 to a high of 39.9 (see Exhibit 11 for the analysis of selected comparable acquisitions).

DPV knew that the valuation would depend upon the state of the U.S. economy. Profits are sensitive to two macroeconomic indicators: residential construction and industrial investment. Consequently, there is a great deal of cyclicality in cash flows, and industry fortunes would depend on how deep the U.S. recession would be and how long it would last (see Exhibit 12 for the trends in key macroeconomic indicators, and projections made by some of the forecasting services). Mr. Leopold Jeorger, Senior Vice President of Corporate Finance at Societe Generale (and the person who signed the bridge loan commitment) was pessimistic about the macroeconomic outlook. He felt that the U.S. recession would last at least a couple of years, and the recovery, when it did come about, would be anemic. Mr. Francois-Poncet of Banque Paribas agreed: this recession was accompanied by a financial crisis in U.S. real estate, a sector on which Square D's sales were highly dependent.

Further, cash flows could be squeezed by the high degree of operating leverage in this industry: fixed costs account for about 50% of the total costs for a company like Square D, and the break-even capacity utilization would be around 60% (Square D's capacity utilization is currently 70%). Yet another worry for DPV was the possibility that Square D could undertake a defensive recapitalization: if he did make the tender offer, the price of the offer would have to be set at a level that would make it difficult for Square D to do this.

Square D's Potential Defenses and U.S. Takeover Legislation

Square D's independence was not a matter of accident: its bylaws offered a plethora of takeover defenses that would potentially deter anyone but the hardiest suitor.

Incorporation in Delaware   Like many U.S. corporations, Square D had sought refuge in the pro-incumbent takeover legislation of the State of Delaware. A key provision under Section 203 of the state's General Corporation Law notes that a Delaware corporation shall not engage in a "business combination" (e.g., merger, sale of more than 10% of assets) with an "interested stockholder" (i.e., holder of more than 15% of the firm's outstanding voting stock) for a period of three years following the date on which the stockholder became an interested stockholder. This provision would be waived if: (1) prior to the date on which someone became an interested stockholder, the firm's board approved the transaction; (2) upon completion of the transaction, the interested stockholder would own at least 85% of the outstanding voting stock (except those owned by directors and Employee Stock Ownership Plan (ESOPs)); or (3) after the date on which someone became an interested stockholder, the firm's board approved the combination and had the approval authorized at a stockholder meeting by at least two-thirds of the voting stock not owned by the interested stockholder.

As of mid-February 1991, Schneider held $15 million, representing less than 2% of Square D's outstanding voting stock.

Rights Plan Square D has a Rights plan that declares a dividend of one Rights share for each outstanding share of common stock. One feature of the plan provided that in the event someone acquires more than 20% of the shares, each Right would become exercisable for that number of common shares having a market value of two times the exercise price of the Right ($100). The Rights of the group that crosses the 20% threshold would be automatically voided. There is another feature which provides that, after someone acquires more than 20%, in the event of a takeover or sale of more than 50% of assets, each Right would become exercisable with the same terms as the first feature.

Further, *before someone crosses the 20% threshold,* the board could redeem all (but not less than all) the Rights at a price of $0.01 per Right. In addition, the terms of the Rights could be amended by the board without the consent of the holders of the Rights.

Supermajority Provisions Square D has no supermajority provisions.

Board Election The board is not classified or staggered; all directors stand for election each year.

Advance Notice of Nominations and Business at Annual Meetings Based on the 1990 meeting dates and current rules, notice of nominations of new board members or proposals of business to be considered by stockholders should be given in writing to the company secretary no later than February 24, 1991. The meeting was currently scheduled for late April, 1991 (though it is not uncommon for firms under siege to attempt to move annual meeting dates in order to gain some breathing room). Considerable information on each nominee has to be provided.

Removal of Directors Directors could be removed by a majority vote of stocks entitled to vote, but could not be removed without cause (however, this rule was inconsistent with Delaware law which provides that, when the board is not classified, directors can be removed without cause).

ESOP In July 1989, Square D put in place an ESOP and issued to it 1,709,400 shares of Series A preferred stock. The ESOP trustee will pass-through to ESOP participants all the voting and tendering rights held in their account. Holders of Series A preferred stock has the same voting rights as holders of common stock (with one vote per share), and they would vote together, as a class. The ESOP shares currency account for about 7% of Square D's voting stock. In order to effect the takeover, DPV would have to add the ESOP shares to the 23.18 million shares currently outstanding

Golden Parachutes   There is an employee severance agreement with seventeen top managers which allows for paying them a lump sum cash payment equal to three times the sum of (a) each individual's salary, and (b) the highest incentive compensation paid to the employee during the three-year period prior to termination. In addition, the benefits package would have to be continued for three years.

There is also a whole set of takeover-related laws at the federal level that Schneider had to consider. The first of these included detailed filings with the Department of Justice (DOJ) and the Federal Trade Commission (FTC) under the Hart-Scott-Rodino Act (HSR) (for details of this and other relevant statutes, see Exhibit 13). Under HSR, if Schneider owned more than $15 million in Square D's stock, it would be subject to a 30-day waiting period in the event that it commenced a tender offer. The FTC and the DOJ would review the transaction for potential antitrust concerns. Often, both agencies can make a request for additional information (also called a second request), which could push the date of the offer back by another twenty days.

There are also antifraud rules under the Securities and Exchange Act of 1934 (overseen by the SEC) which prohibit the use of any "material nonpublic information" in transactions associated with the target's securities. This could be particularly thorny given that a great deal of information had been exchanged between Schneider and Square D during the long joint venture negotiation process. In addition, if the bidder acquired more than 5% of the target's stock, a Schedule 13D would have to be filed with the SEC. Further, under Section 16(a)—often called a "trap for the unwary"—there are complex reporting provisions for transactions in target shares by bidders who own more than 10%. Oversights here could result in transaction profits within a six-month period being recoverable from the bidder.

All in all, lawyers and courts could end up playing an important role in the takeover. Mr. Jean-Rene Fourtou, the CEO of Rhone-Poulenc (a board member of Schneider and a veteran of many takeover battles in the U.S.) said: "Once lawyers get involved, they put you in a situation where you spend 80% of your time worrying about 10% of the details. You end up discussing the worst case, and it ruins the atmosphere. Unlike investment bankers who push to *finish* deals, lawyers are often interested in *continuing* deals. If DPV makes the decision to go ahead with the tender offer, he may not be able to wait around for the lawyers to do their thing."

	1990	1989	1988
Net sales	49,884	45,127	40,493
Cost of goods sold, personnel & admin. expenses	(44,978)	(41,008)	(36,766)
Depreciation and amortization	(1,565)	(1,166)	(1,272)
Operating expenses	(46,543)	(42,174)	(38,038)
Operating income	3,341	2,953	2,455
Interest expense - net	(832)	(757)	(182)
Income before non-recurring items, amortization of goodwill, taxes and minority interest	2,509	2,196	2,273
Non-recurring items			
Gains on disposition of assets - net	419	550	484
Other non-recurring income and expense - net	(367)	(343)	(642)
Income before taxes, employee profit-sharing, amortization of goodwill, and minority interests	2,561	2,403	2,115
Employee profit-sharing	(158)	(130)	(126)
Income taxes	(802)	(912)	(701)
Net income of fully consolidated companies before amortization of goodwill	1,601	1,361	1,288
Amortization of goodwill	(236)	(235)	(345)
Net income of fully consolidated companies	1,365	1,126	943
Groups share of income of companies accounted for by the equity method	4	17	(53)
Minority interests	(445)	(266)	(330)
Net income (SCHNEIDER S.A. share)	924	877	560
Net income (SCHNEIDER S.A. share) per share (in FF)	62.96	63.06	48.85
Net income (SCHNEIDER S.A. share) per	61.65	60.53	N/A
share after dilution (in FF)	701	916	594
Average December share price (in FF)			

EXHIBIT 2 Schneider S.A.: Consolidated Balance Sheet (Data in FF million)

ASSETS	1990	1989	1988
Current assets			
Cash and equivalents	1,841.3	3,400.3	1,579.6
Marketable securities	3,020.9	1,924.3	1,243.7
Accounts receivable - trade	14,597.4	14,987.3	13,998.5
Other receivables and prepaid expenses	4,738.1	3,876.5	4,054.9
Deferred taxes	407.5	290.2	236.9
Inventories and work in process	7,712.6	7,159.0	29,715.3
Total current Assets	32,317.8	31,637.6	50,828.9
Non-current assets			
Property, Plant, and equipment	14,293.9	13,107.5	12,019.7
Accumulated depreciation	(6,691.5)	(6,365.6)	(6,409.5)
Property, Plant, and equipment - net	7,602.4	6,741.9	5,610.2
Investments accounted for by the equity method	175.9	135.7	244.9
Other equity investments	1,727.9	571.3	684.6
Other investments	573.0	618.3	909.8
Total investments	2,476.8	1,325.3	1,839.3
Intangible assets - net	147.5	153.5	115.0
Goodwill - net	7,032.8	6,087.8	5,596.8
Total non-current assets	17,259.5	14,308.5	13,161.3
Total Assets	**49,577.3**	**45,946.1**	**63,990.2**
LIABILITIES AND SHAREHOLDER EQUITY			
Current liabilities			
Accounts payable	9,867.9	9,614.6	8,440.8
Taxes and benefits payable	4,822.5	4,795.8	3,748.4
Other payables and accrued liabilities	5,230.4	4,332.2	3,405.5
Short-term debt	3,120.5	3,165.8	3,081.3
Customer prepayments	2,505.9	3,848.3	27,606.1
Total current liabilities	25,547.2	25,756.7	46,282.1
Long-term debt	9,958.4	7,345.9	7,712.1
of which: convertible bonds	3,950.2	1,108.8	500.5
Provisions for contingencies	3,942.6	3,890.0	3,758.8
Invested capital	24,030.1	20,189.4	17,708.1
Capital stock	1,414.4	1,397.2	1,146.3
Retained earnings	6,091.1	5,344.6	3,046.6
Shareholders equity	7,505.5	6,741.8	4,192.9
Minority interests	2,623.6	2,211.7	2,044.3
Total shareholders equity and minority interests	10,129.1	8,953.5	6,237.2
Total Liabilities and Shareholders Equity	**49,577.3**	**45,946.1**	**63,990.2**

EXHIBIT 3 Schneider S.A.: Business Segments: 1990

Merlin Gerin	Telemecanique	Jeumont-Schneider Industrie	Spie Batignolles
Power transformation transmission and	Automation of industrial control	Nuclear reactant coolant pump sets.	Electrical engineering and contracting.
Extra high, medium voltage and low voltage equipment fo rindustrial, commercial and residential users.	Industrial control components.	Navy propulsion systems.	Industrial engineering development and implementation of manufacturing facilities.
Building maintenance.	Industrial control and protection of electrical motors.	Nuclear power plant and marine maintenance.	Contracting, civil engineering, construction, real estate development.
Safeguarding electrical power users and their property.	Prefabricated busbar distribution.	Power electronics and industrial dive systems.	
Power supply reliability and continuity.			
Sales: PF 18.2 bnNet	Sales: FF 9.98 bn Net income: FP 502 mn Employees: 14,940 operating in 110 countries.	Sales: FF 1.3 bn Net income: FF 61 mn Employees: 2,848.	Sales: FF 22.5 billion Net income: FF 251 million Employees: 35,730 operating in 60 countries.

Activities of Telemecanique:

Limit Switches	Push Buttons	Contactors	Busbars	PLCs	Drives	Electronic Sensors
Telemecanique	*Telemecanique*	Siemens	*Telemecanique*	Siemens	General Electric	Omron
Honeywell	Square D	*Telemecanique*	Square D	Allen Bradley	Reliance	Honeywell
Omron	Allen Bradley	Fuji	General Electric	Mitsubishi	ABB	Allen Bradley
Cutler Hammer	Izumi	Mitsubishi	Pogliano	AEG/Modicon	Siemens	*Telemecanique*
Square D	Cutler Hammer	Allen Bradley	Westinghouse	Omron	Hitachi	
Allen Bradley	General Electric	Klockner-Moeller	Klockner-Moeller	*Telemecanique*	Toshiba	
Klockner-Moeller	Siemens	Square D			Mitsubishi	
	Fuji	General Electric			Emerson	
					Danfoss	
					Leuze	
					AEG/Modicon	
					Telemecanique	

Activities of Merlin Gerin:

Transformers	EHV	MV Breakers	MV Load Break Switches	MCCBs	MCBs	UPS
ABB	ABB	ABB	*Merlin Gerin*	Westinghouse	ABB	Emerson
CI	GEC.Alsthom	*Merlin Gerin*	ABB	Mitsubishi	Siemens	*Merlin Gerin*
GEC.Alsthom	*Merlin Gerin*	GEC.Alsthom	GEC.Alsthom	*Merlin Gerin*	*Merlin Gerin*	Fuji
Merlin Gerin	Mitsubishi	Siemens	Siemens	General Electric	Square D	
Siemens	Siemens	Mitsubishi		Square D	Westinghouse	
Toshiba	Hitachi	Westinghouse		Siemens	General Elec.	
Mitsubishi	Toshiba			ABB	Mitsubishi	
Hitachi	AEG					

EHV: Extremely High Voltage; MV: Medium Voltage; MCCB: Molded Case Circuit Breakers; MCB: Miniature Circuit Breaker; UPS: Uninterruptible Power Supply.

EXHIBIT 5 Square D Company: Five-Year Financial Summary ($ millions, except ratios and per-share data)

	1990	1989	1988	1987	1986
Sales	1653.30	1598.69	1497.77	1330.78	1274.93
Depreciation	59.30	49.44	45.17	42.28	38.55
Non-operating Income	34.74	17.11	17.26	17.59	26.67
Operating Income	153.76	144.64	164.98	171.15	157.55
Interest Expense	28.76	31.44	22.08	19.70	24.98
Taxes	67.78	59.86	63.31	75.74	85.19
Net Income	120.72	101.89	118.93	113.00-	99.03
Common Stock Dividend	50.10	50.59	54.60	53.50	53.20
Cash and ST Investments	244.90	70.20	79.20	100.80	73.90
Receivables	305.20	321.50	279.80	258.20	21 5.90
Total Current Assets	761.60	711.90	588.40	529.90	481.20
Total Assets	1459.70	1372.59	1300.72	1252.82	1178.83
Short Term Debt	123.90	263.70	123.10	79.90	19.30
Accounts Payable	220.60	208.40	199.20	180.50	170.60
Total Current Liabilities	372.10	504.60	375.20	302.80	232.80
Long Term Debt	244.80	123.42	135.47	145.09	166.39
Stockholders Equity	603.60	556.12	636.06	679.71	670.79
Stock Price (year end)	49.00	49.00	46.00	50.00	46.17
Market Value of Equity	1137.21	1143.04	1186.83	1401.12	1338.93
Dividend per Share	2.20	2.00	1.94	1.86	1.84
Earnings per Share	4.94	3.98	4.44	3.82	3.42
Capital Expenditure	94.00	85.80	86.00	43.70	87.70
R&D Expenditure	55.40	44.70	49.50	44.40	41.80
Share Repurchase (Issue)	35.00	126.77	111.39	137.00	n.a.
Total Shares Outstanding (mn.)*	23.18	23.50	25.70	28.00	29.00
Price-to-Earnings (P/E) Ratio (Square D)	9.42	12.22	10.40	13.10	13.50
P/E Ratio (All NYSE Stocks; Dec.)	25.80	14.80	15.00	15.50	16.10

*The figures for 1989 and 1990 exclude 1.71 million (m). ESOP shares. These shares have the same rights as common stock.

EXHIBIT 6 Square D: Product Range

ELECTRICAL DISTRIBUTION	INDUSTRIAL CONTROL

ELECTRICAL DISTRIBUTION

Low-voltage Distribution Equipment.
Load centers and circuit breakers, safety switches, molded case circuit breakers, multi-metering equipment, home wiring systems.

Power Equipment

Low and medium-voltage switchgear (power circuit breakers, switches), motor control centers, switchboards, busways.

Transformers

Dry-type lighting and pad-mounted transformers, oil-filled instrument transformers, low-voltage distribution transformers, control transformers, isolation transformers, uninterruptible power systems (UPS).

Connectors

Transmission, distribution and substation connectors.

Consumer Products

Load Centers and breakers, safety switches, voltage testers and surge suppressors.

INDUSTRIAL CONTROL

Control and Automation Products

Pushbuttons, sensors, relays, pressure switches, control switches, contactors and motor controls (starters, ac drives). Programmable controllers and cell controllers, and data communication networks and systems (hardware and software).

Crane and mill controls, water pump switches, resistance welding controllers and stamping press controls.

Infrared Measurement Division

Infrared thermometers, line scanners and systems for non-contact temperature measurement and control.

Engineered Systems Division

Computerized control and data gathering systems.

Technical Services Division
Service agreements, start-up, training, testing and emergency services.

EXHIBIT 7 Comparative Financial Data on Square D and Competitors (1990)

	Amp Inc.	Cooper Industries	Emerson Electric	WW Grainger	Square D
Sales ($ m.)	3043.6	6222.2	7573.4	1935.2	1653.3
Net Income ($ m.)	287.1	361.4	613.2	126.8	120.7
Sales growth (CAGR[1], 1988-90)	6.8%	20.9%	6.7%	12.3%	5.1%
EBIT Growth (CAGR, 1988-90)	-4.1%	30.2%	8.3%	7.0%	-0.2%
EPS[2] Growth (CAGR, 1988-90)	-4.5%	12.8%	9.1%	8.6%	7.1%
EBIT Margin(%)	16.0%	13.5%	14.6%	10.5%	10.8%
P/E[3] Ratio	17.1	14.4	13.9	14.7	9.4
EPS ($)	1.35	2.81	2.75	4.60	4.94
Long-Term Debt/ Total Book Capital	1.0%	38.6%	11.3%	0.9%	24.2%

n.a. => not available
[1] CAGR = Compound Annual Growth Rate
[2] EPS = Earnings per Share
[3] P/E = Price-to-Earnings

Source: Disclosure databases.

EXHIBIT 8 Square D vs. Schneider: Market Shares in the U.S. and Europe

	UNITED STATES			EUROPE		
	Square D	Merlin Gerin	Telemecanique	Square D	Merlin Gerin	Telemecanique
Residential Distribution	30%	1%	-	2%	25%	-
Industrial Control	15%	1%	-	2%	40%	-
Industrial Distribution	15%	-	5%	<1%	-	25%
Programmable Logic Controls	7%	-	<1%	<1%	-	11%

EXHIBIT 9 Potential Acquirers of Square D

Company Name	Segments (as a % of Sales)	1989 Sales	Net Debt	Total Equity	Net Debt/ Cap (%).
Asea Brown-Boveri	Electrical engineering/power generating (22%), power distribution (19%), power transmission (16%), industry and traffic (20%), and mass products (23%).[a,b]	24,242	4,954	3,308	60
General Electric	[a]Aerospace (9%), aircraft engines (12%), broadcasting (6%), industrial (13%), major appliances (10%), materials (9%), power systems (9%), technical products and services (8%), other (1%), and financial services (23%).	41,677	6,354	21,015	23
Mitsubishi Electric	Electronic products and systems, communications and information processing systems, electronic devices, heavy machinery, industrial products and automotive equipment and consumer products.	19,405	1,185	4,564	21
Rockwell Interna-tional	Electronics (40%), aerospace (32%), automotive (19%) and graphics (9%).	12,357	1,019	4,140	20
Siemens	Energy and automation systems (22%), communication and information systems (17%), power plants (14%), medical engineering (10%), electrical installations and automotive systems (9%), and other (28%).	39,463	(9,851)	11,121	N.A.
Westinghouse Electric[a]	Broadcasting (5%), commercial (18%), electronic systems (20%), energy and utility systems (16%), financing services (9%), industries (23%), and divested and other (9%).	11,652	1,602	4,639	26
AEG	Automation systems (19%), consumer products (21%), electrical systems and components (34%), microelectronics (9%), office and communication systems (12%), and transportation systems (5%).	7,900	1,311	7	N.A.

Note: $ in millions.

N.A. - Not Available
[a] Results exclude finance subsidiaries.
[b] Estimated pro-forma acquisition of Combustion Engineering.

EXHIBIT 10 Schneider's Financing Plan for the Square D Acquisition

- The acquisition will be fully financed through internal cash, existing commitments for perpetual financing (TSDI) and lines of credit from Societe Generale and Banque Paribas.

- Fifty percent will be financed in French Francs (FF) and 50% in U.S. dollars (US$). The FF portion will be hedged with six-month FF/$ currency call options with an exercise price of FF 5.20/US$; the current spot exchange rate is FF 5.075/US$; six-month U.S. interest rates are 5.6%, and equivalent FF rates are 9.3%

- The share of the financing burden borne by the various business units would be as follows: Schneider 50%, Merlin Gerin 45% and Telemecanique 5%.

- The US$ portion would be in the form of a credit facility from Societe Generale and Banque Paribas. Repayment of amounts borrowed under this credit facility would be due one year from the date of borrow-ing; the financing commitment would terminate on December 31, 1991.

- Of the FF Portion, 38% would be raised through the issue of a perpetual subordinated floating rate note called TSDI. Merlin Gerin would be the issuer. The interest rate would be six-month FF Paris InterbankOffer Interest Rate (PIBOR) + 0.7% payable semiannually; issue price at par. The first payment was due March 18,

- The remaining 62% of the FF portion would come from cash reserves within the Schneider group. Most of this cash was raised in June 1990 through the issue of convertible bonds. The convertibles paid an interestof 6.5% annually. Each bond had a share purchase warrant priced at FF 150 and gives investors the right to purchase a Schneider share for FF 1200 by tendering FF 900 in cash together with two warrants; the warrants were exercisable until July 1, 1993. In the event that they were nonexercisable, they would be redeemed at par on January 1, 1988.

EXHIBIT 11 Analysis of Selected Comparable Acquisitions ($ millions)

Announce-ment Date	Business of Acquirer/Acquiree	Acquired Company	Equity Purchase Price	Total Purchase Price	Equity Purchase Price as a Multiple of:		Total Purchase Price as a Multiple of:		
					Income	Book Value	Revenues	EBDIT[1]	EBIT
12/1/87	Imo Delaval Ioc./Income International (IFINT-Income Inc.)	Manufacturer of mechanical and electronic controls and power transmission devices.	$167	$195	N.A.	2.1	0.9	5.5	7.0(f)
9/11/87	Siebe PLC/Barber-Colman Company	Industrial and environmental controls, cutting tools, fasteners.	228	228	N.M.	N.M.	0.9	10.4	15.0
9/7/87	Landis & Gyrag Mark Controls Corp.	Process and environmental controls for industrial use, water systems equipment.	145	159	39.6	2.2	0.6	11.1	16.5
12/24/86	Emerson Electric/Liebert Corporation	Environmental and power control systems.	594	519	27.1	3.2	1.8.	13.2	15.0
12/19/86	Siebe PLC/Ranco Incorporated	Industrial controls, valves, relays, semiconductor devices and sequence controls for refrigeration, air conditioning, home, laundry and automotive.	153	186	22.5	2.1	1.0	8.7	13.4
9/8/86	Rockwell International/Electronics Corp of America	Photoelectric controls and electronic combustion sensors.	96	102	19.9(9)	3	N.A.	N.A.	N.A.
7/15/86	Siebe PLC/Robertshaw Controls Company	Manufacturer of automatic controls and control systems for industry commercial buildings and the home.	472	503	22.0	2.9	1.2	10.5	13.1

NOTES:
(a) Figures are 1990E. Source: Baird/The Gaspar Report, September 5,1989.
(b) Book value and EBDIT figures estimated by James Carrol, a Paine Webber analyst. Finmeccanica is a wholly-owned subsidiary of IRI, the Italian state-owned conglomerate.
(c) Assumes $45 per share and 7.2 million shares outstanding March 31,1988. Also includes 0.5 million shares issuable upon exercise of warrants and options at an estimated average exercise price of $17.50. (Source: Offer ro Purchase dated May 11,1988)
(d) Excludes $1.2 million after-tax ($0.16 per share) gain on Last-In-First-Out (LIFO) inventory liquidation, assumed to be $2 million pre-tax.
(e) Excludes $1.3 million charge resulting from the purchase of the company's shares above the marker price, tax effected at 44%.
(f) Operating income from continuing operations excludes unusual items, depreciation/amortization of asset write-up, and corporate/group expense.
(g) Excludes $1.4 million earnings resulting from resolution of certain tax matters.
[1] EBDIT = Earnings Before Depreciation, Interest, and Taxes

A09-97-0017

EXHIBIT 11 (cont.)

Announcement Date	Business of Acquirer/Acquiree	Acquired Company	Equity Purchase Price	Total Purchase Price	Equity Purchase Price as a Multiple of:		Total Purchase Price as a Multiple of:		
					Income	Book Value	Revenues	EBDIT[1]	EBIT
12/1/87	Imo Delaval Ioc./ Income International (IFINT-Income Inc.)	Manufacturer of mechanical and electronic controls and power transmission devices.	$167	$195	N.A.	2.1	0.9	5.5	7.0(f)
9/11/87	Siebe PLC/ Barber-Colman Company	Industrial and environmental controls, cutting tools, fasteners.	228	228	N.M.	N.M.	0.9	10.4	15.0
9/7/87	Landis & Gyrag Mark Controls Corp.	Process and environmental controls for industrial use, water systems equipment.	145	159	39.6	2.2	0.6	11.1	16.5
12/24/86	Emerson Electric/ Liebert Corporation	Environmental and power control systems.	594	519	27.1	3.2	1.8.	13.2	15.0
12/19/86	Siebe PLC/ Ranco Incorporated	Industrial controls, valves, relays, semiconductor devices and sequence controls for refrigeration, air conditioning, home, laundry and automotive.	153	186	22.5	2.1	1.0	8.7	13.4
9/8/86	Rockwell International/ Electronics Corp of America	Photoelectric controls and electronic combustion sensors.	96	102	19.9(9)	3.3	N.A.	N.A.	N.A.
7/15/86	Siebe PLC/ Robertshaw Controls Company	Manufacturer of automatic controls and control systems for industry commercial buildings and the home.	472	503	22.0	2.9	1.2	10.5	13.1

NOTES:(a)Figures are 1990E. Source: Baird/The Gaspar Report, September 5,1989.
(b)Book value and EBDIT figures estimated by James Carrol, a Paine Webber analyst. Finmeccanica is a wholly-owned subsidiary of IRI, the Italian state-owned conglomerate.
(c)Assumes $45 per share and 7.2 million shares outstanding March 31,1988. Also includes 0.5 million shares issuable upon exercise of warrants and options at an estimated average exercise price of $17.50. (Source: Offer to Purchase dated May 11,1988)
(d)Excludes $1.2 million after-tax ($0.16 per share) gain on Last-In-First-Out (LIFO) inventory liquidation, assumed to be $2 million pre-tax.
(e)Excludes $1.3 million charge resulting from the purchase of the company's shares above the marker price, tax effected at 44%.
(f)Operating income from continuing operations excludes unusual items, depreciation/amortization of asset write-up, and corporate/group expense.
(g)Excludes $1.4 million earnings resulting from resolution of certain tax matters.
1 EBDIT = Earnings Before Depreciation, Interest, and Taxes

EXHIBIT 12 Trends in Key Macroeconomic Indicators and Forecasts

Actual	Real GNP (% Change)	Industrial Production (% Change)	Non-Residential Fixed Investment (Index)	Residential Investment (Index)
1990 Q1	1.3	0.6		
Q2	1.0	0.9		
Q3	1.0	2.2		
Q4	0.3	0.3	522.6	206.7
Forecasts				
1991 Q1	- 0.4	- 1.3	515.9	197.6
Q2	- 0.3	- 2.4	516.2	196.8
Q3	- 0.2	- 2.7	522.3	207.9
Q4	0.9	0.2	531.8	222.9
1992 Q1	2.0	2.4	540.2	233.5
O2	2.5	3.3	548.7	239.8
Q3	2.8	3.5	556.5	244.8
Q4	2.8	3.3	564.1	249.8

Source: Blue Chip Econometric Detail, February 10, 1991.

EXHIBIT 13 Some Relevant U.S. Federal Takeover Statutes

1. No specific rule prohibits pre-bid accumulation of shares. However, anyone who acquires more than 5% of any class of equity registered under the *Securities Exchange Act of 1934* must, under *Section 13(d),* file a report with the SEC, any exchange in which the security is traded, and the issuer, within ten days of the acquisition.

2. The *Securities Exchange Act Rule 10(b)-13* prohibits the bidder from purchasing or agreeing to purchase except pursuant to an announced bid throughout the whole period of the bid.

3. Under the *Securities Exchange Act,* the intention of the bidder with respect to the target must be disclosed in the offering document. If the subsequent conduct of the bidder deviates from the stated intent, the bidder may be subject to suit for fraud if intent or recklessness tantamount to intent is shown.

4. Any merger, acquisition, or joint venture involving corporations whose activities affect interstate commerce may be prohibited if it has adverse effects in a defined geographic and product market. The principal statutory provision for merger control is the *Clayton Act, Section 7,* under which mergers may be declared illegal where their effect is to substantially lessen competition.

5. In general, investigations and injunctive suits challenging mergers may be brought by the Department of Justice (DOJ), the Federal Trade Commission (FTC), and the State Attorney General. Private parties (including takeover targets) may also file suits.

6. The *Hart-Scott-Rodino Antitrust Improvements Act of 1976* (HSR) requires pre-merger notification with the DOJ and FTC in certain cases. It sets up an elaborate investigative mechanism and schedule for mergers subject to notification. Notification must be filed if the following two size thresholds are met: (i)either the bidder or the target has assets or annual sales of $100 mn. or more and the other party has assets or sales of $10 mn. or more; (ii) the bidder would end up holding either 15% of the shares in the target, or would end up with voting securities or assets in excess of $15 mn. In addition, foreign buyers may be subject to review if the target has assets or annual sales exceeding $25 mn. There is a 30-day waiting period (15 days for cash tender offers) before the acquisition may take place. Prior to its expiration, the 30/15 day period may be extended by the DOJ or the FTC by issuing a so-called second request for more documents and information. The transaction is then stayed for a second 20/10 day period, which does not start until the bidder has complied with the second request. Extensive market, financial, and corporate data are usually required under HSR. Transactions are held up for the prescribed periods, and thereafter (by agreement) pending the completion of the investigation by the DOJ and the FTC—90% of the investigations are completed within the waiting periods, but in complicated cases an investigation can stretch up to six months.

GM's Plant X-Brazil (A)

Rio De Janeiro—General Motors Corp. is preparing to build a new small car in Brazil that it plans to offer with one of the lowest sticker prices in the world, giving GM a competitive advantage in developing markets. In addition, according to individuals close to the situation, experimental assembly techniques GM is expected to use in building the car could hold implications for vehicle manufacture in the developed markets. Already, Volkswagen AG has used South America as a testing ground for radical approaches to making cars more efficiently.

GM's Brazilian experiment, code named "Blue Macaw," would fill a gap in the auto maker's lineup in Brazil, where small low-cost cars with 1.0 liter engines—known as "popular cars" here—dominate the market. GM plans to produce the car at a new, $600 million plant being built in southern Brazil.

When opened in about 18 months, the plant is expected to rely heavily on suppliers to deliver major subassemblies of the car to the plant. Employees of the suppliers may be involved in some of the assembly work, using an idea long advocated by J. Ignacio Lopez de Arriortua, the executive who left GM for VW in a cloud of controversy. VW also has been applying some of his ideas in South America. GM officials say the new assembly lines will be the so-called Plant X, a design that was the center of their industrial-espionage dispute with Mr. Lopez.

"GM to Build a Low-Priced Car in Brazil,"
Wall Street Journal, May 19, 1997, pp. A2, A4.

Claudia Teofilo had only a few days to finish the financial structure for GM's new Brazilian plant. The so-called *Plant X* would represent a large investment by GM—and a big risk—which Claudia hoped to counter with a financial structure and budget with margins for error. Claudia knew that the project was already going forward, regardless of her numbers, but the pressure was still on for her to *prove the truth* about the financial legitimacy of GM's major expansion in Brazil. After all, every other major auto manufacturer in the world seemed to be pouring capital into Brazil, so why should GM hesitate?

The Brazilian Auto Market

Cheap was the watchword for competing in the Brazilian automobile market. If GM was to actually garner a large chunk of the new automobile market in Brazil, the new car would have to come in under the price of the major competitors, and competition was heating up.

Volkswagen had traditionally dominated the Brazilian market, producing 700,000 autos of the total 1995 Brazilian output of 1.6 million vehicles (a 44% market share). And Volkswagen was not about to sit idly by as quieter competitors made inroads on their market position.

Specific to GM's target market, Fiat Spa was already well entrenched in the Brazilian market with the *Uno* at a price of R$11,500 (about US$10,750 at the current exchange rate of 1.07 Brazilian real per U.S. dollar). Ford had also recently joined the fray with the *Ka*, a 1.0-liter popular car (also termed "ultra-small") first introduced in Europe.

EXHIBIT 1 Low-Cost Auto Prices in Brazil and the United States, 1997

Brazilian Market	
Model	Price
Blue Macaw (planned)	$9,000
Fiat Uno	$10,000
Ford Ka	$11,000

United States Market	
Model	Price
Geo Metro	$8,580
Hyundai Accent	$8,599
Suzuki Swift	$8,999
Ford Aspire	$9,295
Mitsubishi Mirage	$10,520
Honda Civic	$10,550

Source: "Low Sticker Prices," *The Wall Street Journal,* Monday May 19, 1997, p. A3.

GM believed that if it could undercut the *Ka*, and undercut it by a substantial amount, it could reap huge rewards.

The Brazilian car market had literally exploded in recent years thanks to governmental economic and political reforms aimed at stimulating economic growth. Working primarily through tax reductions on new car sales, policy changes had caused Brazilian car production to rise by 6% in 1996, to over 1.7 million cars. This made Brazil the seventh largest car market in the world.[1] Mrs. Dorthea Werneck, Brazil's trade minister, was now forecasting Brazilian auto production to hit 3.0 million units by the year 2000, which would move Brazil up to the fifth largest auto producer in the world.[2] To double production between 1995 and 2000 would, however, require a massive influx of foreign capital.

Although company after company had announced major new investment initiatives for the Brazilian marketplace, the various Brazilian states were also competing heavily for individual plants. The Brazilian auto manufacturers association, *Anfavea*, had its hands full in trying to cope with the massive influx of capital and development requests.

♦ Renault (France), enticed by a $300 million loan by the state of Paraná, had announced a new Meganes manufacturing facility.

♦ Volkswagen (Germany), already the leading manufacturer of automobiles in Brazil, had announced two new major developments: a $500 million plant to

---

[1] "Foreign Automakers Flocking to Balmy Brazil: Deficit to Demand Expected to Widen," Michael Kepp, *American Metal Market,* November 4, 1996.

[2] "Renault Bucks the Brazil Carmaker Trend: The French Company is the Latest to Move Into the Market, But With a Difference," Simonian Haug, *Financial Times,* April 19, 1996.

produce 100,000 Golfs per year; and a $500 million plant to produce 80,000 Audis per year. Both plants were to be on-line in late 1998. It appeared that the state of Rio de Janeiro had the upper hand, as the State was putting together a $800 million package for VW's benefit.

♦ Honda (Japan) had broken ground on a $100 million facility in São Paulo to produce 30,000 Honda Civics per year beginning in late 1998.

♦ Daimler Benz (Germany) had recently chosen Minas Gercasi for a new $400 million, 80,000 car per year Mercedes manufacturing plant.

♦ Other manufacturers from around the globe were also in some stage of investment planning, including Asia Motors, Hyundai, Peugeot, and Chrysler.

In all, foreign automobile manufacturers had pledged over $10 billion in capital expenditures for Brazil by the turn of the century.

Co-Production vs. Joint Production

Plant X was the realization of a not-really-that-new idea. GM would design the car, recruit and organize the suppliers, build and furnish the basic manufacturing floor, but have the suppliers manufacture their parts and inputs on-site and then assemble the car. The manufacturing floor was literally divided by yellow lines indicating where one supplier stopped and the next started. *Tier 1* suppliers would both manufacture and assemble on-site, while *Tier 2* suppliers would produce only.

The economics of the co-production process were revolutionarily different from those of the customary specialization of production envisioned by Alfred P. Sloan over 70 years ago. It really was no longer General Motors building the automobile, but a consortium of sub-assemblers and input manufacturers with GM as the facilitator, the *conductor* of this increasingly complex *orchestra*. The role of the suppliers, in their willingness to produce on-site, devote capital resources to the placement of manufacturing equipment and workers on-site, and in many ways to then share in the risks simultaneously with GM, was a role few had ever been called upon to play. But, they were no longer simply contract players; they were now integral to the production of the co-designed and co-produced product. They were now subordinated stockholders as well as suppliers and workers.

GM believed that the process as designed for the *Blue Macaw* would allow the manufacture of a world-class economy car—*popular car*—at a price which would devastate the competition. Actual manufacturing costs were estimated to be 30% to 35% less than traditional manufacturing designs. And because the suppliers were on-site, the need for GM to hold massive inventories, or even to invest in capital-intensive electronic data interchange (EDI) systems to support a just-in-time inventory or *kamban* system, was eliminated.

GM would now not only produce the car at lower per unit cost, but it could do so with a fraction of the normal capital required for major new automobile manufacturing units anywhere else in the world. Operationally, because of the just-in-time manufacturing capability, the plant would produce cars on order, not on forecast. Again, this meant that the top half of the firm's Brazilian balance sheet could be substantially reduced. Lower inventories of materials, intermediate inputs, work-in-progress, and finally finished product could be drastically reduced. *Virtual manufacturing* was the way one of the engineers had described it in a meeting in Detroit.

Capital Budget: Plant X

According to GM's revised *corporate capital allocation policies* (CCAP), the project would be evaluated on two different levels:

1. **Project Viewpoint.** This was an in-country capital budgeting analysis in which traditional capital budgeting methods were used. This would require the construction of a complete set of pro forma financial statements, including revenue structure, transfer pricing, capital investment and funding, income statement, statement of cash flows, balance sheet, and finally the capital budget itself. The capital budget, following traditional financial theory, should isolate all net operating cash flows arising from the project, and discount those cash flows by the financial cost (opportunity cost) of that capital back to the present.

2. **Parent Viewpoint.** This was a cross-country capital budgeting analysis which looked more like a cash flow return on investment analysis than the traditional capital budgeting formula followed under part 1 above. The principle was actually quite simple: given the capital put at risk by the parent company (the U.S.-based parent company), did the cash flows returned to the parent over time in the parent's own currency justify such an investment? This required Claudia to identify all individual incremental sources of cash flow and earnings to GM-US arising from the project over time, regardless of whether they were operational or financial in nature.

There were, however, two very distinct differences in this financial analysis from the traditional approaches Claudia had learned in graduate school. First, the project's returns had to justify the investment in no more than five years of operations. Cash flows arising past that date were immaterial to GM as the window for the Blue Macaw would only be open for that short technological life. Secondly, the analysis was to be based on cash flows from actual operations, not from any end-of-period boost from a terminal or sale or salvage value. At the end of the five years, the project would either be highly successful, or not. If not, the manufacturing facility, given its unique construction and co-production format with suppliers, would be worthless.

Plant X: The Numbers

The magnitude of data already collected from the many different project teams was enormous. Claudia had spent the past three weeks collecting, soliciting, and

EXHIBIT 2 Market Forecast for the GM Blue Macaw

Calendar Year	1997	1998	1999	2000	2001	2002
Project Year	0	1	2	3	4	5
Brazil						
New car market	1,800,000					
Growth rate		20.0%	20.0%	20.0%	10.0%	10.0%
Blue Macaw share	—	—	8.0%	12.0%	15.0%	18.0%
Argentina						
New car market	350,000					
Growth rate		10.0%	12.0%	10.0%	8.0%	8.0%
Blue Macaw share	—	—	5.0%	10.0%	12.0%	12.0%
Chile						
New car market	150,000					
Growth rate		8.0%	10.0%	8.0%	6.0%	6.0%
Blue Macaw share	—	—	8.0%	12.0%	15.0%	15.0%

developing the data set. It was now Spring 1997, and the facility would require approximately 18 to 20 months for completion. Operations would officially begin January 1, 1999, and none too soon given the massive influx of manufacturing competitors into the Brazilian marketplace.

Revenues. The driver behind any potential investment, the sales outlook, was by far the most important input. GM's market strategy group had constructed a detailed sales forecast for sales in Brazil, as well as potential export sales to other *Mercosur* members Chile and Argentina. Exhibit 2 lists the market sizes, growth rates, and potential Blue Macaw market share for each of the three countries.

Inflation Rates, Exchange Rates, & Prices. Claudia took a deep breath anytime issues related to prices or exchange rates came up in regard to South America. Brazil's record was not one of the best, but Claudia pinched herself to think positively and look at the recent evidence of the success of the government's economic stabilization plan, the *Plano Real*. Prices, inflation rates, exchange rates—all were better, and had remained so for several years now. GM's biggest brains and computers had churned away for weeks coming up with the estimates on prices and rates for the Blue Macaw project, and the results were condensed in Exhibit 3. These were their best guesses, but were in no way carved in stone. The figures could change, but they would have to serve as the starting point (baseline analysis).

The exchange rate analysis would have to be handled very carefully. The international economics group at GM (and their outside consultants such as Data Resource Inc. in Boston) were forecasting the Brazilian real to depreciate roughly 2.0% per year over the period. That would be nice if true, but the differences in inflation rates between Brazil and the United States would indicate a very different outlook if

EXHIBIT 3 Forecast for Prices, Inflation, and Exchange Rates for the GM Blue Macaw

Calendar Year	1997	1998	1999	2000	2001	2002	2003
Project Year	0	1	2	3	4	5	6
Brazil							
Inflation rates, %:							
consumer	13.4	16.0	17.2	13.4	12.7	10.7	10.7
materials	10.0	12.0	12.0	10.0	8.0	8.0	8.0
labor costs	15.0	15.0	15.0	15.0	15.0	15.0	15.0
Spot rate (R$/$)	1.0700						
Preferred auto import tariffs, %	4.8	7.2	9.6	16.0	16.0	16.0	16.0
Argentina							
Inflation rate, %	0.8	1.7	2.0	2.9	3.7	3.7	3.7
Spot rate (APs/$)	1.0000						
Chile							
Inflation rate, %	6.6	5.7	4.5	4.4	3.9	3.9	3.9
Spot rate (CPs/$)	431.60						
United States							
Inflation rate, %	3.0	3.0	3.1	3.1	3.2	3.2	3.2
Blue Macaw price	—	—	R$10,000				

the currency forecast was based on purchasing power parity (PPP).[3] Claudia knew from the start that although the baseline analysis would use the 2.0% depreciation assumption, a lot of sensitivity and scenario work would be required as well. And that was just for the Brazilian real.

The Argentine peso (APs) was another extreme. Argentina's 100% U.S. dollar reserve monetary system put in place back in 1992 had been extremely successful. Argentina had gone from one of the most hyper-inflationary economies in the world, with one of the weakest currencies, to a stable fixed exchange rate of one peso per dollar, year after year. The question was whether to simply assume the rate would remain fixed over the term or to use purchasing power parity from the start. The project team had wanted to assume a fixed rate for the baseline analysis, but left the door open for additional sensitivity studies.

The Chilean peso (CPs) completed the *Latin triangle*. Here again was a currency of distinct character. The economic reforms of the 1980s combined with the richness of copper resources in Chile had made the Chilean economy the showplace of South America in the 1990s. Economic growth, political stability, low inflation, trade

---

[3] Purchasing power parity assumes exchange rates move in proportion to inflation. For example, if the initial spot rate between the Brazilian real and the U.S. dollar was R$1.0700/$, and Brazilian and U.S. inflation rates were expected to be 16.0% and 3.0%, respectively, the spot rate in one year would be forecast as:

$$\text{Spot rate (year 1)} = \text{R\$1.0700/\$} \times \frac{1 + .16}{1 + .03} = \text{R\$1.2050/\$}.$$

surpluses, all had combined not only to preserve the value of the Chilean peso, but to drive it's value up versus the U.S. dollar. This was not a common sight among Latin American currencies. The baseline analysis called for an annual appreciation of the Chilean peso of 1% versus the U.S. dollar.

The final component of Exhibit 3 which was critical to the Plant X project was pricing. The *Blue Macaw* had to be priced substantially below the *Ka* if it was to capture the market share numbers listed in Exhibit 1. The analysts debate had been ugly; the result was a compromise. The Blue Macaw would hit the market in 1999 at a price of R$10,000. It would then see a price growth which was 6.0% annually less than what consumer prices were expected to do. This meant that if consumer prices rose 13.4% in 2000 as expected, the Blue Macaw's sticker price (MSRP, Manufacturer's Suggested Retail Price) would increase 13.4%-6.0% in the year 2000. The market strategy group had concluded that with this pricing structure the Macaw would be able to capture the market shares needed from other majors like Volkswagen and Fiat—and hold it.

Exchange Rate Pass-Through. Claudia had already expended many hours in working with her colleagues in Argentina and Chile on pricing analysis for those respective markets. The problem was *pass-through*, the ability of a price to reflect underlying exchange rate changes.

The price in the first year of sales, if all went according to plan, was simple enough. The Brazilian real price of R$10,000 (1999) would be converted to Argentine pesos at the current spot rate of APs0.8976/R$, establishing a retail price in Argentina of APs8,975.70.[4]

Claudia and her colleagues know, however, that the price in the second year of sales (2000) would not be allowed by the marketplace to pass-through the full change in the APs/R$ exchange rate to consumers. The pass-through would be partial, possibly only 50%. As illustrated in Exhibit 4, if the Brazilian price rose to

EXHIBIT 4 Claudia's Sample Calculation of Retail Price Pass-Through in Argentina

Calendar Year		1999	2000	
Project Year		2	3	
Exchange rates: APs/$		1.0000	1.0000	
APs/R$		0.8976	0.8796	
Macaw pricing:				
Brazilian price, R$		10,000	10,740	Brazilian retail price
Argentine price, APs:				
100% pass-through		8,975.70	9,447.10	
50% pass-through		8,975.70	9,211.40	Argentine retail price
Effective R$ revenues		10,000	10,472	

Note: In the first year of sales, 1999, the established price is set at the current exchange rate. Partial pass-through initially takes effect in the second year of sales, 2000, where there is an exchange rate change-induced price change possibility from the Brazilian manufactured automobile.

[4] This assumes that as members of Mercosur there would be no tariffs imposed on the Brazilian-manufactured goods, and that any additional distribution expenses were absorbed by GM-Brazil.

EXHIBIT 5 Capital Outlays and Funding for GM's Plant X (R$)

Calendar Year	1997	1998
Project Year	0	1
Cash		30,000,000
Accounts receivable		—
Inventory	=	35,000,000
Current assets	—	65,000,000
Land	20,000,000	—
Plant facilities	25,000,000	60,000,000
Paint shop facilities	20,000,000	30,000,000
Equipment	=	70,000,000
Fixed assets	65,000,000	160,000,000
Investment	65,000,000	225,000,000
Cumulative investment	65,000,000	290,000,000

R$10,740, and the APs appreciated to APs0.8796/R$, the Argentine price should rise to APs9,447.10 per Macaw. But if the Argentine marketplace responded with *partial pass-through* capability, for example 50%, the price the market would bear would be only APs9,211.40:

$$8,975.70 + [.50 \times (9,447.10 - 8,975.70)] = 9,211.40.$$

Although higher than the previous year, this would still result in lower revenues per car in the currency of cost, the Brazilian real. According to Claudia's local market experts, the increasing relative stability of the economies in both Argentina and Chile would most likely allow annual pass-through rates of only 50% to 60%.

Capital Investment. The Macaw might be cheap, but Plant X was not. The total capital outlay was expected to total R$290 million for the two-year construction phase. The entire 1997 capital outlay of R$65.0 million would be an equity investment by GM, with an additional R$105 million in equity in 1998. After-that, a variety of long-term debt took over. As detailed in Exhibit 5, the project would require a total of R$225 million in 1998.

GM was pretty happy with the debt structure, particularly the below market rates provided by the Brazilian government as part of its aggressive package to attract the manufacturing plant to the state of Rio de Janeiro. The state of Rio de Janeiro was providing a 4-year loan of R$40 million at a 16.0% annual rate. A consortium of Brazilian banks, who were working closely with the State, were providing an 8-year loan of R$22 million at a 20% interest rate. Although the rates appeared to most investors from outside Latin America as incredibly high, they were actually quite low compared to comparable commercial market rates, and were fixed for longer periods than normally available. And, they were local currency.

But GM itself would also put debt into the project. The parent company would provide a R$18 million loan for 10 years at a rate of 18% per annum, but would also denominate the loan in local currency—carrying the currency risk itself (the CFO of GM North America had been very unhappy about this minor detail, but had lost the argument).[5] The funding would be rounded out with the issuance of a Eurobond, eight-year maturity, carrying a 10.50% coupon. The principal was a bit tricky given that there would be a 2.0% issuance fee paid up-front from the bond sales proceeds, and it would be denominated in U.S. dollars. As scheduled, net proceeds would need to be R$40 million in 1998, so Claudia made a note to back out the final issuance principal in 1998 so the full debt amortization schedule could be finished up.

Depreciation rates on capital investment in Brazil were largely straight-line and traditional. Standing facilities—the manufacturing plant—were assumed to have 25-year economic lives, and would therefore be depreciated at 4% per year. Equipment life was assumed to be 10 years, but the paint shop had been given preferential treatment with a three-year life. For manufacturing facilities which were multi-shift (Plant X would run two shifts per 24-hour period), the Brazilian tax code allowed increases in normal depreciation rates by 50% for two shifts and 100% for three shifts. Every little bit helped towards taxes and cash flow.

Manufacturing Costs. The entire cost analysis had been conducted for a 1999 startup, with a R$10,000 retail price for the Blue Macaw. On a per unit basis, labor costs were estimated at R$1,650/unit in 1999, and would rise at the estimates for labor costs shown in Exhibit 3.

Power and utilities were contracted with the State, and had been the subject of lengthy debate. The State was clear, it wanted jobs. But since the design of the facility was dependent on supplier/assembler jobs, and not on direct employees of GM itself, the state power authorities had finally settled on a volume-price mechanism. At annual production levels less than 450,000 units, GM would pay R$1,050 per unit in utility fees. When production rose above the 450,000 unit level—which was thought to require the level of employment the State had in mind, power charges would drop to R$850 per unit. In addition, power costs were assumed to rise at the same annual rate as consumer prices in Brazil.

Local materials were the second most expensive manufacturing cost at R$2,150 per unit. This was a substantial part of the manufacturing cost, and represented the majority of the costs payable to the co-production partners, since GM itself actually did not assemble the car. Material costs were expected to rise at the forecasted rates listed in Exhibit 3. However, compared to general price inflation in Brazil, these costs, sub-components and assembly by the suppliers, were expected to rise at relatively modest rates. But that was only the forecast.

It was the imported sub-assemblies from GM itself which had raised a number of eyebrows in the Brazilian government offices. The electronic engine ignition and fuel supply sub-system was manufactured in Ypsilanti, Michigan, at the old Willow Run Plant.[6] The plant had recently been completely renovated, now possessing state-of-the-art computer-aided-design (CAD) systems throughout. The cost per

---

[5] GM had debated the interest rate on the internal loan. Although the Brazilian tax authorities had not yet given a ruling on the issue, GM believed that it could probably set the rate anywhere between 15% and 22% without alarming the Brazilian tax authorities.

[6] The Willow Run plant had gone through a number of lives, not the least of which was as the leading manufacturer of B17 bomber aircraft in World War II. It had also been the home of Rosie the Riveter of women-in-the-war work-effort fame.

unit was estimated at US$1750, to which GM added a 20% markup for arms-length equivalency on third-party sales.[7] The Brazilian government then slapped on a preferential tariff rate on the imported sub-assemblies.[8] Plant X paid in Brazilian real, but the cost was still thought high by international standards (in GM's opinion at least). The sub-assemblies were assumed to rise in price in step with U.S. inflation over the planning period.

Other non-direct costs included general and administrative expenses, estimated at 6.0% of annual sales, distributed overhead expense charges by GM-North America amounting to 1.50% of sales annually, and the Plant X licensing fee, 2.75% of sales. This latter charge by GM-North American to GM-Plant X was for the use of the technological expertise and development held by the parent company. GM in the past had not utilized licensing fees for cash flow repatriation, but their financial strategists were encouraging its use when possible—for example, with a new technology like that of Plant X. Both the distributed overhead charges and the licensing fees represented costs to Plant X but incomes to GM-North America.

Working Capital Management. An area of serious concern to Claudia was working capital management. Claudia's first step was to review what she knew.

- Normal credit terms throughout Brazil were 150 to 180 days. By North American standards, this seemed incredibly long, but it was the norm in Latin America and local suppliers and buyers operated on that basis.

- If, however, a firm in Brazil wished to pay early (60 days was *early*) instead of the standard 180 days, buyers were eligible for a 16% annual discount on payables.

- If Plant X was to push its buyers to pay early, and not follow standard A/R payment terms of 180 days, Claudia estimated that Plant X would suffer roughly 4% annual bad debt expense on these receivables.

- GM in its North American operations was often willing to provide 90-day credit terms to independently-owned automobile dealerships to aid in their inventory financing. GM-North America's representatives had already explained to Claudia that if she wanted non-standard terms (greater than 90 days, and 180 days was the absolute limit), she would pay GM's weighted average cost of capital (WACC) on the transfer balances.

If days sales outstanding (DSO) on receivables were the same as DSO on payables, regardless of what the actual days were, working capital would be largely self-financed. However, given that a large proportion of the payables were to the U.S. parent, and pushing the parent to longer payment terms was costly, Claudia knew that

---

[7] Depending on the transfer pricing cost-accounting methodology applied to different foreign affiliates around the world, GM's margin on similar transfers ranged between 15% and 30%.

[8] See Exhibit 3 for rates designated by the Brazilian government as applicable to preferred producers like GM. Preferred producers, according to the Brazilian regulators were companies with existing manufacturing operations in-country.

the costs of working capital would end up being critical to the project's financial results. In fact, given the lengths of these payment terms, the entire current asset/liability structure of Plant X's balance sheet would be disproportionately large.

The build-to-order concept had a drastic benefit on the balance sheet in the form of inventories. It was estimated that inventory would drop to as little as 8% of current year manufacturing costs—not *following year's* forecast manufacturing costs. This was a major bonus point for the Plant X design.

Assuming all went according to plan (and it rarely does), GM had decided to lower their target cash balance to 1.5% of current year sales. Given the substantial margins on the production and sale, combined with the lower capital burdens and charges of the Plant X design, the assumption was that the Blue Macaw would be generating substantial cash flow in its first year, sufficient to preserve management's goals. Claudia was not so sure. If cash flow was not sufficient in the first year or two of operations (1999 and 2000), then additional capitalization was needed up-front, or additional lines of credit opened down the line. Of the existing long-term debt sources, it appeared that the debt extended by GM itself was the only elastic source. If GM could get access to short-term debt for working capital supplements in Brazil (and it was a big if), the interest rates were likely to approach 30% per annum.

Financial Rates. Claudia had little choice over the capital structure assumptions applied by GM to worldwide investment—they were dictated by corporate policy. GM officially had a capital structure which was 35% debt (average debt cost of 7.40%) and 65% equity. GM's beta, ß, was estimated at 0.80. Current market rates of return, for example the S&P 500 average over recent years, was 14.3%. The 20-year Treasury bond in the United States, the risk free rate, was trading right at 7.00%. GM, like many other multinationals, had used a variety of approaches to measuring risk on foreign investments. Most solutions had not really worked. The current practice was to require an added 6.0% premium over and above GM's capital costs in return on foreign projects.

But Brazil was another issue. Since the *Plano Real* was instituted on July 1, 1994, by then President Cardoso, the Brazilian bolsa had performed quite well, averaging 25.0% per annum. But since even governmental debt issued in-country was currently yielding 16.0%, this was not necessarily phenomenal. But what of Plant X's beta? Claudia's standard procedure was to use the average beta of comparables operating in-country, but there really weren't any in this case. The official guess had been 1.50, but was left open to discretion. At least this would allow her to calculate a weighted average cost of capital for the wholly-owned subsidiary.

Taxes. The Brazilian corporate income tax, like that of the United States, was 35.0% on both ordinary and capital gains income.[9] Withholding taxes were specified by bilateral tax treaties. Unfortunately, Brazil and the United States had never successfully concluded a bilateral agreement, so the U.S. fell into the non-treaty designation category for withholding taxes on dividends (25.0%), interest payments (15.0%), and royalties, license fees, and distributed overhead expenses (10.0%). The tax treaty status was important because GM was planning to have Plant X remit 20% of net income

[9] The actual corporate income tax itself was 25%, but since all firms were also responsible for a 10% income tax for *social contributions*, the effective tax rate was 35%.

annually as dividends to the parent company, and the 25% withholding tax would raise the burden substantially.[10]

As usual, Claudia then had spent a few hours with the controller for international tax, Grøn Pincenez, to review the tax implications of remitting money back to the parent company. Grøn had used a simplified (all in U.S. dollars) example to explain U.S. taxation of foreign-sourced income. (All numbers, including tax rates, are unrelated to Brazil.)

If the foreign subsidiary had income of, say, $100, and paid corporate income taxes of 40%, that left $60 for distribution to stockholders

EXHIBIT 6 Dividend Remittance & Foreign Tax Credits: Hypothetical Calculation

Foreign Subsidiary's Income Statement	
EBT of foreign subsidiary	$100
Less 40% corporate income tax	40
Net income of foreign subsidiary	$60
Dividend declared to parent of 50%	30
Withholding tax on dividends of 10%	3
Net dividend remitted to parent	$27
Gross-up for U.S. Tax Purposes	
Net dividend remitted	$27
Add back foreign taxes paid:	
Withholding taxes on dividends	3
Foreign corporate taxes paid on distributions	20
Grossed-up foreign-source income	$50
U.S. Tax Determination	
Theoretical U.S. taxes due at 34%	$17
Foreign tax credits	23
Additional U.S. taxes due?	0
Excess foreign tax credits?	6

(the parent company). If the parent instructed the sub to distribute 50%, then a dividend of $30 would be declared and remitted to the parent. If there were any withholding taxes imposed on the dividends, say 10%, the $30 would be reduced by $3, leaving a net remittance to the parent of $27. The tax authorities (at least the ones in the United States), would then *gross-up* the dividend remitted, adding back all the taxes already paid on the distribution in order to calculate the theoretical U.S. taxes which would be paid *if* that same income had been generated at home. The U.S. tax authorities would then allow credit, *foreign tax credits*, for those taxes already *paid or deemed paid*. If additional taxes were due, they would be netted from the remittance, reducing the dividend remitted from the subsidiary.

Grøn reminded Claudia that if the firm ended up with excess foreign tax credits, they would be of limited use. The problem was that excess foreign tax credits cannot be applied against domestic-source income tax liabilities, only against other similar foreign-source income tax liabilities. Excess credits can, however, be carried back two years and forward five years, but often when there is an excess one year, there is excess for several years.[11] Claudia made a note to compare how dividend income created foreign tax credits (being after-tax distributions from the subsidiary) compared to other income such as license fees (which were an expense of the subsidiary prior to taxes, and an income to the parent).

[10] Although not in effect in 1997, the Brazilian government was considering the institution of a 10% additional withholding tax on dividend payout rates in excess of 50%.

[11] Claudia remembered a seminar in New York in which the speaker spoke of repatriating earnings in such a way that excess foreign tax credits were minimized by managing the profitability of the subsidiary itself.

Grøn went on to explain (he was now really getting on Claudia's nerves) that *active foreign-source income* (dividends remitted) was treated separately from *passive foreign source income* (interest, royalties, and distributed expenses). The passive income which the parent would earn from the subsidiary would be treated separately and additional U.S. tax liabilities determined. The real bad news was that any excess foreign tax credits in one category, like passive income, could not be applied against tax liabilities due in another category, such as active foreign source income or even domestic source income.

Time is Money

Claudia Teofilo looked down at the calendar, looked up at the clock, and realized time was running short. She had less than three weeks before her financial recommendations had to be in and she had a lot of work to do. Luckily, it was working out to be a hotter and more humid summer than normal in lovely and tropical *Deeetroit*, so to work she would go.

Case Assignment

1. You are Claudia Teofilo, and you work for GM. Using Excel, create a spreadsheet workbook with the complete series of financial statements for both the project and parent capital budget viewpoints.

2. The series of workbook pages should be in the following order:

Name	Exhibit	Contents
Ass	—	Assumption inputs
Ano	—	Assumptions which are made on an annual (ano) basis
Rev	1.	Revenue projections
Cap	2.	Investment, capitalization, and depreciation schedules
Debt	3.	Debt amortization schedules and FX gains (losses)
Cost	4.	Transfer prices & manufacturing costs in Brazil (per unit)
Bal	5.	Plant X's pro forma balance sheet
WACC	6.	Weighted average cost of capital for Plant X and GM
Inc	7.	Plant X's pro forma income statement
Mac	8.	Margin or per unit cost/profit analysis of the Blue Macaw
CFs	9.	Plant X's pro forma statement of cash flows (indirect form)
BRZ	10.	Project Viewpoint Capital Budget
Rem	11.	Remittance worksheet for cash flows to U.S. parent
GM	12.	Parent Viewpoint Capital Budget

3. Now use the financial model to analyze the project. Although we have assumed specific values for a variety of variables, these values could *vary*. It is up to you to determine over what range variables may move (sensitivities), and in what combinations (scenarios).

   Your write-up should summarize the fundamental results, primary and secondary valuation issues, and your recommendations regarding the *tweaking* of the financials. The project has already been accepted, so do not waste your time arguing with it, work with it. (Building the model is only the first step; the assignment is *analysis*.)

SILICA GLASS, INC.

"One day, when a machine stopped because of a technical problem, the western employees went for a coffee break until it was fixed an hour later. The easterners went home, and stayed there until worried Parker managers eventually tracked them down. When machines broke down in East Germany they didn't get repaired for weeks, the workers explained."

- "Parker Hannifan Runs Plant in Germany
That Produces Mostly Misunderstandings"
Wall Street Journal, June 1990.

Mike Harrelson was amazed as he held the crystalline Christmas tree ornament up to the firelight. The sparkle, color, and artistry were mesmerizing. It was December 15, 1990, and the ornament was the product of the world-renowned glass artistry of the Thüringen region of Germany, until recently East Germany. Mike Harrelson is president of Silica, Inc., a U.S.-based firm which had just made an offer for one of the glass manufacturing firms of this Thüringen region. The Treuhandanstalt, the German government agency in charge of the privatization effort for enterprises formerly of East Germany, had not really rejected the offer, but made a counterproposal. The crystal ornament was elegantly simplistic; this acquisition was not. Mike wished to reevaluate his strategy.

Background

Silica Glass Incorporated (U.S.) is a worldwide leader in the production of glass fiber. Silica fiber is a synthetic fiber of proprietary glass composition. The glass fiber is in turn used in many different industrial applications, some of which are in other divisions of the same company.

Silica's products had grown steadily in quality and sales for a number of years; however, the firm itself had undergone a number of significant ownership and strategy changes. The primary product lines had been developed under Silica Products in the early 1980s. The firm was taken over in 1984 by a takeover specialist who used it as a cash cow, milking the enterprise for cash flows but reinvesting little. Two years later, operations were sold to Primavera, a southeastern holding company which had new plans for Silica.

Primavera saw more long-term growth potential for the series of products manufactured by Silica. Primavera's strategy was to expand sales and acquire additional operations which would increase the overall value of the total Silica operation, i.e., grow the firm. Although several of the Silica divisions showed healthy profitability, the product lines were very narrow and market expansion limited. Rapid growth would likely be obtained through merger and acquisition, rather than direct sales growth. Moreover, sales, particularly in the domestic market, were being squeezed by new competitive products.

Silica's Markets

The glass-fiber market is a highly specialized one. Silica's sales were currently split both between intra-divisional sales (50%) and external sales (50%). External sales were in turn divided between the United States (75%), Western Europe (20%), and the Pacific Rim (5%). Silica had grossed nearly $25 million in sales in 1989, and held approximately 25% market share worldwide in these specialized glass-fiber products. World markets in general were expected to grow at a 10-15% per year rate in the coming decade.

The problem was intra-firm sales. While outside sales were expected to grow at nearly 30% per year for the next five years, the internal sales to other corporate divisions were expected to decline nearly 25% annually over the same period. Mike's division was looking at a substantial squeeze. The internal sales decline was fairly certain, as new non-glass synthetics were coming on to the market which would make the products of several other corporate divisions obsolete. Hence, Mike's division needed new sales outside the firm. The solution was fairly clear (or at least Mike had thought so initially): focus on external sales growth through increased market share.

Silica's major competitor, both in the United States and worldwide, was GlassPro, a major midwestern U.S. corporation. GlassPro is a firm of substantially larger size and product scope, but currently had only one glass-fiber production facility, located in Ohio. GlassPro often experienced excess capacity in short periods of sluggish sales. GlassPro would therefore probably not be expanding into European production in the foreseeable future. A third but relatively minor competitor was Sonnenberg Glaswerks GmbH, located in Sonnenberg, East Germany.[1] Although Sonnenberg produced glass fiber, sales were limited to the Eastern Bloc prior to German unification. With unification, however, Sonnenberg could constitute new competition for both U.S. firms throughout Western Europe.

European Production and 1992

Mike Harrelson had concluded that the rapid sales growth Silica was experiencing, both in the United States and Europe, required immediate manufacturing expansion. Initiating production in Europe was a strong possibility.

Silica believed it should locate new production capability in Europe for a number of reasons. First, the recent growth in the European market represented

---

[1] Gesellschaft mit beschränkter Haftung (GmbH) is the German designation of a limited-liability company which is privately held. Aktiengesellschaft (AG) is the German designation for a limited-liability company which is publicly held; only AG-class firms may trade shares publicly.

new opportunities which would be better served by producing within the region. Second, the possibility of a single-Europe, the 1992 program, also created increasing debate over a possible "Fortress Europe." Although the protectionism debate was not considered significant in many industries, Silica had reason to believe it was real. Silica was aware of tentative discussions between the European Commission (EC) in Brussels and a French glass-fiber producer. The French producer was currently a world leader in glass-fiber production, but did not produce the technologically complex fibers of the two U.S.-based firms. The EC's concern was clear: it was interested in fostering European production of high quality (and high value-added) glass fiber. Mike had a suspicion that once European production of glass fiber began, new protectionist legislation might come forward against foreign firms exporting into Europe.

With the support of Primavera Corporation, Mike Harrelson started exploring possibilities for European manufacturing in the spring of 1990. The question was where to produce in Europe, and how to enter. Mike initially explored greenfield investment possibilities, searching first in the United Kingdom, France, western Germany, and Luxembourg for affordable property for plant construction. What Mike found was costly, and not encouraging. A second alternative was then explored: the acquisition of an existing facility—one with a glass furnace in place which might allow a cheaper production start-up.

Mike focused on Sonnenberg Glaswerks in the Thüringen region of former East Germany. Sonnenberg, or what was left of it, was known to have had some of the most advanced technology in the world in glass manufacturing for over four centuries. The fame and product development had stopped with the inception of the Communist government in East Germany in 1945. The following 45 years resulted in little advancement. There had been no new capital investment. The facilities at Sonnenberg were a mix of the technology of different eras. The two 15-ton furnaces in place were of a technology over 50 years out of date.

By the spring of 1990 Sonnenberg was producing a mediocre glass fiber and was badly in need of new capital, technology, and marketing skills if it was to survive the transition to a capitalist market economy. The unification of Germany now provided Mike Harrelson with the opportunity to salvage something of Sonnenberg's history and productive capability while getting Silica's foot in the door of European production.

Privatization and the Treuhandanstalt

Whereas the opening of Eastern Europe produced massive drives for industrialization and privatization for some countries (Poland, Czechoslovakia, Hungary, Bulgaria, etc.), it was different for the former West and East Germanys. Because western Germany was already one of the world's true industrial giants, its economy could provide a jump-start to the revitalization of the east. The east, however, could be absorbed into the whole rather than be independently industrialized like other Eastern European economies. West Germany approached much of the redevelopment with triage analysis, quietly separating the previous East German enterprises into: (1) those which would not be competitive; (2) those which were well-positioned and prepared for competing with western businesses; (3) those which might survive if

---

TREUHANDANSTALT
(German government organization for privatization)

Glasring Thüringen AG
(regional holding company for privatization)

☐ Sühl^{ER} Glaswerke GmbH   ☐ Staaken^{ER} Quarzschmelze GmbH

☐ Rudolstadt^{ER} Thermometerwerk Gmbh   ☐ Schmalkalden Pharmaglas GmbH

☐ Sühl^{ER} Glasmachinenbau GmbH   ☐ Haselbach^{ER} Glaswerk GmbH

☐ Saalfeld^{ER} Glaswerke GmbH   ☐ Naumburg^{ER} Glasfaser GmbH

☐ Zella-Mehlisglas GmbH   ☐ Sonnenberg^{ER} Glaswerk GmbH

☐ Deutsche Schaumglas GmbH   ☐ Langewiesen^{ER} Thermos GmbH

☐ Sonnenberg^{ER} Christbaumschmuck GmbH   ☐ Gotha^{ER} Rhonglas GmbH

☐ Thüringer Glasschmuck GmbH   ☐ Sühl^{ER} Ilmkristall GmbH

☐ Zella-Mehlis^{ER} Metallchristbaumschmuck GmbH

---

provided with infusions of capital, technology, and expertise. The major problem and motivation for selection and action was maintenance of employment. Eastern Germany was rapidly falling into a depression.

To orchestrate the privatization process, a government-constructed holding company was set up—the Treuhandanstalt. The Treuhandanstalt was charged with winding up (selling off or otherwise liquidating from government ownership) over 8,000 firms. The process required the formation of western-style balance sheets and operating statements for every firm. It was also necessary to quickly assess which firms required immediate cash injections in order to stay afloat until they could be sold or closed.

Sonnenberg Glaswerk GmbH was held by a regional holding company known as Glasring Thüringen AG. Sonnenberg was one of 17 different enterprises for which Glasring Thüringen was responsible (see Exhibit 1). Thüringen's role was to follow the directives of the Treuhandanstalt and wind up the 18 firms while doing everything possible to ensure employment.

Proposed Acquisition

After initial exploratory meetings in the spring of 1990, a second visit in September resulted in a tentative arrangement. Silica proposed the acquisition of Sonnenberg Glaswerks, with 75% ownership by Silica, and the remaining 25% remaining with Sonnenberg (actually its present management). The 75% ownership level was necessary in order to obtain tax benefits under European Community law. Although no one had actually owned Sonnenberg in the recent past (under a Communist system), Glasring Thüringen AG would hold the 25% minority ownership under the proposal. Silica would be guaranteed first refusal on the sale of this 25% share (Silica had wanted 100% ownership, but this was unacceptable to Glasring Thüringen). Since Glasring Thüringen was really only a privatization agency, Mike suspected that its 25% ownership would be given to the present management of Sonnenberg. Sonnenberg management still saw itself as owners although they had no equity investment or legal standing. In fact, in the preliminary discussions with management, the chief operating officer of Sonnenberg had wished to discuss a joint venture with Silica in which he would be the other equity holder, albeit with no capital investment.

Silica's offer was to invest approximately DM1,500,000 ($1,000,000 at the present exchange rate of DM1.5000/$) in new capital and technology, and provide all marketing and sales expertise. A fourth of this capital would be required for new plant and equipment, along with an additional 30% subsidy package provided by the German government for specific health, safety, environmental, and machinery needs. The remaining DM1,125,000 would provide working capital for expanded operations. Present contracts such as one with Naumburg Glasfaser would continue. These would provide some minimal cash flows during the transition.

Mike Harrelson returned to the United States to await the completion of balance sheet analysis, feeling positive about the feasibility of the project. Mike waited for financial information throughout October, November, and into December. The process which had moved so quickly and smoothly had ground to a halt. Communication was difficult, and there seemed to be no response to queries for additional information.

Glasring Thüringen AG's Counterproposal

Finally, in mid-December Mike returned to Sonnenberg in order to investigate firsthand the problem. The problems of the Treuhandanstalt and Glasring Thüringen had intensified as unemployment had continued to increase.[2] Glasring Thüringen now proposed an alternative arrangement: Silica would not only acquire Sonnenberg Glaswerks GmbH, but also acquire a second facility 50 kilometers away, Sühl Glaswerke GmbH. The two were to be sold together, and not singly. This was different. Silica would now be expected to split production between the two different facilities, thus adding to direct and indirect operating costs as well as overhead expenses. Mike explored the possibility of consolidating the two operations at one facility, Sühl, but Glasring Thüringen's interests were firmly in the maintenance of regional employment without worker dislocation. In exchange for the acquisition of the second facility, Glasring Thüringen agreed to the same purchase price; two firms for one!

Mike Harrelson now had serious doubts about this rapidly expanding acquisition. This would increase operating costs substantially, costs which he could not identify. There were still no balance sheets or operating statements for either of the two firms.

---

[2] The difficulties which the Treuhandanstalt had been having in finding suitable joint-venture partners were severe. For example, the offer by the West German firm BASF for Synthesewerk Schwarzheide, an East German polyeurethane maker, had been low to say the least: BASF would pay nothing for Synthesewerk Schwarzheide; BASF would not be liable for any environmental liabilities resulting from Synthesewerk Schwarzheide's operations prior to purchase (1945-1990); BASF would be granted ownership by the end of September 1990. The offer was made in August 1990.

He had to decide soon; 1992 was no longer such a distant date. He looked again at the biting quote from the Parker Hannifin executive:

"The luckiest thing that ever happened to us," says Mr. Kaspar, "was when the Treuhand wouldn't give us the plant for nothing." He adds: "Keeping on 600 people would have cost us a fortune."[3]

---

[3] "Parker Hannifan Runs Plant in Germany That Produces Mostly Misunderstandings," *Wall Street Journal*, June 1990, p. A1.

AGUAS MINERALES S.A. & CADBURY SCHWEPPES PLC (A)

In February 1992, the mergers and acquisitions team of the Latin American department of Bankers Trust ("the Bankers Trust team") received the telephone call from Cadbury Schweppes plc: Bankers Trust was awarded the role of sole advisor in its attempt to fully or partially acquire Mexico's Aguas Minerales SA (AMSA). AMSA is the wholly owned mineral water subsidiary of Mexico City-based Fomento Economico Mexicano SA (FEMSA), a producer of beer, mineral water, and other beverages.

This would be one of the largest acquisitions of a Mexican business by an overseas company. The country setting and the fact that Cadbury Schweppes currently competes with FEMSA's soft drink business unit led the Bankers Trust team to conclude that valuation would not be easy.

FEMSA's Background

FEMSA was founded in 1890 by Isaac Garza and his brother-in-law, Francisco Sada as the Cuauhtemoc Brewery in Northeast Mexico. During the first quarter of this century, they expanded to other regions by opening new plants. During World War II Garza, Sada, and their heirs began manufacturing steel to ensure adequate supply of bottle caps. Around that time, they also expanded into financial services by acquiring Banca Serfin, the oldest bank in Mexico. In the 1970s, the brewery operation and Banca Serfin were spun off into a new group of family-owned companies called Valores Industriales SA (VISA). This group was led by Eugenio Garza.

In the second half of the 1970s, Garza, like many Mexican industrialists, got into financial trouble. During the boom years of the 1970s and early 1980s, VISA borrowed freely in order to diversify: it expanded into soft drinks and mineral water, as well as into unrelated fields like hotels, animal feed, and automotive parts. When the price of oil declined in 1982, so did VISA's businesses, which by then had accumulated over $1 billion in debt.

On top of this, President Lopez Portillo's administration nationalized Banca Serfin. Desperate to raise cash, Garza sold VISA's hotels and other businesses unrelated to its core beverage and packaging businesses. In the reorganization of VISA's capital structure, Garza included World Bank's International Finance Corporation, Mexico's state-owned development bank NAFINSA, and Citicorp as new lenders.

In 1988, VISA undertook a debt-for-equity restructuring. The restructuring eliminated three-quarters of VISA's $1.7 billion debt and gave its new creditors approximately 20% of the equity in a newly created, publicly traded beverage and packaging company called Fomento Economico Mexicano, SA or FEMSA. VISA retained 60% of FEMSA, and 20% of the shares traded on Mexico's Stock Exchange (Bolsa de Mexico). Grupo Proa, a private holding company (51% owned by Garza's family), owned around 80% of VISA (Garza's share is currently worth $550 million). The remaining 20% trades on Mexico's Bolsa. Grupo Proa also owns 60% of the insurance group, Valores de Monterrey, S.A. or Vamsa (Garza's share in this is currently worth $200 million). The rest of the shares are publicly traded (see Exhibit 1).

By 1990, FEMSA was Mexico's fifth largest company with 1990 revenues exceeding $1.7 billion and net income in excess of $120 million. It was the nation's largest beverage company, and the 13th largest brewery in the world. This rapid growth was achieved through the acquisition of additional beer (Superior, Dos Equis, and Sol), soft drink, and mineral water brands. FEMSA acquired the Mexico City and Southeastern Mexico Coca Cola franchises and the flagship mineral water brands, Penafiel, Aguas de Tehuacan, and Balseca. FEMSA had a leadership position in all the segments it competed: 51% share of the brewery market; 59% of the soft drink market; and 80% share of the flavored and unflavored mineral water market (see Exhibit 2).

In October 1991, VISA acquired 51 percent of Bancomer, the second largest bank in Mexico with $28 billion in assets, for $2.6 billion. The acquisition was financed with new stock issues worth $1 billion, debt worth $1 billion, and cash. To help finance Bancomer's acquisition, FEMSA announced that it would sell interests in its beverage operations.

FEMSA looked for investors with international beverage experience who could form a joint venture with them, provide marketing and operational expertise, and contribute significant potential for added shareholder value.

In any event, the first divestiture—it was not evident whether it should be a full or partial divestiture—would be FEMSA's mineral water business, AMSA.

AMSA

AMSA bottled and franchised five brands: Penafiel, Balseca, Etiqueta Azul, Catemaco, and Extra Poma. Penafiel was the largest selling mineral water brand in Mexico. Balseca was a strong regional brand in the south eastern Mexico and Etiqueta Azul a discounted regional brand primarily sold through FEMSA's Coca Cola bottling division. In 1991, Aguas Minerales made a pre-tax profit of $24.4 million (pesos 73.1 billion), on sales of $161.6 million (pesos 484.4 billion). AMSA was considered by industry experts to be a well managed company.

AMSA's product line included a portfolio of flavored and unflavored mineral waters positioned as "sourced from famous wells, intrinsically pure, and of high quality." The business owned five bottling plants with natural springs. In the Mexican mineral water industry, as opposed to the U.K. or France, waters are not required to be source-dependent. The law permits it to be sourced with high-quality water from wells anywhere in Mexico.

The Soft Drink Market

In 1991, the Mexican carbonated soft drink market was one of the largest in the world, with annual sales of 2.8 billion gallons (at a price of approximately $1.07 per gallon). Mexico's per capita consumption was 34 gallons per person per year. Colas represented 60 percent of total carbonates and flavored drinks accounted for the rest. Coca Cola and Pepsi had a 47 percent share and 17 percent share, respectively, of total carbonates. The market had grown at 9 percent per year from 1987 to 1990, and had a forecasted growth of 6 percent per year (including the population growth of 2 percent per year) until the year 2000. This indicated a per capita consumption growth of 4 percent per year.

The bottled water market was underdeveloped in comparison to other segments of the carbonates markets, representing only 5 percent of total soft drinks (142 million gallons). However, this market segment has been growing at nearly 12% percent per year since 1985.

Historically, prices for carbonated soft drinks in Mexico have been lower than world prices, and despite the large volume, both franchisers and bottlers experienced marginal profitability. However, there were significant price increases in the last three years.

The Bankers Trust Team's Financial Valuation Assumptions

As a first step, the Bankers Trust team drew up an estimated base-case income statement and balance sheet for AMSA for financial year 1991 (Exhibit 5). From a 1991 base, they assumed sales (volume) growth of 9 percent per year through 1995, 5% per year from 1996 to 2000, and 2 percent per year thereafter. They supported these assumptions with the following arguments:

Advertising: Since 1989, AMSA had supported its 80 percent market share of carbonated waters with national television advertising. In the past, no other Mexican water brand could afford such an investment.

New Products and Packaging: AMSA introduced Penafiel Light in 1990, and the Bankers Trust team believed that this flavored mineral water could grow without cannibalizing the rest of the product portfolio. They believed that plastic bottles would become a key factor in the Mexican carbonated soft drink industry, and saw significant capital expenditures behind this packaging Penafiel represented a major portion of the projected growth rate of 9%.

Pricing: Since 1988, Mexico's inflation had declined in part due to "el Pacto," an annual agreement among government, business, and labor. Price increases at the consumer and retail level were authorized nationally, and transportation services and energy were subsidized. In 1992, the Salinas' administration was expected to lower the IVA tax (value added tax) from 15 percent to 10 percent, which could support a net 4.6 percent price increase.

The Bankers Trust team expected revenues to increase by an achievable price increase. The valuation presumed a 28 percent increase in mineral water prices through December 1992. Assuming a small negative impact on next year's volume, it would increase overall revenues. During the longer term, they assumed price growth roughly in line with inflation. If the North American Free Trade Agreement (NAFTA) came to fruition, it was expected to close the gap between US and Mexican consumer prices, mainly in the beverage and cigarette industries (see Exhibit 6).

Capital Expenditures: Between 1992 and 1996, new capital expenditures would equal approximately 8% of sales. Thereafter, capital expenditures are expected to be at the same level as depreciation.

Currency: Given the considerable presence (and long-term plans) that Cadbury Schweppes had in the US, the Bankers Trust team felt that it would not be inappropriate to undertake the valuation in US$. Data on projected inflation and exchange rates for Mexico are provided in Exhibits 7 and 8.

Tax Rates: Corporate tax rate calculations are complicated in Mexico. There are two basic tax rates, consisting of a regular tax rate of 35%, and a "profit sharing tax rate" of 10%. Moreover, the Mexican government required firms to set up a pension plan from 1992, whereby AMSA would have to set aside 10% of the pre-tax income; however, this amount would be tax deductible. In addition to this, there is a "net asset tax" rate of 2% that is based on a complicated inflation-adjustment formula involving revaluation of fixed and current assets. The Bankers Trust team estimated the net result of these tax rules to be approximately 20% of the post-pension plan income per year till 1995, and approximately 30% per year thereafter.

Mexico's Economic Recovery

The severe economic setbacks of the 1980s—Mexico's "lost decade"—shocked it into abandoning the statism, populism, and protectionism that had crippled its economy since colonial times. Mexico's economic style of the 1980s was to build up infant industries protected with high tariffs (in order to achieve self-sufficiency), to discourage foreign investment seen as "imperialist," to disregard "experts," to allow fiscal deficits to grow, to nationalize near-bankrupt firms where jobs were at risk, and to borrow heavily from the only-too-willing foreign banks.

The cycle ended in August 1982. The administration of President Jose Lopez Portillo proposed a moratorium on the $19.5 billion of principal payments due in 1982 and 1983. His successor, Miguel de la Madrid, had little choice but to embark on a politically costly process of reform.

On December 1, 1988, Carlos Salinas de Gortari took office. He led the current Mexican economic recovery and built closer ties to the US. The reforms established by the Salinas administration were characterized by drastic restructuring of its external debt under the Brady Plan, entering into international trade agreements (joining GATT and negotiating NAFTA with the US and Canada), an aggressive privatization program, and support for Mexico's emerging private capital markets.

The consequence of the structural changes was an overall improvement in most economic indicators. In May 1989, the Salinas government unveiled its national development plan (Plan Nacional de Desarrollo) for 1989-94. The plan had two principal goals: (1) gradual increase in GDP growth from 1.5 percent in 1989 to 6 percent in 1994; and (2) gradual decrease in inflation rates to 9 percent by 1994 (see Exhibit 7). In addition to fiscal restraint, it was hoped that monetary and exchange rate policies would produce stable real interest rates and exchange rates (see Exhibit 8).

The renewed confidence in the Mexican economy meant that Mexican companies could now access international capital markets. Lowered inflation rates and nominal interest rates led to a narrowing of the spreads between eurobonds issued by Mexican companies and US treasuries of similar maturity—the average spread, reflecting country risk, was about 250 basis points (see Exhibit 9).

Mexican companies accessed equity financing not only through the domestic stock exchange (Bolsa de Mexico), and through equity issues in the US through American Depository Receipts (ADRs). By 1991, the P/E gap between US and Mexican companies had narrowed considerably (Exhibit 10). The recent economic reforms had also decreased the cost of borrowing for Mexican companies (see Exhibit 11).

Cadbury Schweppes plc

Cadbury Schweppes plc and its subsidiaries comprise an international group of companies engaged in the manufacturing, marketing, and distribution of branded confectionery and beverage products. Cadbury Schweppes was formed in 1969 through a merger of Cadbury Group Limited and Schweppes Limited. Cadbury was originally formed in 1831 as a family enterprise to produce cocoa and drinking chocolate. The Schweppes business was established by Jacob Schweppe in the late eighteenth century and was incorporated with the name Schweppes, Limited in 1897.

In 1991, Cadbury Schweppes' net sales were $5.6 billion (£3.2 billion, at the current exchange rate of $1.75/£), and operating income was $644 million (£362.5 million; Exhibit 12). The company employed over 35,000 people and its products were sold in more than 140 countries. Its brands included the well-known Schweppes, and Canada Dry lines of carbonated beverages. Other brands included Sunkist carbonated drinks, the Crush line of carbonated orange and other fruit flavors, Hires Root Beer, Sundrop, Pure Spring, and Old Colony carbonates. In the UK, a joint venture between Cadbury Schweppes (51 percent) and the Coca Cola Company (49 percent) bottled, canned, and distributed Coca Cola and Cadbury's soft drinks.

Cadbury Schweppes' subsidiary Cadbury Beverages International manufactured, bottled, and marketed its soft drinks in Europe. The subsidiary aimed to expand its market share in North and South America in both beverages and confections, through joint ventures and acquisitions (see Exhibit 13 for their recent past acquisitions).

Since the early 1980s, Cadbury Beverages International had achieved a healthy presence in Mexico's beverage market with its popular Orange Crush soda and its Canada Dry soft drinks. Acquiring AMSA would reinforce its Mexican presence and would be consistent with its growth strategy. AMSA's sales volume was larger than Cadbury Beverages International's businesses in France, Spain, or Australia.

Potential Synergies

The acquisition provided an opportunity for synergies through a shared distribution system. The key success factor in Mexico was aggressive distribution. With 30 percent of the population living in rural areas and low levels of car ownership even in urban areas, supermarkets played only a small role in soft drink distribution. Therefore, the main channel was the small grocery store and street vendors. Despite an area equal to one-third of the US, distribution channels were more dispersed and consumers more expensive to reach.

Orange Crush represented 77 percent of Cadbury Beverages International's 1991 volume in Mexico. The current Crush bottler network covered around 128,000 outlets out of Mexico's total 810,000 soft drink outlets. This network covered around 19 percent of the Mexican population. AMSA's brands were distributed through the same outlets and had 50 percent penetration. The company expected to increase its Orange Crush penetration up to AMSA's levels by 1996. The current market size for carbonated soft drinks is approximately 2.8 billion gallons, at an average price of $1.07 per gallon, and the casewriters' estimate of Cadbury Schweppes' current sales is approximately 50 million gallons. Further, the casewriters estimate that the net income margin in this business would be approximately 6%.

Considerations in Financing the Acquisition

Cadbury Beverages International was undecided as to how to finance the proposed acquisition. Issuing stock in the London Stock Exchange could have a dilution effect, and unknown signaling effects. The company was worried about the softness of the stock market following the news of the Labor Party's five point lead in the polls in March 19. On March 18, 1992, Cadbury's shares closed at £4.43 on the London Stock Exchange.

On the other hand, a stock issue in the US or London could attract investors looking to diversify their equity interests into the booming Mexican market (during the period 1985-1990, the correlation coefficient between total US$ returns on an index of Mexican stocks and the returns on the S&P 500 was 0.46).

The company had recently undertaken a leveraged recapitalization in order to defend itself against a possible unfriendly takeover by Philip Morris, and as a result, its net debt is expected to rise substantially.

The Bankers Trust Team's Final Concerns

Assessing the appropriate cost of equity for the acquisition presented something of a problem, since AMSA is not a publicly traded company. Firms in lines of business similar to that of AMSA in the US had asset betas[1] that ranged from 0.9 to 1.1. The question that troubled Bankers Trust was whether or not the cost of capital for AMSA

---

[1] The asset beta (β_A) measures systematic risk associated with the business risk of a company. The beta, in turn, is a measure of the percentage movement in the expected share returns of a particular company for each percentage move in the expected returns of a well-diversified portfolio of stocks.

should reflect an appropriate premium for country risk—after all, the bond markets reflected such a premium, so why not equity markets?

Cadbury's management was concerned about the possibility of new competition and about AMSA's source water quality. AMSA's biggest competitive risk would be that Coca Cola decided to launch its own mineral water brand in Mexico. Although Coca Cola was inexperienced in the mineral water market, the passage of NAFTA could be a factor.

Another major concern in selling AMSA to Cadbury was that FEMSA and Cadbury Beverages International competed in the soft drink business—this acquisition could help Cadbury Beverages International strengthen its brands in Mexico by cannibalizing FEMSA's sales.

Bankers Trust was also concerned that completion of the deal was subject to certain commercial and regulatory conditions in Mexico (and Mexican government approvals). Mexico's Foreign Investment Law allows 100 percent ownership of qualifying investments by foreign firms without prior authorization from the Foreign Investment Commission, but only if the investment does not exceed $100 million.

The asset beta is distinguished from the 'equity beta' (β_E) in that the latter includes the effects of *both* business risk and financial risks from financial leverage in a firm. If a firm's debt-to-market value of equity ratio is defined as D/E, then the relationship between the asset and equity betas is expressed as follows: $\beta_E = \beta_A(1 + [D/E])$.

EXHIBIT 1   FEMSA's Ownership Structure

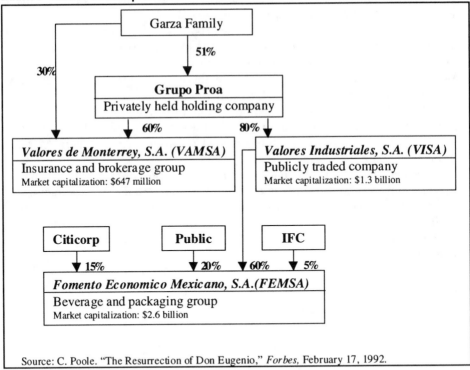

Source: C. Poole. "The Resurrection of Don Eugenio," *Forbes,* February 17, 1992.

EXHIBIT 2 FEMSA's Business Segments

Activity	Main Companies	Main Products	Assets	Sales	Employ
Beer	Cerveceria Cuauhlcinoc Cerveceria Moctezutria Carta Blanca de Occidentc Servicios Industriales y Comerciales	Carta Blanca. Superior, Tecate, XX Lager, Bohemia, Sol. Indio, and Heineken Beers	3,141	2,037	19,213
Beer Division					
Convenience Stores	Cadena Comercial (Oxxo Stores) Vendo de Mexico.	Retailing of Convenience products	84	317	867
Marketing Support	Anuncios y Servicios. Fornento Comercial.	Ice. Coolers, and Panoramic Advertising	32	50	500
Codicome del Sureste / Codicome del Centro					
Cola and Flavoured Soft Drinks	Industria Embotelladora de Mexico	Coca Cola, Diet Coke, Sprite, Fanta, and Sin Rival Soft Drinks	424	529	5,605
Distribucion y Comer dc Hielo y Gas / Embotelladora de Tlalnepantla / Embotelladora del Istmo / Refrescos dc Oaxaca / Embotelladora Sin Rival					
Mineral Waters	Distribuidora de Bebidas del Valle de Mexico, Distribuidora Surena Manantiales Penafiel Extractora y Embotelladora de Productos Balseca Compania Exportadora de Aguas Minerales	Penafel, Balseca, Etiqueta Azul, Extra Poma, and Dietafiel Mineral Waters	257	198	3,727
Mineral Waters Division					
Metallic Packaging	Fabricas Monterrey Partes Industriales Mecanicas	Beverage Cans, Foodstuff Cans, Crown Caps, and Caps	407	361	1,889
Glass	Silices de Veracruz	Glass Bottles and Silicious Sand	105	60	527
Flexible Packaging	Grafo Regia	Labels, Laminations and Wrappers for Cigarettes, Soaps, Chewing Gum Snacks, and Milk	155	87	581
Packaging Division					
Cardboard and Paper	Corrugados Tehuacan	Corrugated Cardboard Boxes	25	44	379
Plastics	Plasticos Tecnicos Mexicanos	Soft Drink Cases, Coolers, Containers, and Chairs	51	32	366
Chemical Products	Quimiproductos	Detergents, Lubricants, and Adhesives	10	17	146
Celulosa y Papel de Xalapa					

Note: All financial data is provided in billions of 1988 pesos.

EXHIBIT 3 FEMSA and Subsidiaries' Financial Statements (A)

Consolidated Income Statement
For the years ended December 31
(amounts in billions of pesos)

	1989	*1990*
Net sales	4,522	4,783
Other operating revenue	67	79
Total revenues	4,589	4,862
Cost of sales	(2.881)	(2,984)
Gross profit	1,708	1,878
Operating expenses:		
Administrative	(556)	(622)
Selling	(746)	(811)
Total operating expenses	(1,302)	(1,433)
Income from operations	406	445
Integral cost of financing:		
Interest, net	(235)	(231)
Foreign exchange loss, net	(133)	(68)
Gain on monetary position	212	278
Total cost of financing	(156)	(21)
Other expenses, net	(47)	(55)
Income before income tax, tax on	203	369
assets, and employee profit sharing		
Income tax, tax on assets, and employee profit sharing	(74)	(177)
Extraordinary credit derived from utilization of tax loss carryforward	24	112
Extraordinary income due to debt prepayment and other	135	39
Net income for the year	288	343

Source: FEMSA Annual Report.

EXHIBIT 4 FEMSA and Subsidiaries Financial Statements (B)

Consolidated balance Sheet
At December 31
(in billions of pesos)

Assets	1989	1990
Current assets:		
Cash and marketable securities	221	105
Accounts receivable:		
Notes	16	19
Trade	239	290
Other	39	47
Total accounts receivable	294	356
Inventories:		
Finished products and in process	150	174
Raw materials and supplies	608	708
Total inventories	758	882
Prepaid expenses	26	27
Total current assets	1,299	1,370
Investments and other assets:		
Shares and securities	26	8
Long-term notes	0	0
Other assets	1	0
Total investments and other assets	27	8
Property, plant, and equipment:		
Land	413	437
Buildings, machinery and equipment, net	4,606	4,874
Construction in progress	127	136
Total property, plant, and equipment	5,147	5,447
Deferred charges, net	38	52
Total assets	6,511	6,877

Liabilities and Shareholders Equity	1989	1990
Current liabilities:		
Bank loans	82	185
Notes payable	3	5
Current maturities of long-term debt	0	68
Accrued interest	22	16
Suppliers	202	291
Accrued taxes	117	107
Accounts payable, accrued expenses and other liabilities	80	115
Total current liabilities	506	787
Long-term liabilities:		
Bank loans and debentures	1042	879
Notes payable	20	10
Current maturities of long-term debt	0	(68)
Total long-term liabilities	1,062	821
Seniority premium and other liabilities	32	31
Stockholders' equity:		
Minority interest in consolidated subsidiaries	8	10
Majority interest:		
Capital stock	253	253
Additional paid-in-capital	2,995	2,995
Retained earnings	989	1,277
Net income for the year	288	343
Holding gain on nonmonetary assets	378	360
Total majority interest	4,903	5,228
Total stockholders' equity	4,911	5,238
Total liabilities and stockholders' equity	6,511	6,877

Source: FEMSA Annual Report.

Estimated Income Statement (all figures in US$ mn)		*Estimated Balance Sheet* (all figures in US$ mn)	
Cases sold (000s)	54,202	Surplus cash	8.00
Annual growth (%)	5.04	Cash for operations	3.50
Sales	161.60	Accts receivable: trade	6.60
Variable manufacturing cost	40.90	Inventories	6.00
Variable selling cost	42.80	Prepaids	2.00
Total variable cost	83.70	Accnts receivable: nontrade	21.00
		Total current assets	47.00
Gross Margin	77.90	PPE	113.50
Gross margin (%)	48.20	Deferred tax assets	
Marketing cost	8.30	Other assets	
Production: salaries	4.90	Total assets	160.60
Production: other	8.30	Short-term debt	2.00
Selling and distín: salaries	7.90	Payables: trade	4.00
Selling and distín: other	7.60	Affiliated creditors	4.00
Admin: salaries	7.20	Payables-nontrade	8.00
Admin: other	5.00		
Depreciation	4.30	Tax payable	5.30
Total Fixed Cost	53.50	Total current liabilities	23.30
Operating pr ofit/sales (%)	15.10	Long-term debt	36.30
Interest expense	3.83	Common stock and paid-in capital	67.30
Interest income	1.83	Preferred stock	0.00
Pre-tax income	22.40	Retained earnings	33.70
Employee profit sharing*	0.00	Treasury stock	0.00
Taxable income	22.40	Total equity	101.00
		Total liabilities and equity	160.60
Income taxes	10.00		
Net income	12.40		

*Will be 10% of pretax income from 1992.

Industry	*Price in Mexico*	*U.S. Price*
Cigarettes	59	200
Beer	32	58
Soft drinks	16	50
Mineral water	19	70

Source: Bankers Trust Company, March 1992.

EXHIBIT 7   Mexico's GDP and Inflation Rates

	Real GDP Growth/ Yr.	*Annual Inflation (%)*
1960-1970	5.5%	5%
1970-1976	6.2	13
1977-1982	6.0	42
1983-1988	-1.0	92
1989-1991	2.9-3.5%	20-25%
1992-1996 est.	5.3-6.0%	15% decreasing to 9%

Source: The Economist Intelligence Unit.

EXHIBIT 8   Mexico's Exchange-Rate Analysis (Note 1)

Year	*1985*	*1986*	*1987*	*1988*	*1989*	*1990*	*1991*	*1992*	*1993*	*1994*	*1995*	*1996*
Exchange rate (note 2)	371	923	2200	2320	2683	2948						
Exchange rate (note 3)		256	611	1378	2272	2474	2831					
Projected (note 4)								3025	3136	3210	3277	3339	3403

Note   1: All exchange rates in peso/US$.
        2: End of period. Source: International Finance Corporation.
        3: Average of period. Source: International Finance Corporation.
        4: Average of period. Source: VISA.

EXHIBIT 9   Major US Dollars Eurobonds Issued by the Mexican Government

Eurobond	*Due Date*	*Basis Point Spread (Note 1)*
2008 Aztec	31-Mar-08	406
Par bonds	31-Dec-19	277
Discount bonds	31-Dec-19	367
MYRA	16-Nov-06	461
Banobras 10.75%	16-Aug-96	282
BNCE 9.875%	24-Jun-96	208
NAFINSA 11.75%	02-Aug-85	276
NAFINSA 10%	14-May-96	217
NAFINSA 10.625%	22-Nov-01	259
Permex 10%	15-Mar-93	222
Pemex 11.625%	25-Oct-93	193
Pemex 17.75%	01-Jun-94	265
Pemex 10.25%	06-Oct-98	209

Note 1: Basis points over U.S. T-bonds of same maturity; the current U.S. T-bill rate is 6%, and yield on long-term U.S. government bonds is 7.9%.

Source: Bankers Trust Company, March 1992.

EXHIBIT 10   Price/Earnings Comparisons between Mexican and U.S. Firms

Industry	Mexican Company	P/E	International Equivalent	P/E
Packaged goods	Bimbo	21	Gerber Products	21
	Tablex	16	CPC	17
Retailing	Cifra	21	Kmart	12
	Commercial	17	Sears	13
Paper	Kimberly Clark	14	Kimberly Clark	15
Cement	Cemex	13	LaFarge	11
	Tilomex	15	Holderbank	12
Container	Vitro	13	Ball Corp.	17

Source: Bankers Trust Company, March 1992.

EXHIBIT 11   Cost of Debt for Mexican Companies

Company	Due Date	Yield to Maturity (%)
Apasco 10.25%	11-Dec-96	9.86
Barton 12%	20-Sep-93	8.29
Cemex 9.41%	21-May-96	10.00
Dynaworld 10.5%	17-Jan-96	9.88
Novum 12%	27-Sep-93	9.97

Source: Bankers Trust Company, March 1992.

EXHIBIT 12 Cadbury Schweppes and Subsidiaries' Financial Statement

Consolidated Statements of Income
For the 52 weeks ended December 30, 1989, December 29,1990, and December 28, 1991
(in £ millions except for share data)

	_1989_	_1990_	_1991_
Net sales	2,777	3,146	3,232
Cost of sales	(1,597)	(l,738)	(l,736)
Gross margin	1, 180	1,408	1,496
SG&A	(906)	(1,705)	(1,130)
Other operating income (expense)	0	1	(4)
Operating income	274	334	363
Equity in earnings of associated companies	3	3	11
Net interest expense	(31)	(57)	(57)
Inc. before taxes, minority interest, and extr. items (note 1)	246	280	316
Taxes on income	(70)	(78)	(88)
Inc. before minority interest and extraordinary items	176	202	228
Minority interest	(17)	(22)	(25)
Income before extraordinary items	159	179	203
Extraordinary items net of tax	14	0	0
Preference dividends	0	(3)	(9)
Net income for ordinary shareholders	173	176	194
Earnings per ordinary share	0.27	0.25	0.28

Note 1: Income before taxes, minority interest, and extraordinary items.

Sources: SEC; Cadbury Schweppes Annual Report, May 1, 1992.

Consolidated Balance Sheet
At December 29, 1990, and December 28, 1991
(in £ millions)

	1990	1991
Assets		
Current assets:		
Cash	63	85
Investments at cost	118	262
Acc. receivable and prepayments	554	579
Inventories	328	332
Total current assets	1,063	1,258
Long-term investments	17	34
Trademarks	304	308
Property, plant, and equipment (net)	979	1, 054
Total assets	2,362	2,655
Liabilities, Minority Interest, and Shareholders' Equity		
Current liabilities:		
Short-term borrowing and current portion of L.T. debt:		
Bank loans and overdrafts	60	72
Capital leases and others	76	66
Income taxes	78	95
Acc. payable and accrued interest:		
Trade creditors	272	275
Accruals and deferred income	255	275
Other taxes and social security costs	66	83
Customer deposits	50	33
Dividends proposed	61	67
Other payable	44	66
Total current liabilities	962	1,033
Long-term debt, less current portion	408	542
Restructuring provisions	83	27
Deferred tax	(4)	(1)
Other long-term liabilities	29	65
Total liabilities	1,479	1,666
Minority interests	116	112
Shareholders' equity:		
Preference shares	0	0
Ordinary shares	174	176
Premiums in excess of par values	382	394
Revaluation surplus	96	100
Retained earnings	116	207
Total shareholders' equity	768	877
Total liabilities, minority interest, and equity	2,362	2,655

EXHIBIT 13 Major Cross-Border Acquisitions by Cadbury Beverages International

Year	Country	Company or Brands	Comments
1987	Australia	Beatrice Australia	
1987	United States	Taylor Food Products	Owns "Red Cheek" apple juice
1988	France	Chocolate Poulain SA	Confectionary manufacturer
1989	United Kingdom	Basset Foods PLC	Sugar, confectionery
1989	Spain	Chocolates Hueso SA	Chocolate, sugar, confectionery
1989	Canada	ED Smith & Sons, Ltd.	
1990	Belgium & Luxembourg	N.V. Gibeco	The Gini franchise
1990	France	Oasis, Atoll & Bali	Perrier's Noncola soft-drink business
1991	Germany, & Austria	Apollinaris Brunnen AG	Mineral water

Source: Cadbury Schweppes Annual Report, 1992.

PART V
MANAGING MULTINATIONAL OPERATIONS

NORTHWESTERN PAPER COMPANY

"I understand your motivation for wanting to source the pulp from Chile, but it is important for the corporation to act as an integrated team on these issues," Bill Ewing, Vice President of International of Northwestern Paper Company, told Arthur Kim, the Director of Northwestern's South Korean subsidiary.

"Maybe you're right," Kim responded, "but I just don't understand why it would make sense to pay $450/ton for pulp when I can get it for $330/ton from Chile. It's tough enough to submit competitive bids to our customers without that kind of markup on raw materials. Besides, our plant is supposed to be a profit center. Shouldn't we be trying to maximize profits?"

"This is a topic that we will be covering in more detail with the finance people at the upcoming International Directors Meeting," Ewing said. "In the meantime, you need to make sure that you meet your pulp allocation from the Everett (Washington state) mill."

Company Background

Northwestern Paper Company, a Portland, Oregon-based firm, was founded in 1916. From a single pulp and paper mill at the company's inception, Northwestern had expanded substantially over the years, opening additional pulp and paper mills across the country. By the 1950s, the company was one of the largest U.S. producers of pulp and paper products. During the 1960s and 1970s, the company made a big push toward overseas expansion, particularly into Western Europe, where there was high demand for paper products. As that market had become increasingly competitive, however, expansion focused on Latin America and Asia. By early 1994, the company had mills and/or distribution facilities in 20 countries around the world. It was one of the largest United States-based manufacturers of market pulp, paperboard, and uncoated paper with 1993 sales of approximately $5.5 billion.

Market pulp was pulp sold on the open market, rather than being converted into paper at the company's own mills. It was shipped from the mill in bales of dry sheets. Paperboard was used to manufacture folding cartons, milk cartons, disposable cups and plates. Uncoated paper was used in office paper, copier paper, tablets, envelopes, and some printing papers.

The early 1990s had proven difficult for Northwestern and other paper companies in the U.S. and Europe. Many of the industry's problems were attributable to the high level of excess production capacity. Industry growth during the 1980s led paper companies to invest heavily in new mills and paper machines. Starting in 1990, however, demand for paper products declined. In an attempt to absorb the high fixed costs associated with investments in plant and machinery, several firms in the industry had tried to maintain relatively high rates of (plant) capacity utilization. This had resulted in a substantial inventory overhang in several product categories.

At the same time, the environmental movement in the United States successfully lobbied for legislation to limit access to government-owned forest lands and to invoke stricter environmental regulations regarding mill operations.[1] European paper companies had also come under increasing pressure from environmental groups. This resulted in higher prices for U.S. and European paper products. This was particularly true relative to other, less-developed regions of the world.

Pulp is manufactured from wood fibers or recycled paper fibers, which are broken down or separated by using a chemical or mechanical process to dissolve away the lignin (glue) which holds them together. In the world market for pulp, North America had been the low-cost supplier for many years. With less-stringent environmental controls and aggressive promotion of the timber and paper industries, however, South America had assumed that position during the early 1990s. A recent long-term analysis of competition in bleached softwood kraft pulp, for example, indicated that Chile was the low-cost producer in the world, mainly due to low pulpwood costs.[2]

In order to keep capacity utilization of its U.S. mills at adequate levels, Northwestern had directed its foreign-based manufacturing facilities to procure pulp from its U.S. mills whenever possible. The company charged overseas subsidiaries the going market rate for U.S. pulp which, as of late 1993, was $450/ton. Incorporated in that price was an allocation of all production costs and operating expenses, as well as a preset percentage markup. Additionally, given cash constraints in the United States, each subsidiary was also responsible for financing its working capital needs from local sources.

The South Korean subsidiary, which operated a combination pulp and paperboard mill (a "board plant" in the industry jargon), supplied paperboard to companies located primarily in South Korea and, occasionally, to other countries in the region. The South Korean mill manufactured a portion of the pulp required to produce the paperboard, and sourced the remainder (predominantly softwood pulp) from Northwestern's U.S. pulp mills or from other external sources.

---

[1] In fact, the domestic industry's expenditures for environmental protection had been over $1 billion annually from 1989 to 1993. Taken from Anderson-Shaw, Carol, "Overcapacity Plagues Paper Producers," *Standard & Poors Industry Surveys*, August 5, 1993, p. B88.

[2] Softwood pulp is produced from softwood trees—primarily spruces, firs, hemlocks and pines. Its fibers are longer than those in hardwood trees, resulting in stronger and more durable products. For many paper products, i.e., paperboard, softwood and hardwood pulps are mixed together to capitalize on the attributes of both. From Correa, Salvador, "Chile as a World Competitor in Forest Products," *Global Issues and Outlook in Pulp and Paper*, (Seattle, Washington: University of Washington Press); 1988, p. 158.

The Bid Conflict and Northwestern's Transfer Pricing System

In early 1994, Suffolk Ltd., an Australian manufacturer, submitted a request for bids for a large quantity of bleached paperboard which they intended to use in manufacturing food cartons.[3] A total of 15 companies submitted bids for the project, including the South Korean subsidiary of Northwestern and another of the company's subsidiaries, which was located in Indonesia. Bids ranged from a low of $640/ton up to $780/ton.

Northwestern's South Korean subsidiary was awarded the contract based on price considerations and quality specifications. In determining the bid price, the South Korean company had calculated the cost of the pulp to be used in manufacture of the paperboard at $330/ton. The pulp was to be acquired from a Chilean supplier, rather than from Northwestern's U.S. mills. On the other hand, the Indonesian subsidiary had developed their bid submission on the basis of raw pulp priced at the $450/ton rate that it was charged by Northwestern's Everett, Washington mill.

Transfer Pricing at Northwestern

Transfer prices between subsidiaries at Northwestern were based on a resale price method in which prices were set at the average sales price charged to unrelated entities. With the majority of Northwestern's market pulp production in the United States, this policy had resulted in pulp prices charged to subsidiaries being set at the prevailing U.S. market rate of $450/ton.

As part of the annual planning process, each of Northwestern's foreign subsidiaries was assigned a certain amount of pulp that it was required to purchase during the year from one of the company's U.S. mills. In evaluating the financial performance of each subsidiary, the Finance Department allocated income generated by the mill in manufacturing and selling the pulp allotment to the subsidiary. The allocation process involved no transfer of funds to the subsidiary; it was merely a book entry made by the corporate office to evaluate the performance of each manufacturing facility or subsidiary.

The mill income applied to the subsidiaries was calculated by taking the sales price of the shipment to the subsidiary less the direct cost and freight charges incurred by the mill. In early 1994, the average Northwestern U.S. mill shipped at a price of $450/ton, and had a direct cost of $280/ton, which provided a contribution margin of $170/ton at the U.S. mill.[4] Freight costs to South Korea and Indonesia were $60/ton and $70/ton, respectively, given shipping distances and routes. In the event that the subsidiary did not order its full allotment of pulp during the year, the resulting down-time expense at the mill was also allocated to the subsidiary in determining financial performance.

---

[3] Folding carton was used to package food, milk, toiletries and cosmetics, as well as other consumer goods. Paperboard had to meet strict product specifications with regard to folding and printing characteristics.

[4] Many of Northwestern's U.S. pulp mills sourced raw wood from the company's wholly owned forest division. Transfer prices were set at market rates.

Comparison of the Bids

South Korean Subsidiary. The South Korean subsidiary won the contract for the paperboard shipment with a bid of $655/ton Delivered Duty Paid (DDP) to Suffolk's Australian plant. Although lower bids had been received by Suffolk's purchasing director, this represented the lowest bid from a firm with the reputation of providing the desired level of quality. In the preparation of the bid package, the Chief Financial Officer at the plant in South Korea calculated that the variable cost relative to the project would be approximately $463/ton, which included acquisition of the raw pulp at $330/ton from the Chilean supplier, a 10% wastage charge on the purchased pulp, and $100/ton in other direct conversion costs. Exhibit 1 provides a breakdown of the bid.

Indonesian Subsidiary. The bid submitted by the Indonesian subsidiary was for delivery of the paperboard at $780/ton DDP to Suffolk's Australian plant. Variable costs were considerably higher than those of the South Korean bid, totaling $575/ton. This variable cost included a $450/ton cost of pulp purchased from the Everett Mill in the United States, a 10% pulp wastage cost applied to the pulp transfer price, and direct conversion costs of $80/ton.[5]

Although not a part of the subsidiary's calculations in determining the bid, in the event that the Indonesian subsidiary had won the contract, its financial performance measurement would have included the allocation of the U.S. mill contribution margin of $170/ton less delivery costs of $70/ton, adjusted for wastage at the Indonesian location. Had the Indonesian subsidiary gone through the Chilean supplier, the pulp could have been acquired for $320/ton DDP. Due to differentials in shipping distance, the cost quoted by the Chilean pulp supplier for the Indonesian subsidiary was slightly less than that of the South Korean subsidiary.

International Directors Meeting

As Bill Ewing prepared the agenda for the upcoming International Directors Meeting, he penciled in a presentation by representatives of the Finance Department with

EXHIBIT 1 Competitive Bids of the South Korea and Indonesian Subsidiaries

Subsidiary	South Korean	Indonesian
Delivered Duty Paid	$655.00	$780.00
Less variable costs:		
Market pulp	(330.00)	(450.00)
Wastage costs (@10%)	(33.00)	(45.00)
Conversion costs	(100.00)	(80.00)
Gross profit or contribution margin	$192.00	$205.00

*All values in U.S. dollars per ton of paperboard.

---

[5] Conversion costs include utilities and other material inputs. Wastage costs are based on the fact that 110 tons of market pulp are consumed for every 100 tons of paperboard produced.

respect to the issue of transfer pricing at Northwestern. Among the issues that he believed needed clarification were the following:

1. Given the high degree of competition in bidding for contracts that subsidiaries had encountered, should some alteration be made in the process of calculating bids?

2. What were the advantages and disadvantage of the allocation process used by the corporate office in determining subsidiary performance? Was the process fair to the subsidiaries? Was it fair to the company as a whole?

3. Given that some of the subsidiaries were located in low-tax jurisdictions, wouldn't it be logical to set transfer prices from the U.S. to those subsidiaries at lower rates?[6]

As Ewing thought about the system that was in place, he began to empathize with Kim's position. He knew that the recent economic boom in Asia had created a situation in which Northwestern's subsidiaries in that region were growing rapidly (in the 8% per annum range), had high capacity utilization rates, and were operating profitably. Perhaps the company did need to review its approach to transfer pricing. Hopefully, the representatives from the Finance Department would be able to offer some suggestions to resolve the apparent problems.

---

[6] As of early 1994, the federal corporate tax rate in the United States was 34%, with South Korean taxes ranging from 20% to 34%, and Indonesia from 15% to 35%, on a progressive basis.

MARTIN GUIDES, INC.

If we do nothing to our current products and do not publish a European product, we will experience an increase in sales, though it will be a gradual increase each year. Our European distributors are predicting a surge in CD-ROM equipped computers over the next few years. In order for us to take advantage of the size of the installed base of CD-ROM drives we must adapt our products to the European marketplace. Last year we had sales outside the U.S. of $950,000. At the current rate we will very probably do $1,250,000 this year (maybe $1,500,000). I would project for 1996 $2,100,000 (tops $2,500,00) if we do nothing to our current products.

—Mike Timmons, European Sales Agent, Martin Guides

As Controller of Martin Guides, Inc. (MG), Cathy McCloud had been assigned by Jeff Martin, the CEO and owner, to research the tax implications of establishing a European sales subsidiary. International tax regulations were not her specialty, but she had invested hours of research, consulted colleagues, and was now fairly confident she could outline the firm's main alternatives.

Many changes had taken place at Martin Guides since her arrival there three years before, in 1992. At that time MG was a relatively small company in Duckbay, Massachusetts, that produced guide books for forty-five of the fifty states. A few months after Cathy's arrival, Jeff Martin unveiled plans to make the guides available on CD-ROM. The new format combined video clips, sounds, and user-interactivity with the text information from the paper guides. Jeff Martin's vision turned out to be very good timing as the multimedia boom had just begun. Sales began to grow at 40% per year after the launch of several widely acclaimed CD-ROM products.

Suddenly, Martin had begun to attract foreign demand with its *WorldGuide* and *TourUSA* CD-ROM products. While the products were in English, European buyers were attracted by their high-quality content, colorful images, accurate maps, and simple user interface. But no one at the company had true international business experience, and the prospect of expanding into Europe had become the subject of several meetings between department leaders and Jeff Martin.

With five more minutes to go, Cathy trudged across the snowy field to the new annex. She smiled upon entering the room in an attempt to appear at ease, although she knew her boss would not be pleased with the results of her research. At the last meeting, Jeff Martin had been enthusiastic about the prospect of establishing a subsidiary in Ireland or the Netherlands, where he believed the company would face low tax rates. At the meeting, Cathy had expressed doubt that the company could benefit from low tax rates offered in those countries. Now those doubts were confirmed.

Mike Timmons, MG's European sales agent, was back from Germany. He would play an important role in the site selection for the European subsidiary due to his in-depth knowledge of the market. Jeff was genuinely friendly, a good person to work for, but he was demanding. When Jeff had an inspiration, everyone was expected to feel it with him and make it happen.

Jeff: Okay, Mike, Cathy, I've only got a few minutes until I have to go over and see the architect for the west building, so let's get down to business. At last month's meeting, Cathy and I had decided that a sales subsidiary in Europe was the best way to address our most immediate problems without putting up a large investment. Mike, you had sent us a fax that outlined some problems we're having in Europe. Since you're here now could you recap what the problems are?

Mike: Sure. Our European distributors are dissatisfied with our export terms and with the fact that our products are not adapted to the market there. Last week, we lost a French distributor because he didn't like FOB Duckbay. And that's not just a French reaction. Many distributors are complaining about having to send faxes back and forth to establish an all-in price. He also said sales were low because the product wasn't translated into French. Several people asked me at the CeBIT convention why we were showing the same version of WorldGuide for the third year in a row, and when we would have European products. I get the feeling that European customers are getting a bad image of us, one that's totally out of line with our U.S. image of being customer-oriented. If we have long-term plans in Europe, we shouldn't risk damaging our image before we even really get into the market. It's bad enough we don't have a European product or version. I polled our distributors and got their estimates of sales over the next two years for both products (see Exhibit 1.)

Jeff: Okay. So really we're dealing with two distinct problems here. One is a marketing problem. Customers aren't totally satisfied with what we're selling. The other is an operational problem. Our distributors want simpler, more direct service. Mike, you've mentioned many times before that customers would like to see a European version. I'd like to see those projections for translated products. As I've explained before, we don't have the resources right now to do the translation well. I want to do a good job on that. That's why I've decided to set up a subsidiary in Europe as a sales office and warehousing center, and we'll leave the republishing operation for later. We have more than enough sales in the U.S. to occupy us for now.

Mike: So, you're talking about invoicing in Europe for the first time?

Jeff: Yes. As you all know, the main reason we have avoided invoicing sales in Europe is to avoid the expense of a European subsidiary. With a mobile agent like Mike, who works out of his house in Germany, we can do everything very inexpensively. We

EXHIBIT 1 Mike Timmons' Sales Projections for ADAPTED Products

Country	Pieces	Euro Guide Sales @ $35	Pieces	WorldGuide Sales @ $42.50	Combined Sales
Germany/Austria/Switzerland	60,000	$2,100,000	70,000	$2,975,000	$5,075,000
UK/Ireland	14,000	490,000	11,000	467,500	957,500
France	10,000	350,000	11,000	467,500	817,500
Scandinavia	7,000	245,000	4,000	170,000	415,000
Netherlands	5,000	175,000	4,000	170,000	345,000
Belgium and Luxembourg	6,000	210,000	2,000	85,000	295,000
Spain and Portugal	2,000	70,000	1,500	63,750	133,750
Italy	9,000	315,000	3,500	148,750	463,750
Projected sales, 1996	113,000	$3,955,000	107,000	$4,547,500	$8,502,500
Projected sales, 1997	226,000	$7,910,000	214,000	$9,095,000	$17,005,000
Estimated sales, eoy 1995	$1,500,000				
Project sales in Europe, 1996	$2,500,000				
Source: Poll of MB's current distributors.					

don't have to pay social welfare costs for German staff, and because Mike arranges sales but does not invoice them, we pay no German taxes. This method has worked well for a few years, but now seems inadequate.

Mike: Where were you thinking of putting the sales office, Jeff? Germany?

Jeff: Well, we talked about this last time, Mike, and we're thinking about putting it somewhere else. I like Ireland. The tax rate in Ireland is 10%, guaranteed until 2010. I talked to Sean Ferguson at the Irish Development Agency (IDA), and he said we would qualify for that rate with a sales subsidiary. Also, the IDA offers grants for investment, training and R&D if the operation is large in size. German tax rates—as you know—are higher than 50%, and the government there is not offering us any breaks. Am I correct, Cathy? You've been researching this issue.

Cathy: Actually, it's a little more complicated than what we've been thinking. Last time I told you I was afraid we wouldn't be able to benefit from the low Irish tax rates, and unfortunately, that's probably the case.

Jeff: You mean, the IDA is giving misleading advice?

Cathy: Well, no, not really. They were just looking at it from an Irish perspective. You see, our company would pay the Irish government only 10%, assuming no withholding tax. Upon repatriation to the U.S. of a dividend from the sales subsidiary, we would pay an additional tax to the U.S. government that would bring the total tax paid up to the same amount we pay now, the U.S. rate.

Mike: Why is that?

Cathy: The U.S. government taxes U.S. companies on their worldwide income at the U.S. tax rate. That means that whenever a dividend is repatriated to the U.S., it is taxed at 34%. Because the U.S. government has treaties with most countries to eliminate double taxation, the U.S. government taxes you only on the amount over and above what you paid in the foreign country on the income before it was repatriated. So in Ireland, you paid $10 on $100 of income, and the U.S. government asks for $24 more, so that in the end, you've paid a total of $34. That's all part of the U.S. tax authorities' goal of tax neutrality. The government doesn't want U.S. domestic companies to pay a higher tax rate than U.S. companies that are operating abroad.

Mike: I see, but what about if you have a company in Germany, where the tax rate is higher? Is that where tax credits come in?

Cathy: Exactly, Mike. In that case, the Internal Revenue Service (IRS) grants tax credits to the company for the amount of foreign tax over and above what the company would have paid in the United States. So in Germany ... can I have a piece of paper? Thanks. Okay. Say Martin Guides makes $100. We would pay German tax of $53 and would get tax credits of $19.

Jeff: So I pay $53 cash out of my pocket and get only $19 in non-cash credits back; doesn't sound like a good deal.

Cathy: Right. But the tax credits can be used to cancel out the excess tax the United States government charges for income in countries with a tax rate lower than ours. So if we made the $100 in Ireland, and the $100 in Germany, we could use the $19 of tax credits in Germany to cancel out $19 of the excess tax paid on the Irish dividend. That would mean that we paid $53 to German tax authorities, $10 to Irish tax authorities, and $5 to the IRS. That's a total of $68, which makes for a 34% tax rate on income of $200.

Jeff: Wait, how are we making money in two places? Now you're talking about two subsidiaries. I don't like this at all. We just decided we only need one subsidiary.

Cathy: Actually, Jeff, we could guarantee a 34% tax rate in Germany with just one subsidiary if we designated it a branch of MG. Branches pay 34% on their earnings because they are considered just an extension of the parent and are outside the German tax jurisdiction.

Mike: So in effect, for our purposes, Germany, Ireland, or the Netherlands are on an equal playing field. We end up paying 34% regardless.

Cathy: Right.

Jeff: Isn't there any way to take advantage of the low Irish tax rate? What if we didn't repatriate our earnings from Ireland. Couldn't we defer taxes for as long as we wanted, until we repatriated the dividend? I mean, paying 10% now and 24% later would be better than paying 34% now.

Cathy: I am afraid we won't be able to do that with a sales subsidiary.

Jeff: Why not? That doesn't make much sense.

Cathy: That's a whole deeper level of IRS complexity. Do you have time for it now, Jeff?

Jeff: I guess. I really want to hear all this. How can the IDA advertise a 10% Irish tax rate if it's not really true?

Cathy: Okay. The IRS says that certain companies have to pay taxes on a dividend even if they didn't pay one out.

Jeff: Whoa. How does that work?

Cathy: Well, I need to start writing some stuff on the board, because it's going to become difficult to remember everything. If the company is classified as a controlled foreign corporation (CFC) and earns Subpart F income, it will be taxed on a dividend deemed paid on the sub's income for that year, even if there is no dividend actually paid. The normal tax credit rules would then apply on that deemed dividend.

Jeff: Would our sales sub fall under those categories?

Cathy: Yes, most likely it would. Here's why. Let me define the terms CFC and Subpart F income. A CFC is a company for which more than 50% of the voting power or value of stock is held by U.S. shareholders. In our case, given our concern with control, I doubt we would have less than a 50% share in our sales subsidiary. The tax is levied on any shareholder of the CFC who holds at least a 10% share. Since we are a small company with few shareholders, I don't think we could get around the tax.

Jeff: Could we structure the ownership such that we could hold 50% directly, and then hold the other 50% indirectly?

Cathy: Don't think so, Jeff. Ownership is looked at constructively. The IRS looks at the whole organizational diagram and adds up all the percentages of ownership until it reaches the ultimate shareholder, in order to see who really controls things. Subpart F income is passive income that results from the resale of related party goods. That's actually only the simple definition, since many other types of income fall under that category. For our purposes we've defined Subpart F sufficiently. It means that if we sell our CD guides to our European sub—and it resells them—the sub earns Subpart F income.

Jeff: So our sales subsidiary in Ireland would meet the conditions that allow the IRS to tax us on income that is not remitted. Is that right?

Cathy: Right. Our sub would be a CFC that earns Subpart F income.

Jeff: That's unbelievable! The IRS taxes you even though the money is still over in Europe?

Cathy: Remember, the purpose of the IRS is not to tax you beyond 34%, but it will make sure you're paying your fair share. They'll just tax you as if you've remitted all retained earnings as a dividend to the parent. It's true that a lot of U.S. companies used to set up sales subs in low tax areas just to shift profits out of the U.S. tax jurisdiction. They would keep the earnings over there and avoid paying U.S. taxes. So the IRS closed the loophole.

Jeff: I guess we have no chance at the Irish tax rate then, even for deferral purposes, unless we can avoid earning Subpart F income and reinvest in European operations.

Cathy: Not with a sales subsidiary as we have envisioned it. However, we could escape Subpart F if we resold only to unrelated parties in the country of incorporation of the sub.

Mike: For example, if we had a sub in Germany that sold only to the German market.

Cathy: Right, but what would be the point? We wouldn't be benefiting from Irish tax rates then.

Mike: Oh, yeah.

Jeff: If we did establish something in Germany, we'd have to set up a sub somewhere else to offset the excess tax credits. That would be expensive, and not likely to work, since we'll probably earn much more in Germany than in, say, Ireland. We'd still pay at least 34%.

Cathy: That's exactly right, Jeff. My guess is that we would have trouble setting up such a system, though it would be possible. Besides, there's another major catch. Even if we could avoid earning any sort of Subpart F income, we couldn't retain earnings in the CFC in excess of 25% of total assets. So really, deferral would be fairly limited anyway unless we were planning to reinvest in Europe.

Jeff: It keeps getting worse. Basically, Cathy, what you're telling us is that there's not really a practical way for MG to get the low Irish rates with a sales subsidiary.

Cathy: Unfortunately, no, there isn't. At least not using a sales subsidiary. We would really have to make a much bigger investment in Ireland to take advantage of the 10% rate. With a manufacturing sub, we could earn non-Subpart F income and then reinvest the rest back into the Irish sub, or into other European operations.

Jeff: I see. And that would allow us to defer paying any taxes until a dividend was remitted from the sub. Hmm... that sounds like a possible loophole. Maybe we could just do some very light manufacture. How do they define manufacture in the U.S. tax code?

Cathy: According to the tax digest I was referring to, manufacture was considered adding 20% to the market value of the goods.

Jeff: Could we work repackaging or translation in such a way that it adds 20% more to the value of the product we ship to the subsidiary?

Cathy: I wondered the same thing, but I could not find any reference to that type of operation in the digests I was reading, so I asked my friend Jack Vance at Overture Software. Jack is the Tax Director for Overture, which has a subsidiary in the Netherlands. He has a lot of experience with this sort of question. He said that the IRS doesn't interpret the 20% test literally. In fact, to qualify for the manufacturing exclusion, the product shipped from the U.S. cannot be commercially viable. Jack said that the reproduction and translation of software abroad does not constitute manufacture. That opinion is based on actual court cases involving the IRS and U.S. firms.

Jeff: So basically, the IRS can decide what really constitutes manufacture.

Cathy: Yes, if the activity being performed is shaky. If we were writing the software over there, that would probably constitute manufacturing even by their definition. As Jack told me on the phone, the IRS looks at what's really going on, not necessarily what we report to them. In any case, all decisions ultimately go to tax court where they can be decided either way, for us or against us.

Jeff: Does the IRS even know anything about what goes into making a software package?

Cathy: Actually, yes. Jack was telling me they have special off-shore software agents who are quite knowledgeable on the differences between manufacture and packaging for our industry. There's a lot of potential tax revenue at stake.

Jeff: So we could probably only benefit from the low Irish tax rate if we located our whole development process over there. Is that the case?

Cathy: Right, and remember we would have to reinvest the earnings in the sub anyway in order to avoid accumulating excess passive earnings, which would be currently taxed. So we would want to have something to invest in; a translation operation alone might not provide enough opportunity.

Jeff: Well, as we said before, I'm not ready to manufacture there yet. Actually, I'm not sure if I ever want to put the research and development over there. I like the process right here at Duckbay, where I can see it.

Let me see if I've got this all straight. We're back at square one, paying 34% unless we locate development in Ireland. Even if we do locate development in Ireland, we can at best defer paying taxes on 24% of the income until it's repatriated. On top of it all, we have to reinvest abroad to keep the IRS from levying a tax on the passive earnings.

Cathy: You've pretty much summed it up as far as I know. There is one more possibility which might be helpful. The U.S. tax code provides for a special type of subsidiary, a Foreign Sales Corporation (FSC), to help U.S. firms export by giving them permanent exemptions from part of the tax on foreign profits. In other words — this is not a deferral — this is permanent forgiveness. The firm never has to pay a certain portion of its tax liability.

Jeff: How much of an exemption is it?

Cathy: That depends on a fairly involved formula, but the results of it are actually quite straightforward. Most companies using FSCs pay around 5 or 6% less than the U.S. rate on their foreign profits. Legally, both the FSC and its parent corporation are exempt from taxes on a percentage of their export earnings. The U.S. company may then repatriate the income from the FSC in the form of a dividend that is completely free of U.S. tax.

Mike: That's not bad, considering what we've heard today, but what's the catch?

Cathy: There isn't much of a catch at all. Setting up an FSC is just a paper transaction. The only requirements are that the FSC is located in a country that has a special treaty with the U.S., and that the U.S. firm meet certain "economic process" requirements. For example, the FSC must have at least one non-U.S. board member, and at least one board meeting per year must be held in the country of the FSC. Those rules are designed to prevent the FSC from being counter to the GATT. In fact they are fairly easy to fulfill. The countries most commonly used are U.S. possessions, such as the U.S. Virgin Islands, because they have little or no income or withholding tax. There are companies, including our own accounting firm, that will arrange the FSC and administer it for a fee of around two or three thousand dollars a year.

Mike: It sounds like an off-shore operation. I am amazed it's legal. How does it work?

Cathy: There are two ways the transaction is structured. Usually, the U.S. parent passes title of the goods to the FSC, which then resells them and takes a fee for the transaction. Sometimes, the transaction is arranged so that the FSC buys the goods outright and resells them for a profit. The transfer prices and fees are set according to special rules in the U.S. tax code so that the parent can't shift all its profits to the FSC. The income of the FSC is partially exempt from U.S. taxes. The earnings of the FSC can then be repatriated to the U.S. parent with no additional tax by the U.S. government. Usually, the country of incorporation of the FSC has no income or withholding taxes and the result is a 5 or 6% reduction in the tax rate paid on foreign income.

Jeff: Wouldn't selling goods through the Caribbean complicate operations even more?

Cathy: Well, the goods aren't actually routed through the FSC. The FSC only takes care of the paper work. The goods can go directly to distributors.

Jeff: That sounds a little better. So we just set up a paper company, pay an annual fee to our accounting firm, and reduce our tax rate to around 28%. Amazing. Why don't other companies use this?

Cathy: A lot of large firms do use FSCs. I spoke to a friend of mine who is a tax expert at the Department of Commerce who said that many smaller firms just don't know about FSCs.

Mike: I have a question, Cathy. Aren't we forgetting the purpose of the meeting here? Don't we really want to improve customer relations in Europe by having a presence there? How does an FSC help us with that?

Cathy: I suppose you're right. I mean, we don't want to minimize taxes at the expense of other aspects of the business.

Jeff: Can't we use an FSC and a European sales subsidiary? That way we would both lower our tax rate and improve contact with distributors.

Cathy: Hmm... You know, I really don't know. That would be a very good option if it's possible. The only thing that worries me is that we might be selling from the FSC to another related party, either a branch or a subsidiary.

Jeff: Could you find that out for next week. Even if that's not possible, I'd be eager to know how much an FSC would save us over the next few years, if we implemented one.

Cathy: Okay. I could have a spreadsheet by then (see Exhibit 2), and the answer to whether the FSC can be used with a sales subsidiary.

EXHIBIT 2 Calculation of Benefits to Martin Guides of Using a Foreign Sales Corporation (FSC)

	1995	1996	1997
Foreign revenues	$1,500,000	$2,500,000	$4,000,000
Foreign cost of goods sold	259,760	432,933	692,693
Foreign or other direct & indirect costs	796,224	1,327,040	2,123,264
Foreign income before tax	$ 444,016	$ 740,027	$1,184,043
FSC expenses, first year			
Formation fee	$ 1,500		
Incorporation costs: US Virgin Islands	400		
Business license: US Virgin Islands	100		
FSC annual expenses			
Annual FSC management fee	$ 1,500	$ 1,500	$ 1,500
Annual business license USVI	100	100	100
Minimum annual franchise tax USVI	400	400	400
Estimated exemption as a result of FSC	$ 26,641	$ 44,402	$ 71,043
Less expenses to implement FSC	(4,000)	(2,000)	(2,000)
Total savings to Martin Guides	$ 22,641	$ 42,402	$ 69,043
Tax without FSC	$ 150,965	$ 251,609	$ 402,575
Tax rate without FSC	34 %	34 %	34 %
Tax with FSC	$ 128,325	$ 209,208	$ 333,532
Tax rate with FSC	29 %	28 %	28 %

Jeff: If so, then the right decision appears to be the use of an FSC. If not, then we might have to do without any change for now. We talked a lot about taxes today. But I agree with Mike in that we should also start looking at the other benefits and costs of each location. If we use branches, all three countries are on an equal footing with regard to taxes. If the U.S. tax rate is the best we can do then we'll have to accept that.

HOZHO (A)

I am a Navajo and I belong to the earth. The earth is my mother, my provider, and my caretaker. I am her child. She nourishes me from her body and her soul. I belong to the land. I am rooted in my mother earth. Her deserts, canyons, and mesas encircle me. Her mountains, fields, and forests are a part of me. I am one with nature, and she is one with me.

I belong to my people, the Diné, meaning The People. Our clans live between the four sacred mountains. These mountains protect us. On this land between these mountains we strive for unity and balance. When all is in balance with our Earth Mother, our Sky Father, and The People, then there is hozho, or harmony.

- Danny K. Blackgoat
from *Time Among The Navajo*

Hozho (U.S.) is the parent corporation of a newly incorporated subsidiary Diné, located in the United Kingdom (U.K.). Hozho has seen substantial growth in its sales in recent years, both in the United States and the United Kingdom. The primary product — the only product — consists of a series of reproductions of Navajo rugs. For the past twelve years, Hozho has serviced its British buyers directly through exports from the United States. British sales have grown so large, however, that Hozho has now decided to create a wholly-owned subsidiary in the United Kingdom. The new British subsidiary will purchase partially-completed rugs from the U.S. parent and finish them for the local market. Jim Begay, Treasurer of Hozho, has been asked to consider the best way(s) to repatriate earnings from the British subsidiary, and to present his strategy to the CEO at the Chinle, Arizona headquarters next week.

Hozho (U.S.) sources its inputs from the U.S. market. The raw rug product — a line of approximately twenty different imitation Navajo rug designs — is then sold in the United States and the United Kingdom after additional finishing. The Navajo rug designs are named for either the trading posts around which the designs originated (Teec Nos Pos, Two Grey Hills, Wide Ruins, Ganado, Klagetoh, Burntwater, Chinle) or for the image depicted (Two-Faced Yeibichai, Yei, Diamond Twill, Storm, Eyedazzler, Crystal, Pictorial, Sandpainting). Hozho's rapid growth and success comes from successfully reproducing the original designs at a much lower price for the average buyer. Whereas authentic Navajo rugs range in price from as little as $1,000 to as high as $30,000 each, Hozho's rugs sell for only $600 a piece in the United States and $645 in the United Kingdom.

Hozho (U.S.) is expected to produce a total of 2,500 raw rugs this year, 800 units for sale in the U.S. and 1,700 units for sale — *transfer* — to Diné (U.K.) to be sold in the British market. These raw rugs require additional dyeing and finishing prior to sale which is performed in the country in which they are sold.

Morning Meeting

Begay arrived at his morning meeting in his usual unceremonious way — a cloud of dust and burning 10W-40 billowing from his '62 Ford pickup. As he slammed the door shut (twice), he greeted his assistant, Joe Grayson, with the customary *Yateéh* Navajo welcome.[1] Grayson was the tax expert — a skill picked up from the *belaganaas*.[2] Begay assumed — and had been doing a lot of the computer work for Hozho and Diné in order to evaluate the tradeoffs of income, earnings, and assorted intra-firm cash flows. Begay wanted to review these financials with Joe Grayson before the 10 AM conference call to Manchester to talk with (discuss them with) Chamisa Tsosie, the newly exported controller for Diné in the United Kingdom. They filed into Begay's office.

"Without spending too much time, let's build up the basic P&L from scratch here so that I know what's what," Begay began. "I know Chamisa has done all her homework, and I don't want to waste any of her — or AT&T's — valuable time once we get on the phone."

Grayson leaned back and closed his eyes to concentrate. "It goes like this. It costs us — here in the States — $125 per unit for labor, $75 per unit for local materials, and $50 per unit for a variety of other expenses such as lease fees, electrical power and water usage. If we finish the rugs here, for sale in the States, it costs about another $50 per unit. Hozho's non-direct expenses include $35,000 for general and administrative overhead and an annual depreciation charge of about $15,000. We have essentially no debt — well, any that bears interest — and our corporate income taxes in the United States are 34%. While net income has been steady — and healthy — we have been very disciplined in distributing only 40% of earnings to owners and reinvesting the rest. It is this reinvestment strategy that is largely responsible for our lack of debt."

Grayson opened his eyes, shifted in the old hard wooden chair, closed his eyes again, and continued. "Our current proposal is to have Diné purchase about 1,700 partially finished rugs from us, paying a transfer price of $360 per unit. The transfer price is pretty conservative, because the profit margin is only 33% on these internal sales." Grayson pursed his lips, blinked, and went on. "After looking at the numbers, we might consider changing that margin, maybe pump it up to about 40%." He stopped, and opened his eyes indicating to Begay he was, at least for the moment, finished.

---

[1] *Yateéh* is pronounced as a cross between Ya-ta-hey and Ya-ta-eh. Navajo became a written language only after World War II.

[2] *Belaganna* is the Navajo term for whites, or generally all European peoples of non-Navajo origin.

"Can we do that, can we change the margin on those transfers and not have the IRS crawling all over us?" Begay asked.

"Well, since there aren't any really comparable products out there, what the IRS calls "arms-length comparisons," I think we have room for some fine-tuning." Grayson shifted in his chair again, it was obviously becoming harder and less comfortable by the moment. He continued.

"In order to complete the partially finished rugs purchased from us, Diné will pay roughly $20 per unit in direct labor, $20 per unit in local materials, and $15 per unit in power and water in Britain. Those are what we could call the U.K. finishing costs. We estimate general and administrative expenses for Diné at $25,000 per year, and depreciation charges at $8,500."

The phone buzzed, indicating that Begay's secretary had Chamisa Tsosie on the line from Manchester. Begay leaned forward and spoke out loudly. "Yateéh. Chamisa, Joe and I are here on the speakerphone. Can you hear us okay?"

"Loud and clear. In fact, you can lean back in your chair Jim, before I go deaf," Chamisa responded. Begay noted Chamisa was her usual charismatic self.

Begay grimaced and shifted back in his seat. "Okay, good. Ah, how did the meeting with the British tax authorities go?"

"The Inland Revenue Service has concluded their pre-audit determination. They had some specific concerns. First, royalty fees charged by Hozho have to be kept to a maximum of 8% of sales — at least if you want them to be deductible expenses. Personally, I think a rate of 3% would be sufficient. Secondly, although you are providing a lot of the management and administration — which obviously saves us a lot of trouble — the fees you charge us cannot exceed 5% of our sales here in the United Kingdom. I know the U.S. Internal Revenue Service requires that we be charged, but we better keep it down."

Begay looked over at Grayson, who only nodded affirming Chamisa's points. He did not seem at all surprised by Inland Revenue's concerns. "Chamisa, Joe, uhh, did they also confirm the tax rates we had talked about?"

"Hey Joe. Yep. Inland corporate taxes are paid at 30%, but there are withholding taxes on dividends distributed to non-resident stockholders — you guys — of 15%, if the dividend payout is kept below 50%. If dividend payout rises above 50%, the withholding tax on dividends remitted rises to 25%. Nothing new there. All withholding tax rates are specified by the United States-United Kingdom bilateral tax agreement. Withholding taxes on royalties are 15%, interest payments 10%, and distributed expenses are zero percent.[3] And we have still not been able to get them to back-off the import duty on textiles of 17% of fully-landed value.[4] Same-ole-same-ole," Chamisa chanted.

Begay shrugged and unconsciously leaned forward again. "Okay, what about financing?"

---

[3] Withholding taxes are deducted from the nominal payment, thus the receiver, in essence, pays the tax in the form of a reduced remittance received.

[4] The United Kingdom charges an import duty, *tariff*, of 17% of the fully-landed value of the textile good. In this case, the value would consist of the transfer price plus ocean

Grayson responded first. "Although Hozho itself is relatively debt free, the Diné subsidiary will require debt financing of $1 million to establish operations. We had planned on putting roughly $600,000 of equity in, and coming up with local loans and parent-loans for the balance."

Chamisa interrupted. "You mean total *capital* of a million, only $400,000 in actual debt, right? And, while we're on it, what interest rate are we going to get from you guys? I think the going rate is about 12% around here."

It was Grayson's turn to grimace. He had of course meant total *capital*, and Chamisa was as usual acting more like a *belaganna* than a Navajo by interrupting. "Yes, capital. We would probably prefer if you could get most of the debt there, but I don't know if those doors will be open even if we post a guarantee from this end. What's your read on that?"

"I don't know yet. I would prefer to start building a credit reputation here, but you may be right. It may be hard to get much debt here before we really have cash flows to show for it. Before I left, you guys had talked of interest anywhere between six and 14%. What's it going to be?" Chamisa pursued. She was not going to let the point die.

Begay's eyes met Grayson's as he chose his words. "No decision on that yet. In the event we did provide a lot of the debt-financing, we would be sure and stretch out the maturity so that — at least initially — you would only have to worry about interest payments." Begay surreptitiously slipped in a glance at his watch, as if Chamisa could see him. "Okay. You look into the financing and we will do a bit more head-scratching over the explicit structure. We'll talk early next week."

"Whoa Chief," Chamisa chimed. Begay cringed when anyone called him Chief and Chamisa knew it. "I want you guys to remember that cranking those royalty and management fees up may put pennies in your pockets, but it takes *pence* out of mine. What about my profitability? I have people here that need to know they have a fair shot at those performance bonuses which we talked about back in Chinle before I caught my flight. Somehow *that* hasn't come up in this conversation." Chamisa's voice had started to rise.

Begay sighed. "Chamisa, I am well aware of those facts and very important details. Thanks. We'll talk next week." Click.

Lunch Discussion

Over a lunch of lamb stew at the Thunderbird Cafe down by the entrance to Canyon de Chelly, Begay and Grayson had roughed out a diagram (see Exhibit 1) of the ways in which cash would flow between the two units of the newly created multinational firm. Clearly, there were a number of decisions to be made regarding the rates for specific cash flows (royalties, distributed overhead, etc.) as well as fundamental decisions regarding the level of debt acquired from the parent and at what interest rate. And the transfer price itself, given that there was really no real substitute or arm's-length price for the rugs, could be adjusted a bit to either increase or decrease the profitability of Diné. As Grayson droned-on, Begay stared out the window

EXHIBIT 1   Cash Flows Between Hozho (U.S.) and Diné (U.K.)

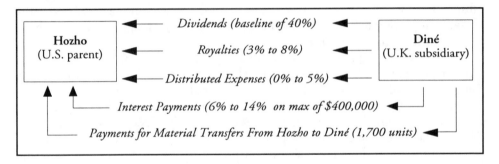

wondering how it could still be dusty though snowing at the same time. His mind returned to the continuing soliloquy of Joe Grayson.

"Another problem is taxes. The United States Internal Revenue Service requires that taxes be paid on all income derived from foreign sources — in this case Diné — but foreign tax credits are allowed only for taxes already paid or *deemed paid* in the foreign country." Begay did remember that this procedure applied only to income which was actually *remitted* in the current period, that is, paid to the parent as dividends.

When Begay got back to the office, he sat down and scratched out the gross-up procedure as he remembered it (see Exhibit 2).

If the subsidiary had income of, say, $100, and paid corporate income taxes of 40%, that left $60 for distribution to stockholders (the parent company). If Hozho instructed Diné to distribute 50%, then a dividend of $30 would be declared and remitted to the parent. If there were any withholding taxes imposed on the dividends, say 10%, the $30 would be reduced by $3, leaving a net remittance to the parent of $27. The tax authorities (at least the ones in the United States), would then gross-up the dividend remitted — adding back all the taxes already paid on the distribution in order to calculate the theoretical U.S. taxes which would be paid *if* that same income had been generated at home. The U.S. tax authorities would then allow credit, *foreign*

EXHIBIT 2   Dividend Remittance & Foreign Tax Credits: Hypothetical Calculation

Foreign subsidiary's Income Statement	
EBT of foreign subsidiary	$100
Less 40% corporate income tax	40
Net income of foreign subsidiary	$60
Dividend declared to parent of 50%	30
Withholding tax on dividends of 10%	3
Net dividend remitted to parent	$27
Gross-up for U.S. Tax Purposes	
Net dividend remitted	$27
Add back foreign taxes paid:	
Withholding taxes on dividends	3
Foreign corporate taxes paid on distributions	20
Grossed-up foreign source income	$50
U.S. Tax Determination	
Theoretical U.S. taxes due at 34%	$17
Foreign tax credits	23
Additional U.S. taxes due?	0
Excess foreign tax credits?	6

tax credits, for those taxes already *paid or deemed paid (all these italics were starting to make Begay very nervous)*. If additional taxes were due, they would be netted from the remittance, reducing the dividend remitted from the subsidiary.

Grayson reminded Begay that if the firm ended up with *excess* foreign tax credits, they would be of limited use. The problem was that excess foreign tax credits cannot be applied against domestic-source income tax liabilities, only other similar foreign-source income tax liabilities. Excess credits can, however, be carried back two years and forward five years, but often when there is an excess one year, there is excess for several years.[5] Begay made a note to compare how dividend income created foreign tax credits (being after-tax distributions from Diné) compared to other income such as royalties (which were an expense of Diné prior to taxes, and an income to Hozho).

Grayson went on to explain (he was now really getting on Begay's nerves) that *active foreign-source income* (dividends remitted) was treated separately from *passive foreign source income* (interest, royalties, and distributed expenses). The passive income which Hozho would earn from Diné would be separately grossed-up and additional U.S. tax liabilities determined. And (it seemed to never stop), any excess foreign tax credits in one category, like passive income, could not be applied against tax liabilities due in another category, such as active foreign source income or even domestic source income.

Late Afternoon

As the day wound down, Begay was left alone with his thoughts. Alone, that is, until the fax machine started spewing forth a fax from Chamisa.

FACSIMILE TRANSMISSION

TO:	Jim Begay, Treasurer Hozho, Inc.	**FROM:**	Chamisa Tsosie Diné, Inc.
CITY:	Chinle, Arizona	**CITY:**	Manchester
COUNTRY:	U.S.	**COUNTRY:**	England

Yateéh Jim. A quick note. It occurs to me that we should agree on the goal of the financial structure before we start choosing rates at random. Grayson and I were discussing this the other day and agreed (believe it or not) that the goal is to maximize the consolidated earnings of the two units, Hozho and Diné, after-tax. This means we have to pay very specific attention to how we get the money back to Chinle so that we don't end up with a lot of excess foreign tax credits. That's all for now. Talk to you next week. Chamisa.

P.S. Don't forget to check out that interest rate on the debt Hozho is going to provide to us here in the land of palefaces. C.T

Although they had worked together on the project a number of hours already, Begay and Grayson could still not agree on what exactly they were trying to *minimize* or *maximize*. Begay thought that the goal of the financial construction should be to

---

[5] Begay remembered a seminar in New York in which the speaker spoke of repatriating earnings in such a way that excess foreign tax credits were minimized by managing the profitability of the subsidiary itself.

minimize the global tax bill (total taxes paid in the United States and the United Kingdom), while simultaneously maximizing the net income of Hozho itself, not the net income of Diné. Grayson and Chamisa argued that the "taxes should not wag the dog" and that the goal was the maximization of consolidated earnings after taxes (the net income of the U.S. and U.K. units combined), or maybe some other equally confusing combination. Chamisa, as much as she hated it, had agreed with Grayson (which they both agreed must have been the first time since *Kokopelli*, the dancing flute-player depicted on canyon walls throughout the desert Southwest, had wandered the earth).

It looked like this was going to be the first discussion on the agenda next week, so Begay put on a fresh pot of coffee to brew and sat back down at his computer. He started constructing pro forma income statements side-by-side for Hozho and Diné, as well as tax worksheets for Hozho's foreign source income, hoping it would help him understand the relationships between the two, and what tradeoffs must be considered in setting the various intra-firm rates. The first attempt was nearly finished when Begay realized he had not included, anywhere, the profits to Hozho from the raw rugs sold to Diné; Begay concluded that they were domestic income, although the sales were actually exports. Exhibit 3 provides the basic structure for the pro forma income statements (Begay's third try), and Exhibit 4 is the associated tax worksheets for the tax calculations on foreign source income.

Taking a break at about 11 PM, Begay chuckled to himself as he stared at the old wooden chair on the other side of the desk. Best idea he had ever had, making sure that old chair was always there — and always uncomfortable. Kept people from hanging out. But, he was already tired — the previous week had been spent at a Night Way, a sing for his maternal uncle's health — and he was already short of sleep. It would be a long night.

Case Questions

1. Whose side would you take in terms of the goal(s) of multinational financial management? What is the appropriate goal (other than "the maximization of stockholder wealth"), minimization of global taxes, minimization of U.S. taxes, minimization of the effective tax rate, maximization of global income before tax, maximization of global income after tax, maximization of U.S. income before/after tax, or something else? Why?

2. Complete the spreadsheets depicted in Exhibits 3 and 4 which allow the calculation of different management determined variables on the relative incomes and taxes of the two units, Hozho (U.S.) and Diné (U.K.). Be careful in the construction of taxes due on foreign-sourced income, as the parent company Hozho must first gross-up earnings from Diné and then determine whether additional taxes are due above and beyond identified foreign tax credits for both active and passive income categories. For the basic analysis, assume a dividend payout of 40%, a royalty rate of 3%, a distributed expense of 2%, an intra-firm interest rate of 6% on parent provided debt of $400,000, and a margin of 33% on transfers from Hozho to Diné.

3. If you assume that Diné (U.K.) will distribute 40% of net income to the parent, Hozho (U.S.), what would you recommend regarding the other managerially determined variables (royalty rates, management fees, etc.) for Diné's operations? Would you recommend changing the dividend payout rate itself?

EXHIBIT 3 Pro Forma Income Statements for Hozho (U.S.) and Diné (U.K)

Line Item	Hozho (U.S.)	Diné (U.K.)
Revenues:		
External sales	$ 480,000	$1,096,500
Internal sales	612,000	
Costs of goods sold:		
Purchases from Hozho		612,000
Freight charges for imported rugs		
Import duties on imported rugs		
Local labor		
Local materials		
Other variable costs		
Hozho's finishing costs		
Total COGS		
Other costs:		
Royalties and license fees		
General & administrative expenses		
Distributed charges due Hozho		
Depreciation		
Total other costs		
EBIT		
Interest expenses:		
Interest on local debt		
Interest on parent-provided debt		
EBT		
Corporate income tax on domestic income		
Taxes due on foreign-source active income		
Taxes due on foreign-source passive income		
Total taxes due		
Foreign-source income (net of withholding taxes)		
Dividends received from Diné		
Royalties received from Diné		
Distributed charges received from Diné		
Interest earnings from Diné		
Total net foreign-source income		
Total income (domestic + foreign)		
Retained earnings		
Distributed earnings		

EXHIBIT 4   Tax Worksheets for Hozho's Foreign Source Income

ACTIVE INCOME (dividend repatriation)

Dividend remittance:

Dividends paid by Diné (U.K.)
        Less withholding taxes
Net dividend remitted to Hozho (U.S.)

Gross-up of dividend remitted for U.S. tax purposes:

Net dividend remitted to Hozho (U.S.)
        Add-back foreign taxes paid
                Witholding taxes on dividends
                U.K. corporate income taxes paid on distributions
Grossed-up dividend income
Theoretical U.S. taxes due
Credit for foreign taxes paid
Additional U.S. taxes due?
Excess foreign tax credits?

PASSIVE INCOME (royalties, interest, distributed charges)

Passive income remittance:

Royalties paid by Diné (U.K.) to Hozho (U.S.)
        Less withholding taxes paid
Net royalties remitted to Hozho (U.S.)

Interest paid by Diné (U.K.) to Hozho (U.S.)
        Less withholding taxes paid
Net interest remitted to Hozho (U.S.)

Distributed charges paid by Diné (U.K.) to Hozho (U.S.)
        Less withholding taxes paid
Net interest remitted to Hozho (U.S.)

Gross-up of passive income remitted for U.S. tax purposes:

Total passive income remitted (royalties, interest , charges)
        Total foreign tax credits
Grossed-up foreign source passive income
Theoretical U.S. taxes due
Credit for foreign taxes paid
Additional U.S. taxes due?
Excess foreign tax credits?

TEKTRONIX (C)

In September 1999 Jerry Davies, Treasurer, Tektronix (Tek) and Randahl Finnessy, Worldwide Cash Manager, needed to make some urgent decisions about Tek's foreign exchange risk management strategy.

On June 24, 1999 Tek had announced its decision to split itself into two separate, publicly traded companies. One company would be comprised of Tek's Measurement Business Division (MBD) and would retain the Tektronix name. The other company would be comprised of Tek's Color Printing and Imaging Division (CPID) with a new name to be announced later. It would be capitalized with an initial public offering (IPO) of 15% of its shares. The remaining shares would be distributed tax-free to Tek's existing shareholders. Tek also announced that it intended to sell or find a strategic alliance for its Video and Networking Division, excluding Video Tele.com business unit, which had just been merged into MBD.

On August 10, 1999 Tek announced that it had agreed to sell its video and networking division to a private investment group. Tek will retain a 10% interest in this group.

The split up would result in individual foreign exchange risk profiles for each new company that differed from the existing combined profile. It meant rethinking the strategies and instruments to be used in managing the new operating, transaction, and accounting exposures. The instruments that had been used by the combined company included forward contracts, foreign currency options, a risk sharing agreement, a multilateral netting program, and a reinvoicing center.

The Decision to Split Up

The decision to split up was motivated by the need to improve focus. This generic strategy is the current fad in the academic literature, and promoted heavily by management consultants and security analysts. Management would be able to focus its efforts on a single business line of competency. Shareholders and analysts would gain transparency; the ability to analyze and invest in a pure business line—a pure play.

Tek's timing was motivated by its recent stock price performance. As shown in Exhibit 1, it had underperformed the market, as measured by the S&P500, since March 1998. (Appendix 1 illustrates Tek's share price alone.)

Splitting up Tek to gain focus is a divestment strategy that could reverse some of the economies of scale and synergies that accrue to firms from mergers and

EXHIBIT 1 Tektronix (TEK) Share Price Performance Versus the SP500

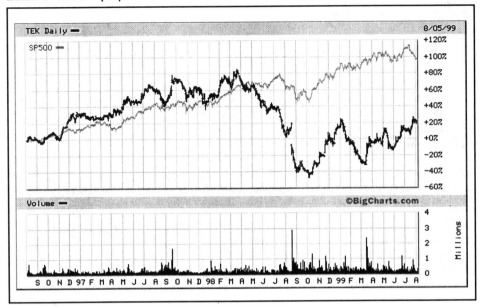

acquisitions. The immediate problem being analyzed by Jerry Davies and Randahl Finnessy related to the foreign exchange risk management strategy, but other potential financial repercussion's were also important. These included such items as the effect on the cost and availability of capital for the two surviving entities. What should be their optimal financial structures? There would be a need to duplicate and compete for internal (and external) personnel with financial experience and expertise. Another problem would be the division of the existing firm's assets and liabilities.

In addition to the financial repercussions of a divestment strategy, there could be serious effects on strategies in marketing, production, distribution, research and development, and other links in the value chain. These are beyond the scope and responsibility of Treasury executives but are obviously critical to the overall success of a divestment strategy. In summary, there is a price to pay for pursuing a divestment strategy, but gains could accrue from a strategy that focuses a company more narrowly on its core competencies.

Background

Tek is a U.S. corporation, headquartered in Wilsonville, Oregon. It designs, manufactures, and markets worldwide three major product lines: measurement instruments (MBD), color printing and imaging products (CPID), and video and networking products. Tek had 7571 employees worldwide as of May 31, 1999, and maintains operations in 29 countries outside the United States (see Appendix 2). Tek's stock is listed on the New York Stock Exchange under the symbol TEK.

Measuring Instruments		
Fiscal 1999 Facts		**Geographic Sales (in millions)**
Sales (thousands): $844,882		Japan $59.2
Headquarters: Beaverton		Europe $226.6
Number of employees: 3,600		Americas $38.0
		Pacific $112.3
		United States $408.8
Principal Products		**Global Market Focus**
Protocol analyzers and simulators		Focuses on high-growth segments;
Network monitoring systems		communications, computers, and
Transmission and cable test products		semiconductors. Includes telecommunications
RF and communication products through alliances		public network equipment manufacturers
Windows-based logic analyzers and systems		and operators; electronic design engineers and
Broad range of oscilloscopes and accessories		prototype developers; television
		equipment manufacturers; content
		providers; broadcasters;cable network providers.
Color Printing and Imaging		
Fiscal 1999 Facts		**Geographic Sales (in millions)**
Sales (thousands): $725,334		Japan $15.9
Headquarters: Wilsonville		Europe $243.4
Number of employees: 2,100		Americas $35.4
		Pacific $42.8
		United States $387.9
Principal Products		**Global Market Focus**
Phaser workgroup color printers use either color		Business office market; graphic arts/
laser or solid ink printing technology. We also		publishing; science/engineering data analysis;
market a complete line of printer consumable		and on-demand printing.
products such as ink, toner, and transparencies.		
Source: *Tektronix Annual Report*, 1999.		

Products and Markets   A description of Tek's products and markets, excluding the video and networking division, is presented in Exhibit 2. About half of Tek's sales are outside the United States. Europe, the Pacific, Japan, and the Americas are the most important markets in declining order of importance. About 45% of total sales in 1999 was produced by MBD, 39% by CPID, and the remaining 16% by the Video and Networking Division.

Financial Results

In fiscal 1998 and 1999 (year ending May 31st), Tek took non-recurring pre-tax charges of $79 million and $120 million, respectively. In 1999 diluted earnings per shares fell to a negative ($1.07) from $1.60 in 1998 and $2.29 in 1997. The decline in earnings was mainly due to the downturn in Asian markets, flat U.S. markets, and restructuring to cut costs and to anticipate the split-up. Exhibit 3 presents selected financial data for the 1995-1999 period.

	1999	1998	1997	1996	1995
Net sales	$1,861.5	$2,085.8	$1,940.1	$1,768.9	$1,498.0
Gross margin	38.2%	41.5%	42.9%	41.9%	45.3%
Excluding NRC	39.7%	43.3%	42.9%	41.9%	45.3%
R&D expenses	11.0%	9.7%	9.7%	9.3%	11.1%
Selling, G&A expenses	25.8%	24.4%	24.8%	24.8%	26.7%
Operating margin	(3.7)%	5.5%	8.5%	8.1%	7.7%
Excluding NRC	2.8%	9.3%	8.5%	8.1%	7.7%
Pretax margin	(4.0)%	5.9%	8.7%	8.0%	7.4%
Excluding NRC	2.4%	9.7%	8.7%	8.0%	7.4%
Earnings margin	(2.7)%	3.9%	5.9%	5.6%	5.4%
Excluding NRC	1.7%	6.5%	5.9%	5.6%	5.4%
Net earnings (loss)	$(51.2)	$82.3	$114.8	$99.6	$81.6
Excluding NRC	$30.8	$135.2	$114.8	$99.6	$81.6
Basic earnings (loss) per share	$(1.07)	$1.63	$2.32	$2.00	$1.67
Excluding NRC	$0.65	$2.68	$2.32	$2.00	$1.67
Diluted earnings per share	$(1.07)	$1.60	$2.29	$1.95	$1.64
Excluding NRC	$0.64	$2.63	$2.29	$1.95	$1.64
Weighted average shares outstanding:					
basic	47.7	50.4	49.5	49.8	48.9
diluted	47.7	51.3	50.2	51.0	49.8
Dividends per share	$0.48	$0.46	$0.40	$0.40	$0.40
Cash and cash equivalents	$39.7	$120.5	$142.7	$36.6	$31.8
Total assets	$1,359.4	$1,389.2	$1,316.7	$1,328.5	$1,218.3
Long-term debt	$150.7	$150.7	$151.6	$202.0	$105.0
Total debt	$266.4	$156.1	$157.7	$246.6	$192.6
Total capitalization	$621.6	$784.9	$771.3	$675.3	$604.2
Return on equity	(7.3)%	10.6%	15.9%	15.6%	15.2%
Excluding NRC	4.0%	16.8%	15.9%	15.6%	15.2%
Ending shares outstanding	46.9	50.3	50.1	49.0	49.6
Book value per share	$13.25	$15.59	$15.39	$13.77	$12.18
Capital expenditures	$107.5	$155.1	$112.0	$106.7	$103.8
Depreciation expense	$71.4	$65.9	$59.6	$47.1	$40.9
Square feet in use	3.7	4.0	3.8	4.1	4.3
Employees	7,571	8,630	8,392	7,929	7,712
Net sales per employee (000s)	$246.1	$241.7	$231.2	$223.1	$194.2
Revenue from new products	71%	74%	73%	67%	62%

NRC = non-recurring charges. Source: www.tektronix.com

Foreign Operations

Tek was founded in 1946, but had already established its first foreign distribution agreement (in Sweden) by 1948. In the succeeding years Tek established numerous sales subsidiaries, a 50-50 joint venture with Sony of Japan (Sony-Tek), and for a period, manufacturing facilities in the U.K., the Isle of Guernsey, and The Netherlands. The latter have been replaced more recently by manufacturing facilities in Berlin (Germany), Padova (Italy), and Penang (Malaysia). It also has a joint venture in China. Despite the large number of foreign entities, Tek still manufactures 85%

of the value of its production in the United States and only 15% abroad. However, foreign sales account for 50% of Tek's total sales

MBD products are mostly produced and exported from Beaverton, Oregon (Tek's original location), but specialized products are manufactured in Berlin with support from Padova. CPID products mostly originate in Wilsonville, Oregon, although the purpose of acquiring manufacturing facilities in Penang, Malaysia was to shift some color printing manufacturing to that location. The Video and Networking Division that will be divested also had foreign sales, but it transacted all of its business in U.S. dollars, both with respect to sales and purchases. Therefore, it's sales are expected to have a neutral effect on any foreign exchange exposure strategy.

Exhibit 4 shows how Tek (Oregon) is related to its foreign operating affiliates. Tek also utilizes a Foreign Sales Corporation (FSC), located in Vancouver, British Columba, that enables it to reduce U.S. taxes on export sales from the United States. All exports with U.S. content greater than 50% go through the FSC.

The majority of Tek's exports from Oregon utilize its reinvoicing center, Tek Europe International (TEI). The products are invoiced to TEI in U.S. dollars but TEI then invoices the foreign subsidiaries in local currency. Thus the foreign exchange risk is assumed by TEI and is managed at Tek's Wilsonville, Oregon headquarters. TEI is a legal entity that has no physical presence. Its transfer prices to foreign subsidiaries are adjusted for each country to reflect the customary local margins in each location. The margins employed by local independent distributors are used as a proxy for customary local margins. Tek (Oregon) both buys and sells to Sony-Tek (Japan). Sony-Tek sells to their own customers in Japan and the rest of Asia. Yangzhong buys from Tek (Oregon) and sells in China. It also manufactures and sells some of its own product types in China.

EXHIBIT 4. Organization of Tek (Oregon) and Its Foreign Affiliates

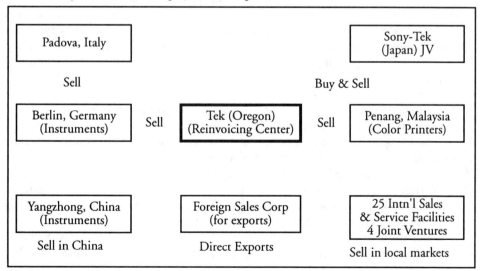

Foreign Exchange Exposure

Manufacturing in Oregon and selling abroad in local currencies creates significant structural operating and transaction exposures. When the U.S. dollar strengthens relative to its foreign sales locations, Tek's products become less price competitive. If prices are maintained in local currency terms, foreign exchange losses occur when the local currency proceeds are converted to dollars. If prices are maintained in U.S. dollar terms, foreign sales decline. This phenomenon led to large losses on foreign sales during the 1980-1985 period, when the U.S. dollar appreciated by as much as 50% against European currencies. It is also partly responsible for the most recent losses due to declining sales in Asian markets, where local currencies plunged in value. The U.S. dollar has even strengthened somewhat compared to the euro, but not yet to the point of the 1980-1985 disaster.

Exhibit 5 presents Tek's foreign exchange exposures as of May 31, 1999. Equity exposure measures the net exposed assets of Tek's foreign affiliates from an accounting exposure perspective. It is the dollar value of the shareholder equity account on the balance sheet of the foreign affiliates. Gains and losses on equity exposure are placed in an equity reserve account. Earnings exposure is a measure of the Tek's existing transaction exposure. Backlog exposure measures foreign-currency-denominated contracts or orders that have been accepted by Tek but not yet delivered or invoiced. Current exposure is foreign exchange contracts for vendor payables. Anticipated exposure springs from expected future transactions, not actually contracted for, which in this case are primarily an ongoing commitment for Tek to import components from a major Japanese supplier.

Tek has experienced modest foreign exchange losses every year (1995-1999) despite efficient risk management programs. Not every exposure is hedged since that would be very costly. The main reason for Tek's continuing foreign exchange losses is its operating exposure. Some transaction gains (losses) could also result from the use of the U.S. dollar as the functional currency for Sony-Tek and Tek's Hong Kong subsidiary. All the other foreign subsidiaries use their local currency as the functional currency, so that the foreign exchange gains and losses on these subsidiaries are closed to an equity reserve account (the Cumulative Translation Adjustment or CTA) and do not affect earnings. Appendix 3 presents the functional currency designation and buy currency for each of Tek's subsidiaries.

Operating Exposure All of Tek's foreign exchange exposures shown in Exhibit 5 are positive because it has structural foreign currency operating exposure. Tek produces mainly in Oregon, USA, but sells half of its output abroad. Most foreign sales are invoiced in foreign currencies. The imbalance is most severe in Europe even though Tek manufactures to a limited extent in Berlin, Germany (which sources inputs from Padova, Italy). Centralized manufacturing in Oregon has the advantages of gaining economies of scale, close coordination with Tek's R&D activities, and the supporting external infrastructure which has built up over the years.

Tek's main worldwide competitors are predominantly much larger MNEs that can and do enjoy economies of scale in multiple foreign manufacturing locations. For

EXHIBIT 5 Tektronix Foreign Exchange Exposures, Fiscal Year-end 1999, and Foreign Exchange Losses in Recent Years (thousands of US dollars)

	Equity	Earnings	Backlog	Current	Anticipated
European Exposures					
Belgian francs	$2,543	$839	$673		
Danish krone	1,655	497	851	1,675	
Deutschemark	33,935	4,072	7,236		
Dutch guilder	1,372	926	713		
Italian lira	17,923	3,838	4,500		
Austrian shilling	2,125	3,838	547		
British pound	72,888	371	8,073		
French franc	23,658	4,859	4,052		
Norwegian krone	374	2,900	191		
Spanish peseta	8,255	0	2,669		
Swedish krona	926	3,126	1,007		
Swiss franc	15,199	132	1,267		
Total European	$180,833	$25,398	$31,780	$1,675	--
AM/PAC Exposures					
Australian dollar	$5,894	$2,301	$5,152		
Brazilian real	9,135	-6,170	207		
Canadian dollar	10,362	2,805	3,329		
Japanese yen	1,682	1,004	12,744	995	50,000
Mexican peso	3,982	- 380	81		
Total AM/PAC	$31,055	-$439	$21,514	$995	$50,000
Exposure Summary					
European	$180,833	$25,398	$31,780	$1,675	------
AM/PAC	31,055	- 439	21,514	995	50,000
Total exposure	$211,889	$24,959	$53,294	$2,670	$50,000

Foreign Exchange Gains & Losses (thousands of US dollars)	
1995	($2,230)
1996	($1,341)
1997	($ 753)
1998	($ 278)
1999	($3,448)

Source: Tektronix Treasury Group

example, Hewlett-Packard (HP) is the longtime competitor that most closely matches Tek in both product lines and historical development. HP, based in Palo Alto, California, has manufacturing plants in 20 foreign countries, besides the United States. HP is therefore not as severely affected by operating exposure as is Tek.

In March 1999 HP also announced a strategy to sharpen its "focus." It too will split into two companies, named Agilent and Hewlett-Packard. Agilent will focus on the traditional measuring instruments products and markets. It has existing sales of $7 billion (much larger than all of Tek combined). The other company, keeping the HP name, will focus on computer and printing operations with sales of $40 billion worldwide.

Exhibit 6 is an attempt to profile Tek compared to its competitors from the perspective of foreign exchange operating exposure. In addition to HP, Siemens is an immense European MNE, with particularly strong manufacturing in Germany

EXHIBIT 6 Profile of Tek's Global Competitors and their Structural Operating Exposures

	Main Listing Exchange	1998 Sales (millions)	1998 Income (millions)	1998 Employees	Main Mfg. Locations	Admin. & R&D Locations	Equipment Source
Measurement							
Tektronix (US)	NYSE	$ 1,863	$ (51)	8,630	U.S.	U.S.	Global
Hewlett-Packard (US)	NYSE	$47,061	$2,945	124,600	Global	U.S.	Global
Siemens (Germany)	European	$70,551	$ 550	416,000	Ger/Neth	Germany	Global
National Instruments (US)	NYSE	$ 274	$ 37	1,658	U.S.	U.S.	not avail
Color Printers							
Tektronix (US)	NYSE	$ 1,863	$ (51)	8,630	U.S.	U.S.	Global
Hewlett-Packard (US)	NYSE	$47,061	$ 2,945	124,600	Global	U.S.	Global
Compaq Computer (US)	NYSE	$31,169	$(2,743)	71,000	U.S.	U.S.	Global
Eastman Kodak (US)	NYSE	$13,406	$ 1,390	86,200	Global	U.S.	Global
Xerox (US)	NYSE	$19,449	$ 395	92,700	Global	U.S.	Global
Lexmark (US)	NYSE	$ 3,021	$ 243	8,800	U.S.	U.S.	Global

and the Netherlands. However, it has its own operating exposure depending on the fortunes of the euro. In the color printing and imaging sector, Tek faces giant U.S.-based MNEs such as Xerox, Eastman Kodak, Compaq, and of course HP. These MNEs all have multiple manufacturing operations worldwide even though they are headquartered in the United States. It should be noted, however, that some elements of the value chain are equally exposed, especially among Tek's U.S. competitors. These elements include the location of administration and a large part of research and development in the United States. All firms also source a number of their major inputs and much of their equipment at world prices. They all have access to a global cost and availability of capital, shown by their listing on the NYSE, NASDAQ, and European stock exchanges (Siemens). They all sell worldwide and therefore have ongoing exposure to foreign currency receipts.

Foreign Exchange Risk Management   Tek uses a number of complementary strategies to manage its foreign exchange risk. The most important tools are: (1) matching cash flows; (2) risk sharing; (3) forward contracts and currency options; (4) reinvoicing; and (5) multilateral netting.

Matching Cash Flows   As a combined company Tek has been able to mitigate part of its Japanese yen exposure by natural matching of cash flow's. CPID imports components from a major supplier in Japan and is invoiced in yen. MBD and CPID have healthy sales invoiced in yen. These yen cash flows can be matched at the present time, but not in the future after the split up. Wherever possible, Tek tries to match cash flows as a primary foreign exchange risk management technique.

Risk Sharing   CPID also had a risk sharing agreement with its major Japanese supplier that it canceled a few years ago. The agreement required Tek to assume the foreign exchange risk for the Japanese yen/U.S. dollar (¥/$) exchange rate for a limited range of movement. Beyond the range, Tek and its Japanese supplier shared the foreign exchange risk for the ¥/$. It worked in favor of the Japanese supplier when the yen was at ¥165/$, but badly for Tek. After the risk sharing agreement was canceled the yen strengthened to around ¥114/$. Tek needs to come up with a replacement for this agreement especially without future matching yen cash flows. Appendix 4 illustrates the typical structure Tek uses in its currency risk sharing agreements.

Forward Contracts and Currency Options   Tek's policy is for TEI, the reinvoicing center, to hedge selectively with forward contracts where natural currency matching strategies are ineffective. It can only hedge known commercial exposures including backlog exposures. It cannot hedge anticipated exposures. At the end of 1999 and 1998, the notional amounts of Tek's currency contracts were $75.3 million and $127.4 million, respectively.

TEI has also utilized covered options but does not write any uncovered options. In general, Tek has historically been quite conservative when it comes to the use of exotic financial instruments to hedge foreign exchange exposures. This is in tune with its other historical financial policies, which favor a low debt ratio and a high level of risk aversion.

Multilateral Netting   Tek employs an internal multilateral netting system to minimize the transaction cost of too many small infrequent internal transfers of cash between operating units and between countries. The birth of the euro should greatly simplify the netting process for subsidiaries located in Euroland (11 participating countries). However, the split up will probably necessitate duplicating the netting system unless an alternative can be found. For example, at one time Tek used Citibank in London to run its multilateral netting system.

Decision Time

Jerry Davies and Randahl Finnessy need to finalize a foreign exchange risk management strategy for each of the two new companies even though they could personally stay with only one of them. Higher level approval could also be a challenge, since Carl Neun, the Chief Financial Officer for Tek, is already slated to be the Chief Executive Officer (CEO) of the continuing Tek that was formerly MBD. The present CEO of Tek, Jerry Meyer, was picked to be the CEO of the new company that was formerly CPID. The existing Presidents of the two divisions were to continue as Presidents of the successor companies.

When Tek is split up, the two new companies will each need to redefine their contractual hedging policies. They will also need to recruit the financial expertise to run possibly two reinvoicing centers and execute the necessary hedging activities. The synergies of centralized foreign exchange exposure management will be diluted by having to duplicate this function.

Appendix 1   Tektronix Share Price, 1997-1999

Appendix 2   Tektronix Corporate Information

Corporate Office
Tektronix, Inc.
Wilsonville, Oregon

Manufacturing	**Subsidiary Companies**	**Joint Ventures**
Beaverton, Oregon	England	Japan (Sony/Tek)
Chelmsford, Massachusetts	Wilsonville, Oregon	China (Yangzhong)
Nevada City, California	Beaverton, Oregon	Madison, Wisconsin
Penang, Malaysia	The Netherlands	Beaverton, Oregon
Wilsonville, Oregon	Agana, Guam	
Yangzhong, China	Bangalore, India	
Berlin, Germany	Penang, Malaysia	
	Padova, Italy	
	Berlin, Germany	

International Sales and Service

Argentina	France	Norway
Australia	Germany	Poland
Austria	Hong Kong	Singapore
Belgium	India	Spain
Brazil	Italy	Sweden
Canada	Japan	Switzerland
China (PRC)	Korea	Taiwan (ROC)
Denmark	Mexico	United Kingdom
Finland	The Netherlands	

Appendix 3   Functional and Buy Currencies for Tektronix Subsidiaries

Subsidiary	Functional Currency	Buy Currency	Subsidiary	Functional Currency	Buy Currency
Asia (U.S.)	USD	USD	Berlin (CTE)	DEM	DEM
Australia	AUD	AUD	Bouwerij (Neth's)	NLG	NLG
Beijing	CNY	CNY	Denmark	DKK	DKK
Brazil	BRL	BRL	Europe B.V. (Neth's)	NLG	NLG
Canada	CAD	CAD	Europe Ltd. (U.K.)	GBP	GBP
China	CNY	CNY	Finland	FIM	FIM
Fed Systems (U.S.)	USD	USD	France	FRF	FRF
FSC (U.S.)	USD	USD	Germany	DEM	DEM
GV Japan	JPY	JPY	Holding Co. (U.K.)	GBP	GBP
Hong Kong	USD	USD	Italy	ITL	ITL
India	INR	INR	Norway	NOK	NOK
India Engineering	INR	INR	Poland	PLZ	PLZ
International (U.S.)	USD	USD	Research Ltd. (U.K.)	GBP	GBP
Korea	KRW	KRW	Spain	ESP	ESP
Mexico	MXP	MXP	Sweden	SEK	SEK
Singapore	SGD	SGD	Switzerland	CHF	CHF
Sony/Tek (Japan)	USD	USD	TEI EAME (U.S.)	USD	USD
Taiwan	TWD	TWD	TEI Americas (U.S.)	USD	USD
TDC (U.S.)	USD	USD	TEI Pacific (U.S.)	USD	USD
YTK (Yangzhong)	CNY	CNY	Tek Holland (Neth's)	NLG	NLG
Austria	ATS	ATS	UK	GBP	GBP
Belgium	BEF	BEF			

Note: "Functional Currency" is identified by Tek in accordance with guidelines provided by FAS#52. "Buy Currency" is the currency of denomination for purchases from Tek (Oregon) or other suppliers.

(Sample structure used by Tektronix)

1. **Payment in dollars**

   Prices for products are set in Japanese yen. Payments for products will be made in U.S. dollars at an adjusted foreign exchange rate (yen per U.S. dollar). The adjusted foreign exchange rate shall be calculated monthly for each month's shipments based on the following formula:

$$\frac{\text{Price in Japanese yen}}{[(\text{Average JPY Spot Rate} + \text{JPY Base Rate}) \times 1/2]}$$

   Base rate = Value of Japanese yen per one U.S. dollar at contract signing

   Average Spot Rate = Based on the New York edition of the *Wall Street Journal*, the yen to dollar exchange rate for the calendar month two months prior to the actual shipments, e.g. for shipments for the month of April 1999 the average exchange rate for the month of February, 1999 will be used.

2. **Payment in yen**

   The U.S. dollar Base Unit Price (BUP) for each item uses a Base Exchange Rate (BER) (value of Japanese yen per one U.S. dollar at contract signing) to determine the yen price. On four (4) consecutive Tuesdays in each month of December, March, June, and September, SELLER shall record the spot JPY rate as published in the New York edition of the Wall Street Journal. The average rate of these four Tuesdays shall be defined as the Average Exchange Rate (AER).

   If the difference between the AER and the BER for a specific item is greater than 5%, then the price of that item for the calendar quarter following the month of each calculation shall be adjusted using the following Yen based formula:

   If AER - BER > (some amount of foreign currency), then

   Revised BUP Price = BUP x AER / [(AER + BER) x 1/2]

   Else,

   If BER - AER > (some amount of foreign currency), then

   Revised BUP Price = BUP x AER/[(AER + BER) x 1/2]

   After the revised BUP price is calculated, it is applied against the BER to determine the new JPY payment.

   If the absolute value of the difference between the AER and the BER for a specific item is greater than (some amount of foreign currency)/Dollar, then BUYER and SELLER shall upon the request of either or both meet and discuss a revision of the BER and/or the PUP.

   Source: Tektronix Treasury Group

INSEAD

GREAT EASTERN TOYS (A)

It was late July 1998. Mr. Paul Cheng, sole owner of Great Eastern Toys, was getting ready to leave his office. An hour earlier, Mr. John Li, the company's general manager, had dropped on Cheng's desk the company's financial statements for the year ending on June 30, 1998 as well as several other reports (see Exhibits 1 to 5). Paul Cheng decided to take these documents home with him. He wanted to examine them in detail before meeting with Li tomorrow morning. Two issues were on Paul Cheng's mind. First, he wanted to determine the effectiveness of the policies and efforts of John Li whom he hired as general manager nearly two years earlier. Second, he wanted to review the evolution of his company's financial condition and prepare for a meeting with his banker in the next few days.

Great Eastern Toys was established in Hong Kong almost thirty years ago by Paul's father to create and design children's toys and books. It had few production facilities itself, but relied mainly on a number of local suppliers who manufactured to its specifications. Less than 5% of the firm's business was local with the remainder of its sales to export markets. Its customers included both toy companies as well as department stores and other large retail chains. Dollar markets [mainly the United States and Canada] accounted for slightly more than 50% of total sales, with Western Europe accounting for the rest.

Paul Cheng took over the business after his father's death during the Summer of 1994. The two fiscal years ending June 1995 and June 1996 of his tenure were considered good years for the industry but the performance of Great Eastern Toys was disappointing in comparison to the year ending in June 1994, while Paul's father was still running the company. In late Autumn of 1996, Paul decided to hire a general manager to help him turn things around. He attracted John Li into the company by offering him a share of the profits in addition to a salary. Li had been the general marketing and sales manager of another Hong Kong firm that exported sporting goods and various other consumer products to markets in Asia and North America. Both men agreed that as general manager, Li would have full authority to execute any changes he desired.

Since his father's death, Paul Cheng had been troubled by the question of whether his family should retain their interest in the company or sell out. He had heard his father speak of the steadily declining margins in the toys-and-books business in recent year and, while he and his family enjoyed considerable wealth, he had been wondering whether they shouldn't sell out and invest the proceeds in an enterprise of greater promise, or in the stock market and real estate. In fact, he told Li at their first meeting that he might be interested in finding a buyer for the company because operating margins had been so drastically reduced in recent years: "My father worked on an average pre-tax operating margin of about 10 percent not many years ago" he said. "Now we are lucky to average about 5 percent. My feeling is that, if the trend of the last few years keeps up, this business will soon be dead".

Li replied that he was certainly familiar with the declining margins problem and that he had given it a great deal of thought. He was convinced, he said, that the answer lay in doing a high-volume business. "I don't think we'll ever see average pre-tax operating margins of 10 percent in the business again, but I do think we can maintain an adequate return on investment by building volume and controlling costs. It's not easy, but I think it can be done". Li's confidence had been an important element in Paul Cheng's decision to leave the family money in the company, at least for the present.

During his first few weeks in the company, Li reviewed in detail the records of the operating and sales departments with the help of his staff : Mr. Peter Gray (the company's accountant), Mr. Ignacius Tang (the operations manager) and Mr. Robert Ho (the sales manager). He was particularly concerned with their lack-luster exports to European markets achieved by the company in 1995-1996 in relation to the estimated potential. And with some more effort, he believed that sales could be substantially increased in the United States and Canada. Li was also interested in the trends in operating margin and in the net profit shown by product lines. Finally, he noted the financing of the company, a mixture of short and medium term loans in both Hong Kong dollars and Japanese Yen. Concerned with the potential risk from borrowing in Yen, the accountant explained that this funding had been used since it provided by far the cheapest funds available.

As a result of his review, and with the aid of the operations manager and the general sales manager, Li submitted to Paul Cheng the following short memo:

To: Paul Cheng   From :   John Li

Re: Outline of our action plan for fiscal year 1998 (July 1997 to June 1998)

Date:March, 1997

1.   We intend to control costs in order to improve margin and profitability. Higher profits should allow us to sustain faster growth rates during the coming years.

2.   We will build up volume by:

(a) reviving older (but potentially profitable) products

(b) introducing new products, particularly in the video game sector.

(c) make a major campaign to increase sales to the European markets.

3.   We will review our portfolio of products with the objective of discontinuing products that do not contribute adequately to the overall profitability of the company.

4.   We will make every effort to speed up the collection of our accounts receivable and to obtain overall inventory turns of ten times in order to get the most use of the company's supply of capital.

Exhibit 1 Great Eastern Toys Income Statements (Millions of Hong Kong Dollars)

	Year Ending June 1996		Year Ending June 1997		Year Ending June 1998	
Sales revenues [net]	171.275	100.00%	187.500	100.00%	244.900	100.00%
Cost of sales [COS]	131.295	76.66	143.810	76.70	187.225	76.45
Selling and administrative expenses [S&A]	27.800	16.23	29.700	15.84	36.765	15.01
Depreciation expense	4.650	2.71	4.800	2.56	5.700	2.33
Earnings before interest and taxes [EBIT]	7.530	4.40	9.190	4.90	15.210	6.21
Interest expense	1.960	1.14	2.970	1.58	6.125	2.50
Earnings before taxes [EBT]	5.570	3.26	6.220	3.32	9.085	3.71
Taxes	0.919	0.54	0.995	0.53	1.454	0.59
Earnings after taxes [EAT]	4.650	2.72	5.225	2.78	7.631	3.12
Dividends paid	3.100		4.810		4.810	
Retained earnings	1.550		0.415		2.821	

Shortly after, in the Spring of 1997, Li began to put his plan into action. Additional personnel were added to the staff and, as the monthly sales reports were received, Paul Cheng observed a substantial overall increase in sales in comparison to the previous year. With the increased activities, however, the company was experiencing serious difficulties in controlling the growth of its working capital. Since most of this was financed with short term debt, the firm's bankers became more and more concerned. As the economic situation in Hong Kong and other Asian countries deteriorated

Exhibit 2 Great Eastern Toys Balance Sheets (Millions of Hong Kong Dollars)

	30 June 1996		30 June 1997		30 June 1998	
Cash & marketable securities	6.588	8.17%	7.750	9.43%	2.400	2.45%
Accounts receivable	22.475	27.88	24.800	30.19	33.325	33.99
Inventories	27.125	33.65	29.450	35.85	42.550	43.40
Prepaid expenses	0.387	0.48	0.925	1.13	1.163	1.19
Net fixed assets	24.025	29.81	19.225	23.40	18.600	18.97
TOTAL ASSETS	80.600	100.00%	82.150	100.00%	98.038	100.00%
Short term debt[1]	17.900	22.21%	18.580	22.62%	27.774	28.32%
Accounts payable	14.610	18.13	15.500	18.87	19.850	20.25
Accrued expenses [operations]	3.100	3.85	3.705	4.50	5.108	5.21
Long term debt[1]	6.240	7.74	5.200	6.34	3.320	3.39
Owner's equity	38.750	48.08	39.165	47.67	41.986	42.83
TOTAL LIABILITIES & NET WORTH	80.600	100.00%	82.150	100.00%	98.038	100.00%

[1]Short-term debt consists of bank loans in Hong Kong dollars, a Japanese Yen revolving credit facility, plus the current repayment portion of long- term debt. The long term debt was a 7-year note denominated in Yen, repayable ¥ 10 million each 6 months.

Exhibit 3

To:	Paul Cheng	From:	Robert Ho (Sales Manager)
Cc:	John Li		Ignacius Tang (Operations Manager)

Re: **Report on sales, receivables and inventories**

Date: July 1998

1. **Accounts Receivable**

   Our receivables are in good condition with 92% current in June. Doubtful accounts have increased marginally and hence our bad debt reserve should be maintained at the same level as last year.

	June 1998	May 1998
Current	92%	94%
Past due :		
1 to 60 days	5%	4%
61 to 90 days	2%	$3^1/2$%
91 days and over	1%	$^1/2$%

2. **Inventories**

   Our inventories as of June 1998 amounted to HK$ 42.55 million. They are up considerably from a year ago, primarily as a result of the addition of the video games, our newest product. Our inventory position and corresponding operating margins are as follows:

Item	Sales Budgeted	Sales Actual	Cost of Sales Actual	Inventory Actual
Books	55.800	61.225	46.092 (75%)	9.250
Toys	69.750	73.470	52.932 (72%)	10.710
Board games	37.975	36.735	31.233 (85%)	8.965
Video games	38.750	39.138	27.435 (70%)	3.875
Other products	34.100	34.333	29.533 (86%)	9.750
TOTAL	236.375	244.900	187.225 (76%)	42.550

3. **Accounts Payable**

   Our payables are settled promptly, usually no later than 6 to 7 weeks, in order to maintain a good relationship with our suppliers and ensure rapid delivery of goods in the future.

during the second half of 1997, and with the crisis getting worse in 1998, banks were facing up to the prospect of widespread default from their lending.

During his telephone conversation with his banker, Cheng learned that since all banks were caught in a severe credit squeeze, the current size of the short term borrowing could not be maintained and that in any event it was highly unlikely that the bank would be willing to lend Great Eastern Toys more than HK$ 25 million beyond the end of the current quarter. Interest rates had skyrocketed during the past months and lending by the banks was being sharply cut back as the Hong Kong monetary authorities had taken drastic steps to defend the currency.

Late in July 1998, John Li gave Paul Cheng copies of the company's Profit and Loss Account and Balance Sheet for the 12 months ended June 30, 1998, together with a memo from the sales and operations managers (see Exhibits 1, 2 and 3). For

Exhibit 4 BENCH MARKING : June 1998 - RECREATIONAL INDUSTRY SAMPLE

	Company A	Company B	Company C
Current ratio[STAssets/STLiabilites][1] 1.7		2.0	1.6
Short term/Total debt	60%	75%	65%
Average collection period [days of sales]	32 days	29 days	30 days
Average payment period [days of purchases]	30 days	32 days	37 days
Inventory turnover [based on cost of sales]	8 times	10 times	9 times
Pre-tax operating margin [EBIT/Sales][2]	6.0%	6.8%	6.5%
Return on invested capital [EBIT/Invested capital][3]	20.5%	28.1%	24.2%
Pre-tax return on equity [EBT/Equity][4]	18.4%	24.6%	21.9%
Effective tax rate	15%	16%	16%

[1] ST = Short term [or current] assets / liabilities

[2] EBIT = Earnings before interest and taxes

[3] Invested capital = Cash + Working capital requirement + Net fixed assets

[4] EBT = Earnings before taxes

Exhibit 5 QUARTERLY SALES FORECAST FISCAL YEAR 1998/1999 (Millions of Hong Kong Dollars)

Second Quarter	*1998*	*58.125*	*(Actual)*
Third Quarter	1998	100.700	
Fourth Quarter	1998	80.100	
First Quarter	1999	48.250	
Second Quarter	1999	59.700	
Total for July 98–June 99		288.750	

comparative purposes Mr. Peter Gray, the company's accountant, gave Paul Cheng selected financial and operating statistics for three companies in the recreational products industry (see Exhibit 4) whose operations, he stressed, were only partially comparable. On receipt of these reports, Paul Cheng began to analyze the effectiveness of Li's plans and operations during the fiscal year 1998.

In the meeting with his banker, when Cheng explained that he did not expect sales to grow as fast as in the past year, he was told that even with slower growth, the bank's lending to Great Eastern would have to be reduced. Much more of its funding needs would have to be generated internally through the retention of profits and a better management of the firm's assets.

Finally, he wondered whether—on the basis of Li's performance to date and the long-term prospects of the business—the Cheng family might be justified in investing additional funds of their own in the company by reducing the dividend and, if necessary, through an injection of new equity. This probably would not be well-received since he knew that his family would be unhappy by any substantial cut in the cash dividend. Over the past several months, the company was forced to borrow Hong Kong dollars at rates as high as 19 percent at times, although recently they had hovered around 12 percent. Most people believed bank loans would return to more normal rates of 8% to 10% or less once the economic situation improved and the currency crisis calmed down.

But selling the company was still on his mind. In the past, Mr. Cheng had considered a return of 16% to 18% on the family's investment to be acceptable. But given the economic crisis and other uncertainties since the Summer of 1997, Mr. Cheng felt that this was not high enough to justify the risk of having all of their wealth invested in the company; they now needed, he believed, an average return on capital of at *least* 20 percent. This they had not achieved since his father's death. If someone made him a tempting offer he was ready to seriously consider selling the business.

INSEAD

GREAT EASTERN TOYS (B)

Mr. Paul Cheng, the sole owner of Great Eastern Toys, and Mr. John Li, the firm's general manager, are currently considering whether to extend its existing product line of plastic dolls. Dolls have been among Great Eastern's most successful products for over 20 years.

Mr. Li recently proposed that the company enter the market for relatively high-margin, high-quality, *designer* dolls. A consulting firm was hired to do a preliminary study of that market. Its report indicated that the new dolls could be sold, net to Great Eastern, for HK$300 per unit. Sales volume was projected at 3,000 units per month over a period of at least five years at the same price. The consultant's market study cost the firm HK$500,000 which was paid shortly afterwards.

While most of Great Eastern's production was sub-contracted, this new doll would be manufactured in its own facilities. A study undertaken by the production department showed that new equipment would be needed costing a total of HK$16 million delivered and installed. Resale value of this equipment was uncertain, but estimated at HK$800,000 if disposed of any time between 5 and 10 years after beginning production. The new equipment, assuming proper maintenance was carried out, should allow Great Eastern Toys to produce at least 3,000 dolls per month for the next 10 years. The study also indicated that raw materials needed to produce the doll would be HK$95 per unit; the value of raw material inventory was estimated to amount to one month's production. Although the production cycle of a doll is rather uncomplicated, the study estimated that inventories of work-in-process and finished goods would need to be increased by HK$150,000 to allow for smooth and efficient manufacturing. Direct labor costs would rise by HK$100,000 per month and energy costs by HK$30,000 per month.

A building owned by the firm, currently unoccupied, would be used to produce the new designer doll. Recently they had received a letter from the manager of a nearby department store offering to rent the building for use as a storage area. At current market rates the building could be rented at HK$80,000 a year.

To take account of overhead costs, the accounting department had a standard charge of 1% against sales revenues of new projects. An additional annual financing charge equal to 10% of the book-value of assets employed in the project would be levied.

These preliminary figures were assembled by Mr. Peter Gray, Great Eastern's accounting and finance manager. John Li asked Gray to make an economic and financial evaluation of the designer-doll project.

Gray took note that recently, the firm expected accounts receivable to be collected, on average, within 50 days. Accounts payable, on average, were settled in 36 days. Great Eastern Toys's cost of debt was estimated at 10% and its cost of equity at 20%. The company used straight-line depreciation for computing operating earnings. Company financing was 40% debt, 60% equity. Income taxes were 16% for Hong Kong companies. Currently, there was no tax on capital gains.

Learning of the project, the sales manager, Mr. Robert Ho, was concerned that the proposed designer doll would possibly "erode" sales of the existing standard dolls produced by Great Eastern Toys. He feared that those potential losses could actually reduce after-tax operating cash flow by as much as HK$ 600,000 per year.

INSEAD

GREAT EASTERN TOYS (C)

Following his review of the company's operational and financial performance, Mr. Paul Cheng remained unsure whether or not he should try to sell the business. After discussion with members of his family, he agreed with them that he did not have enough expertise himself to put a value on the firm and should turn to his bankers for advice. His wife had reminded him that taking his salary, perks, and dividends together, they had been earning between HK$ 5 and 6 million per year since he took over after his father's death in 1994. If they were to sell Great Eastern, she argued, they should continue to enjoy at the least that level of income. Agreeing with her, Paul Cheng felt confident that they should be able to earn on average a 10% net return if the proceeds from an eventual sale were invested in the stock market and in real estate. This meant that they would have to realize over HK$ 50 million for the company in order to maintain their current level of income. However, he believed the company was worth considerably more and hoped that he would find this confirmed by his bankers.

Meeting with them, he was told that there were two principal ways of putting a value on a company: either a valuation based on accounting data, or one based on future earnings. Prospective buyers would be looking at the firm in much the same way. The main difference was that they would be trying to pay as little as possible whereas Cheng would aim to get as much as possible.

The bankers pointed out that using an accounting valuation such as *book value* would surely be inadequate since it ignored the company's real sources of value: the creation and design of its products and the supplier and customer network built up over many years. The only way that these could be properly evaluated would be to consider their earnings potential.

One way of doing this was what the bankers called the *comparative valuation approach.* Here one would try to find how much firms in related businesses had sold for in terms of price compared to net earnings, cash earnings, or book value. The difficulty with this method is finding relevant data There were no firms listed on the Hong Kong stock exchange that could provide a benchmark, but the bankers believed they could find one or more firms traded on a foreign stock exchange that might have some similarities to Great Eastern. The bank had arranged the sale in 1997 of a Hong Kong company in the toy business called *Allied Toys Distributors.* But it was a much smaller firm with its markets mainly in South East Asia. Its owners had wanted to retire and decided to sell when an attractive offer was made to them. Some benchmark data on this firm and a sample of several foreign companies in related businesses appears in Exhibit 1. Additional selected data for large companies in a number of world markets appears in Exhibit 2.

Exhibit 1 Great Eastern Toys [C] Comparative Data - Selected Firms in the Book, Games, and Toy Business, Latest Fiscal Year

Company	Sales HK$ Millions	Profits HK$ Millions	Cash Earnings HK$ Millions†	Book Value HK$ Millions	Beta	Market Capitalisation HK$ Millions	Debt to equity ratio	Tax Rate
Great Eastern	244.9	7.6	13.3	42	n.a.	n.a.	0.74	16%
Allied Toys	65	0.63	1.02	3.95	n.a.	12.25‡	1.5	16%
Nintendo [Japan][4]	34247	5361	n.a.	40556	n.a.	98642	0.34	45%
Bandai [Japan][5]	18460	64	n.a.	6053	n.a.	3263	1.46	45%
Maruzen [Japan][6]	9222	33	n.a.	882	n.a.	1914	9.26	45%
Mattell [USA][7]	37470	2248	3292	14125	0.7	86157	1.02	30%
Hasbro [USA][8]	25606	1713	3022	15074	0.8	37680	0.67	32%
Marvel Enterprises [USA][9]	2248	loss	negative	1375	1.63	2339	0.71	0%
Education Insights [USA][9]	312.6	loss	negative	164.8	1.21	105.7	0.23	0%
Play by Play Toys [USA][9]	1185	31.8	48.8	692.1	0.93	301.2	0.49	30%
Grand Toys Int'l [USA][9]	235.8	loss	9.8	37.8	1.34	64.2	1.57	0%

† Cash earnings = earnings after tax + depreciation
‡ Value of the transaction
[2]1997 data; [4]Electronic games; [5]Games and toys; [6]Book retailing; [7]Toys [Barbie doll]; [8] Toys [Pokemon]; [9]Similar to Great Eastern's range of products.

The other way to properly value a company like Great Eastern was what the bankers called the *discounted cash flow approach*. This required making forecasts of the firm's future operations. First, a considerable number of assumptions would have to be made covering sales growth, profit margins, investment in working capital and fixed assets, depreciation, tax rates, as well as the time horizon over which these variables would be estimated. These assumptions would then be used by the analyst making the valuation to forecast cash flows over a certain number of years into

Exhibit 2 Great Eastern Toys [C] Averages - Large Companies in Selected Markets, Latest Fiscal Year[9]

Market	Price/Book	Price Earnings	Yield	ROE %
Hong Kong	1.8	10	5.4%	17.8%
Singapore	2.2	16	1.6%	13.3%
Taiwan	2.8	24	0.8%	13.6%
Malaysia	2.3	13	1.7%	21.0%
Australia	3	22	3.1%	15.2%
Japan	3	55	0.9%	6.9%
Great Britain	1.2	24	2.4%	19.4%
Germany	5.4	32	1.8%	15.9%
United States	5.6	28	1.4%	22.4%

[9]Source: Business Week, 29 May 1998. Certain averages shown are medians since the data included too many extreme values for the mean to be representative.

Exhibit 3   Great Eastern Toys [C] DCF "As is" Valuation Assumptions

1. Sales growth forecasts: 1998/1999: 20%; 1999/2000: 15%; 2000/2001: 10%; 2001/2003: 5%; 2004 onwards: 3%
2. Operating earnings [EBIT]: based on 1998 - 6.2% of sales
3. Efficiency of WCR management: same as 1998 - 21% of sales
4. New capital investment equal to annual depreciation
5. Average cost of debt - 12%; estimated cost of equity - 17.8%
6. Debt to equity ratio: 40% debt, 60% equity
7. Corporate tax rate: 16%

the future. The cash flows would then be discounted to determine how much they would be worth today, that is, their *present value.* This, in turn, would require the analyst to determine a suitable discount rate or *cost of capital.* Again, cautioned the bankers, it was no easy task determining what this should be. The cost of debt was straight-forward enough—the future cost of borrowing. Much more debatable was how to estimate the cost of equity capital. The cost of both types of capital was closely related to the firm's operating risk which could affect the size and timing of its cash flows, and to the amount of debt in its capital structure. When Paul Cheng told them that he believed a 20% return was needed on his family's investment in the company, given the risk of the business, his bankers replied that while it wasn't unreasonable, it was worth having a closer look.

A first set of assumptions appears in Exhibit 3. The bankers stressed that one set would not be sufficient. Any valuation based on *discounted cash flow* should rely on several scenarios, each with different growth, investment, or profit assumptions.

Paul Cheng left the meeting with his bankers, intending to ask them to prepare a valuation of his firm once he had conferred with his wife and family. In the meantime, he planned, with the help of Peter Gray, his accountant, to make a tentative valuation himself using the financial data appearing on Exhibits 1 to 3, the company's financial statements, and his knowledge of the business and its future prospects.

GREAT EASTERN TOYS (D)

During the meeting with their banker, Mr. Jason Wu, in late July 1998, Paul Cheng, the principal shareholder of Great Eastern Toys, and John Li, the company's general manager, intended to focus discussion on the financing needs of the business. The banker explained to them that all of the banks in Hong Kong were facing a severe credit squeeze and that he had no choice but to cut back lending. He added that Cheng's firm was not being treated differently from the bank's other clients. For the past two years, Great Eastern had been borrowing large amounts of short term debt to finance working capital needs, especially during the four months from August through November when over half of annual sales were made. In October of the previous year, total short term debt had exceeded HK$ 50 million for a short period. Mr. Wu made it clear that such an amount was completely out of the question now: the bank would be forced to limit its lending to HK$ 25 million.

At the end of June 1998, the firm had borrowed about HK$ 24.45 million. Besides the short-term debt denominated in Hong Kong dollars, the firm had other loans totalling ¥ 120 million [HK$ 6.64 million[1]] outstanding. A 7-year note paying 6% interest had been taken in 1994. It was being amortized ¥ 10 million every six months. On 30 June 1998, ¥ 60 million was still outstanding. The short term Yen debt consisted of the current portion of long term debt [¥ 10 million] and a 6-month EuroYen loan [¥50 million] at a $4^{1}/2$% rate of interest. This loan had been reduced at the beginning of 1998 from an original ¥ 150 million, and Paul Cheng was concerned that his Japanese bankers would ask for the remaining amount to be repaid by the end of the year.

After reviewing its financial situation, the banker next raised an issue that the firm's management had paid little attention to up to now. About half of sales were made in U.S. dollars to the North American market. For the 1997–1998 fiscal year, this amounted to the equivalent of about HK$ 125 million. Slightly less than half of its annual sales [HK$ 115 million equivalent] were to markets in Europe. Up to now, these had been invoiced in various currencies with Deutsche Marks, Sterling, and French Francs accounting for most of the sales. Great Eastern's European distributors indicated that with the advent of the Euro in January 1999, they would expect to be invoiced in the new currency unit.

Completely occupied with expanding their business, Great Eastern's management had never given much thought to currency risk. For more than 10 years, the Hong Kong dollar had been firmly pegged to the U.S. dollar, so effectively, they were immune from currency risk on half of their sales. This had not been the case with European currencies. Nor would it likely be in the future with the Euro. In fact,

---

[1]HK$ equivalent value is based on the 30 June 1998 spot exchange rate of ¥18.1 per HK$.

---

during the past three years, the major European currencies, with the exception of Sterling, had depreciated by over 15% against the U.S. dollar [and because of the peg, also to the HK$][2] . This had been part of the reason for falling profit margins over the past few years. The banker went on to point out that the Yen loans also gave rise to currency risk. This had been in Great Eastern's favor for the past two or three years since the Yen had depreciated continually against the dollar during that time. Although the amount at risk was much smaller than that for the European currencies [only HK$ 6.64 million equivalent], a 10% increase in the value of the Yen would still make a noticeable impact on the firm's earnings. All-in-all, the banker concluded, the company faced significant risk from possible changes in both the European currencies and the Yen, and should seriously consider doing something about it. Asked to elaborate on this, the banker set out a number of things he thought Cheng and Li might think about.

To begin, he agreed that because they had up to now ignored their currency exposures, this "do nothing" approach turned out to be lucky in the case of their Yen borrowing since it resulted in much cheaper funding than if the rate had been fixed. The depreciating Yen meant that it had taken fewer HK$ to service these loans. On the other hand, he was certain that the firm's export earnings had suffered from the general weakness of the European currencies over the past few years. At the same time, he recognized that currency risk was not an issue with their dollar exports thanks to the peg. And even if the peg were to change, which was periodically rumored, it would almost certainly mean a stronger U.S. dollar.

Listening to the banker, Cheng reflected on what his father had always remarked about financial markets: *"Prices rise and fall. That you can be sure. Its all in the timing."* Both the Yen and the European currencies had been depreciating since 1995 against the dollar. Perhaps it was about time that this trend would reverse. The banker suggested that this could happen, especially with the Japanese currency, since at ¥140 per U.S. dollar many observers believed it to be oversold. But with the Europeans adopting the Euro as their common currency, he believed they were moving into uncharted waters. A potentially positive factor would be if the Euro were to become a reserve currency. This could create a strong worldwide demand for it. However, many other forces would be at work that could limit any potential rise in the Euro—differences in economic growth and interest rates, or political dissent among the member states. At the moment, the banker cautioned, European currencies appeared to be at more or less fair value.[3]

The same could not be said about the Hong Kong dollar, which appeared to be substantially over-valued. Inflation in Hong Kong was running about double the rate in the U.S. and most of Europe, but the HK$ was tightly locked into the U.S. dollar. This meant that wages and many other costs were rising faster in Hong Kong than elsewhere, but competition, together with a fixed exchange rate, prevented them from increasing export prices to compensate. Therefore, operating margins were being squeezed with bottom-line profits further eroded by recent high interest rates for

---

[2]See Exhibit 1 for currency trends: ECU & Yen agasinst HK$. The ECU is shown as representative of the major European currencies.

[3]By "fair value," the banker meant that their exchange rates, adjusted for inflation, had not significantly changed for the past few years. See Exhibit 2.

most of their financing [see Exhibit 4]. The firm could not afford to take chances on something as unpredictable as the exchange rate. Because of this, the banker suggested that it would be unwise to continue "doing nothing" about their currency risk: his advice was to hedge their export sales to Europe as well as their remaining Yen loans, but leave open the exposure from the export sales in U.S. dollars.

According to the banker, there were two basic choices when hedging. One could "lock-in" today an exchange rate that would be close to the current spot rate; a forward contract provided this type of hedge. Or they could enter into an option contract that would fix a minimum rate on the currency, but allow them to take advantage of an increase in value if that should happen by the time the invoices were paid. The currency option would provide some of the advantages of not hedging, but limit the disadvantages—but at a cost.

To "lock-in" an exchange rate, the banker went on, meant that the future price of a foreign currency—*the future spot rate*—would in effect be set today—in other words, the hedge was a bet that the currency would weaken. Obviously, there would be no point in hedging if the currency used for pricing exports were expected to strengthen. This type of hedge insures that whatever the future spot rate might turn out to be, the *effective* price received for the currency would still be that which was agreed today. There were three ways to "lock-in" an exchange rate: a forward contract, a money market transaction, and a currency futures contract. Each of these carried precisely defined terms with regard to price, maturity, and certain other characteristics. Any modifications in the terms of the contract, such as changing its maturity, would have to be negotiated and agreed with the party providing the hedge, possibly resulting in additional cost.

Great Eastern's exports to the European markets were invoiced in several currencies. Mr. Wu explained that, until recently, each currency should have been hedged separately, an approach that would have been cumbersome to administer and led to relatively high transaction costs. However, since May 1998, the parities of most currencies in the *European Monetary Union* had been fixed. Therefore, as a practical matter, he thought that the firm should use the Deutsche mark as its hedging currency. DEM hedging instruments were widely traded and highly liquid. In any event, this would only be a temporary measure because starting in January 1999, exports to the European market would be invoiced in Euros. Almost as an afterthought, Wu reminded Cheng and Li that while his bank would be prepared to offer some DEM hedges against the HK$, for the more complex instruments a hedge against the U.S. dollar would be slightly cheaper and much easier to unwind if that turned out to be desirable. Thanks to the peg, he added, there would be practically no risk in doing so.

The *forward contract hedge* was an arrangement by which it sold to the bank a specified quantity of foreign currency to be delivered at a specified date in the future—normally when the sales invoice was to be settled. The exchange rate was fixed at the outset. At HK$ 4.3535 per DEM [DEM 0.2297 per HK$], the 90-day forward rate was at present about $1^{1}/4$ % more "valuable" than the spot rate of HK$ 4.3085 per DEM [DEM 0.2321 per HK$]. The forward DEM was trading at a premium to the HK$, explained Wu. With this hedge, Great Eastern would receive the foreign currency [DEM[4]] from its clients on the agreed maturity date, pay these to the bank in exchange for Hong Kong dollars at the forward exchange rate agreed earlier [HK$ 4.3535 per DEM].

The ***money market hedge*** was also an arrangement with the bank. Great Eastern would borrow DEM today from a bank then sell them immediately on the spot market for HK$. These funds would be used to finance working capital needs or to pay down existing loans. When the DEM were received from the customer, they would be used to repay the loan. The cost of this hedge would be the difference between the interest paid on the DEM loan and the interest saved on the HK$ loans that were repaid. The banker reminded them that Great Eastern was currently paying 400 *basis points*[5] above HIBOR[6] [9.25 percent] or an all-in cost of 13.25% for its short-term HK$ loans; a three-month DEM loan could be arranged at an all-in cost of 7.875% p.a.

A ***futures hedge*** could be provided by an instrument traded on the *Chicago Mercantile Exchange* [CME][7], but would be unwieldy and, in the opinion of Mr. Wu, impractical. DEM futures were traded on the CME, but were generally of little interest to corporations. Plans called for the Euro to be traded on the CME beginning in January 1999. Currency futures were priced in U.S. dollars against the other currency. Therefore, the futures hedge would introduce a small amount of additional risk since the Hong Kong—U.S. dollar peg might change during the period of the contract, Wu reminded them once again. As protection against loss from currency fluctuations, this hedge was very similar to the forward contract provided by the bank. To create the hedge, a firm would *sell* a sufficient number of currency futures to create the hedge. It could then wait until the futures contracts came to maturity and use the currency received from customers to settle up the contracts. Alternatively, if it decided the hedge was no longer needed *before* the futures contracts reached maturity, the position could be liquidated. This would create an accumulated profit or loss depending on how the currency had moved against the dollar. However, the mechanics of futures contracts differ considerably from forwards. The contracts are made through a member of the futures exchange, usually a broker. Currency futures come in standard contract sizes [for the DEM 125,000], and standard maturity dates [the third Wednesday of March, June, September, December]. They are revalued daily [*marked-to-market*] with any profit or loss immediately settled between broker and client. To trade on the futures market, the client must open and maintain collateral [margin account] with the broker. This changes from time to time, but

---

[4]Recall that the Deutsche mark was suggested for the hedge. Other European currencies besides teh DEM would actually be received, but since the parities had already been fixed, the net effect would be as if all were in DEM.

[5]A basis point is 1/100 of a percent, ie., 0.0001. Basis points are generally used in pricing loans and certain other financial instruments. Rates are usually quoted on an annual basis.

[6]HIBOR—Hong Kong inter-bank offer rate: The rate of interest charged between international banks on short-term HK$.

[7]Currency futures are also traded on exchanges in London [LIFFE], Singapore [SIMEX], Sidney, and elsewhere in the world.

at present, is a minimum of around $1,500 per contract. In addition, the broker will charge a small commission.

The ***currency option contract*** was available from either banks or exchanges. Option contracts give the *right but not the obligation* to buy [a **call**] or to sell [a **put**] currency or some other asset within a specified period and at a predetermined price known as the *strike* or *exercise price*.

Bank or OTC[8] options can be tailored to meet the clients precise needs for maturity, amount, or currency. They are usually "European" type options, that is, they may only be exercised at maturity when they expire. Most bank options are on spot currency. Great Eastern's banker pointed out that besides dealing in "plain vanilla" [standard] call and put options, he could also offer them *synthetic* or *exotic* instruments, although these might only be available in U.S. dollars. *Synthetics* were combinations of calls, puts, and sometimes forward contracts that were designed to meet particular risk/return objectives of a client. A so-called *zero-cost option* is one of the more widely used of these. *Exotics* were options that had some particular feature that gave the buyer a lower premium at the price of a more risky payoff.[9]

Like futures, *exchange traded* options have standardized maturities and amounts. The expiration dates are similar to those for futures: March, June, September, and December. In addition, the American exchanges offer some "near-by" expiration dates. For example, at the end of June, contracts on major currencies against the U.S. dollar were offered for July and August expiration as well as for the September and December standard months. Only a few major currencies are available—the HK$ not being among them. Most are priced in U.S. dollars—even those traded on European or Asian exchanges. They are usually so-called "American" type options, in other words, they may be exercised at any time before expiration. Recently "European style" options have been introduced on some exchanges; they can only be exercised at maturity. Those traded on the Philadelphia exchange are on spot currency. Chicago's CME and London's LIFFE contracts are on currency futures. To buy an option on an exchange, the full premium[10] must be paid in advance. To sell [or write] an option requires a specified margin to be maintained with the broker. Again, Mr. Wu reiterated that for the same reason as futures, *exchange traded* options would be impractical for Great Eastern's needs.

Besides explaining the hedging instruments to his clients, Wu raised a number of other issues for them to consider. The company exported goods to its European customers on a continuous basis throughout the year. If they did decide to hedge these sales, should it be when the goods were ordered? Or should they wait until the time when the shipment was made and the invoice actually sent? What about hedging periodically for a longer period of 6 to 12 months once operating plans and sales budgets were agreed? Finally if they do decide to hedge, should it be for the entire amount at risk, however it was measured, or only some portion of it?

---

[8]OTC is over-the-counter.

[9]Among the most popular were average rate and barrier or knockout options.

[10]The LIFFE exchange uses a margin system similar to that for futures trading. Hence, a specified minimum margin is maintained with the broker rather than paying a cash premium up-front.

Great Eastern's banker concluded by stressing there was no "correct" hedging approach. It depended on the particular needs and financial position of the company, and the attitudes of its management and shareholders towards risk. Whether or not the hedge was profitable would only be known *ex post*—when the proceeds from the sales were collected. In their case, hedging the Yen loans during the past months would have been the wrong decision; in contrast, it would have been the correct decision for the European currency exposures. If instead, Yen had strengthened against the dollar, "locking-in" the rate would have been the correct decision. Since it is usually impossible to predict how the rates will move, he was not prepared to advise them when to hedge and when not to. Further, he cautioned that hedging, under some competitive situations, could actually increase risk rather than decrease it.

The discussion left Mess. Cheng and Li somewhat overwhelmed. On leaving, they told the banker a few days were needed to decide what to do. Back at the office, Cheng told Lu that he was pretty much convinced that they should begin to devote a bit more time and thought to managing their currency position. Realizing they had "lost" a considerable amount during the past several months from a "do-nothing" policy, there was clearly too much potential for further losses if they continued as they had been doing. The problem was to decide quickly what to do?

Anxious to resolve this matter quickly, Paul Cheng asked Lu to prepare a brief report on how their company's currency risk should be managed. In particular, he asked him to set out the relative advantages in terms of cost and risk for each of the alternatives that had been described to them by the banker. To provide a practical example, he could use the exposure arising from the DEM 4 million worth of goods that been ordered by their European distributors in July to be delivered in September and paid for in October, 90 days from then. He suggested Lu use the July 15 market rates which they had picked up at the bank [Exhibit 1] and, for the purpose of the analysis, assume that their customers would pay them, and the hedges unwound on the 15th of October. He himself intended to give some thought to broader policy issues including whether they should hedge only the European exports, or also the Yen loans? When should they hedge, and under what conditions?

EXHIBIT 1 Current Market Data, Exchange Rates & Interest Rates

Spot exchange rates:	HK$ 4.3085 - 4.3122 per DEM
	DEM 0.2319 - 0.2321 per HK$;
Three-month forward outright rate:	HK$ 4.3535 - 4.3706 per DEM
	DEM 0.2288 - 0.2297 per HK$;
September DEM—U.S. dollar futures:	$0.5579 per DEM
December DEM—U.S. dollar futures:	$0.5650 per DEM
Three-month HIBOR:	$8^7/8\%$ - $9^1/4\%$
Three-month DEM LIBOR:	$3^3/4\%$ - $3^7/8\%$
Three-month USD LIBOR:	5 9/16% - 5 11/16%
Three-month DEM OTC put option:	strike price - HK$ 4.3103 per DEM; DEM 0.2320 per HK$; Premium: HK$ 0.0630 per DEM

EXHIBIT 2 Currency Developments, Exchange Rate Trends, 1995/1998

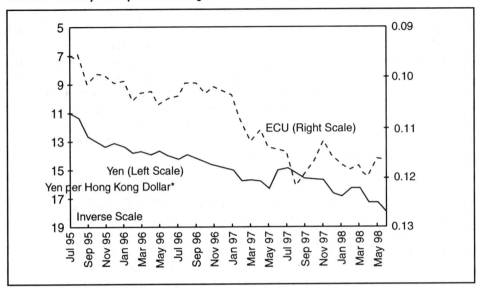

EXHIBIT 3 Currency Developments, Real Effective Exchange Rates

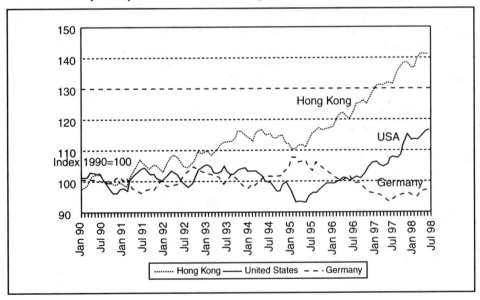

EXHIBIT 4 Short Term Interest Rates

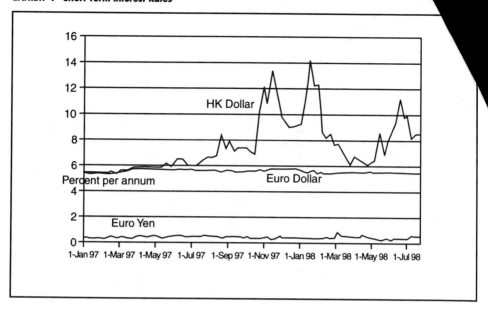

EXHIBIT 5 Great Eastern Toys, Income Statements (Millions of Hong Kong Dollars)

	Year Ending June 1996		Year Ending June 1997		Year Ending June 1998	
Sales revenues [net]	171.275	100.00%	187.5	100.00%	244.9	100.00%
Cost of sales [COS]	131.295	76.66	143.81	76.7	187.225	76.45
Selling and administrative expenses [S&A]	27.8	16.23	29.7	15.84	36.765	15.01
Depreciation expense	4.65	2.71	4.8	2.56	5.7	2.33
Earnings before interest and taxes [EBIT]	7.53	4.4	9.19	4.9	15.21	6.21
Interest expense	1.96	1.14	2.97	1.58	6.125	2.5
Earnings before taxes [EBT]	5.57	3.26	6.22	3.32	9.085	3.71
Taxes	0.919	0.54	0.995	0.53	1.454	0.59
Earnings after taxes [EAT]	4.65	2.72	5.225	2.78	7.631	3.12
Dividends paid	3.1		4.81		4.81	
Retained earnings	1.55		0.415		2.821	

...ern Toys, Balance Sheets (Millions of Hong Kong Dollars)

	35245		35610		35975	
...curities	6.588	8.17%	7.75	9.43%	2.4	2.45%
...le	22.475	27.88	24.8	30.19	33.325	33.99
	27.125	33.65	29.45	35.85	42.55	43.4
...expenses	0.387	0.48	0.925	1.13	1.163	1.19
...t fixed assets	24.025	29.81	19.225	23.4	18.6	18.97
TOTAL ASSETS	**80.6**	**100.00%**	**82.15**	**100.00%**	**98.038**	**100.00%**
Short term debt[1]	17.9	22.21%	18.58	22.62%	27.774	28.32%
Accounts payable	14.61	18.13	15.5	18.87	19.85	20.25
Accrued expenses [operations]	3.1	3.85	3.705	4.5	5.108	5.21
Long term debt[1]	6.24	7.74	5.2	6.34	3.32	3.39
Owner's equity	38.75	48.08	39.165	47.67	41.986	42.83
TOTAL LIABILITIES & NET WORTH	**80.6**	**100.00%**	**82.15**	**100.00%**	**98.038**	**100.00%**

[1]Short-term debt consists of HK$ 24.45 million in bank loans denominated in Hong Kong dollars, a Japanese Yen revolving credit facility, plus the current repayment portion of long-term debt totaling ¥ 60 million [HK$ 3.32 million]. The long term debt was a 7-year note denominated in Yen with ¥ 60 million outstanding on 30 June. Amortization schedule was ¥ 10 million each 6 months.